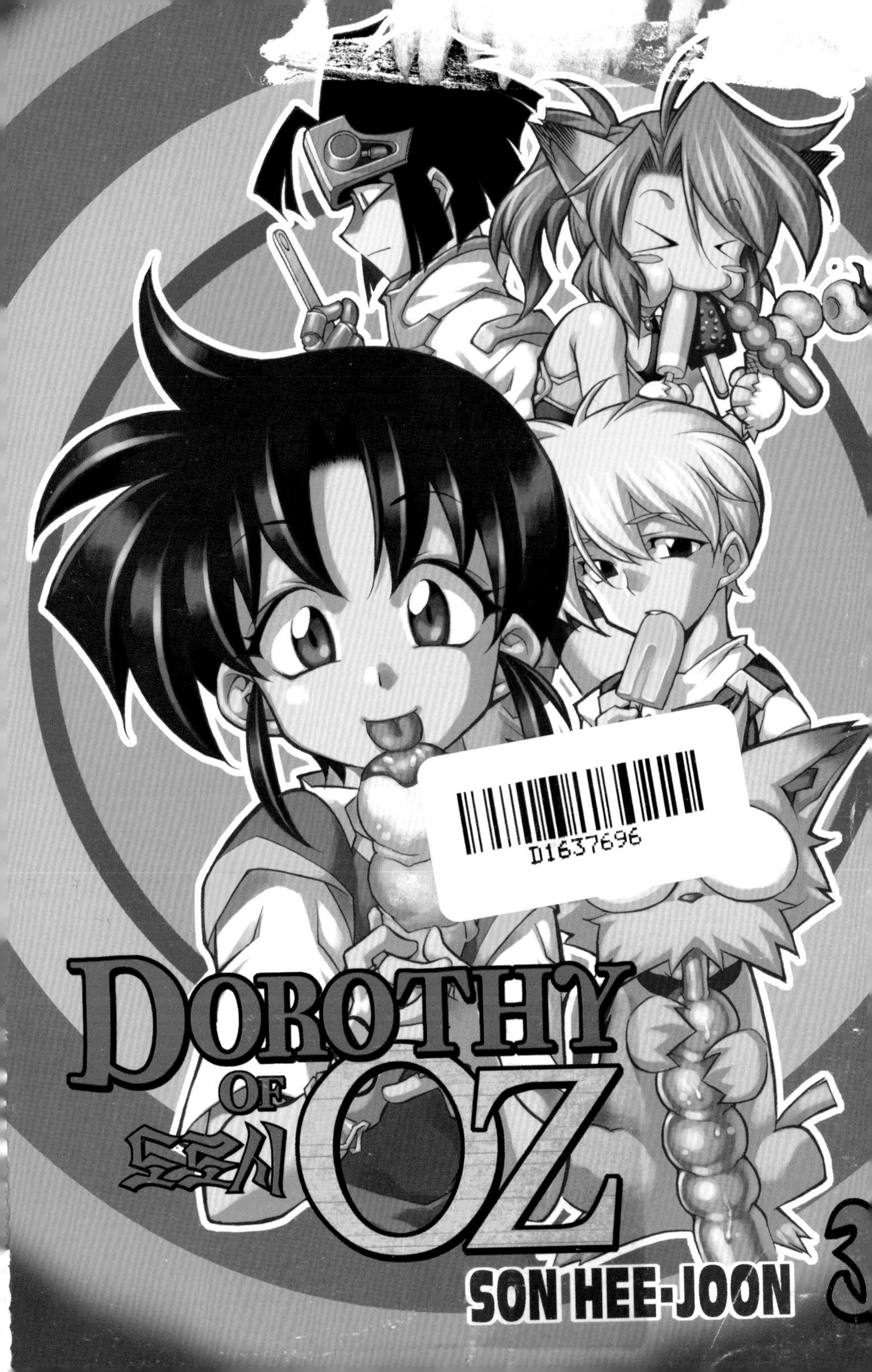
DOROTHY
OF
OZ
SON HEE-JOON
3

DOROTHY OF OZ 3

CONTENTS

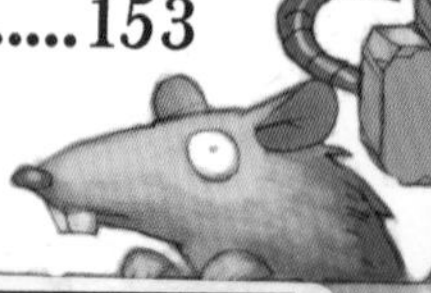

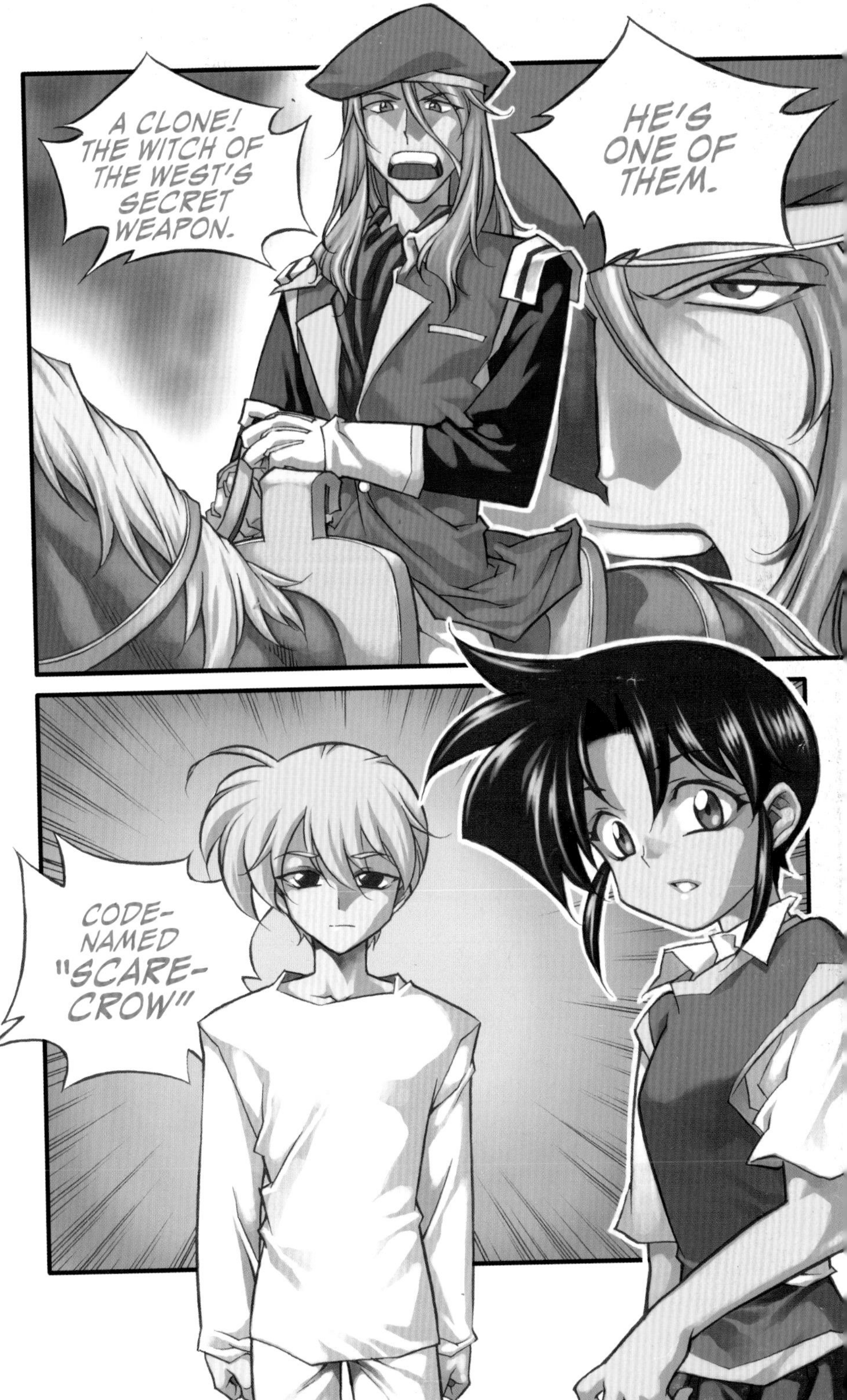
A CLONE! THE WITCH OF THE WEST'S SECRET WEAPON.
HE'S ONE OF THEM.
CODE-NAMED "SCARE-CROW"

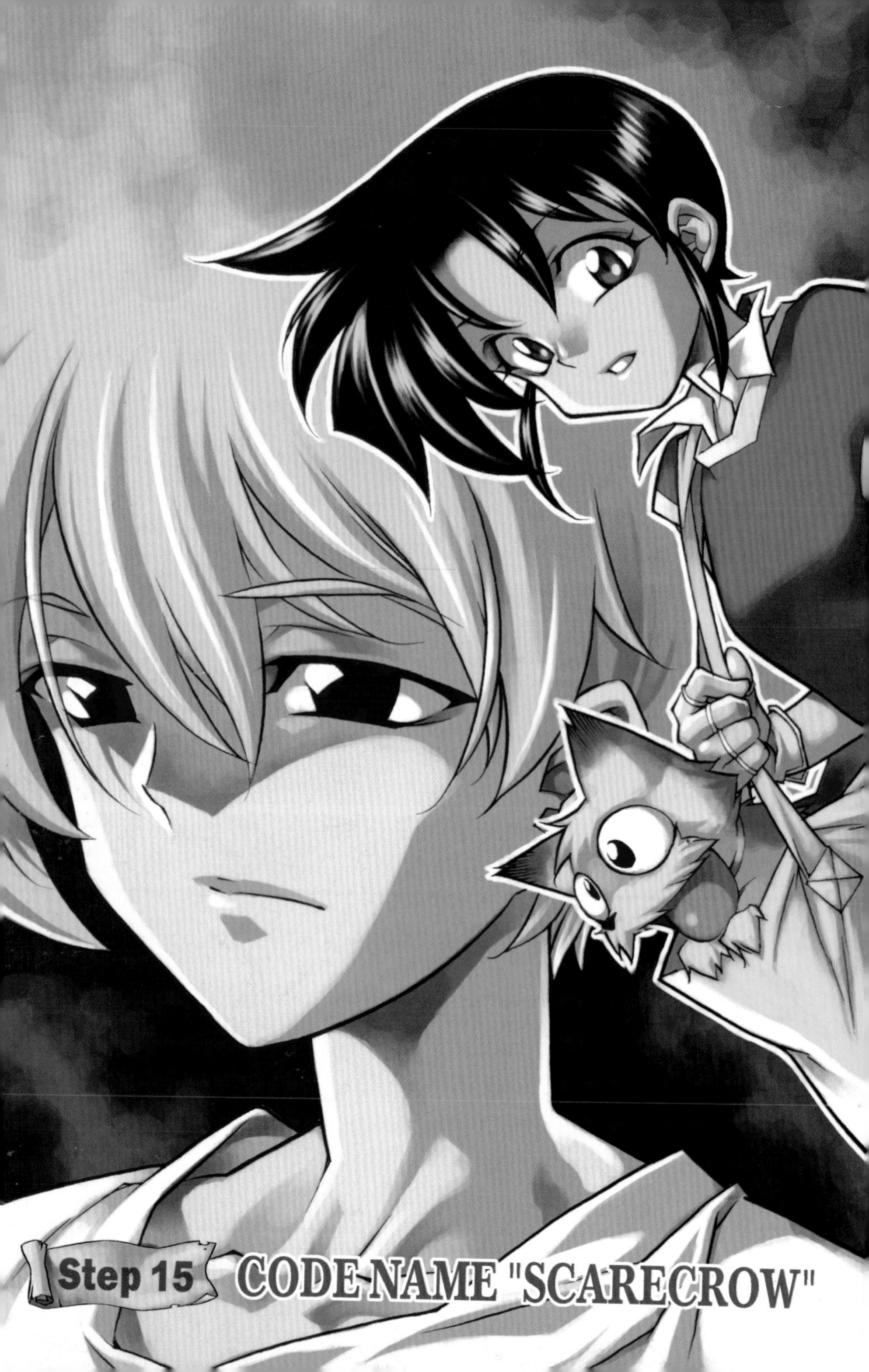
Step 15
CODE NAME "SCARECROW"

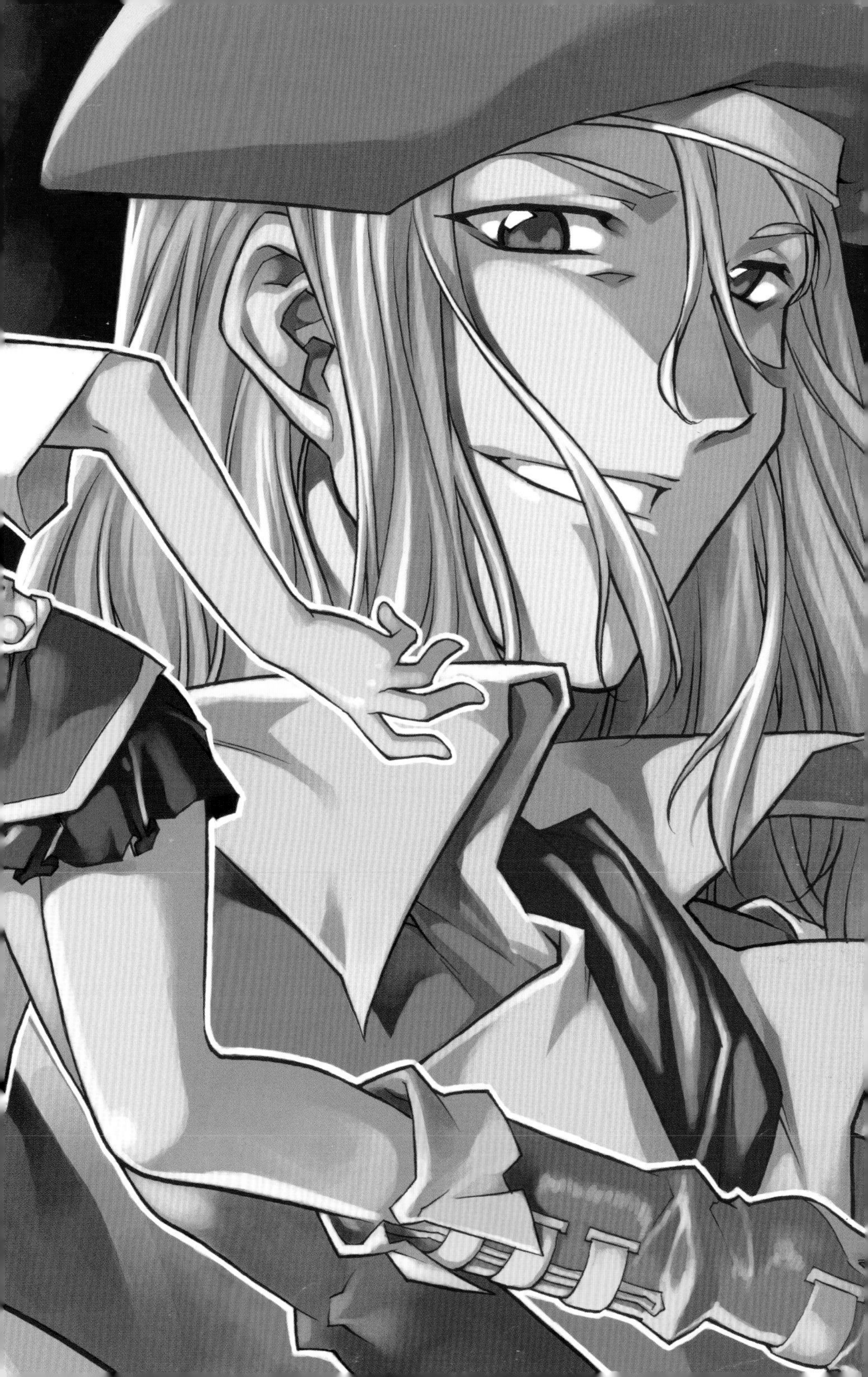

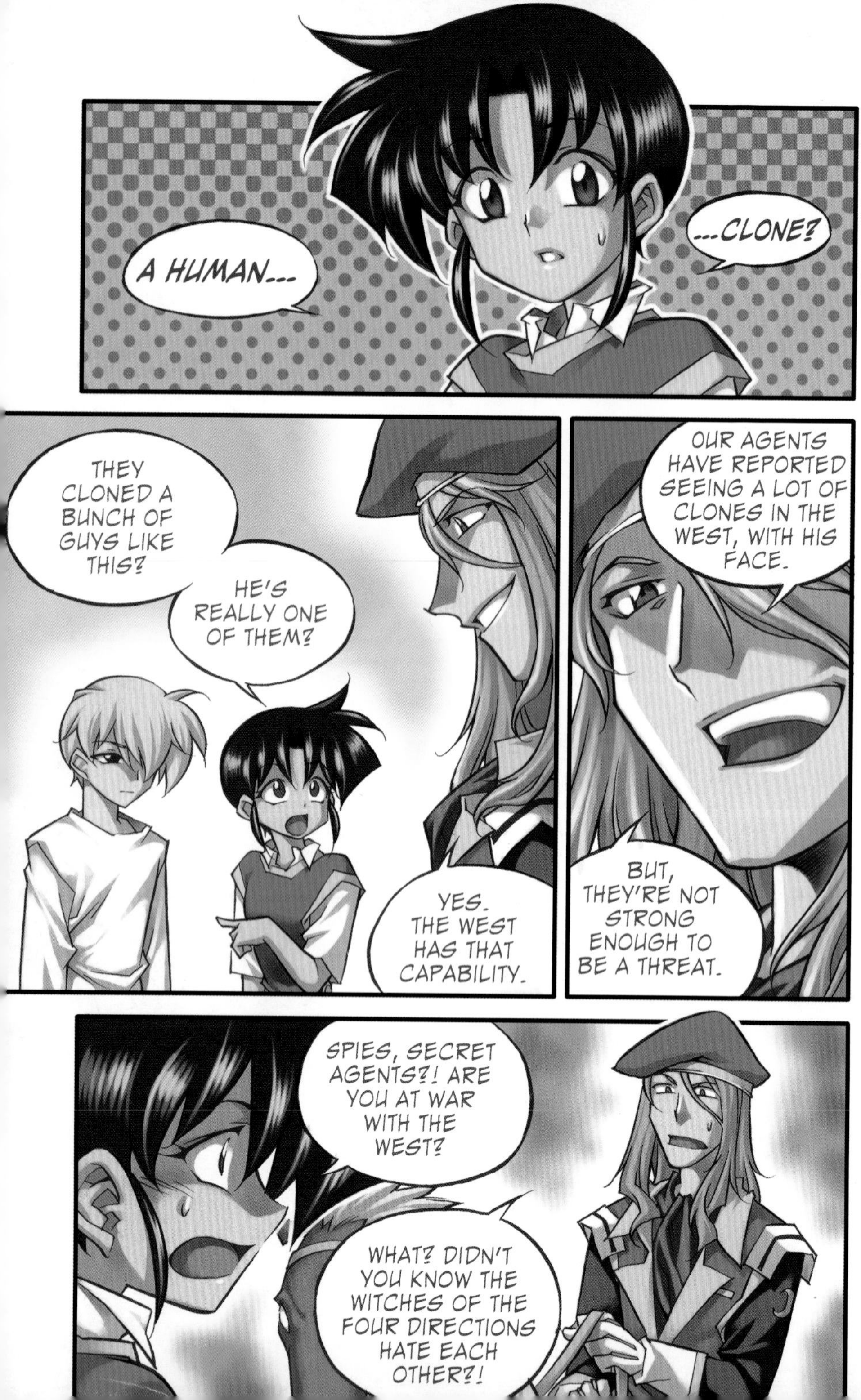
A HUMAN...
...CLONE?
THEY CLONED A BUNCH OF GUYS LIKE THIS?
HE'S REALLY ONE OF THEM?
YES. THE WEST HAS THAT CAPABILITY.
OUR AGENTS HAVE REPORTED SEEING A LOT OF CLONES IN THE WEST, WITH HIS FACE.
BUT, THEY'RE NOT STRONG ENOUGH TO BE A THREAT.
SPIES, SECRET AGENTS?! ARE YOU AT WAR WITH THE WEST?
WHAT? DIDN'T YOU KNOW THE WITCHES OF THE FOUR DIRECTIONS HATE EACH OTHER?!

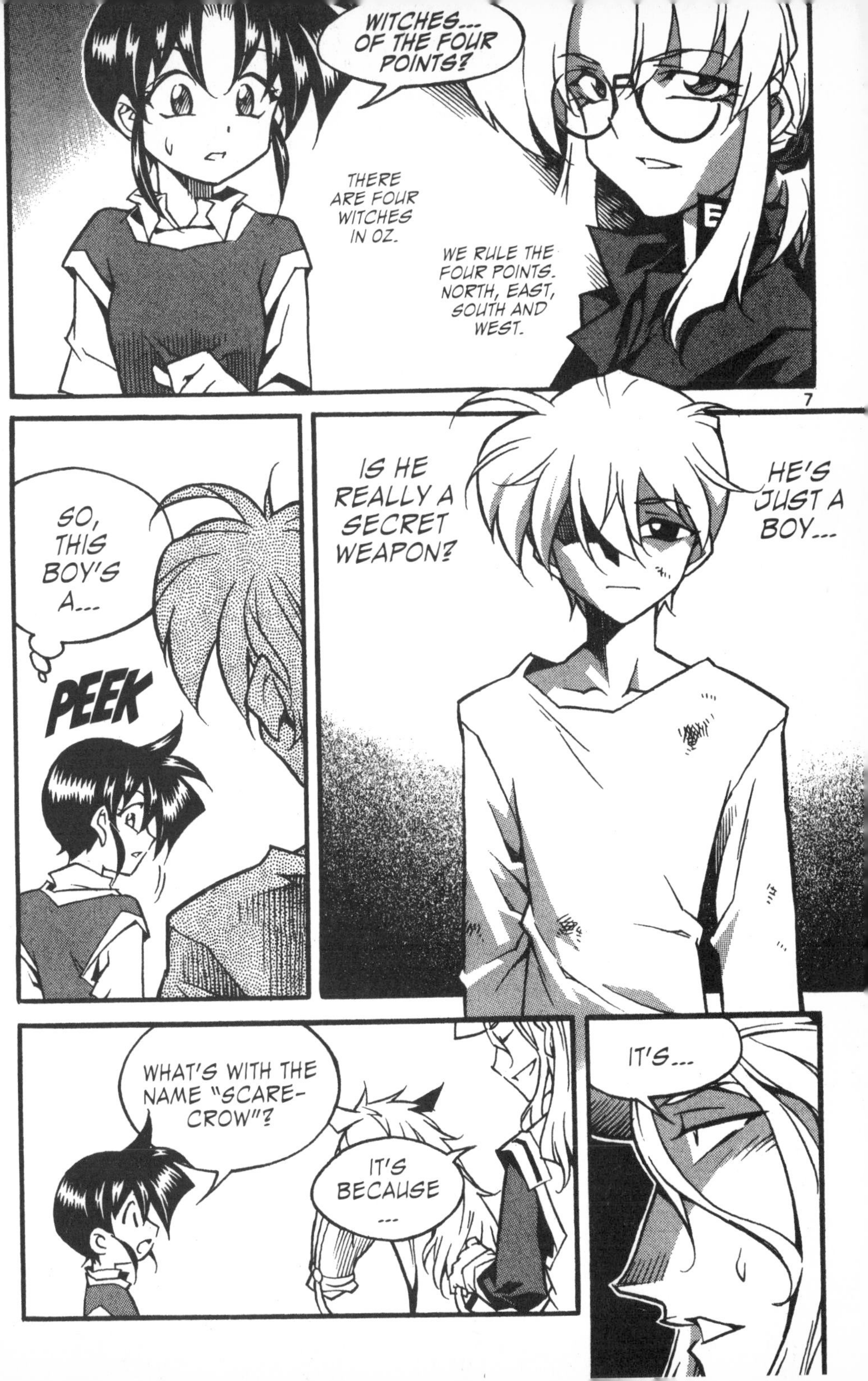
WITCHES... OF THE FOUR POINTS?
THERE ARE FOUR WITCHES IN OZ.
WE RULE THE FOUR POINTS. NORTH, EAST, SOUTH AND WEST.
SO, THIS BOY'S A...
PEEK
IS HE REALLY A SECRET WEAPON?
HE'S JUST A BOY...
WHAT'S WITH THE NAME "SCARE-CROW"?
IT'S BECAUSE ...
IT'S...

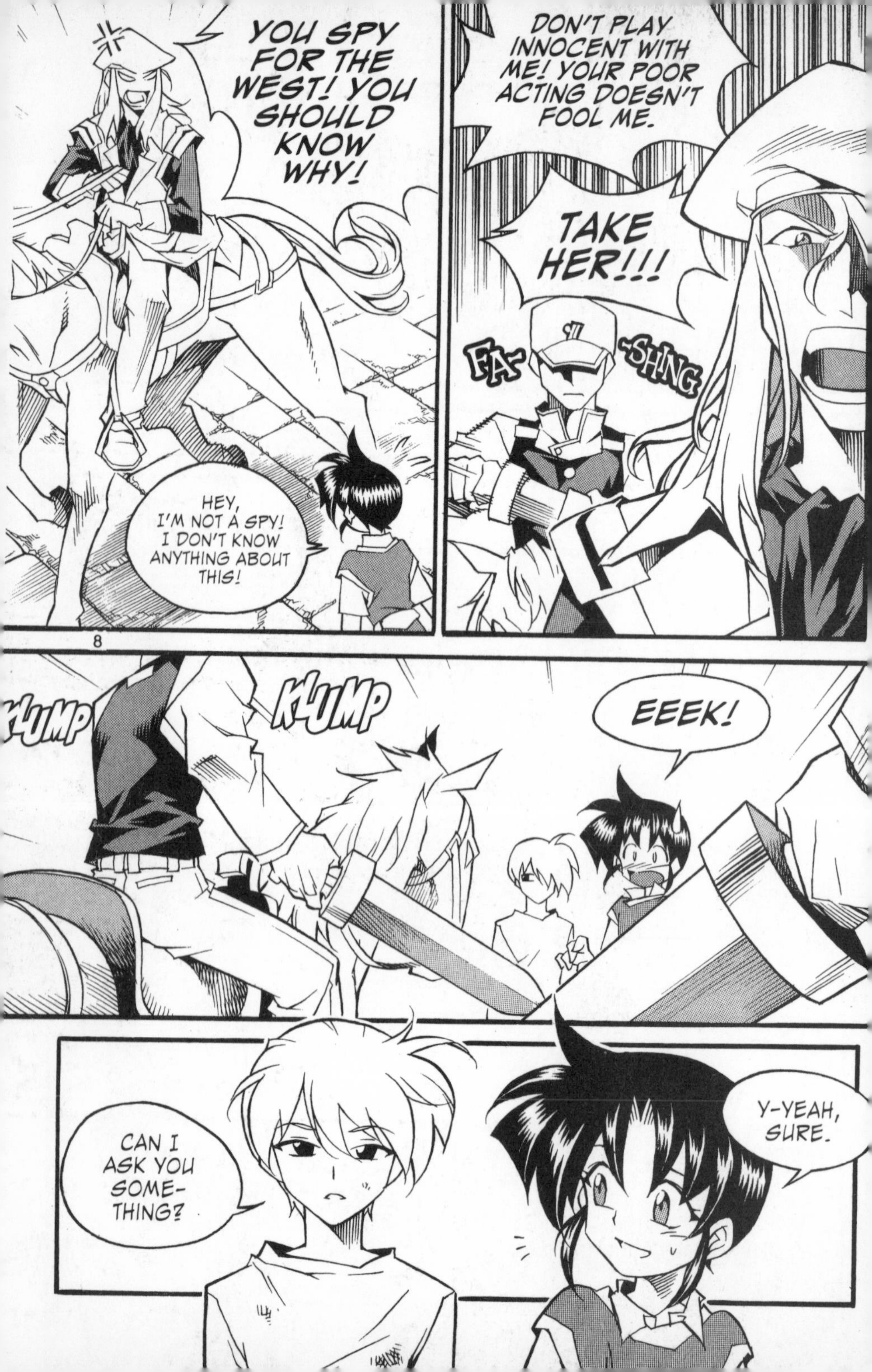
YOU SPY FOR THE WEST! YOU SHOULD KNOW WHY!
HEY, I'M NOT A SPY! I DON'T KNOW ANYTHING ABOUT THIS!
DON'T PLAY INNOCENT WITH ME! YOUR POOR ACTING DOESN'T FOOL ME.
TAKE HER!!!
FA-
-SHING
KLUMP
KLUMP
EEEK!
CAN I ASK YOU SOME-THING?
Y-YEAH, SURE.

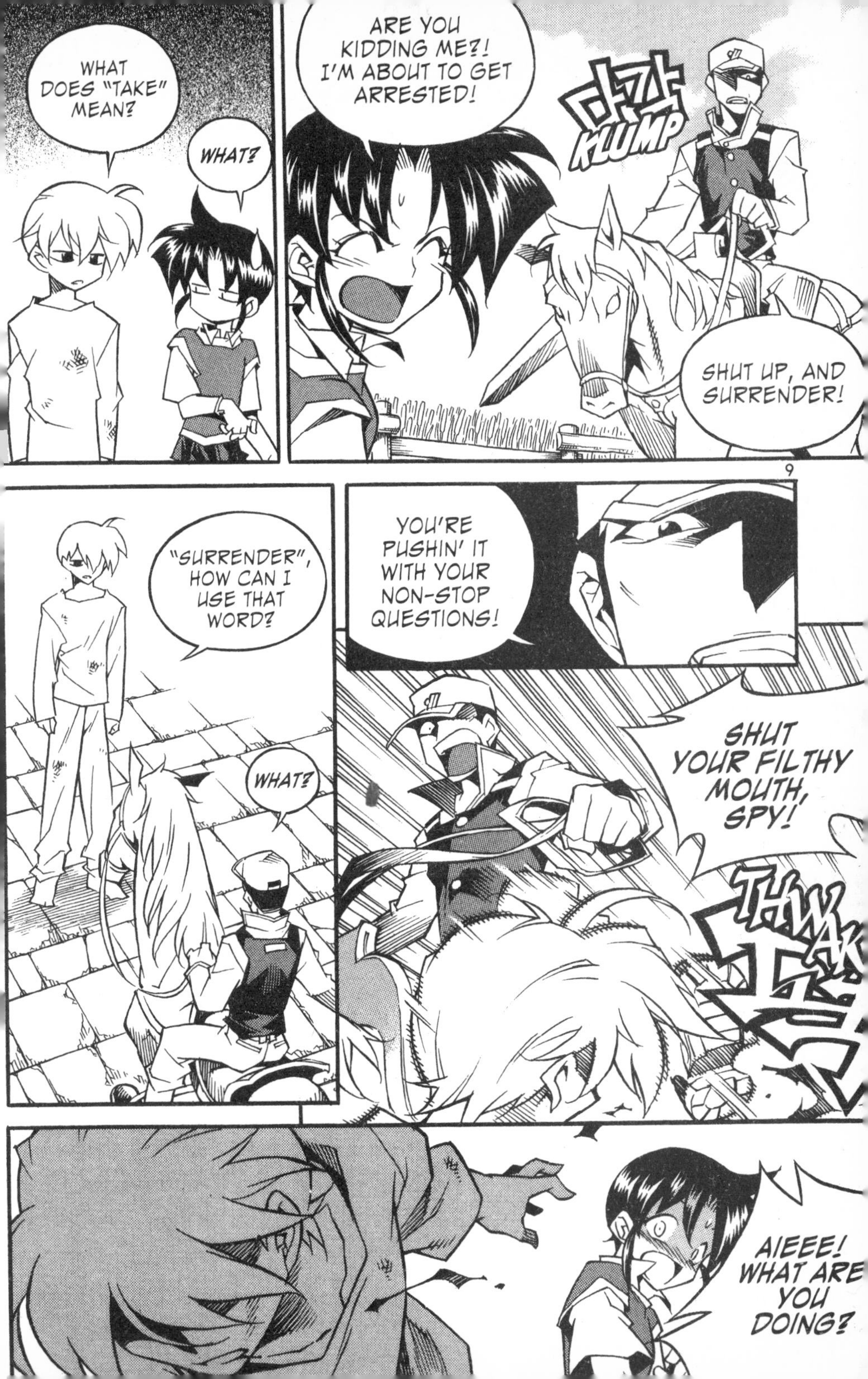
WHAT DOES "TAKE" MEAN?
WHAT?
ARE YOU KIDDING ME?! I'M ABOUT TO GET ARRESTED!
KLUMP
SHUT UP, AND SURRENDER!
"SURRENDER", HOW CAN I USE THAT WORD?
WHAT?
YOU'RE PUSHIN' IT WITH YOUR NON-STOP QUESTIONS!
SHUT YOUR FILTHY MOUTH, SPY!
THWAK
AIEEE! WHAT ARE YOU DOING?

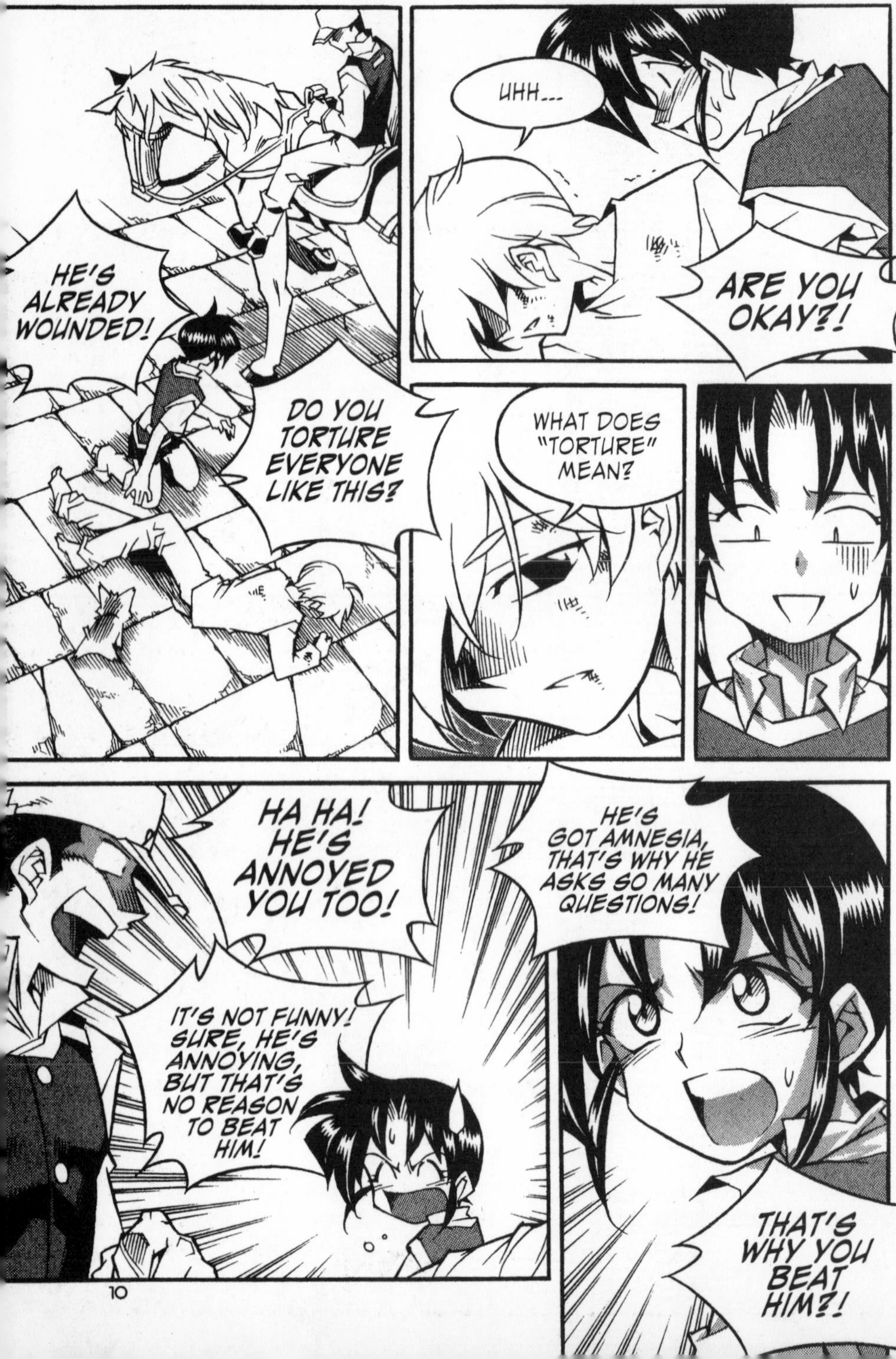
HE'S ALREADY WOUNDED!
DO YOU TORTURE EVERYONE LIKE THIS?
UHH...
ARE YOU OKAY?!
WHAT DOES "TORTURE" MEAN?
HA HA! HE'S ANNOYED YOU TOO!
IT'S NOT FUNNY! SURE, HE'S ANNOYING, BUT THAT'S NO REASON TO BEAT HIM!
HE'S GOT AMNESIA, THAT'S WHY HE ASKS SO MANY QUESTIONS!
THAT'S WHY YOU BEAT HIM?!

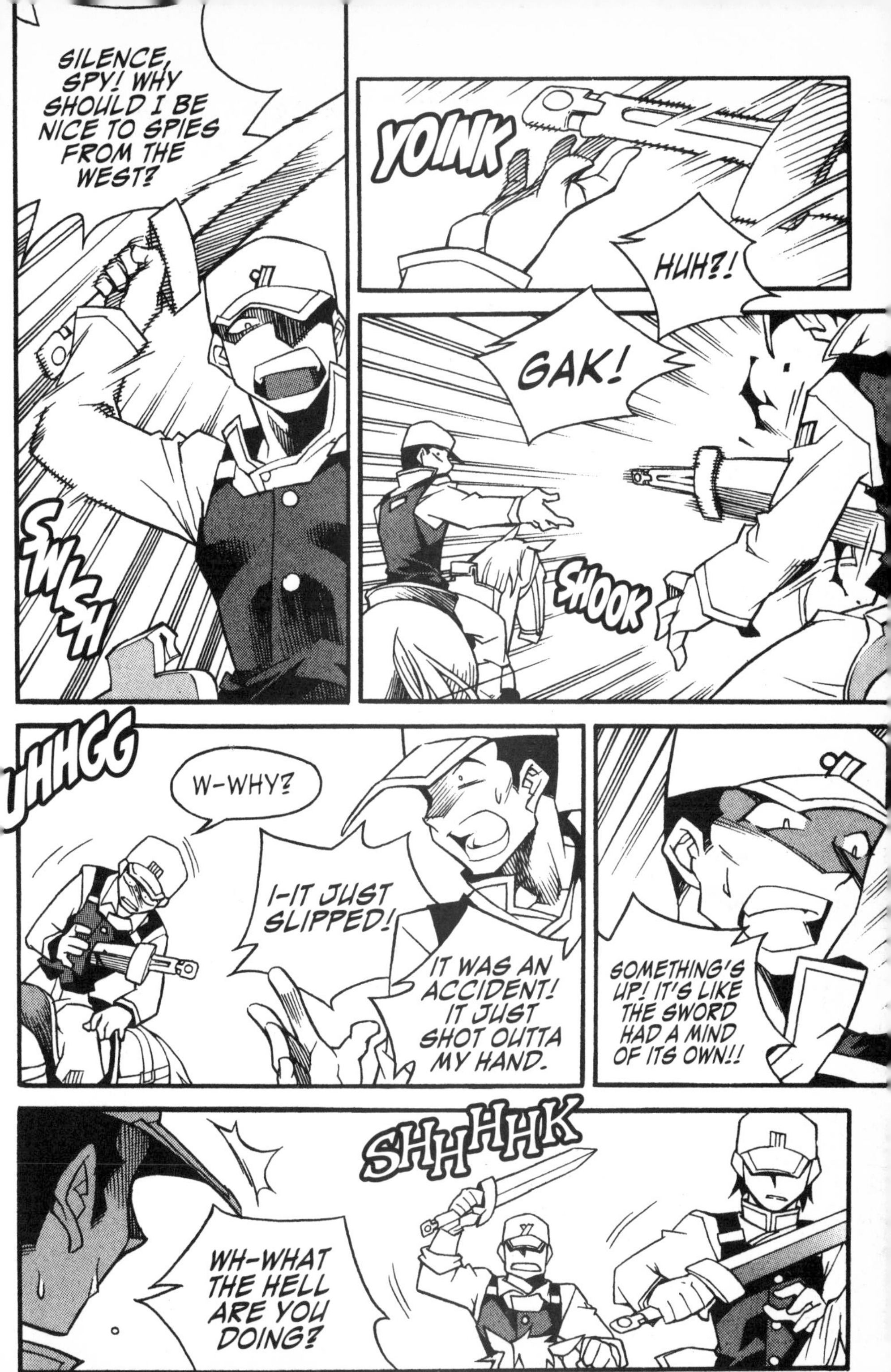
SILENCE, SPY! WHY SHOULD I BE NICE TO SPIES FROM THE WEST?
SWISH
YOINK
HUH?!
GAK!
SHOOK
UHHGG
W-WHY?
I-IT JUST SLIPPED!
IT WAS AN ACCIDENT! IT JUST SHOT OUTTA MY HAND.
SOMETHING'S UP! IT'S LIKE THE SWORD HAD A MIND OF ITS OWN!!
WH-WHAT THE HELL ARE YOU DOING?
SHHHHK

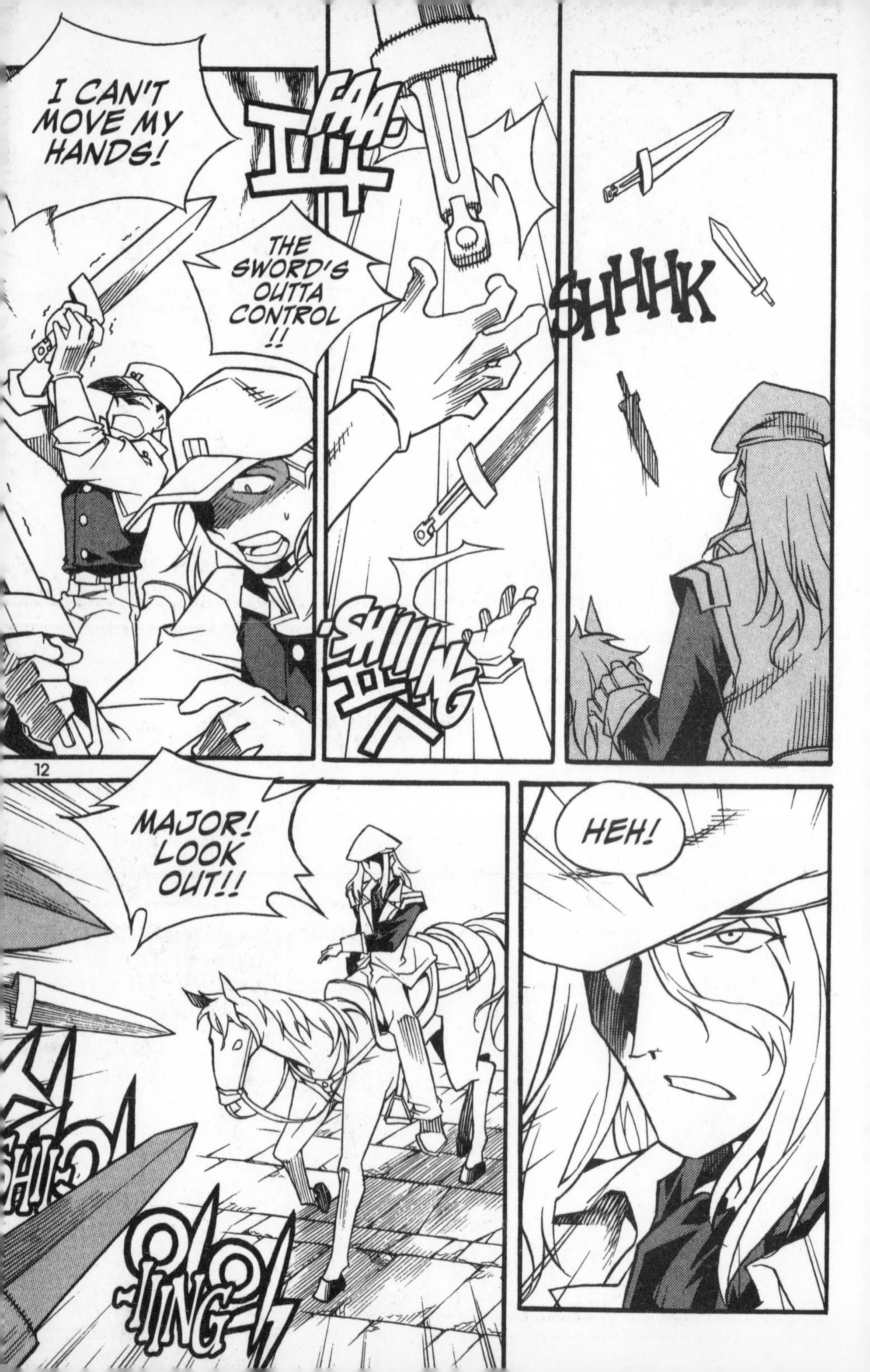
I CAN'T MOVE MY HANDS!
THE SWORD'S OUTTA CONTROL!!
SHHHK
MAJOR! LOOK OUT!!
HEH!

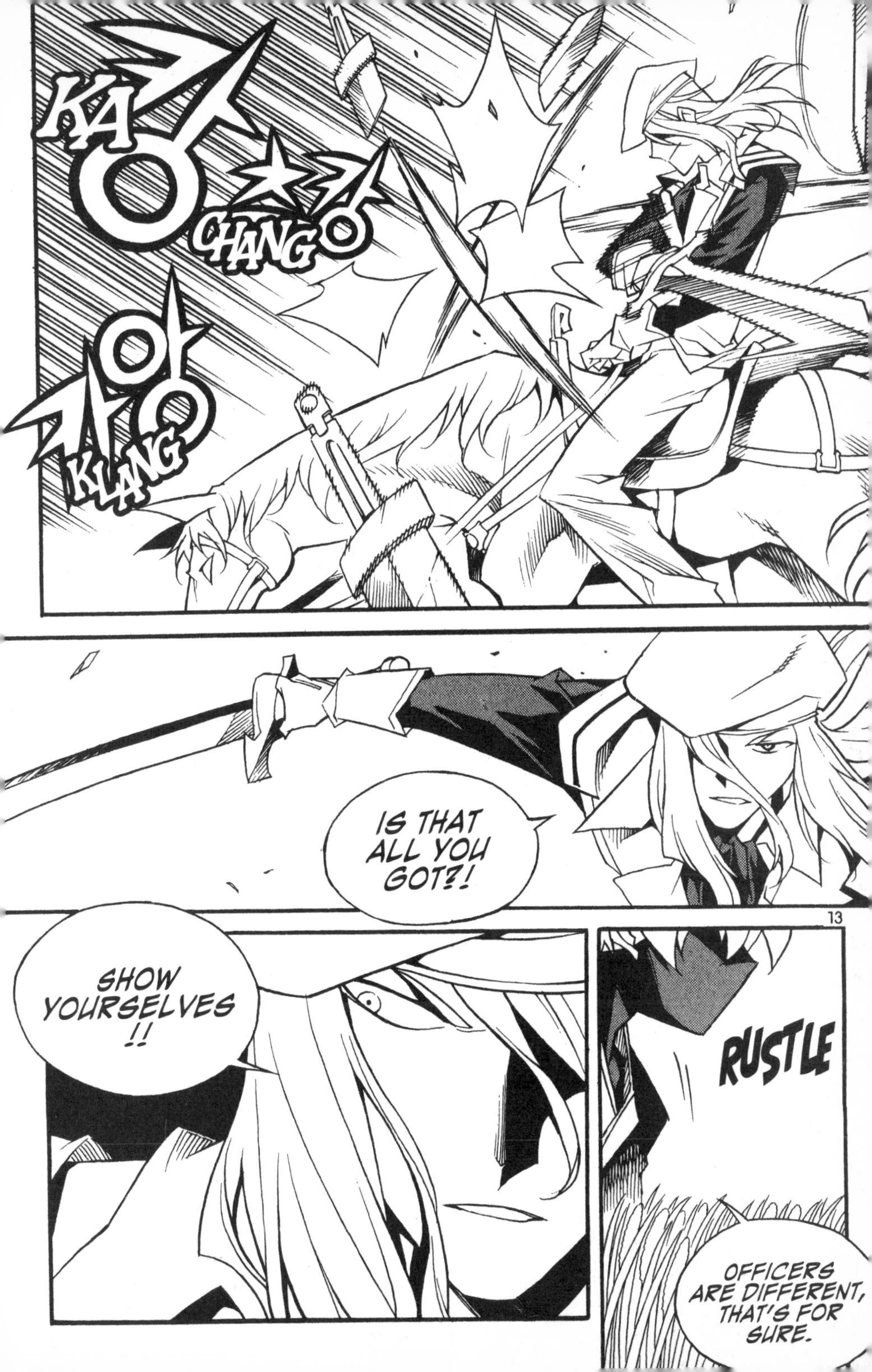
KA
CHANG
KLANG
IS THAT ALL YOU GOT?!
SHOW YOURSELVES !!
RUSTLE
OFFICERS ARE DIFFERENT, THAT'S FOR SURE.
13

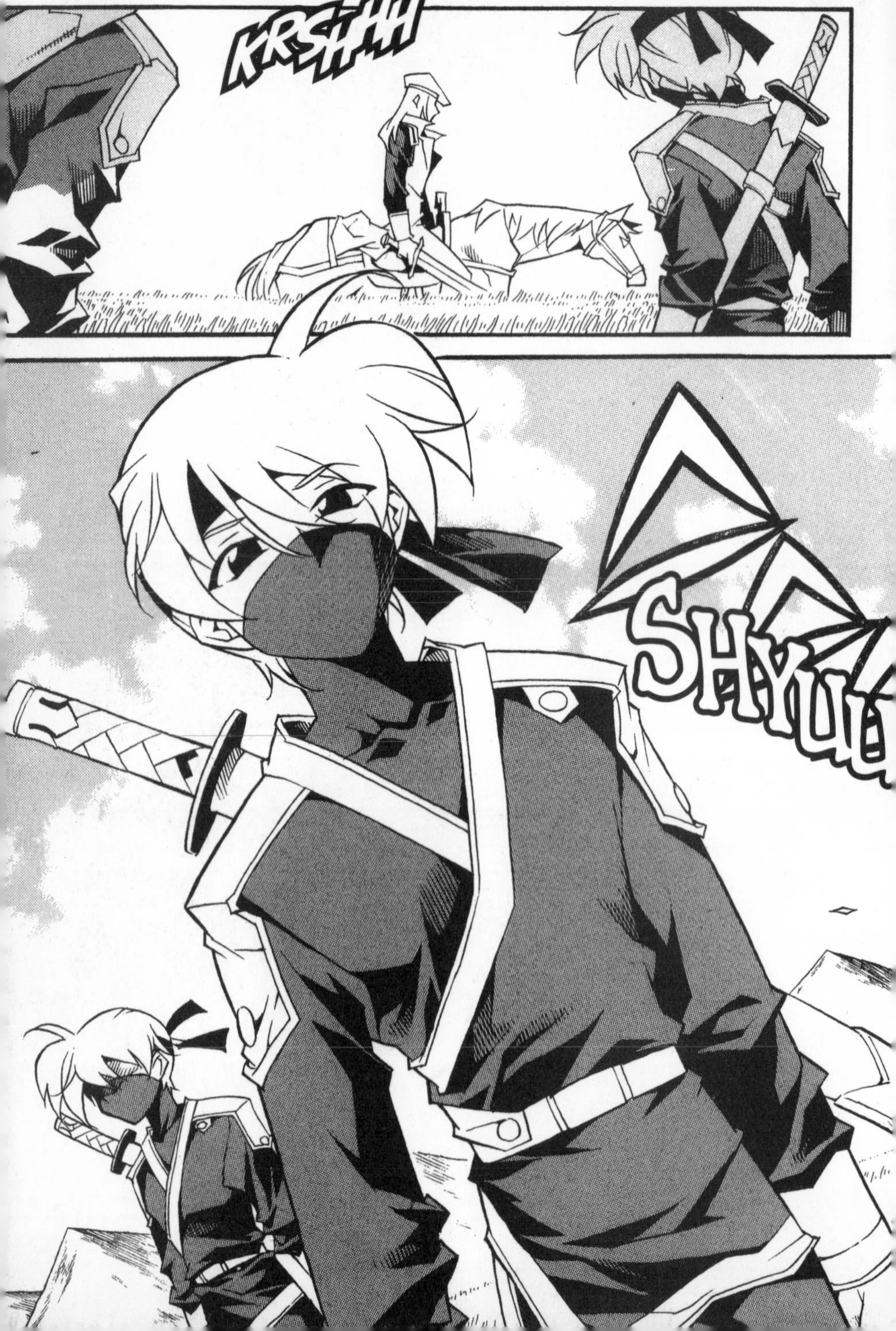
KRSHHH
SHYUU

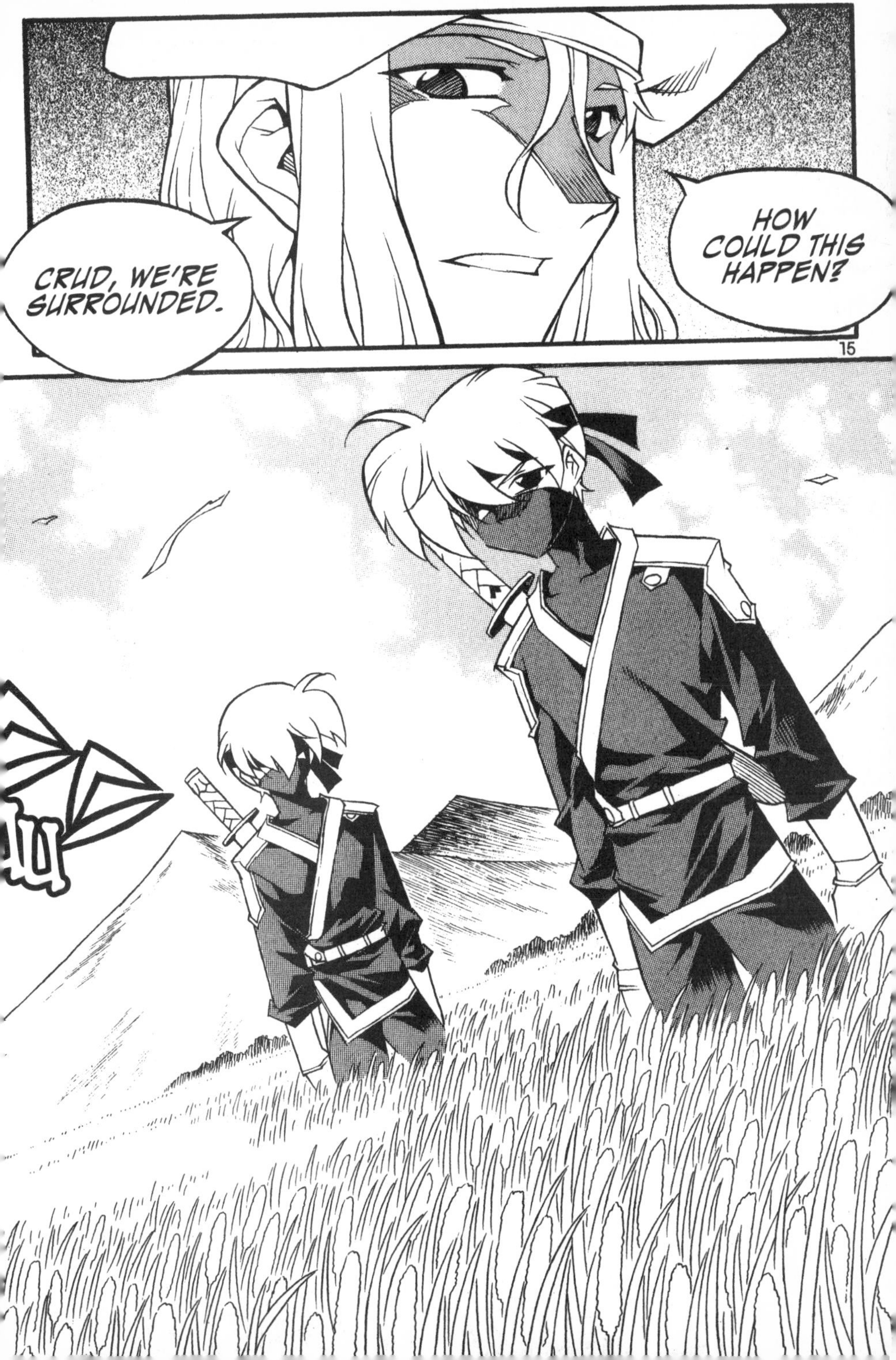
CRUD, WE'RE SURROUNDED.
HOW COULD THIS HAPPEN?

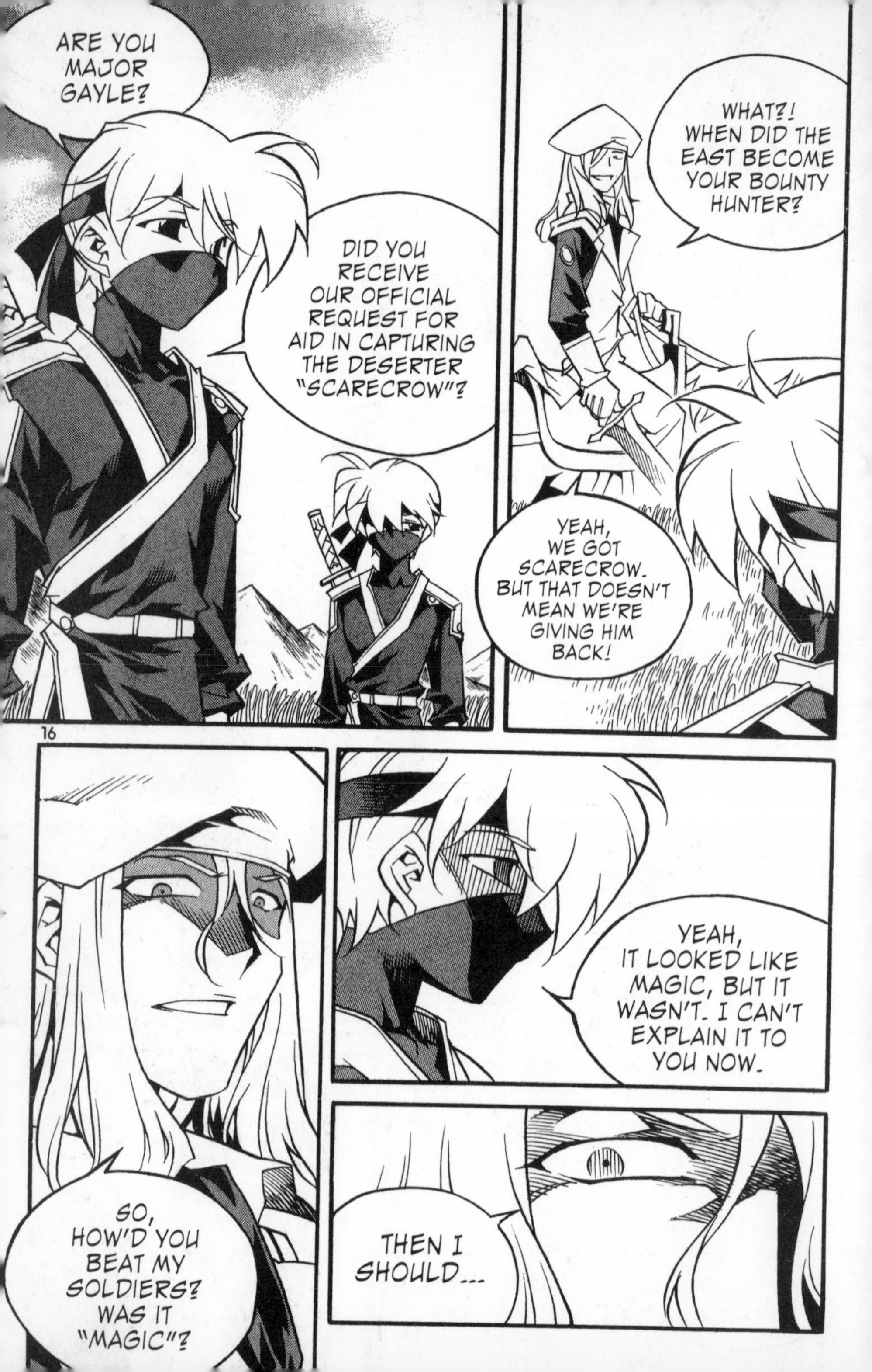
ARE YOU MAJOR GAYLE?
DID YOU RECEIVE OUR OFFICIAL REQUEST FOR AID IN CAPTURING THE DESERTER "SCARECROW"?
WHAT?! WHEN DID THE EAST BECOME YOUR BOUNTY HUNTER?
YEAH, WE GOT SCARECROW. BUT THAT DOESN'T MEAN WE'RE GIVING HIM BACK!
SO, HOW'D YOU BEAT MY SOLDIERS? WAS IT "MAGIC"?
YEAH, IT LOOKED LIKE MAGIC, BUT IT WASN'T. I CAN'T EXPLAIN IT TO YOU NOW.
THEN I SHOULD...

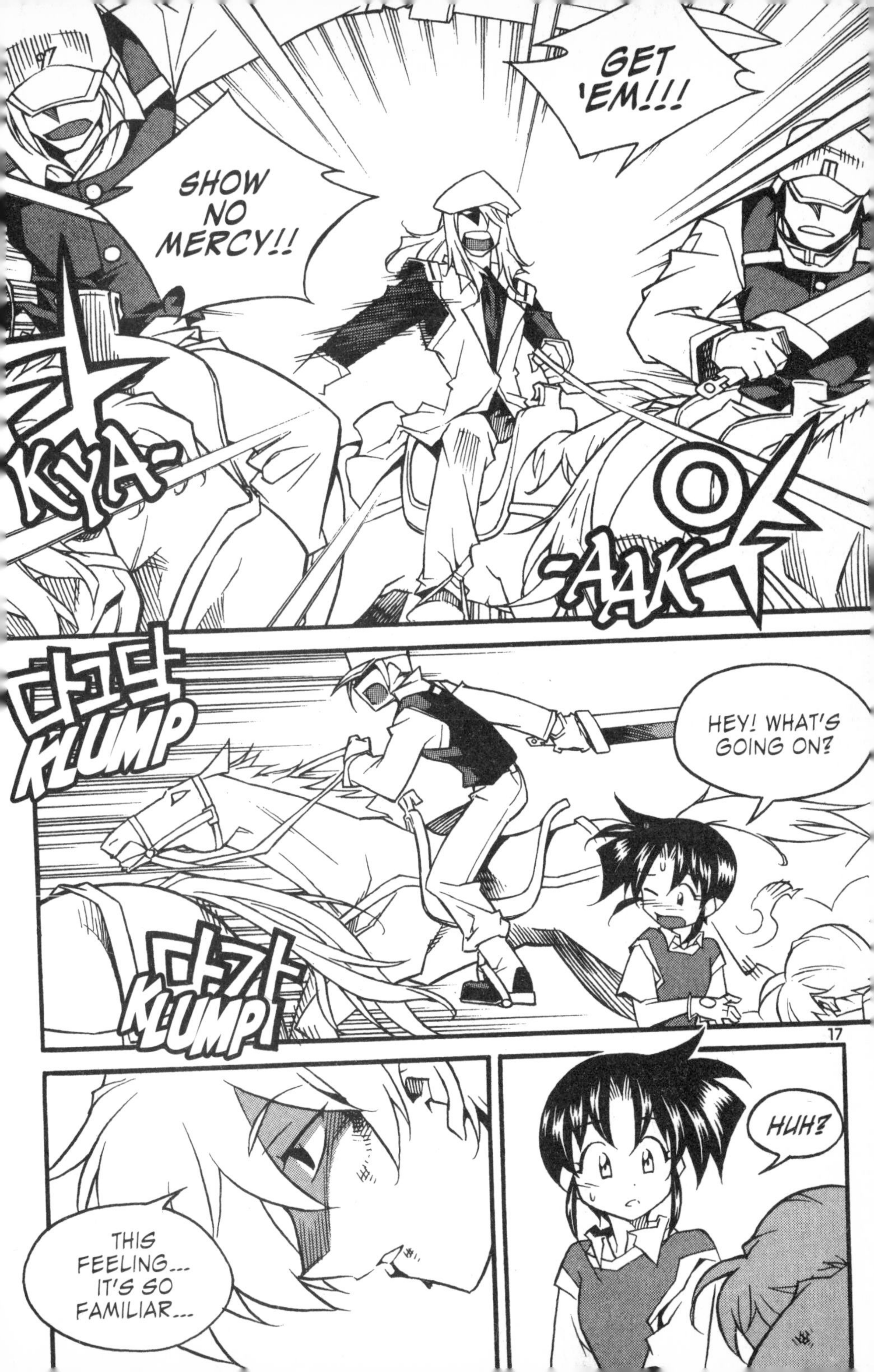
SHOW NO MERCY!!
GET 'EM!!!
KYA-
-AAK
다그닥
KLUMP
HEY! WHAT'S GOING ON?
KLUMP
THIS FEELING... IT'S SO FAMILIAR...
HUH?

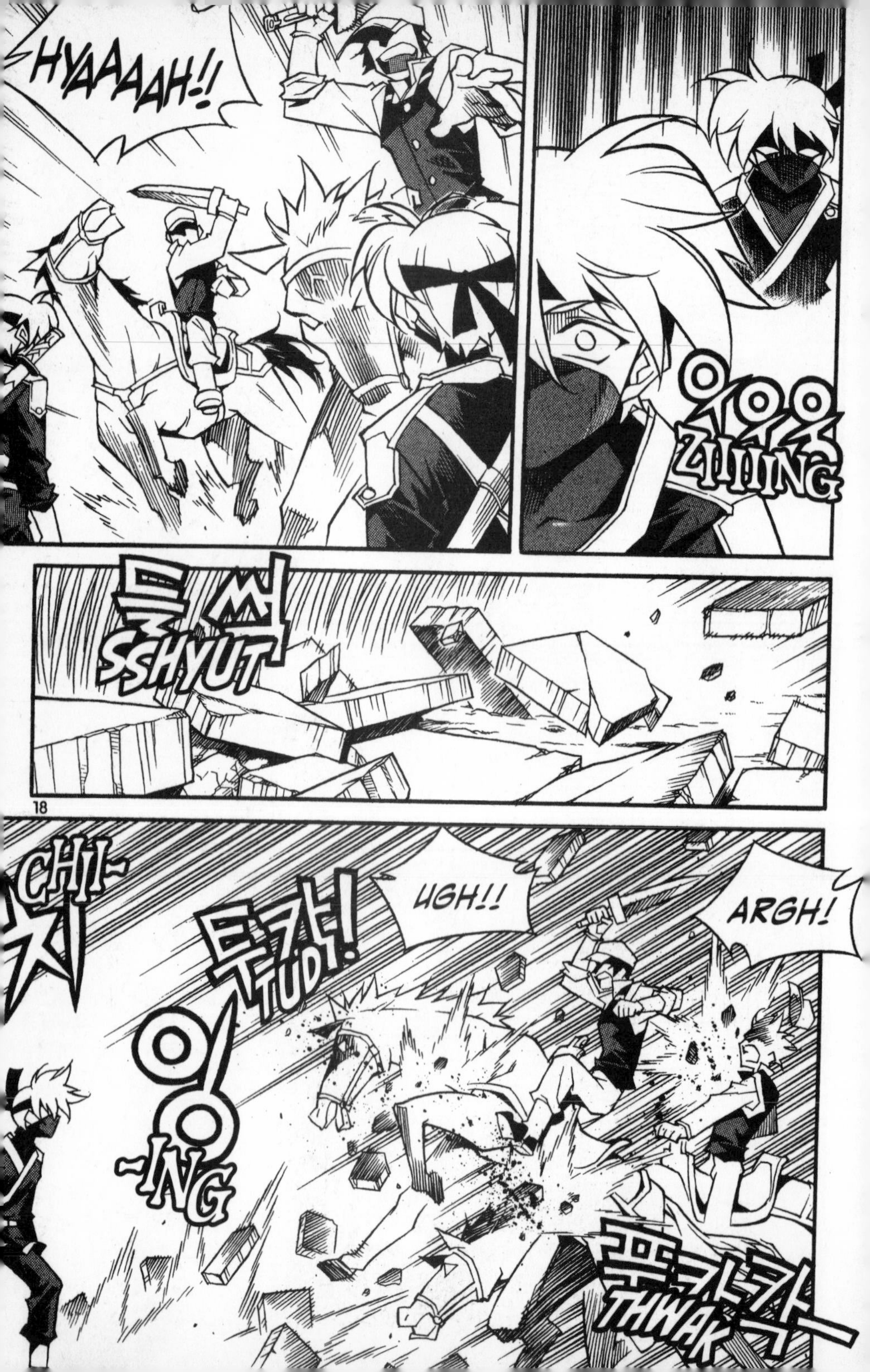
HYAAAAH!!
ZIIING
SSHYUT
CHI-
TUD
UGH!!
ARGH!
-ING
THWAK

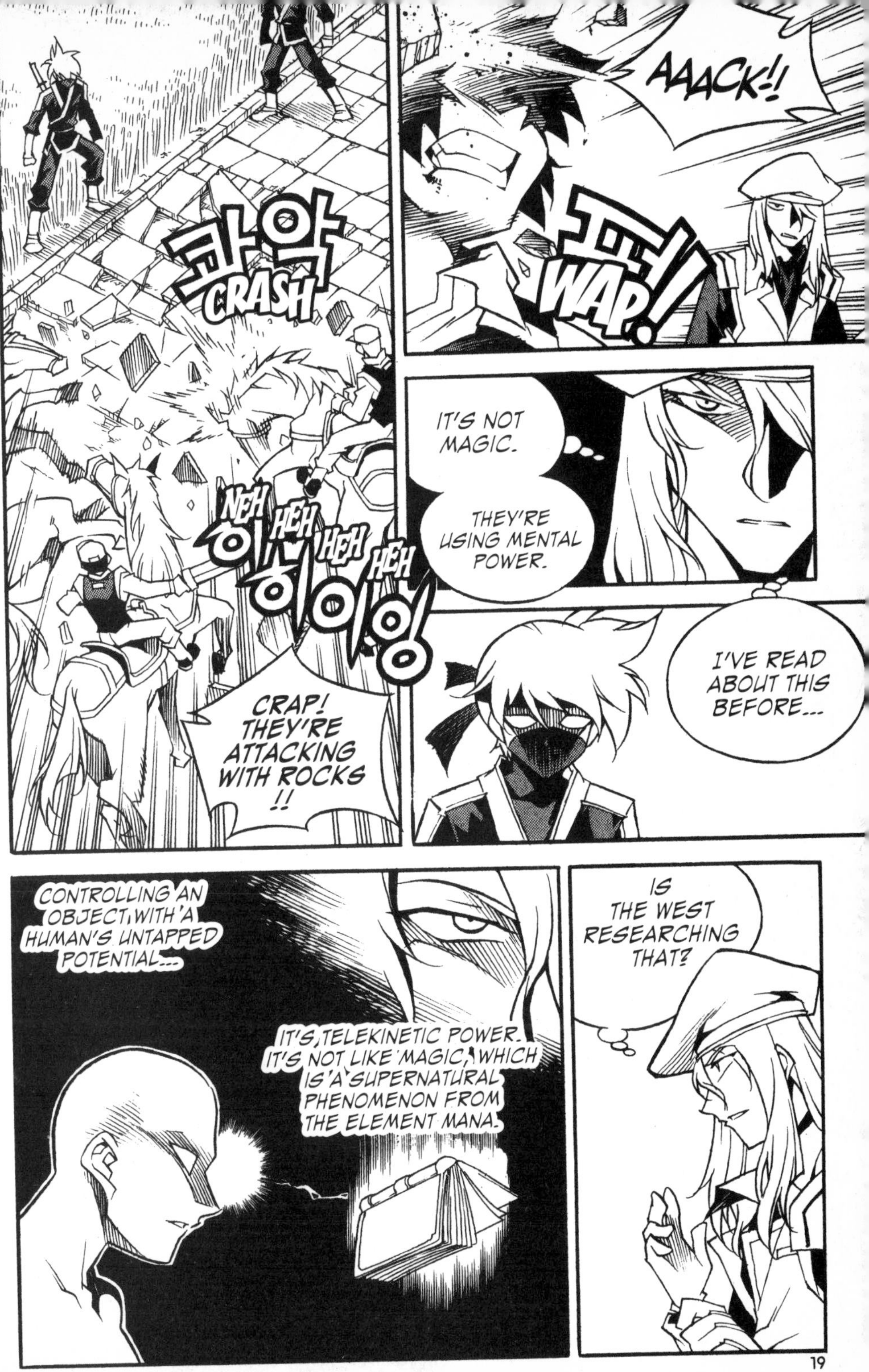
CRASH
NEH HEH HEH HEH
CRAP! THEY'RE ATTACKING WITH ROCKS!!
AAACK!!
WAP!
IT'S NOT MAGIC.
THEY'RE USING MENTAL POWER.
I'VE READ ABOUT THIS BEFORE...
CONTROLLING AN OBJECT WITH A HUMAN'S UNTAPPED POTENTIAL...
IT'S TELEKINETIC POWER. IT'S NOT LIKE MAGIC, WHICH IS A SUPERNATURAL PHENOMENON FROM THE ELEMENT MANA.
IS THE WEST RESEARCHING THAT?

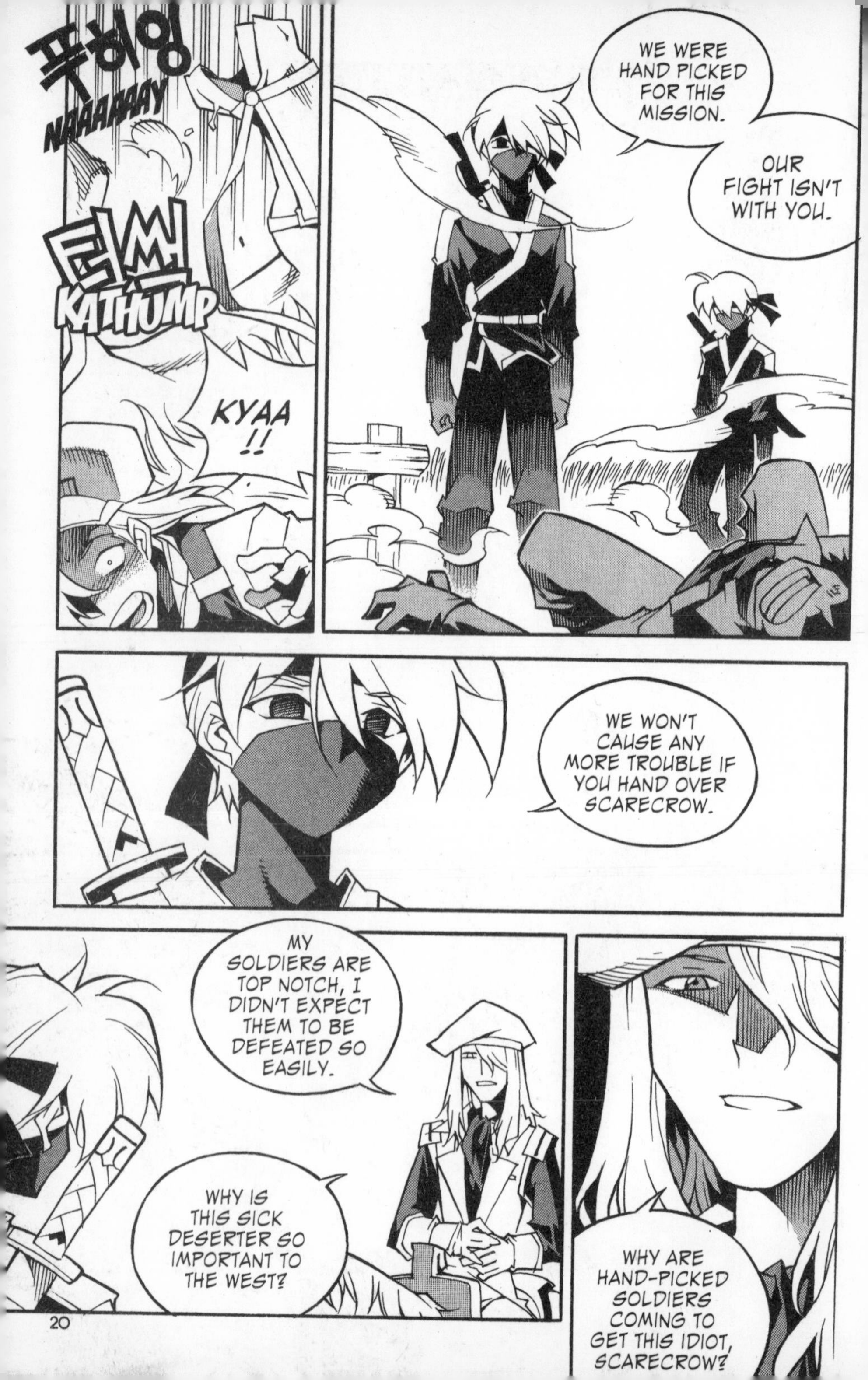

푸히잉
NAAAAAY
덜썩
KATHUMP
KYAA !!
WE WERE HAND PICKED FOR THIS MISSION.
OUR FIGHT ISN'T WITH YOU.
WE WON'T CAUSE ANY MORE TROUBLE IF YOU HAND OVER SCARECROW.
MY SOLDIERS ARE TOP NOTCH, I DIDN'T EXPECT THEM TO BE DEFEATED SO EASILY.
WHY IS THIS SICK DESERTER SO IMPORTANT TO THE WEST?
WHY ARE HAND-PICKED SOLDIERS COMING TO GET THIS IDIOT, SCARECROW?

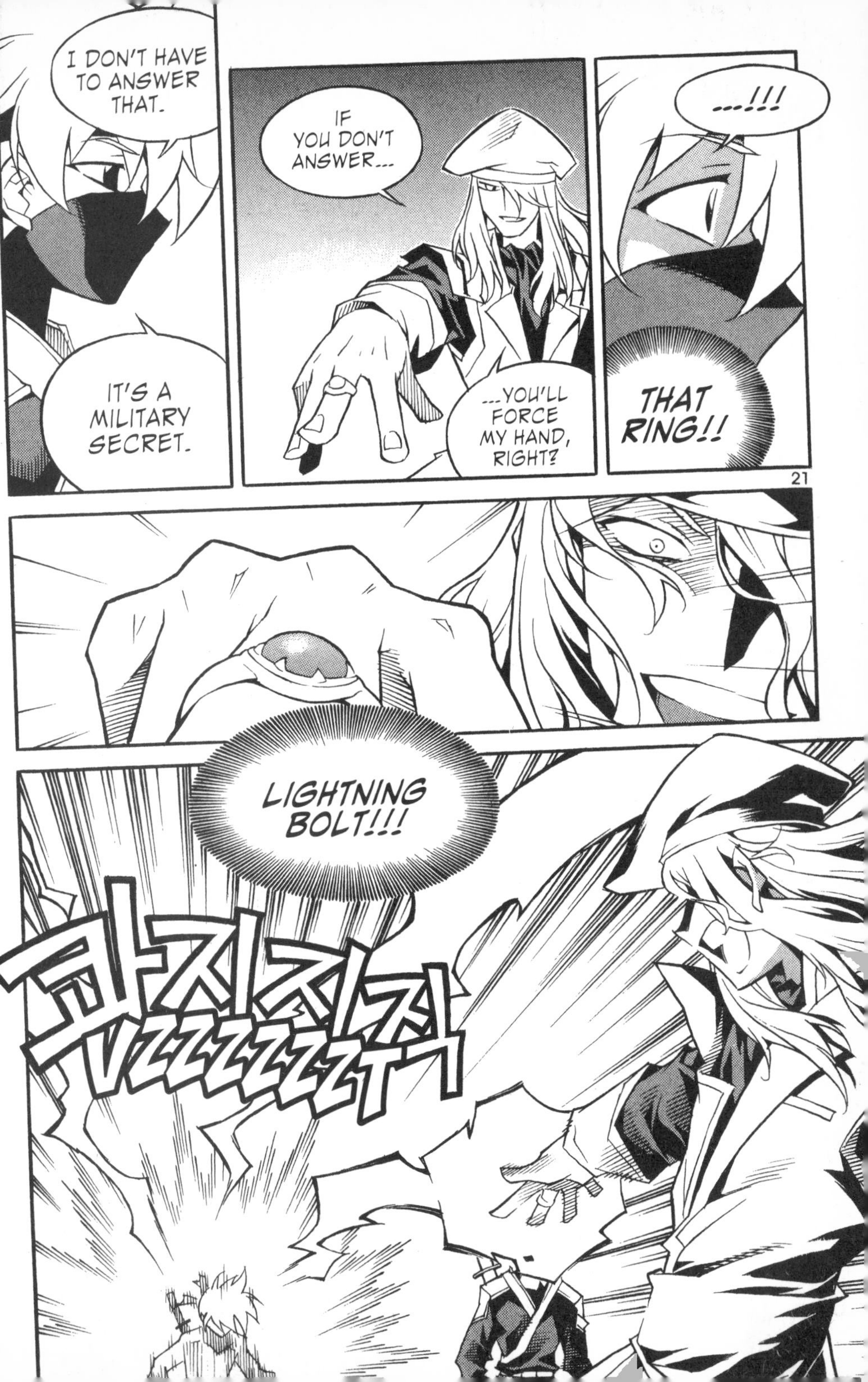
I DON'T HAVE TO ANSWER THAT.
IT'S A MILITARY SECRET.
IF YOU DON'T ANSWER...
...YOU'LL FORCE MY HAND, RIGHT?
...!!!
THAT RING!!
LIGHTNING BOLT!!!
VZZZZZZZT

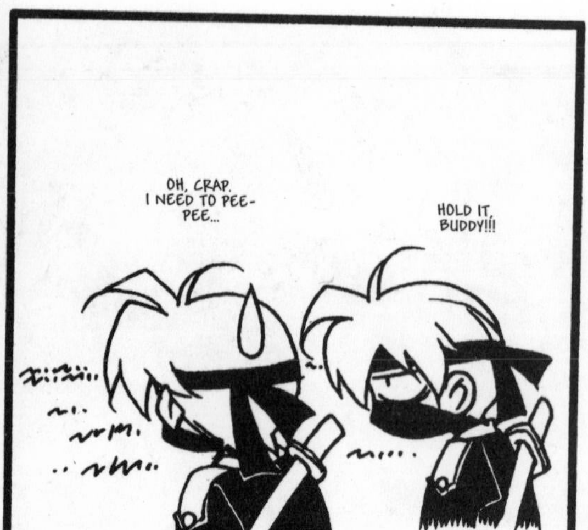
OH, CRAP. I NEED TO PEE-PEE...
HOLD IT, BUDDY!!!

Step 16 IT'S NOT THE SAME

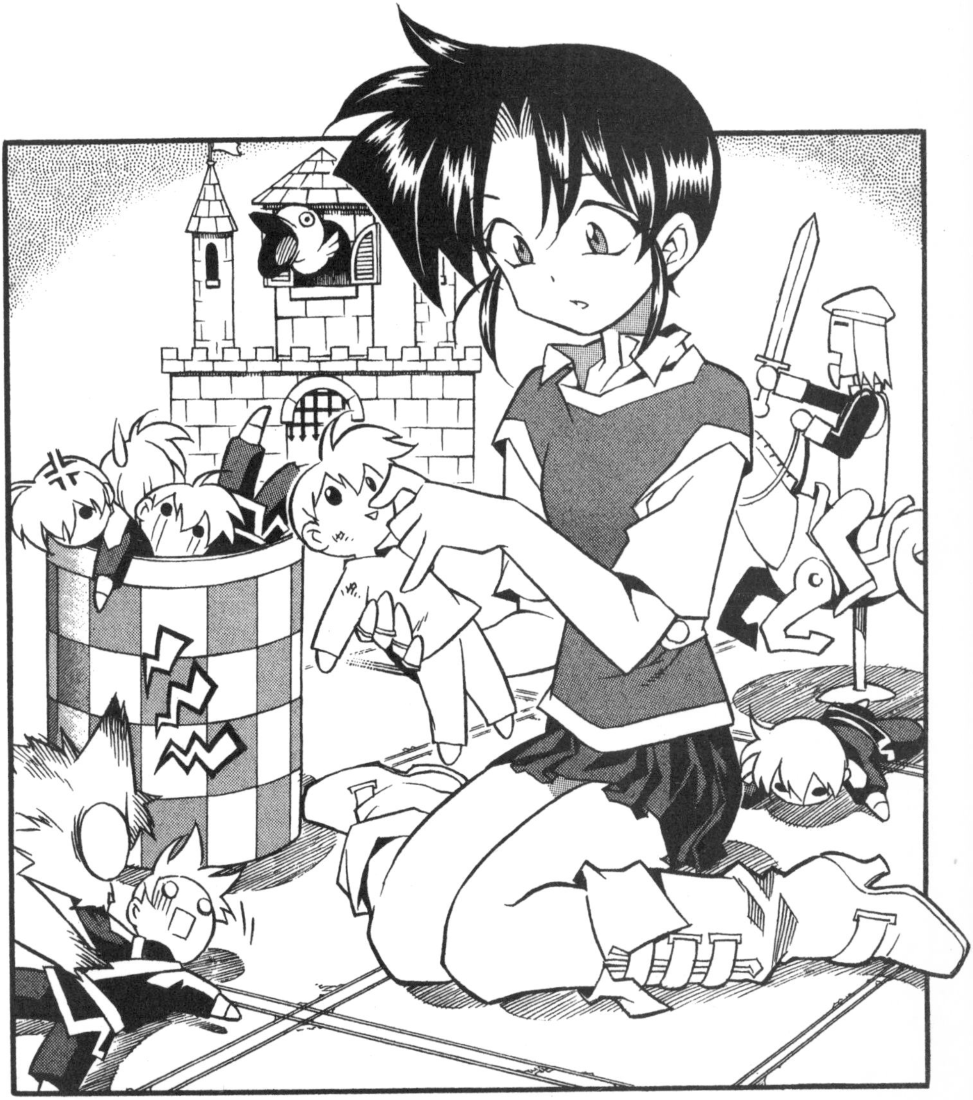

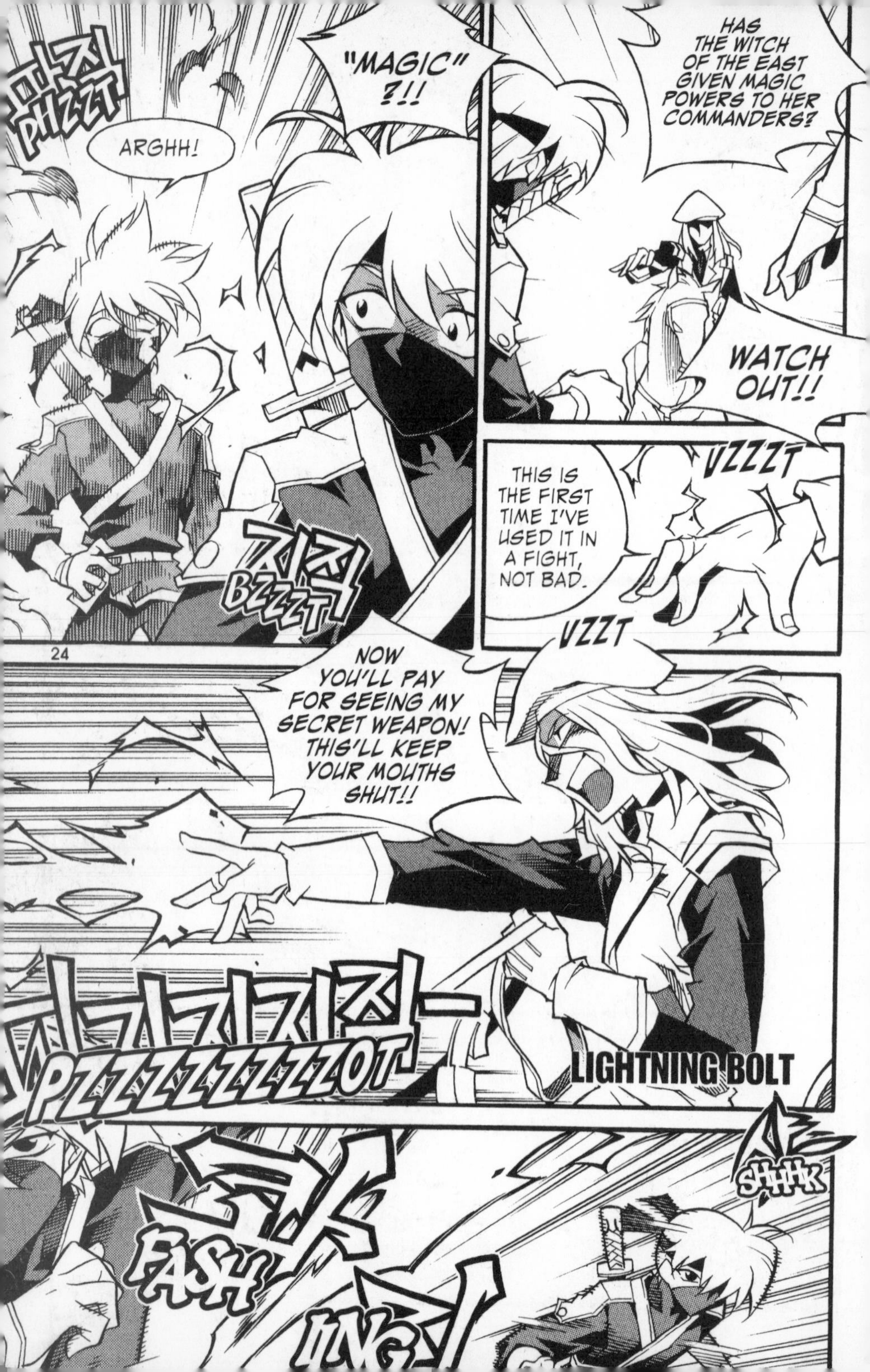
PHZZT
ARGHH!
"MAGIC" ?!!
BZZZT
HAS THE WITCH OF THE EAST GIVEN MAGIC POWERS TO HER COMMANDERS?
WATCH OUT!!
VZZZT
THIS IS THE FIRST TIME I'VE USED IT IN A FIGHT, NOT BAD.
VZZT
NOW YOU'LL PAY FOR SEEING MY SECRET WEAPON! THIS'LL KEEP YOUR MOUTHS SHUT!!
PZZZZZZZZOT
LIGHTNING BOLT
SHHHK
FASH
ING

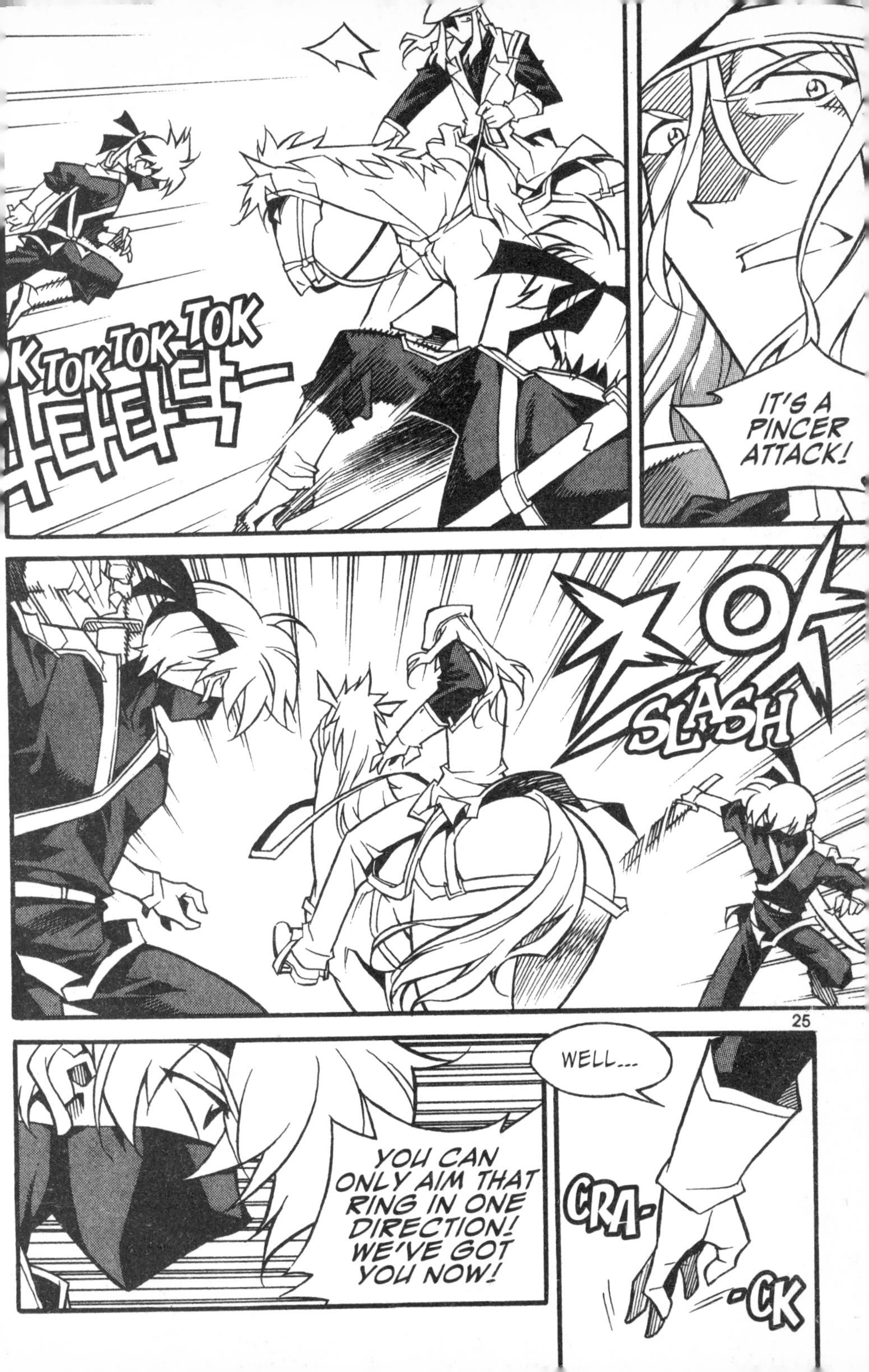
K TOK TOK TOK
IT'S A PINCER ATTACK!
SLASH
YOU CAN ONLY AIM THAT RING IN ONE DIRECTION! WE'VE GOT YOU NOW!
WELL...
CRA-
-CK

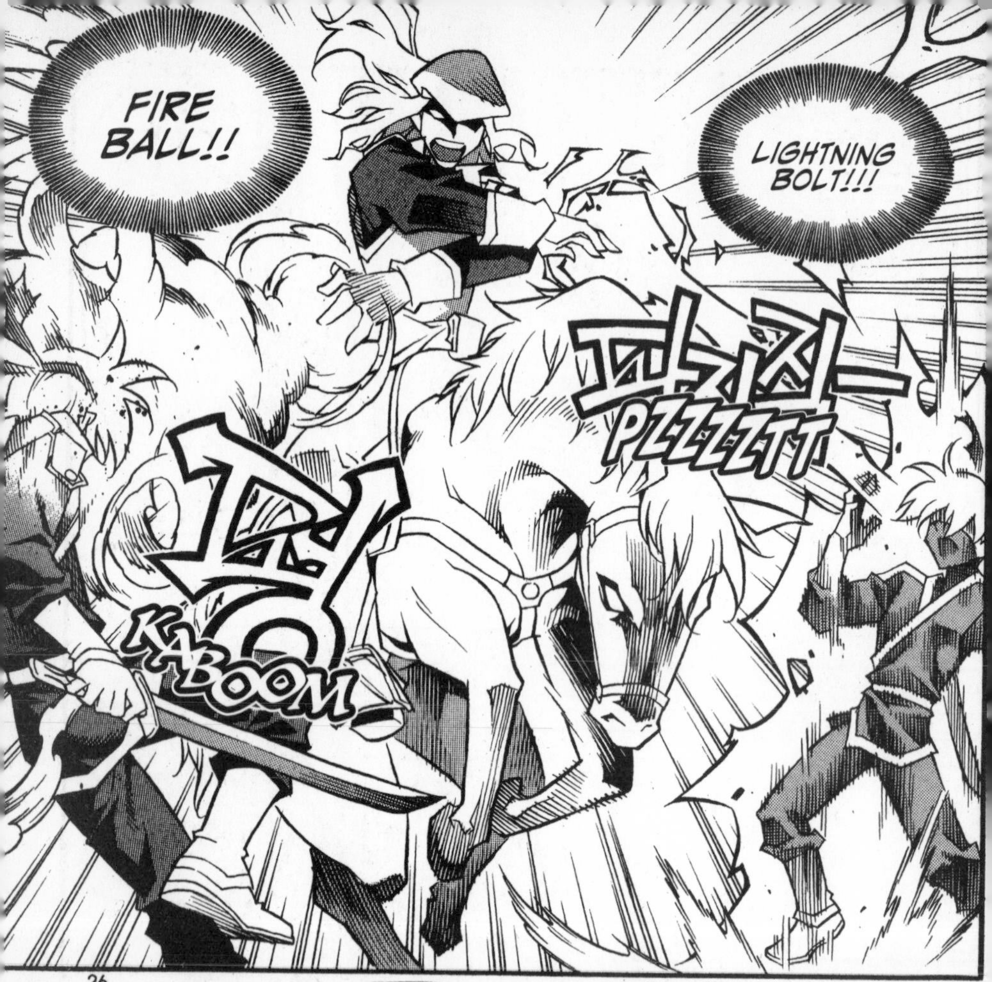
FIRE BALL!!
LIGHTNING BOLT!!!
KABOOM
PZZZZZTT

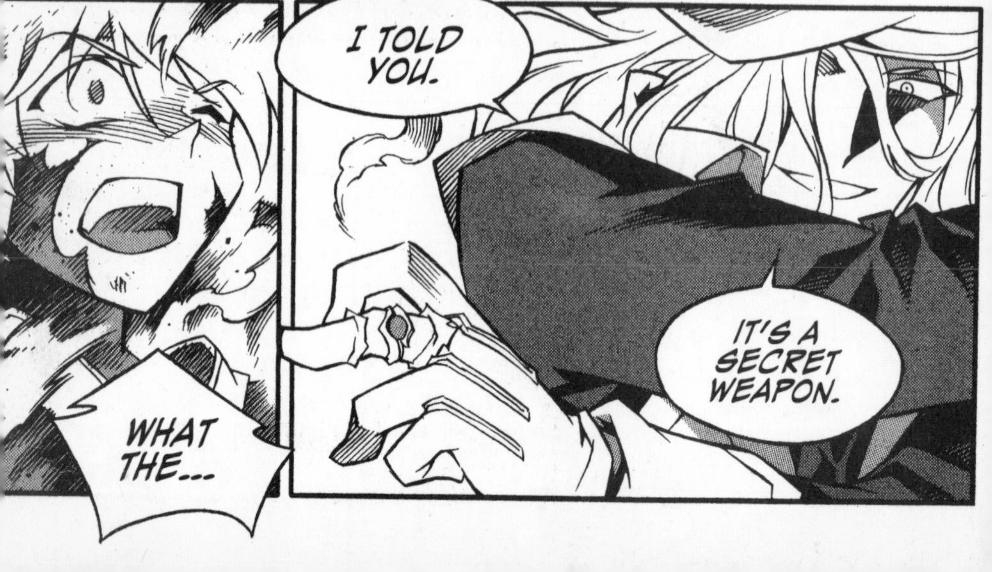
WHAT THE...
I TOLD YOU.
IT'S A SECRET WEAPON.

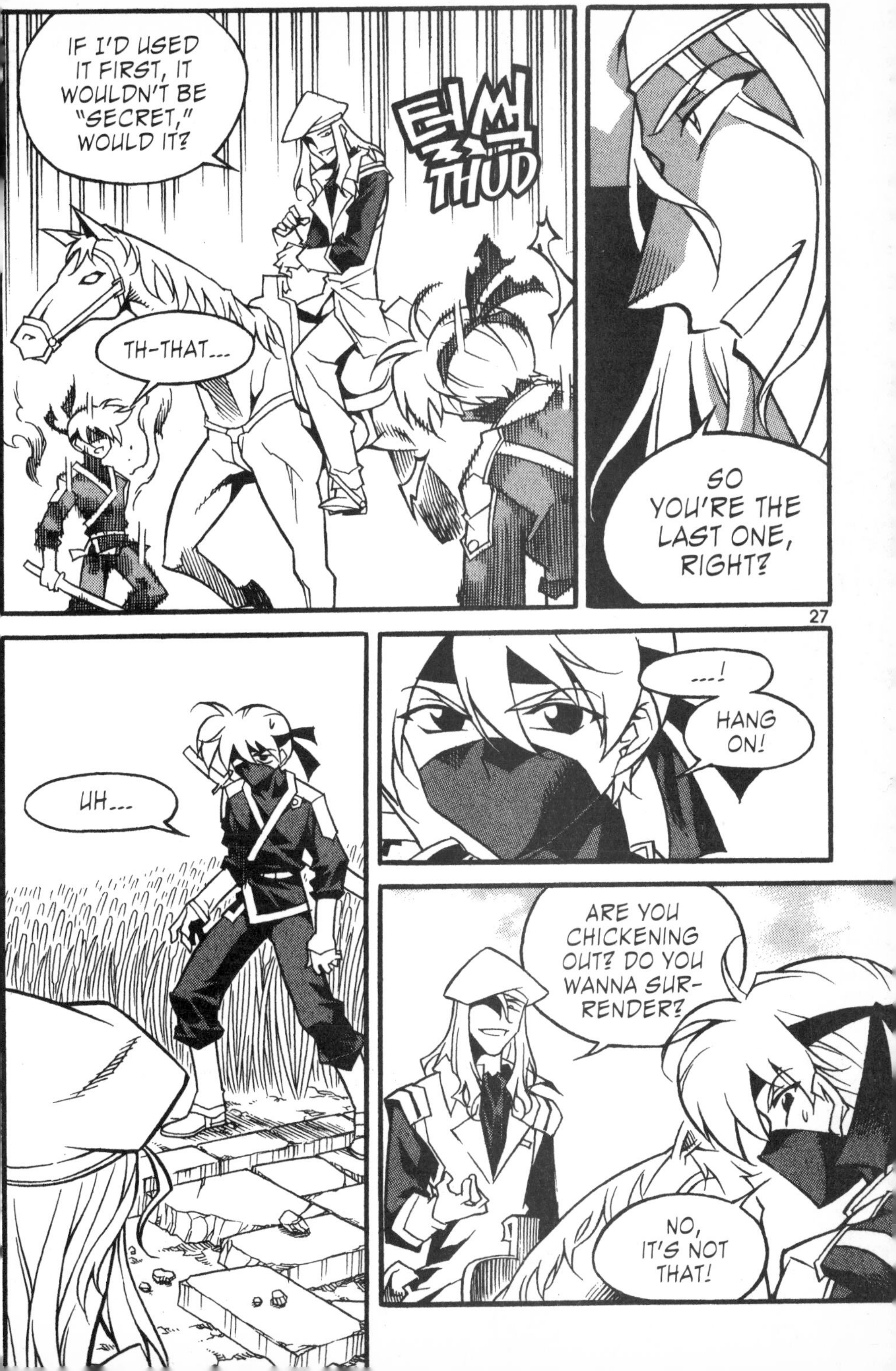
IF I'D USED IT FIRST, IT WOULDN'T BE "SECRET," WOULD IT?
THUD
TH-THAT...
SO YOU'RE THE LAST ONE, RIGHT?
UH...
...!
HANG ON!
ARE YOU CHICKENING OUT? DO YOU WANNA SUR-RENDER?
NO, IT'S NOT THAT!

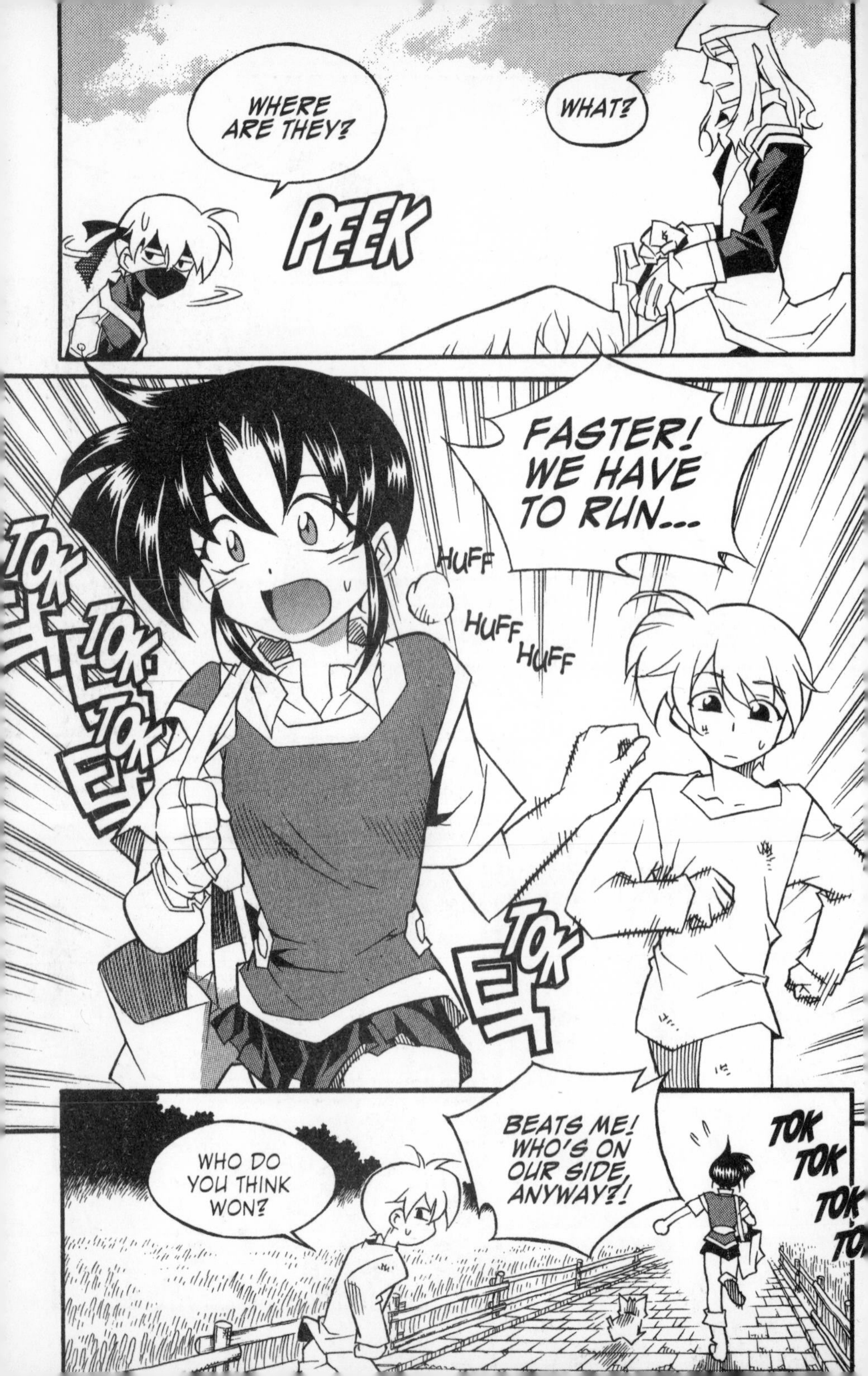
WHERE ARE THEY?
WHAT?
PEEK
TOK TOK TOK
FASTER! WE HAVE TO RUN...
HUFF HUFF HUFF
TOK
WHO DO YOU THINK WON?
BEATS ME! WHO'S ON OUR SIDE, ANYWAY?!
TOK TOK TOK TOK

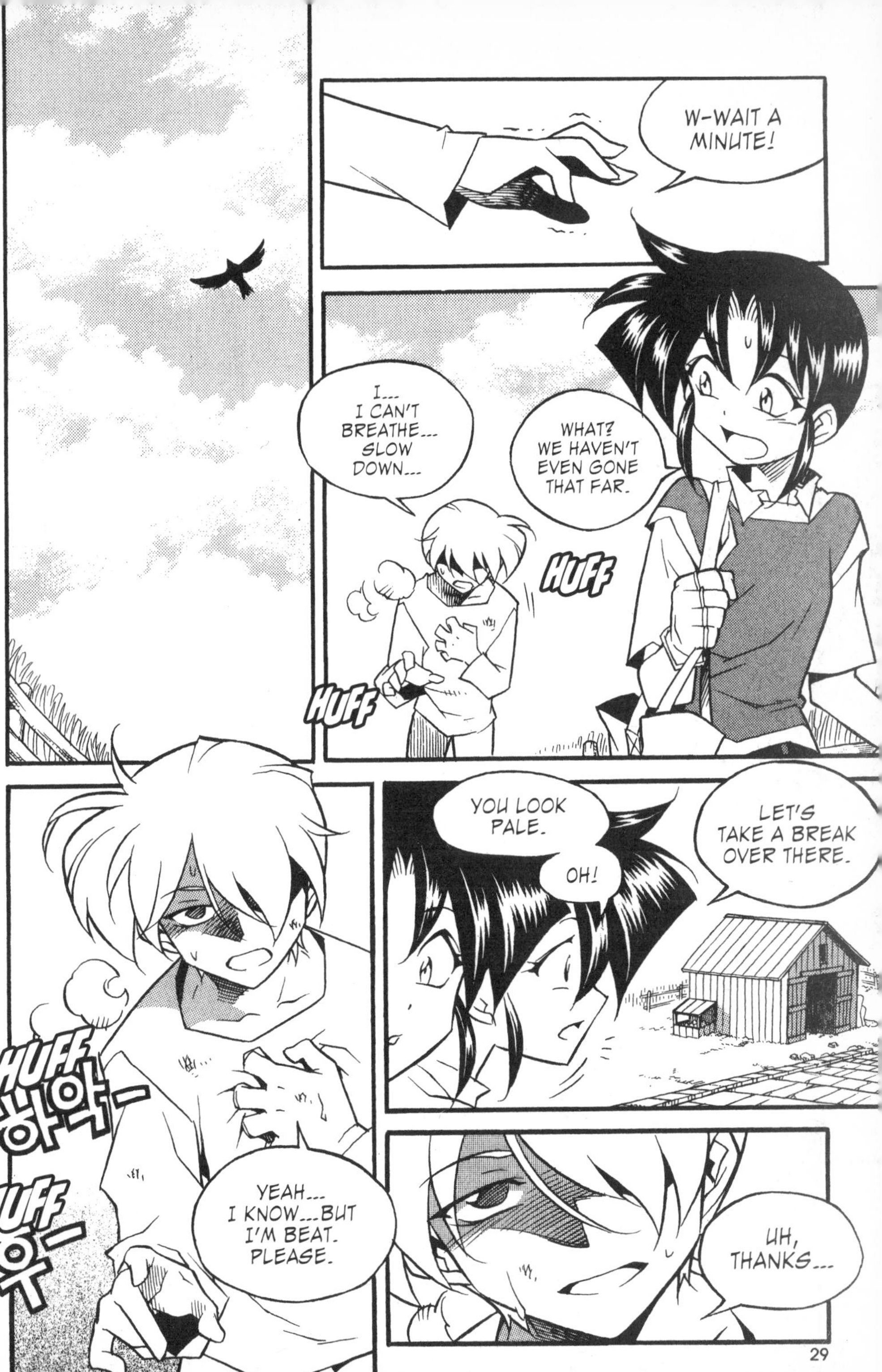
W-WAIT A MINUTE!
I... I CAN'T BREATHE... SLOW DOWN...
WHAT? WE HAVEN'T EVEN GONE THAT FAR.
HUFF
HUFF
HUFF
하악-
UFF
우-
YEAH... I KNOW... BUT I'M BEAT. PLEASE.
YOU LOOK PALE.
OH!
LET'S TAKE A BREAK OVER THERE.
UH, THANKS...

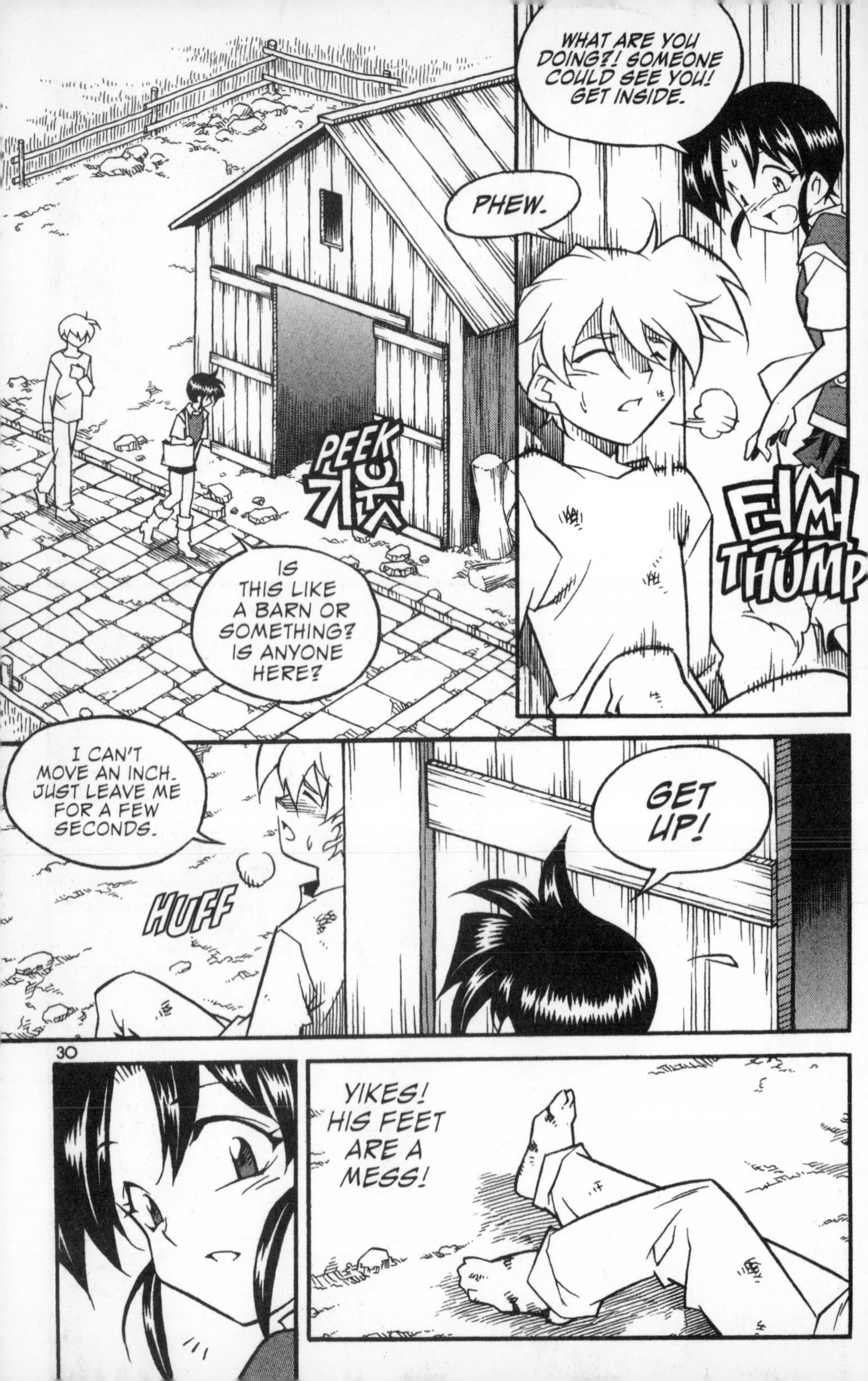
PEEK
기웃
IS THIS LIKE A BARN OR SOMETHING? IS ANYONE HERE?
WHAT ARE YOU DOING?! SOMEONE COULD SEE YOU! GET INSIDE.
PHEW.
THUMP
I CAN'T MOVE AN INCH. JUST LEAVE ME FOR A FEW SECONDS.
HUFF
GET UP!
YIKES! HIS FEET ARE A MESS!

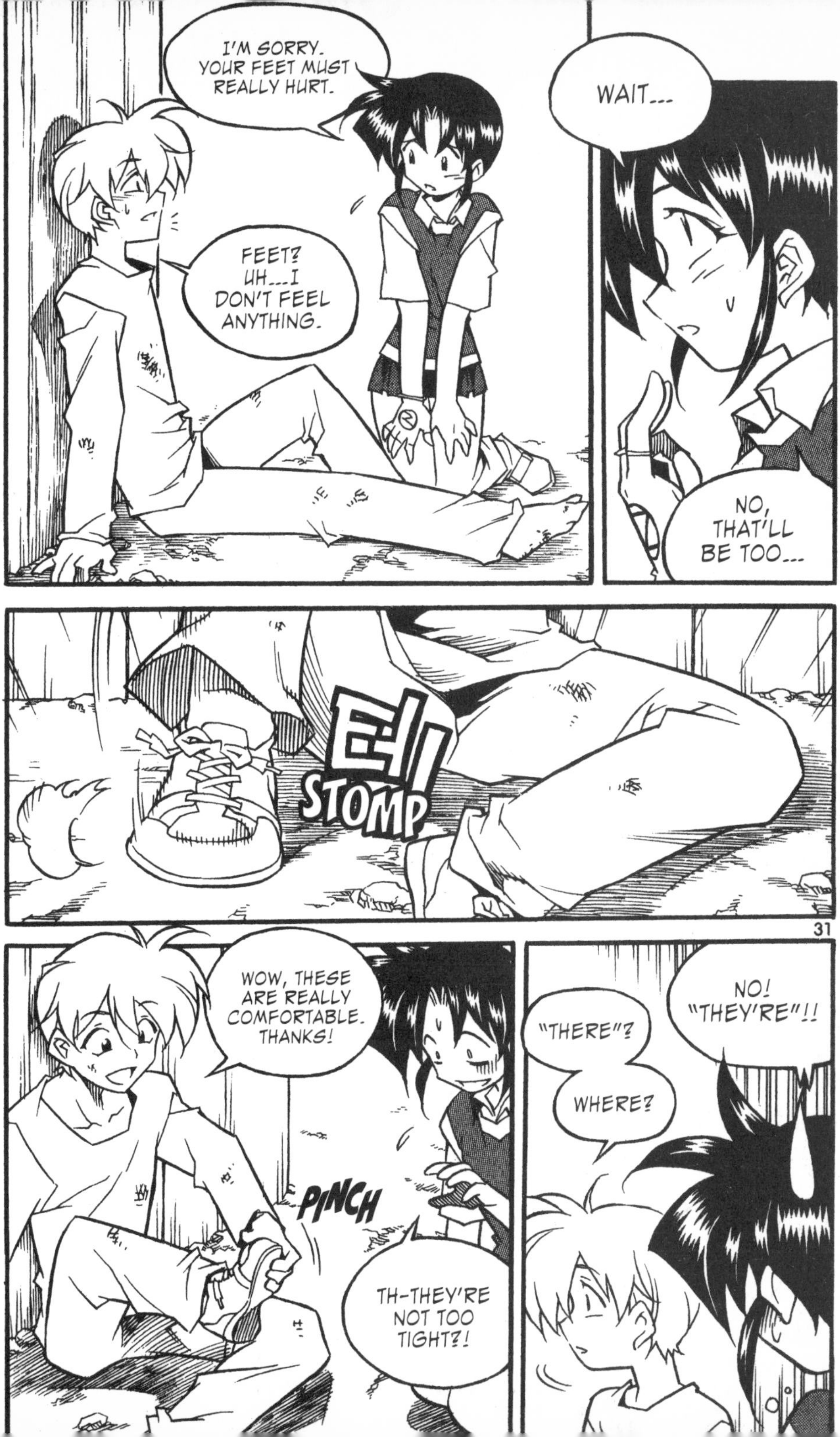
I'M SORRY. YOUR FEET MUST REALLY HURT.
FEET? UH...I DON'T FEEL ANYTHING.
WAIT...
NO, THAT'LL BE TOO...
STOMP
WOW, THESE ARE REALLY COMFORTABLE. THANKS!
PINCH
TH-THEY'RE NOT TOO TIGHT?!
"THERE"?
WHERE?
NO! "THEY'RE"!!

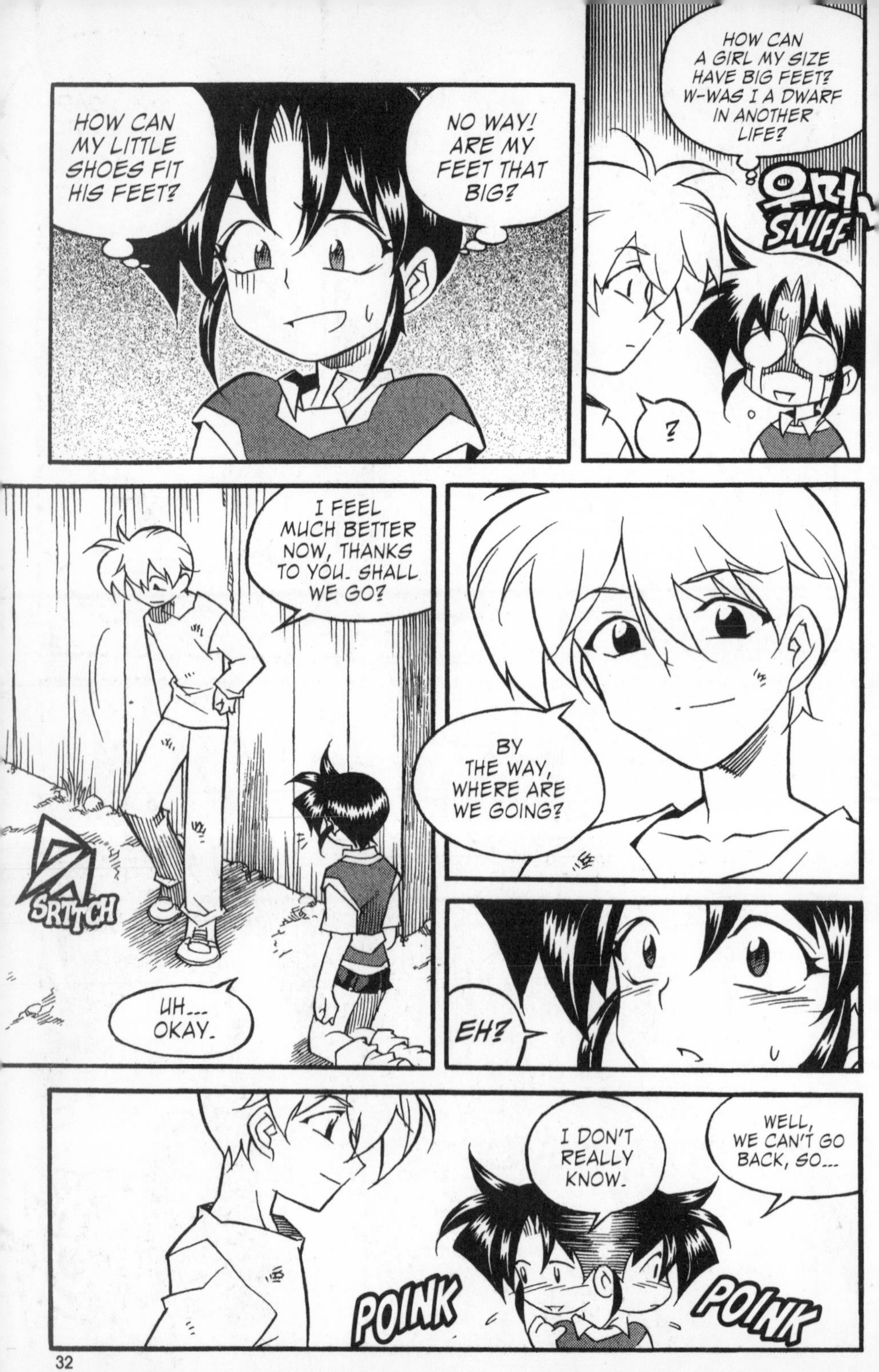
HOW CAN MY LITTLE SHOES FIT HIS FEET?
NO WAY! ARE MY FEET THAT BIG?
HOW CAN A GIRL MY SIZE HAVE BIG FEET? W-WAS I A DWARF IN ANOTHER LIFE?
우럭
SNIFF
?
I FEEL MUCH BETTER NOW, THANKS TO YOU. SHALL WE GO?
SRTTCH
UH... OKAY.
BY THE WAY, WHERE ARE WE GOING?
EH?
I DON'T REALLY KNOW.
WELL, WE CAN'T GO BACK, SO...
POINK
POINK

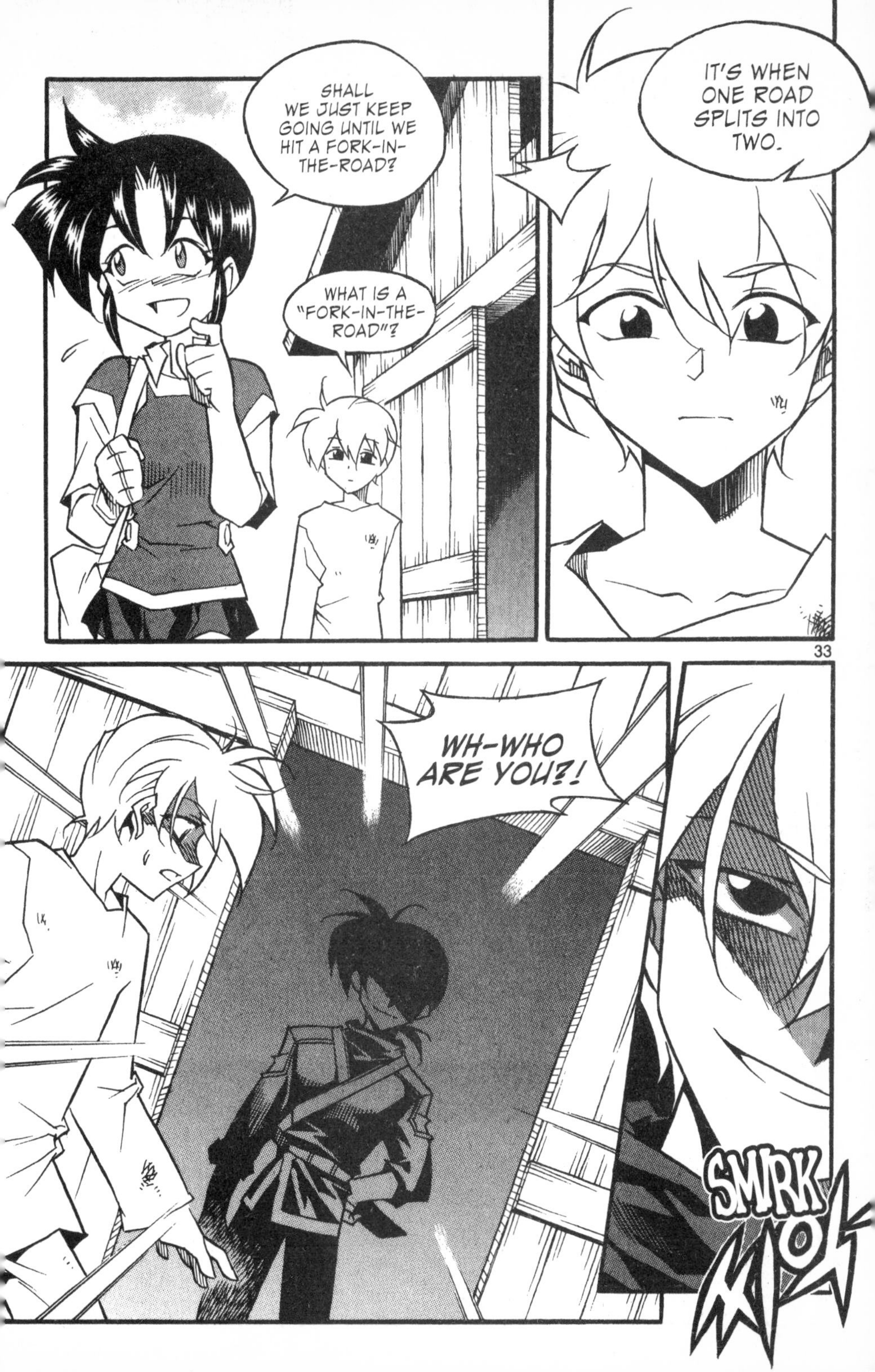
SHALL WE JUST KEEP GOING UNTIL WE HIT A FORK-IN-THE-ROAD?
WHAT IS A "FORK-IN-THE-ROAD"?
IT'S WHEN ONE ROAD SPLITS INTO TWO.
WH-WHO ARE YOU?!
SMIRK

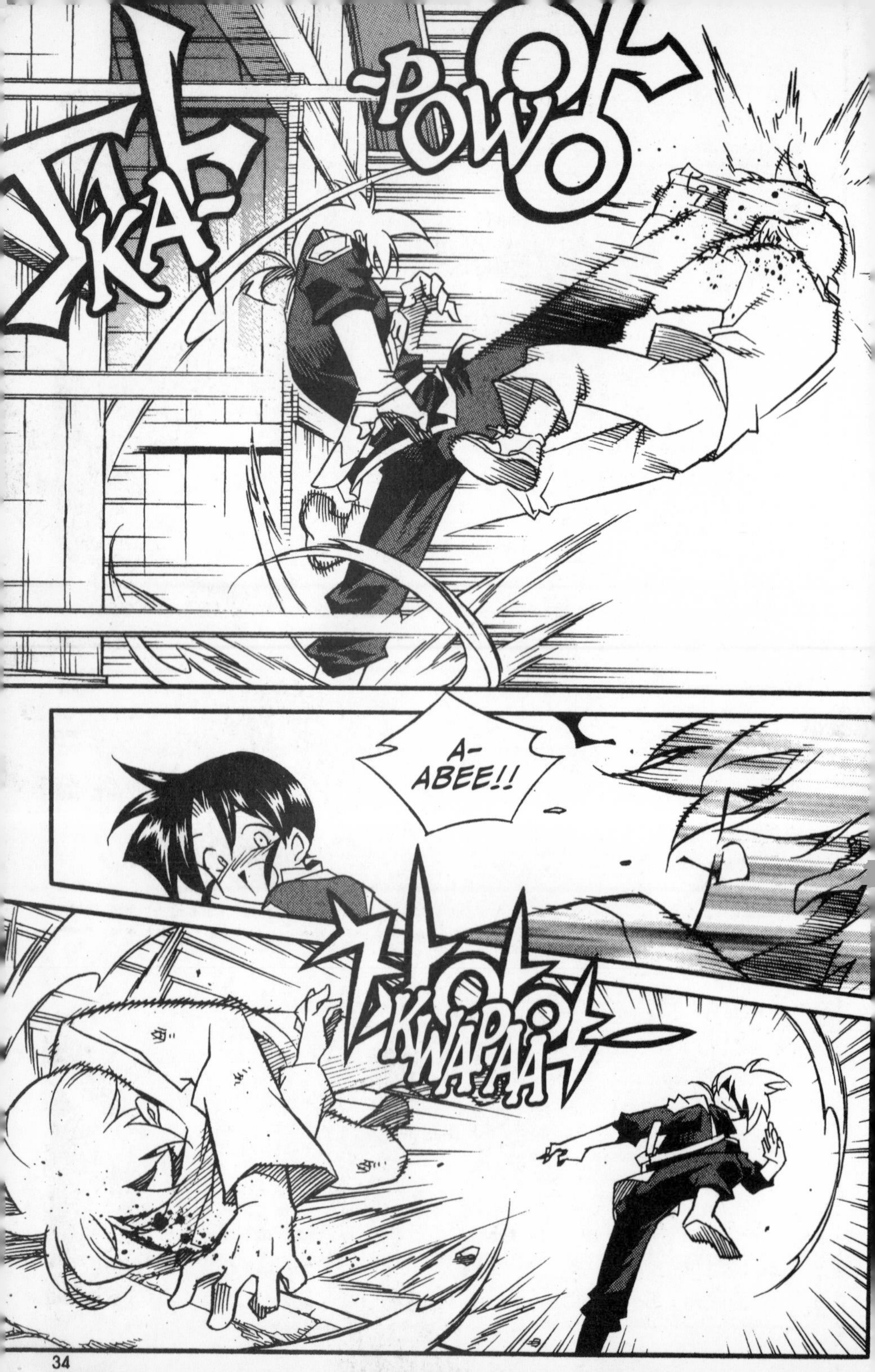
KA-
-POW
A-
ABEE!!
KWAPAA

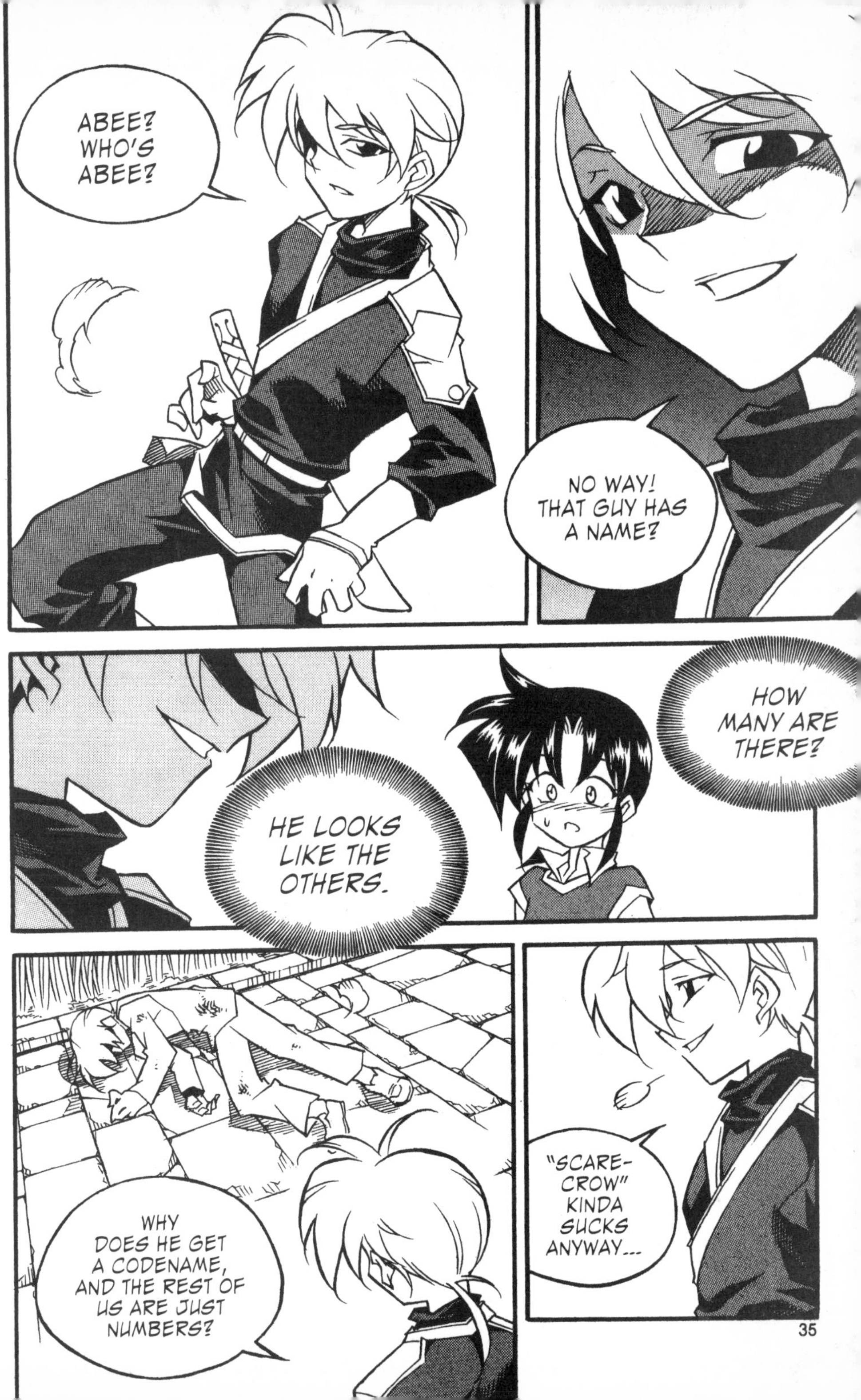
ABEE? WHO'S ABEE?
NO WAY! THAT GUY HAS A NAME?
HE LOOKS LIKE THE OTHERS.
HOW MANY ARE THERE?
WHY DOES HE GET A CODENAME, AND THE REST OF US ARE JUST NUMBERS?
"SCARE-CROW" KINDA SUCKS ANYWAY...

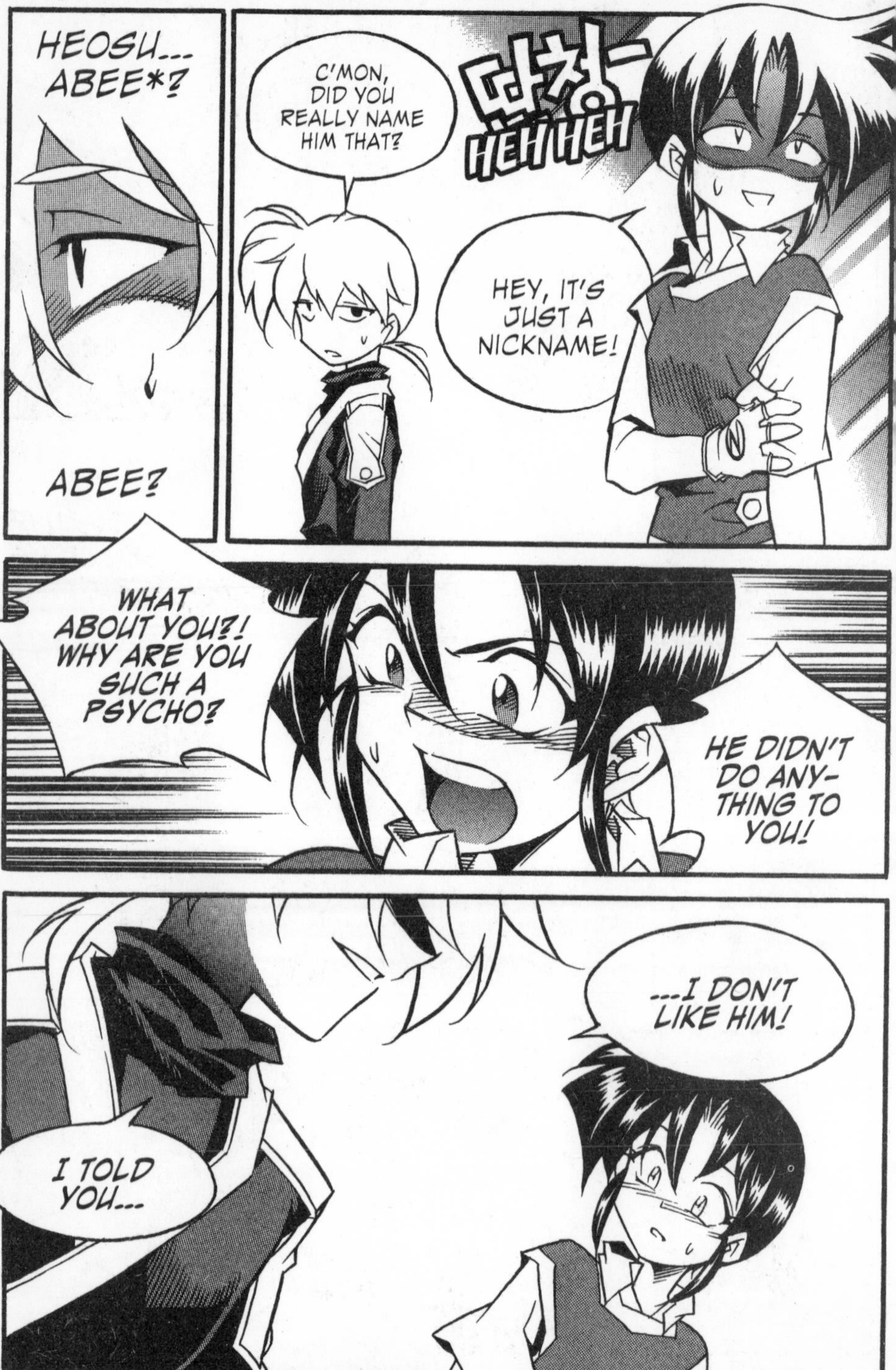
HEOSU... ABEE*?
ABEE?
C'MON, DID YOU REALLY NAME HIM THAT?
따치
HEH HEH
HEY, IT'S JUST A NICKNAME!
WHAT ABOUT YOU?! WHY ARE YOU SUCH A PSYCHO?
HE DIDN'T DO ANY-THING TO YOU!
I TOLD YOU...
...I DON'T LIKE HIM!

*"ABEE" IS MARA'S SHORTENING OF "HEOSUABEE" OR SCARECROW IN KOREAN

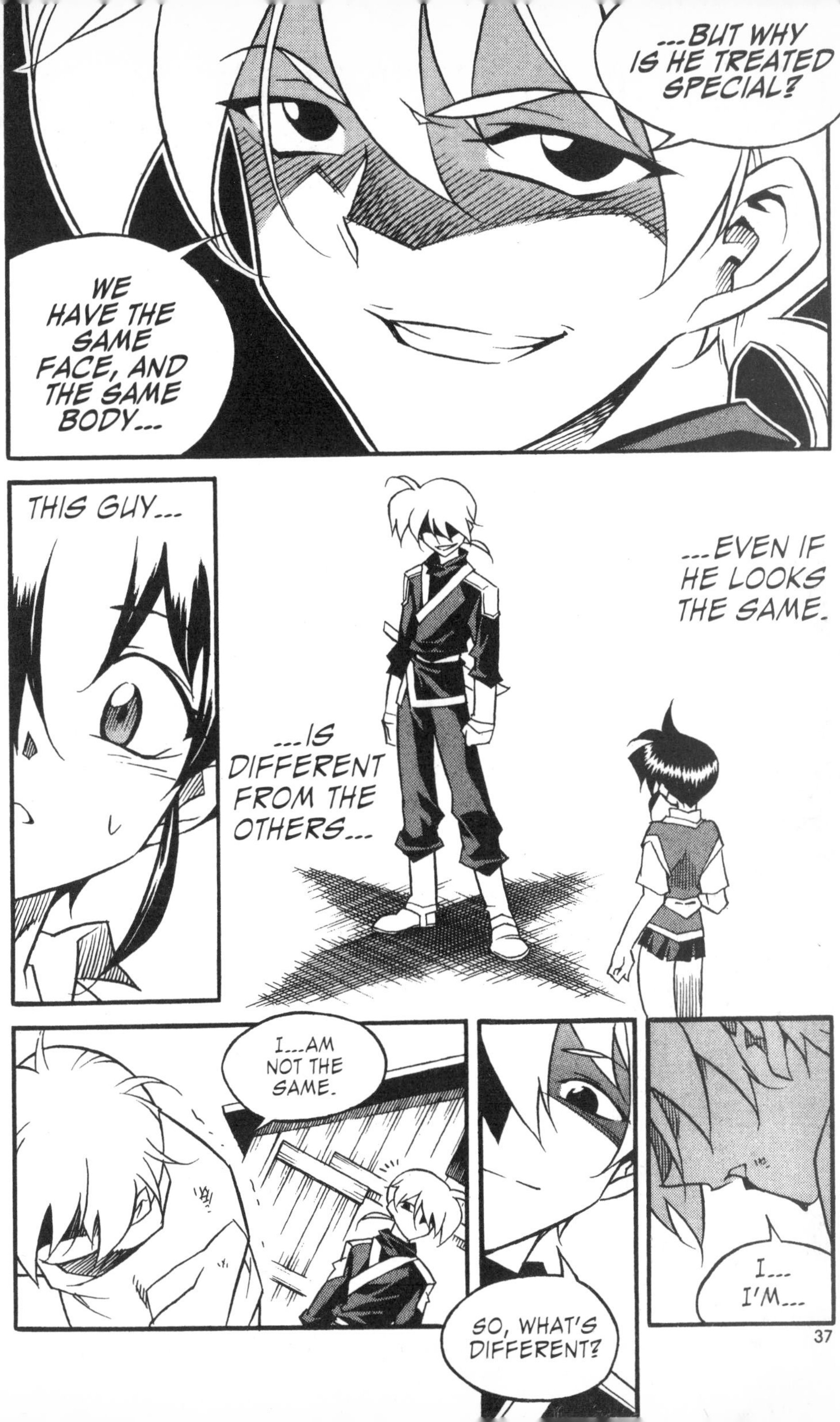
WE HAVE THE SAME FACE, AND THE SAME BODY...
...BUT WHY IS HE TREATED SPECIAL?
THIS GUY...
...IS DIFFERENT FROM THE OTHERS...
...EVEN IF HE LOOKS THE SAME.
I...AM NOT THE SAME.
SO, WHAT'S DIFFERENT?
I... I'M...

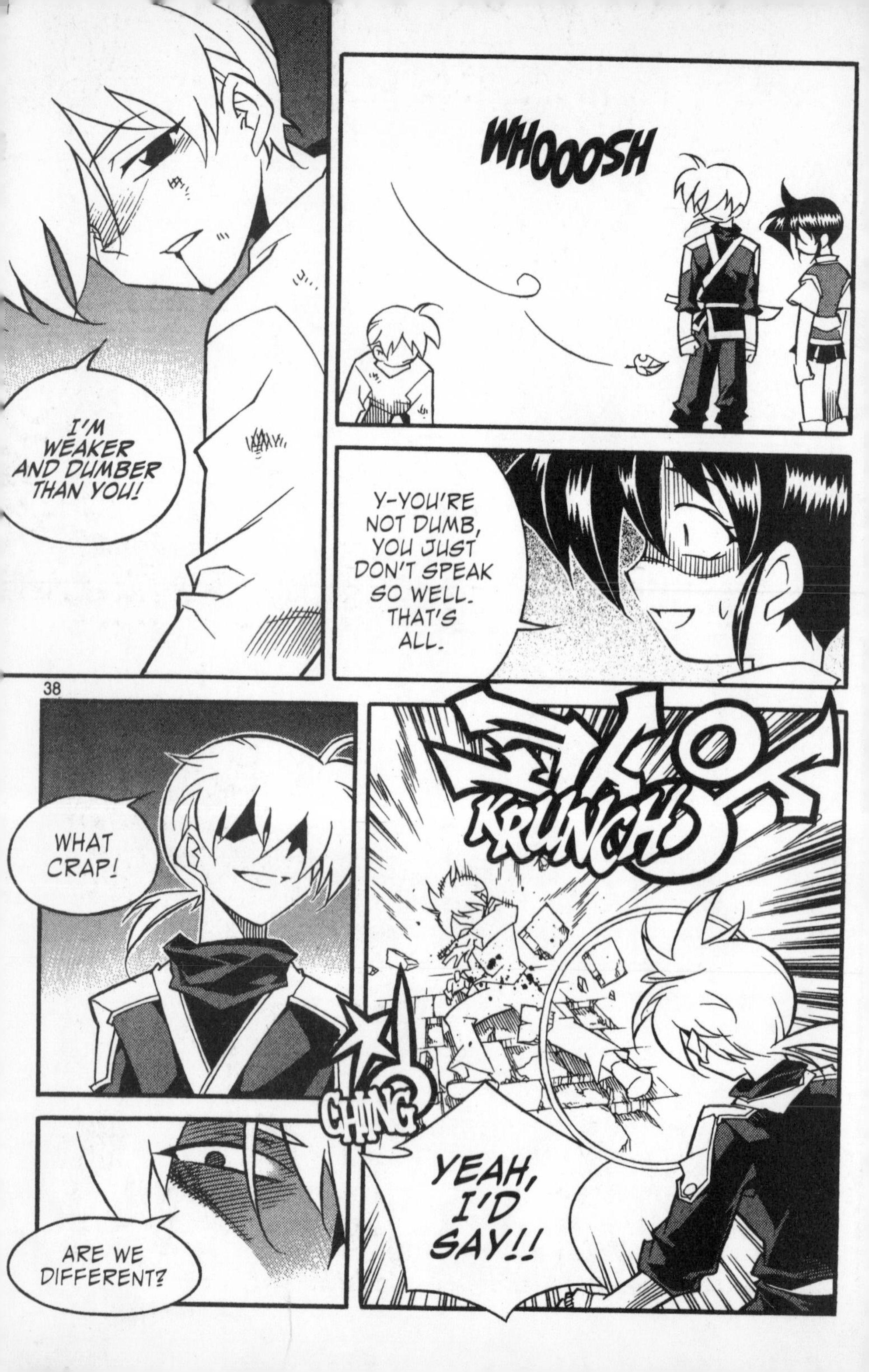
I'M WEAKER AND DUMBER THAN YOU!
WHOOOSH
Y-YOU'RE NOT DUMB, YOU JUST DON'T SPEAK SO WELL. THAT'S ALL.
WHAT CRAP!
ARE WE DIFFERENT?
KRUNCH
CHING
YEAH, I'D SAY!!

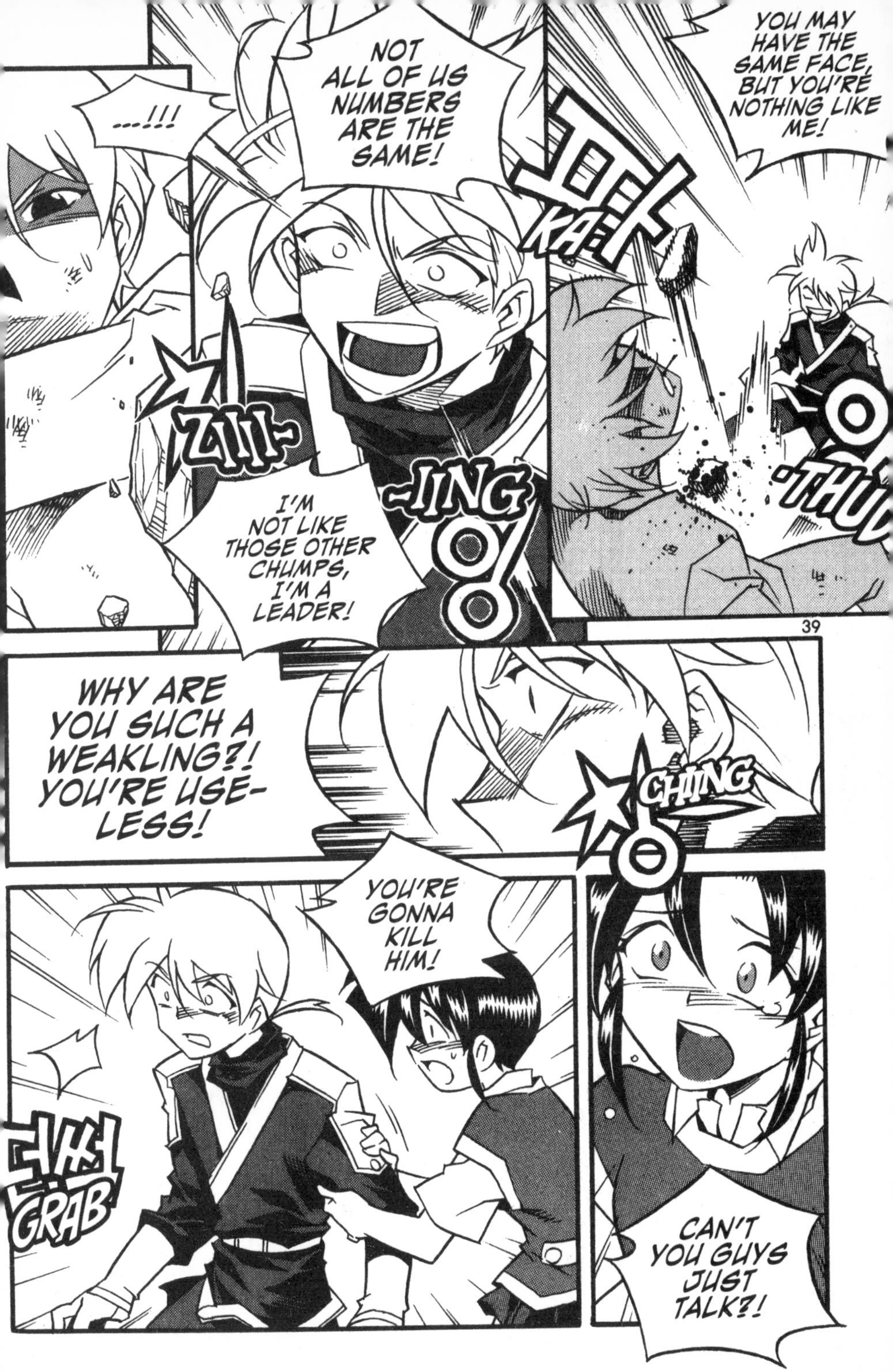

...!!!
NOT ALL OF US NUMBERS ARE THE SAME!
ZIII-
-ING
I'M NOT LIKE THOSE OTHER CHUMPS, I'M A LEADER!
YOU MAY HAVE THE SAME FACE, BUT YOU'RE NOTHING LIKE ME!
KA-
THUD
WHY ARE YOU SUCH A WEAKLING?! YOU'RE USE-LESS!
CHING
GRAB
YOU'RE GONNA KILL HIM!
CAN'T YOU GUYS JUST TALK?!

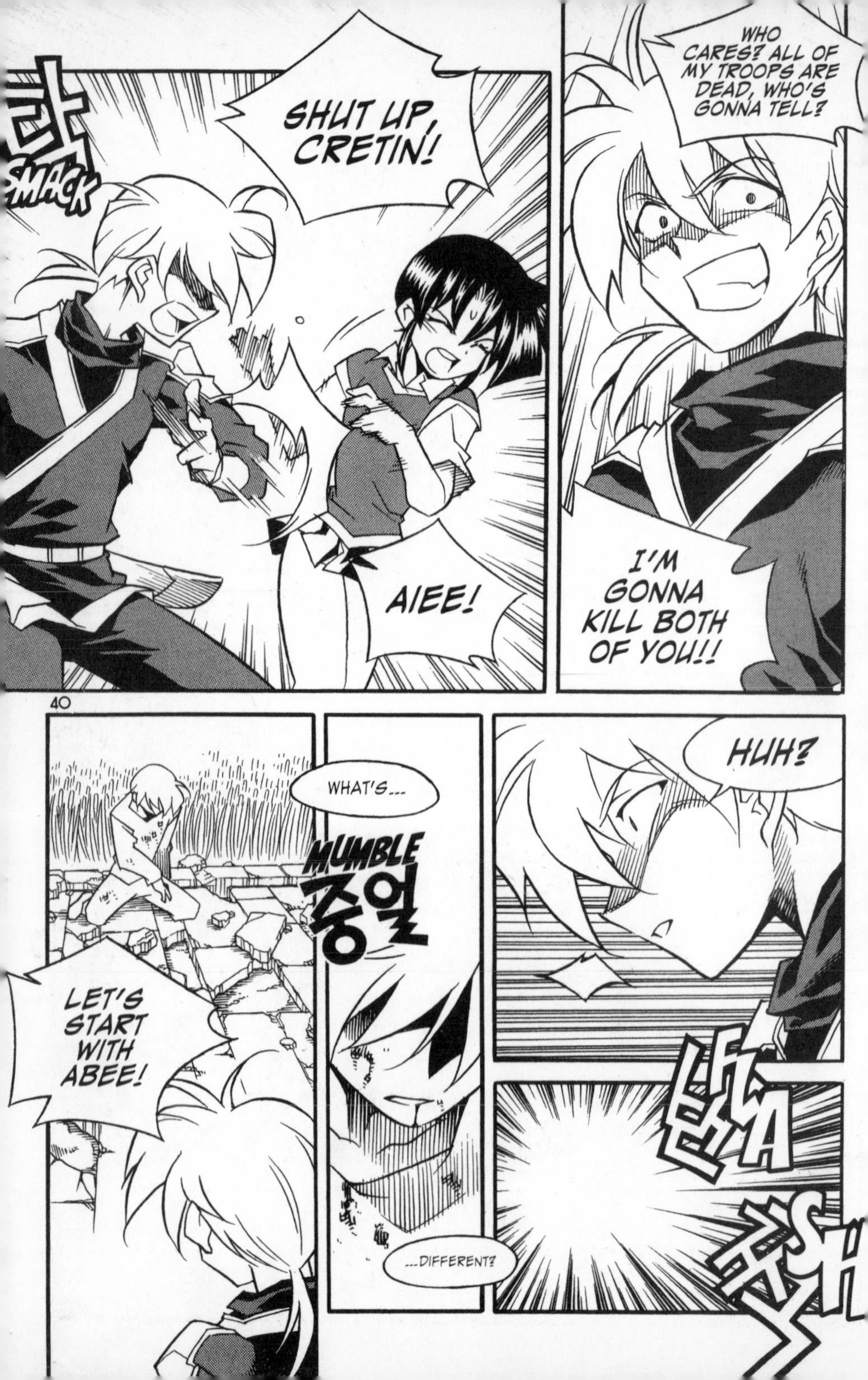
SMACK
SHUT UP, CRETIN!
AIEE!
WHO CARES? ALL OF MY TROOPS ARE DEAD, WHO'S GONNA TELL?
I'M GONNA KILL BOTH OF YOU!!
LET'S START WITH ABEE!
WHAT'S...
MUMBLE
중얼
...DIFFERENT?
HUH?

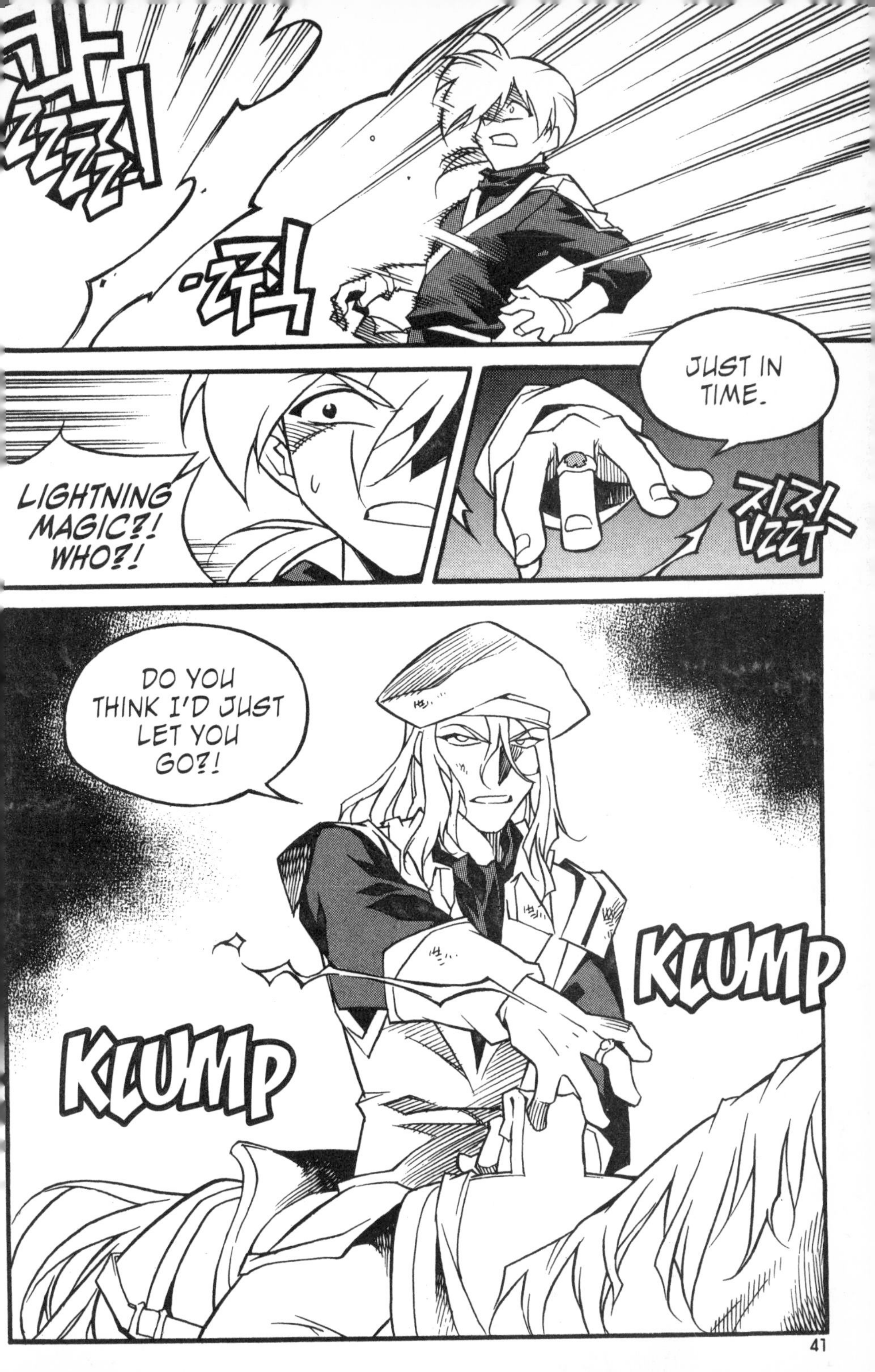
LIGHTNING MAGIC?! WHO?!
JUST IN TIME.
지직 VZZT
DO YOU THINK I'D JUST LET YOU GO?!
KLUMP
KLUMP

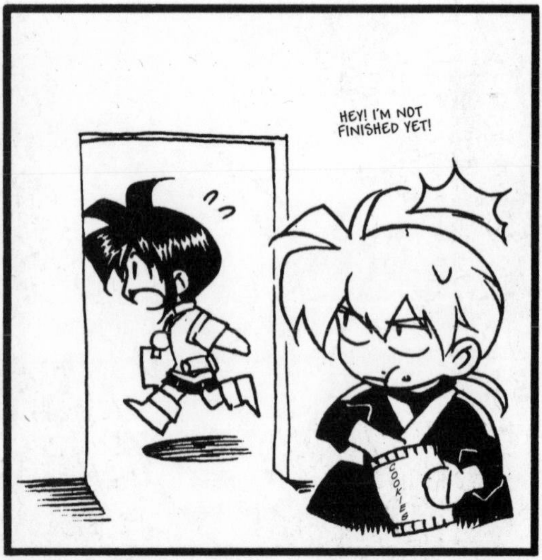
HEY! I'M NOT FINISHED YET!
COOKIES

Step 17 I REMEMBER!

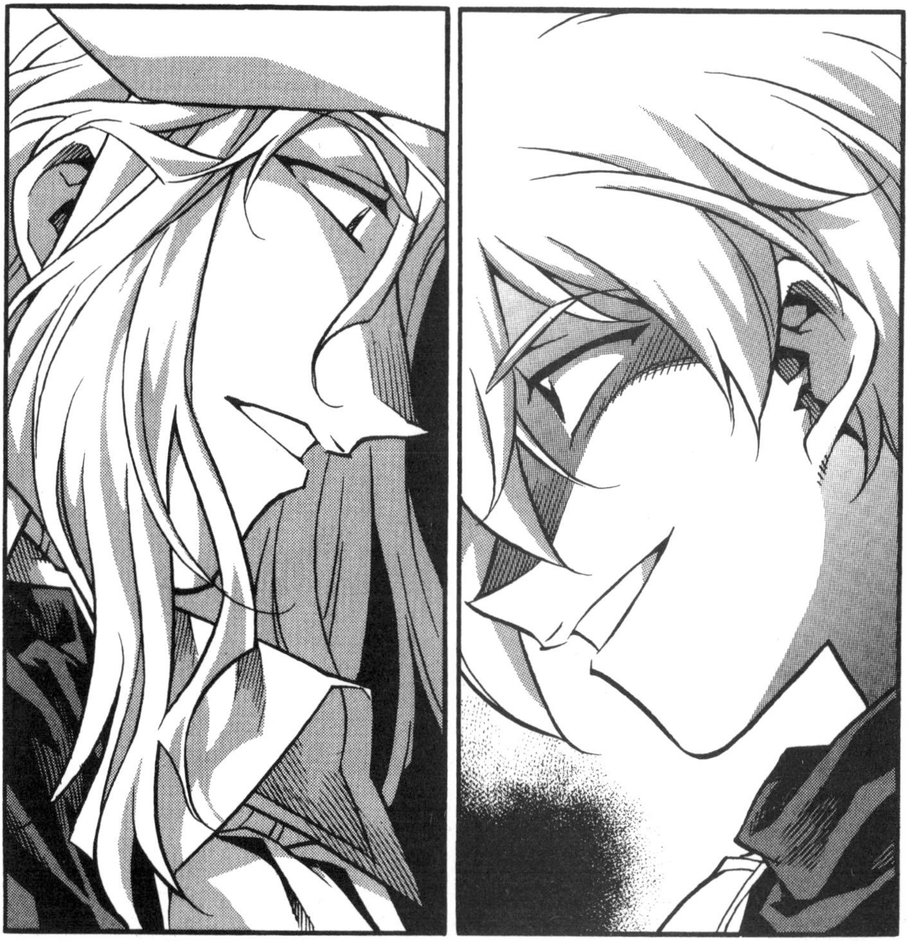

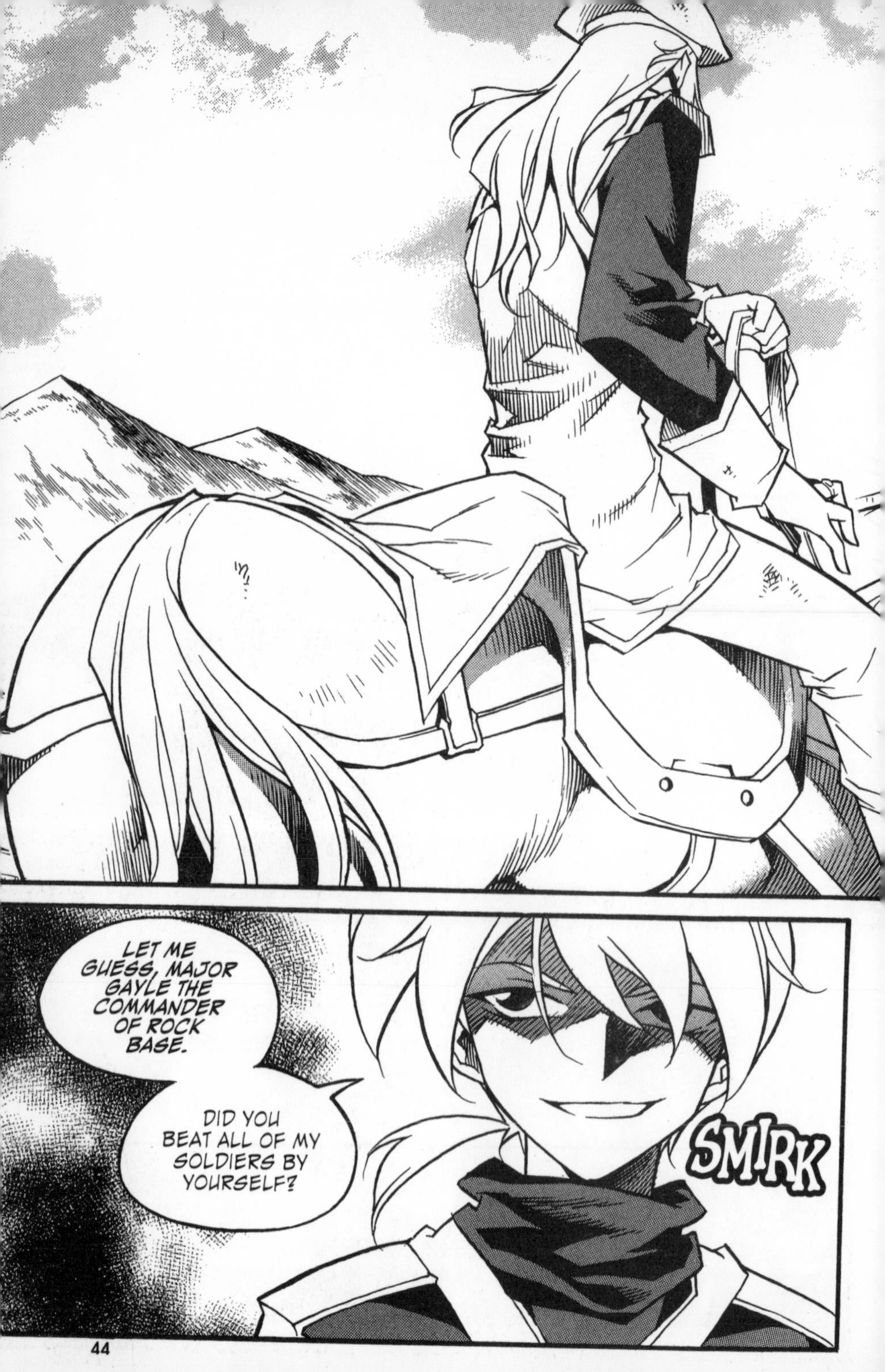
LET ME GUESS, MAJOR GAYLE THE COMMANDER OF ROCK BASE.
DID YOU BEAT ALL OF MY SOLDIERS BY YOURSELF?
SMIRK

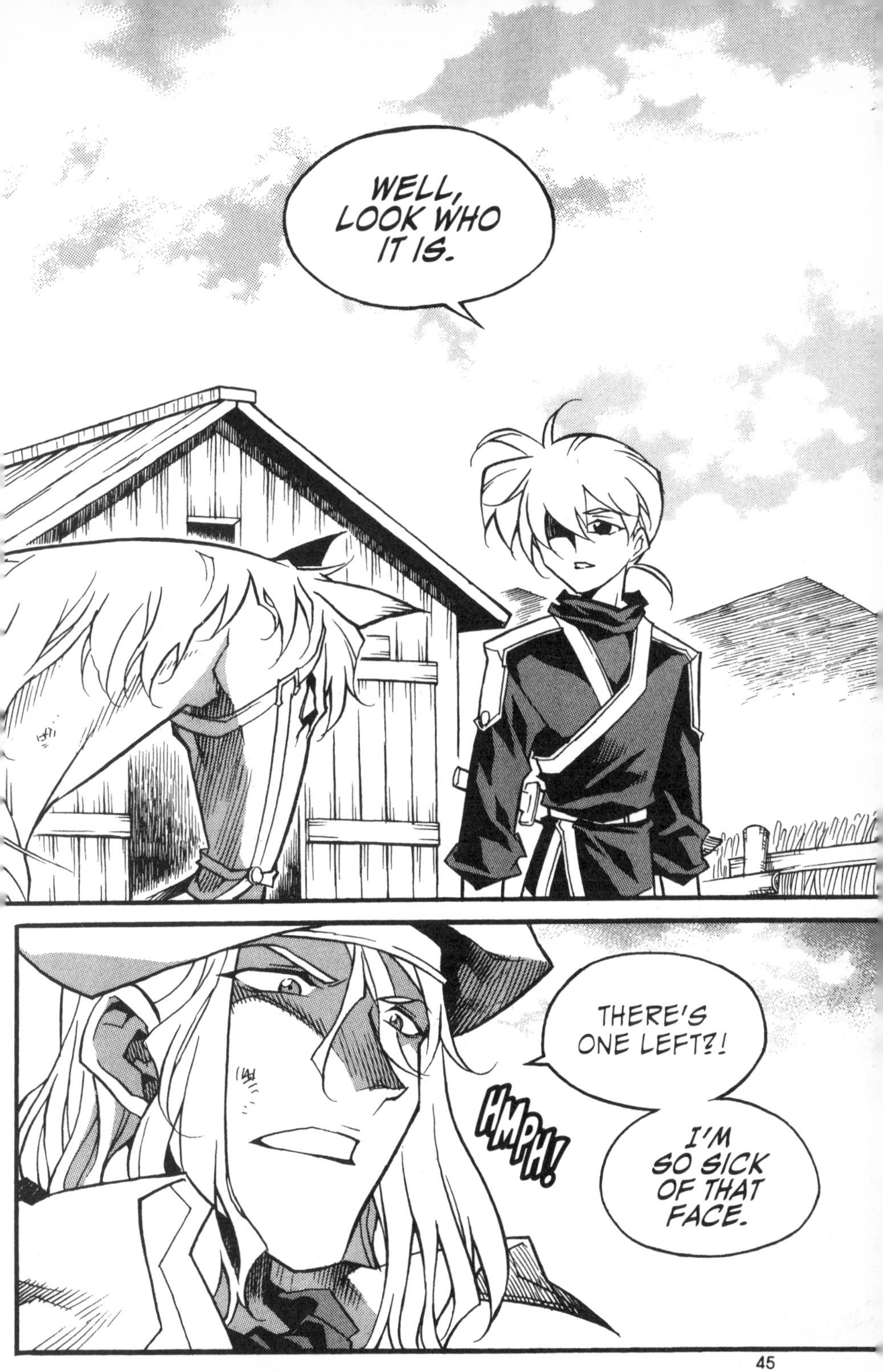
WELL, LOOK WHO IT IS.
THERE'S ONE LEFT?!
HMPH!
I'M SO SICK OF THAT FACE.

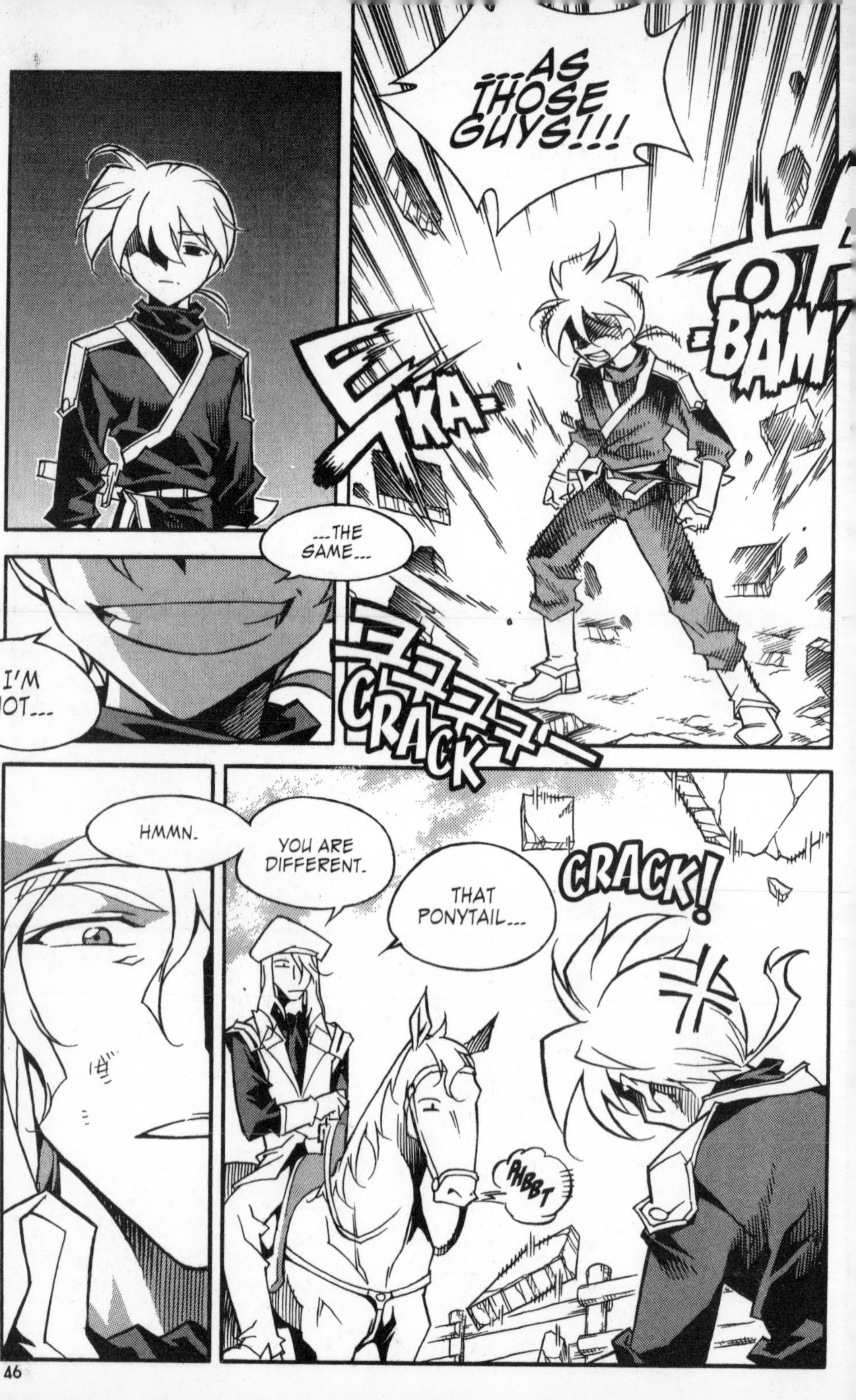
I'M NOT...
...THE SAME...
...AS THOSE GUYS!!!
KA-BAM
CRACK
HMMN.
YOU ARE DIFFERENT.
THAT PONYTAIL...
CRACK!
PHBBT

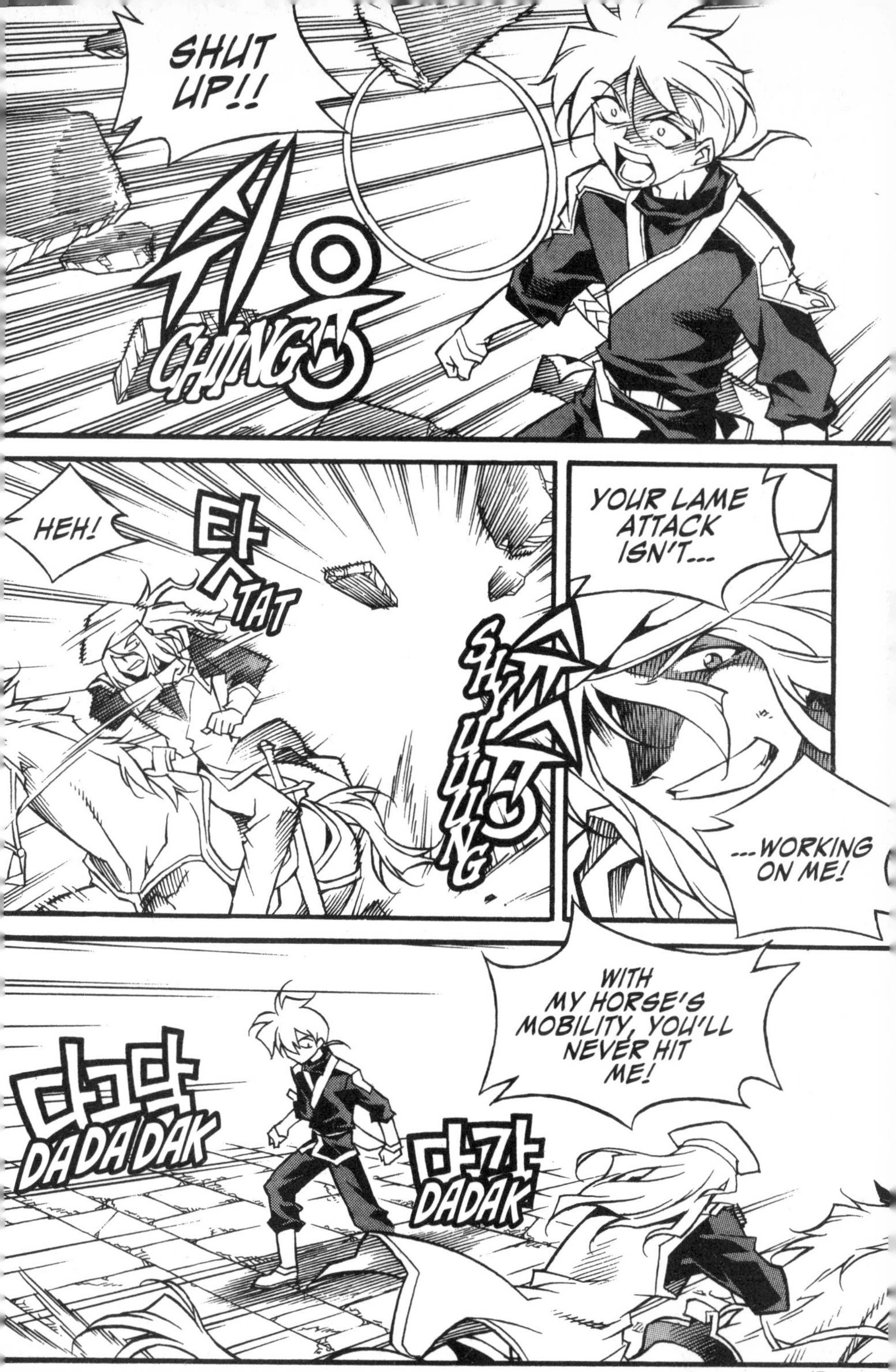
SHUT UP!!
CHING
HEH!
탁
TAT
YOUR LAME ATTACK ISN'T...
SHUUUNG
...WORKING ON ME!
WITH MY HORSE'S MOBILITY, YOU'LL NEVER HIT ME!
DA DA DAK
DADAK

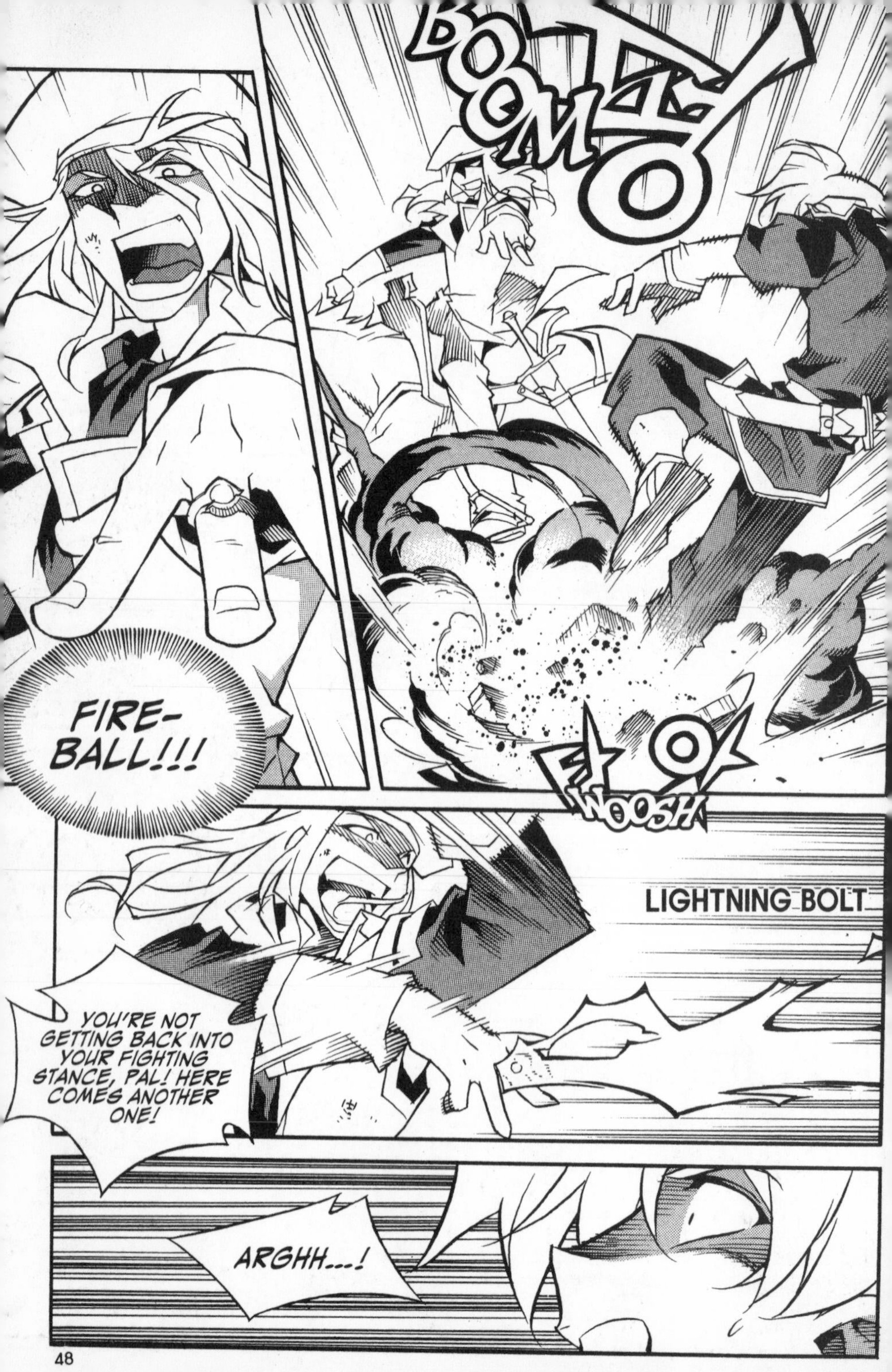
FIRE-BALL!!!
BOOM
FWOOSH
LIGHTNING BOLT
YOU'RE NOT GETTING BACK INTO YOUR FIGHTING STANCE, PAL! HERE COMES ANOTHER ONE!
ARGHH...!

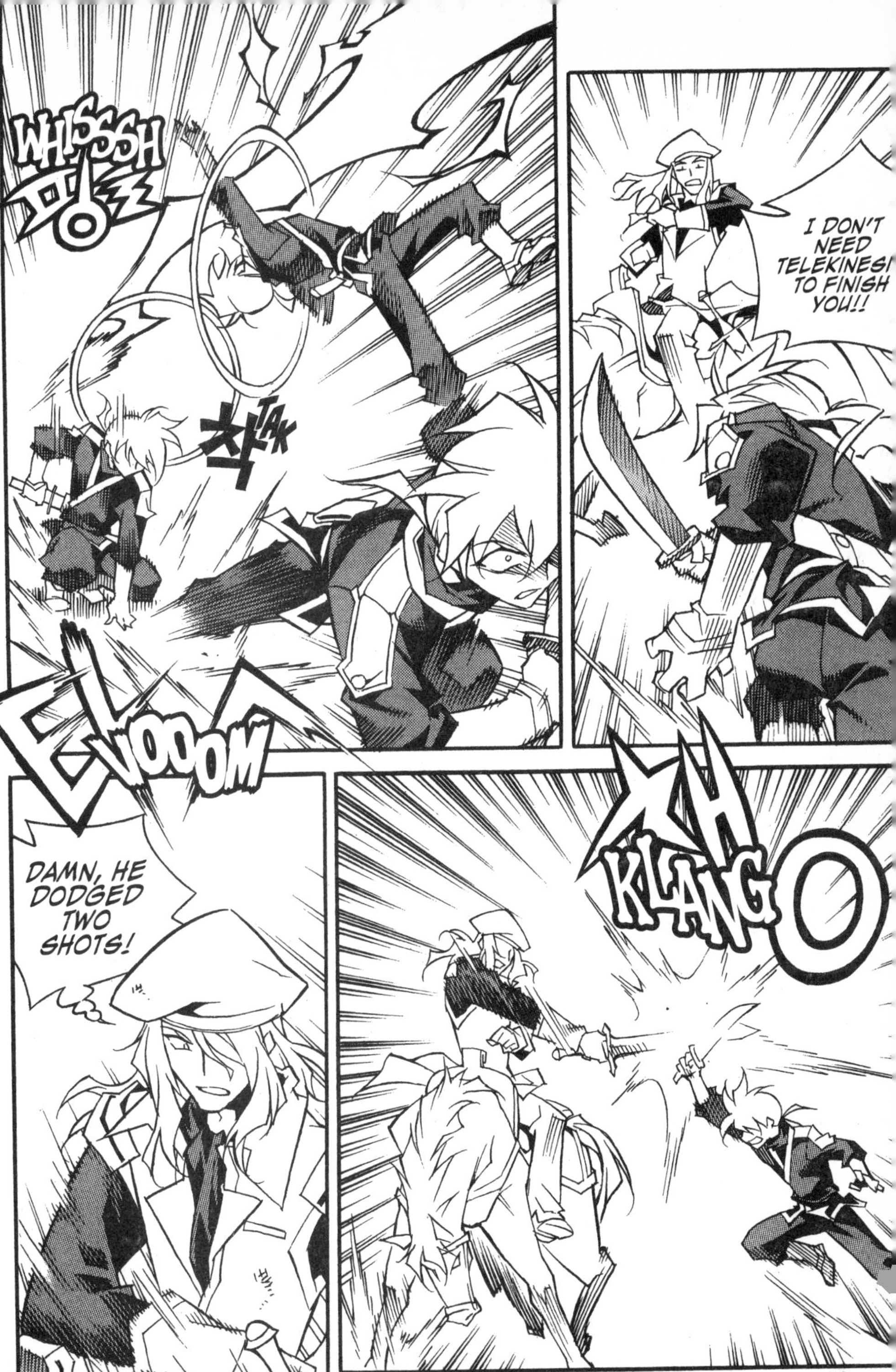
WHISSSH
TAK
EVOOOM
I DON'T NEED TELEKINESI TO FINISH YOU!!
DAMN, HE DODGED TWO SHOTS!
KLANG

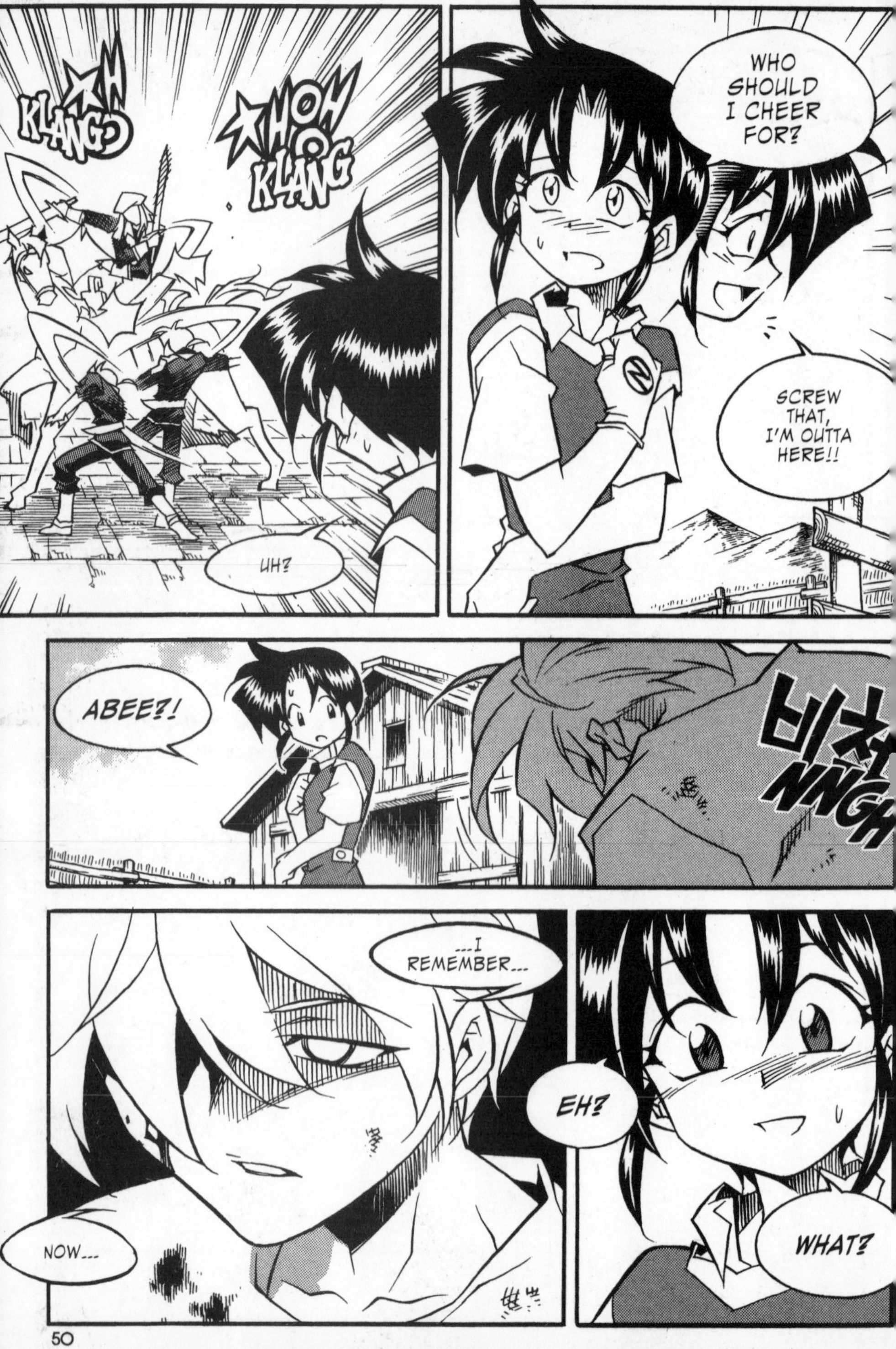
KLANG
HOH
KLANG
UH?
WHO SHOULD I CHEER FOR?
SCREW THAT, I'M OUTTA HERE!!
ABEE?!
비척
NNGH
...I REMEMBER...
NOW...
EH?
WHAT?

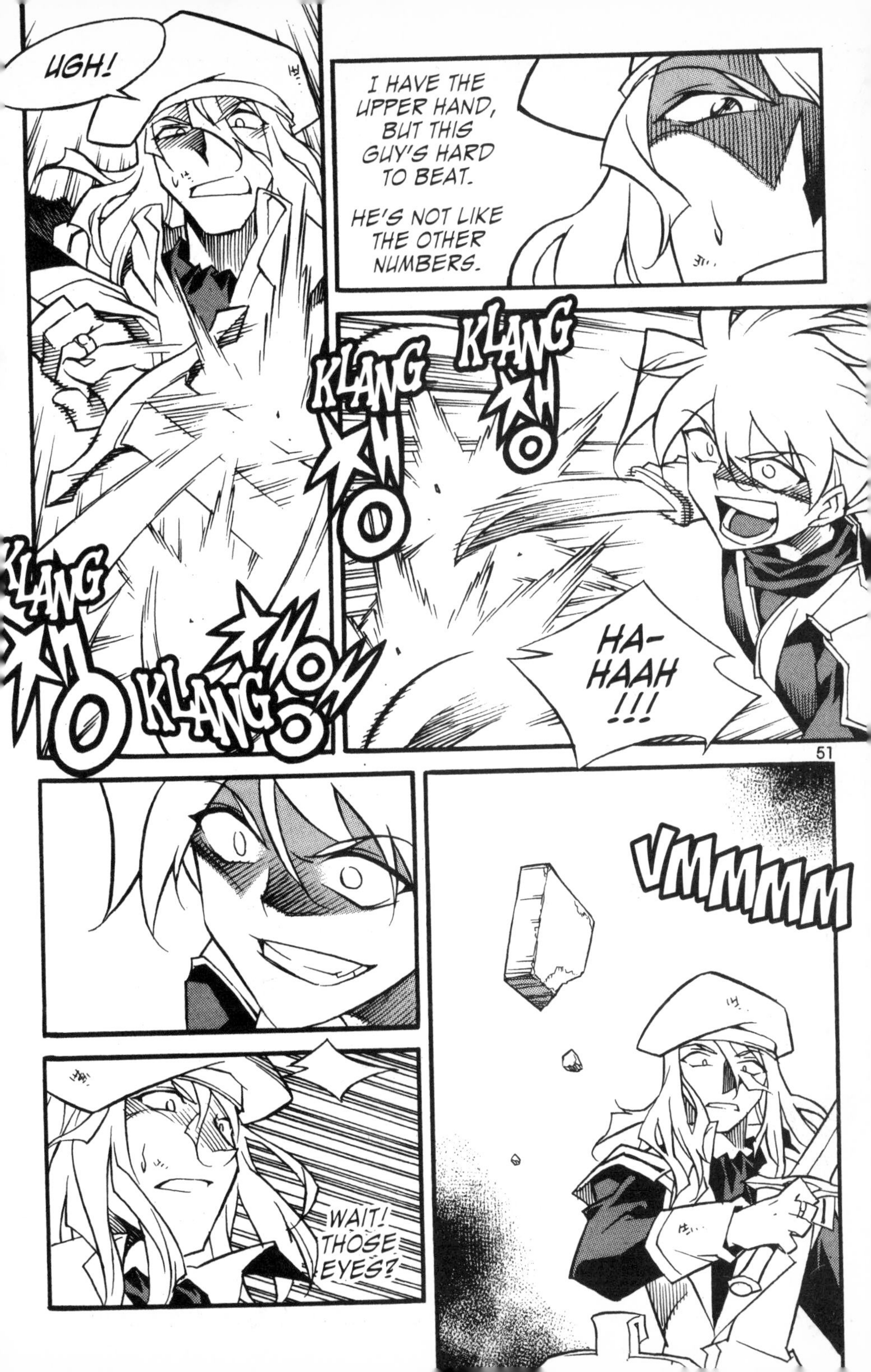
UGH!
I HAVE THE UPPER HAND, BUT THIS GUY'S HARD TO BEAT.
HE'S NOT LIKE THE OTHER NUMBERS.
KLANG
KLANG
KLANG
KLANG
HA-HAAH!!!
VMMMMM
WAIT! THOSE EYES?

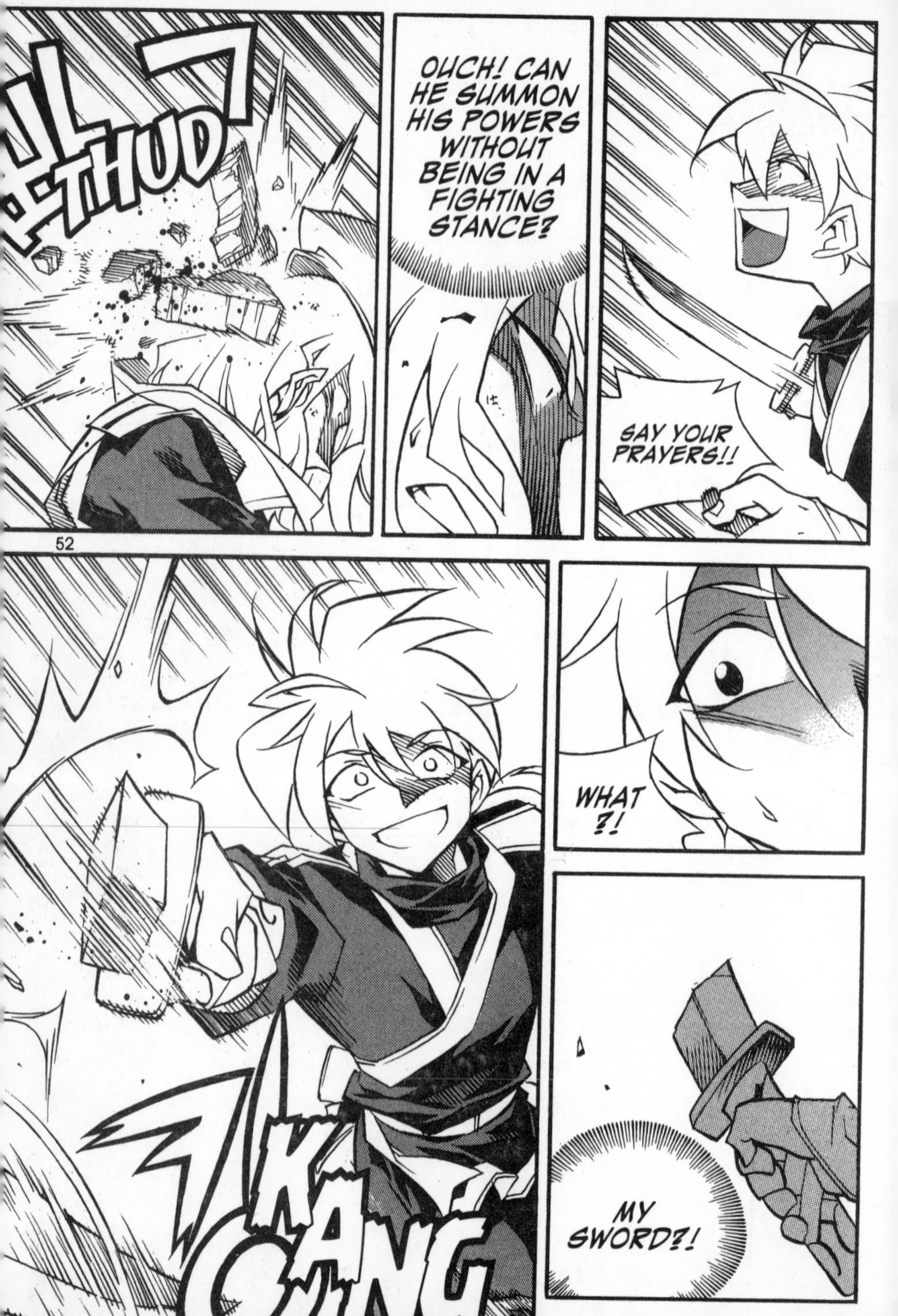
THUD
OUCH! CAN HE SUMMON HIS POWERS WITHOUT BEING IN A FIGHTING STANCE?
SAY YOUR PRAYERS!!
KA
CANG
WHAT?!
MY SWORD?!

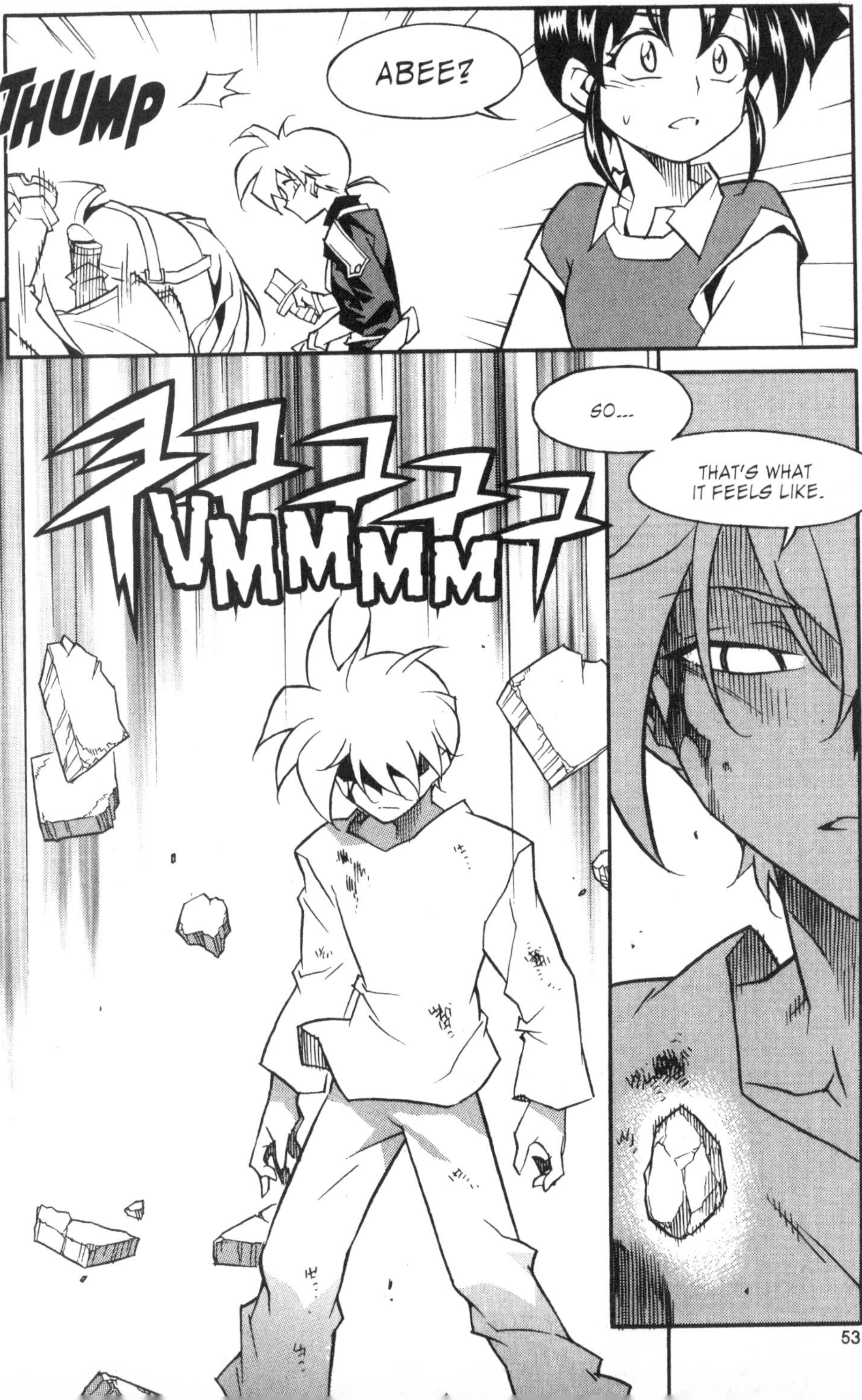
THUMP
ABEE?
VMMMMM
SO...
THAT'S WHAT IT FEELS LIKE.

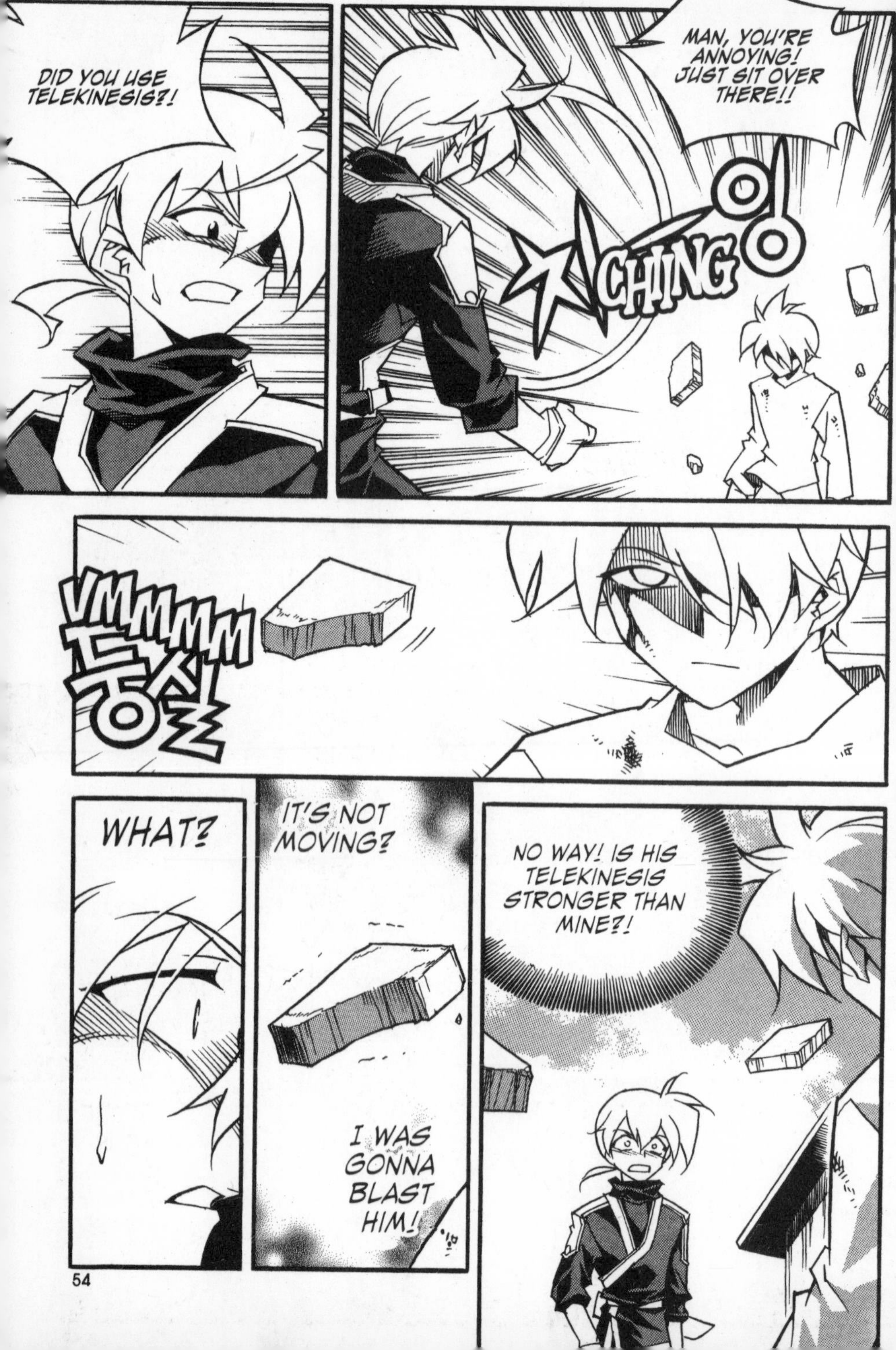
DID YOU USE TELEKINESIS?!
MAN, YOU'RE ANNOYING! JUST SIT OVER THERE!!
CHING
VMMMMM
WHAT?
IT'S NOT MOVING?
I WAS GONNA BLAST HIM!
NO WAY! IS HIS TELEKINESIS STRONGER THAN MINE?!

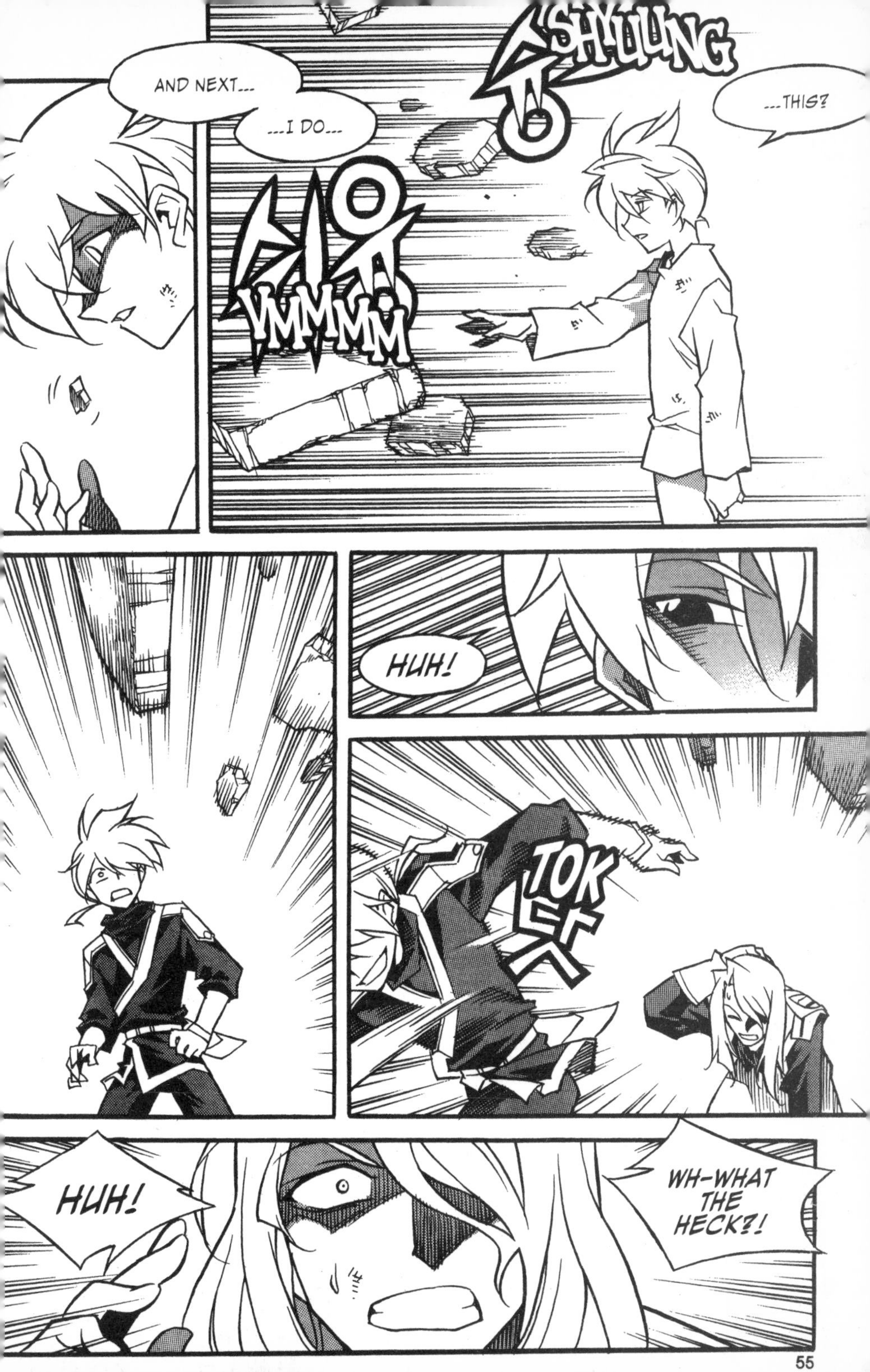
AND NEXT...
...I DO...
SHYUUNG
...THIS?
VMMMMM
HUH!
TOK
HUH!
WH-WHAT THE HECK?!

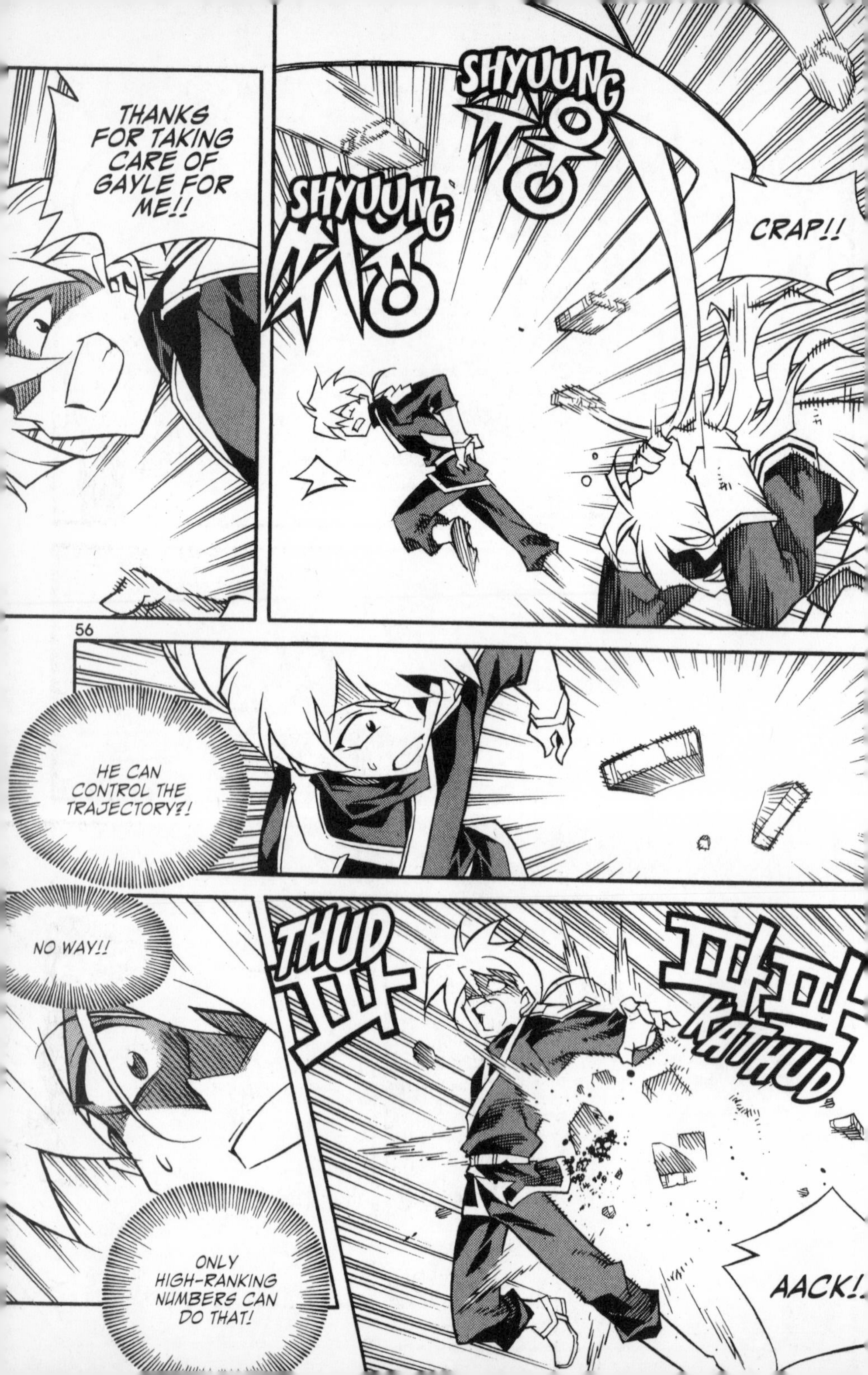
THANKS FOR TAKING CARE OF GAYLE FOR ME!!
SHYUUNG
SHYUUNG
CRAP!!
HE CAN CONTROL THE TRAJECTORY?!
NO WAY!!
ONLY HIGH-RANKING NUMBERS CAN DO THAT!
THUD
KATHUD
AACK!!

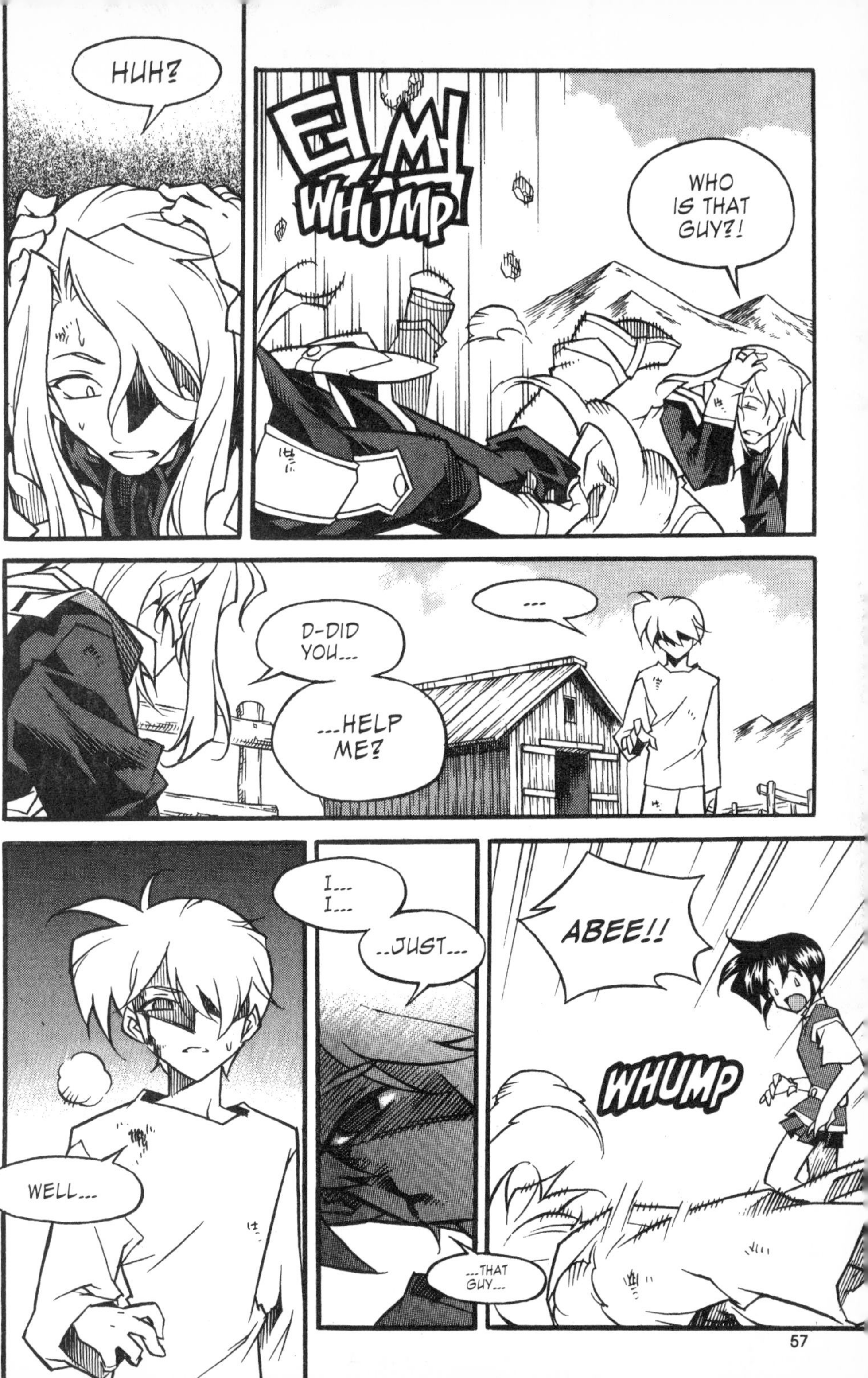
HUH?
WHUMP
WHO IS THAT GUY?!
D-DID YOU...
...HELP ME?
...
WELL...
I... I...
..JUST...
...THAT GUY...
ABEE!!
WHUMP

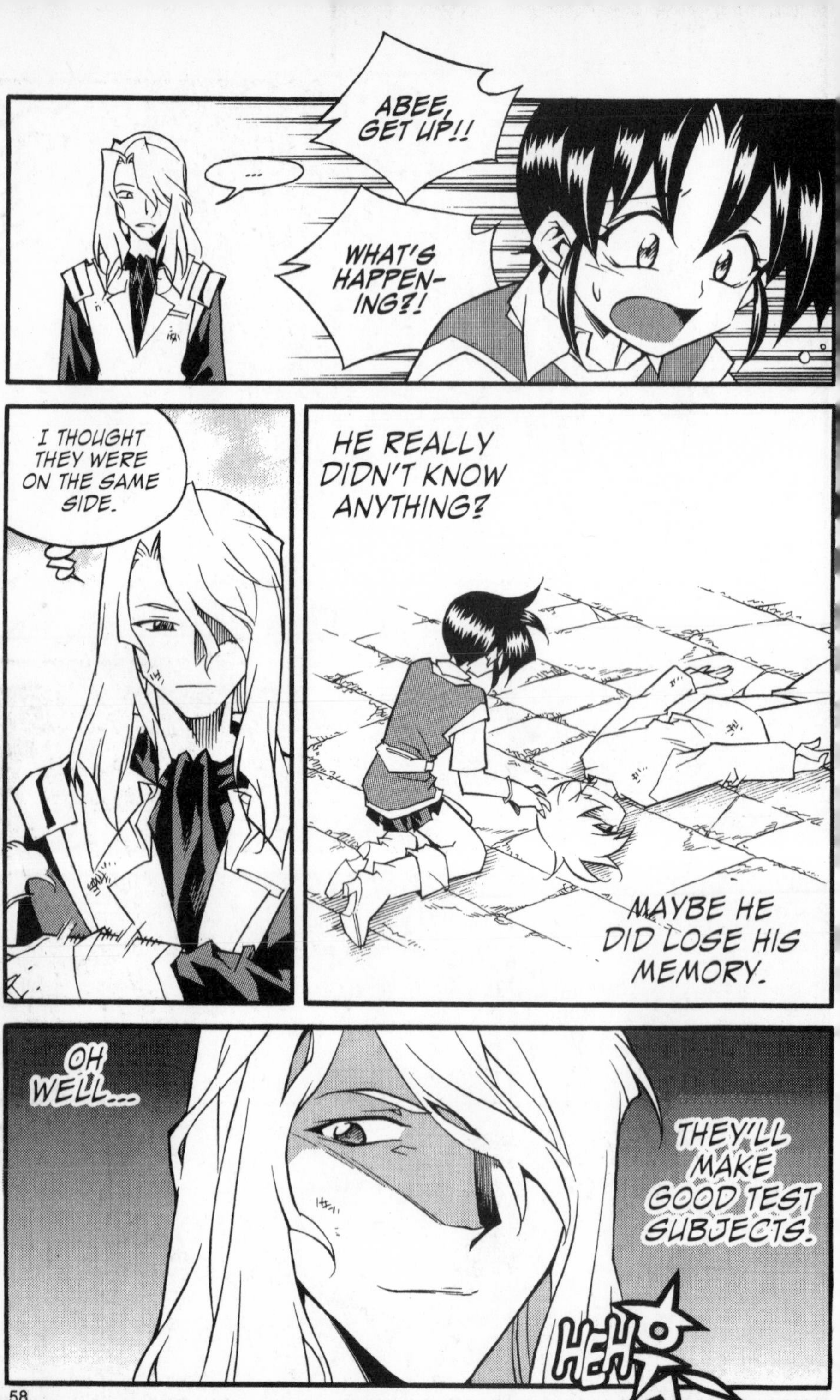
ABEE, GET UP!!
...
WHAT'S HAPPEN-ING?!
I THOUGHT THEY WERE ON THE SAME SIDE.
HE REALLY DIDN'T KNOW ANYTHING?
MAYBE HE DID LOSE HIS MEMORY.
OH WELL...
THEY'LL MAKE GOOD TEST SUBJECTS.
HEH

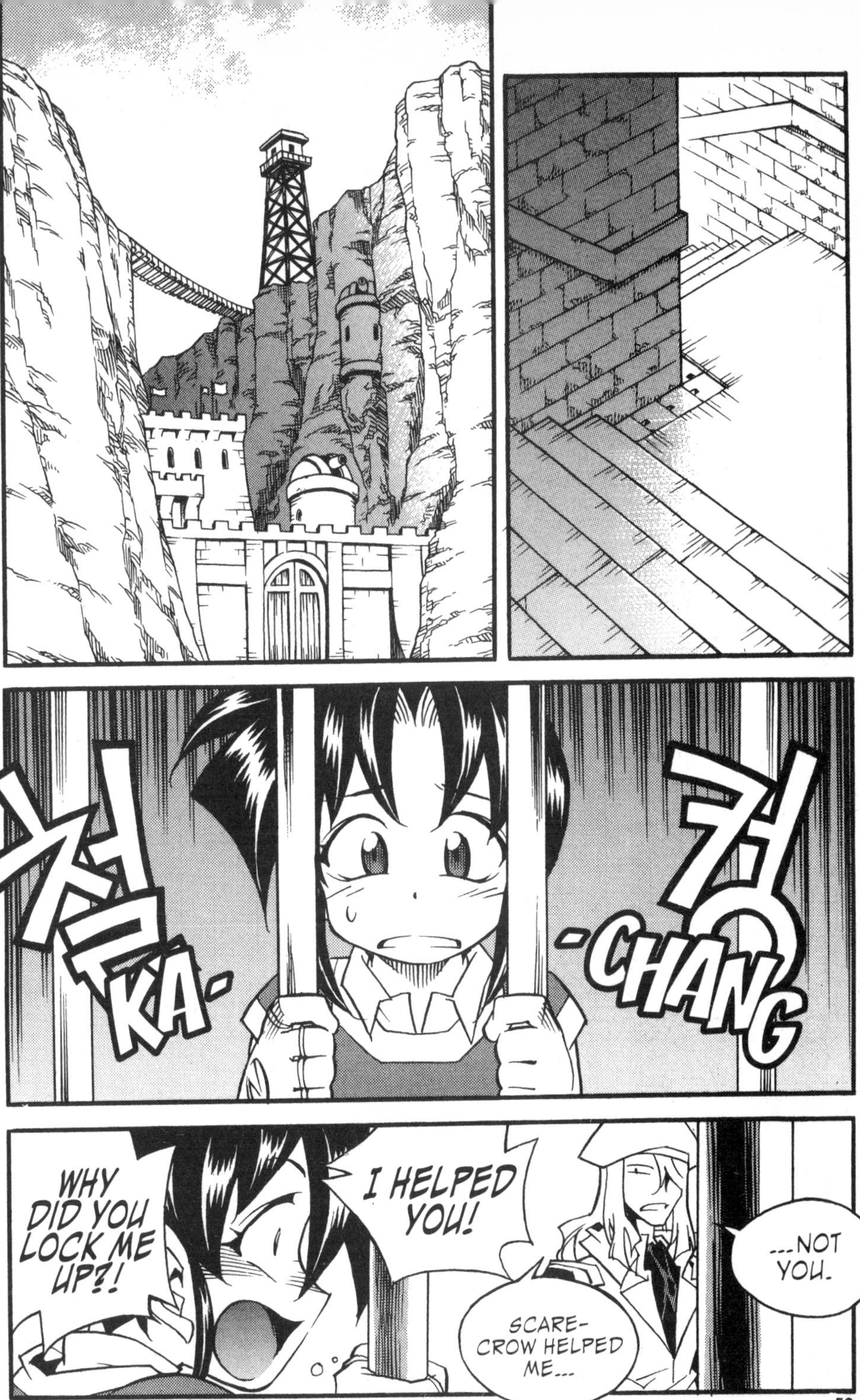
KA-
-CHANG
WHY DID YOU LOCK ME UP?!
I HELPED YOU!
SCARE-CROW HELPED ME...
...NOT YOU.

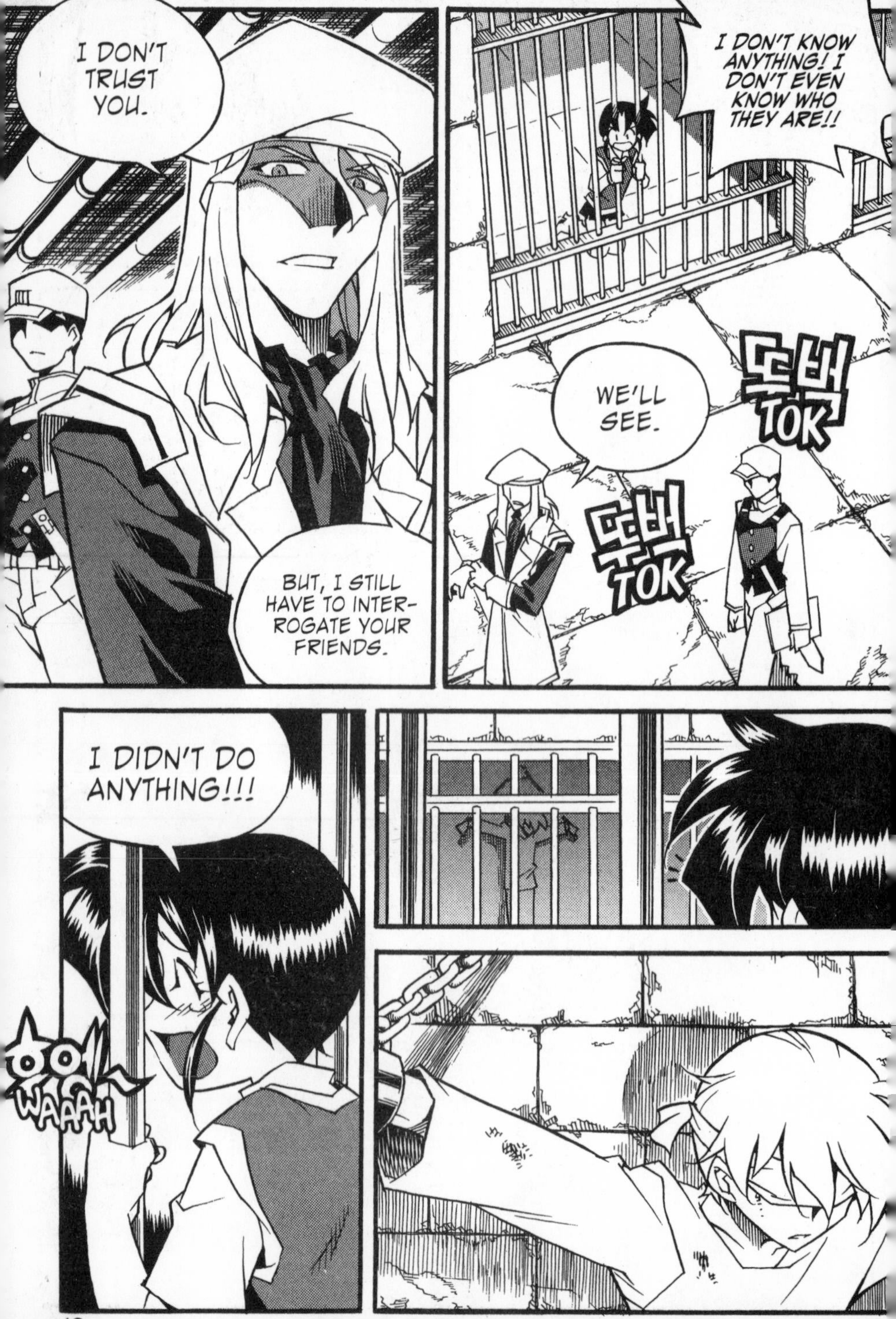
I DON'T TRUST YOU.
BUT, I STILL HAVE TO INTER-ROGATE YOUR FRIENDS.
I DON'T KNOW ANYTHING! I DON'T EVEN KNOW WHO THEY ARE!!
WE'LL SEE.
또박 TOK
또박 TOK
I DIDN'T DO ANYTHING!!!
WAAAH

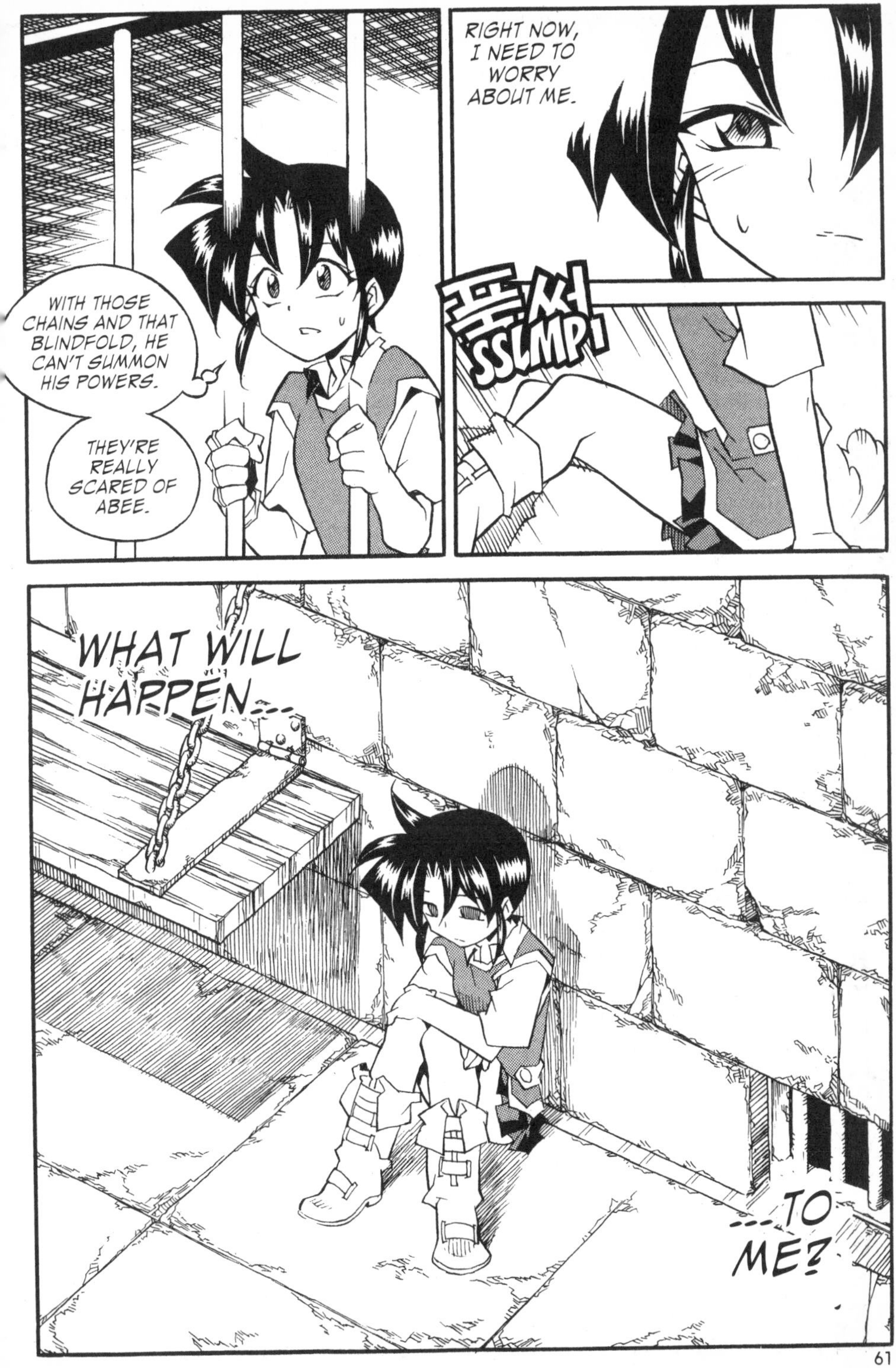
WITH THOSE CHAINS AND THAT BLINDFOLD, HE CAN'T SUMMON HIS POWERS.
THEY'RE REALLY SCARED OF ABEE.
RIGHT NOW, I NEED TO WORRY ABOUT ME.
SSLMP!
WHAT WILL HAPPEN...
...TO ME?

STAY ALERT! THEY'RE DANGEROUS!

MAJOR!!

I'VE BEEN LOOKING FOR YOU, SIR.

YES, SIR!

타타타
TOK TOK TOK

WHAT'S GOING ON?

WELL, SIR...

IT'S URGENT, SIR! FROM SAPPHIRE CITY.

URGENT? IS IT WAR?!

I'M NOT SURE, BUT....

....IT SOUNDS WORSE.

WHY DON'T YOU READ IT, SIR.

WHAT'S GOING ON?

RRSTL

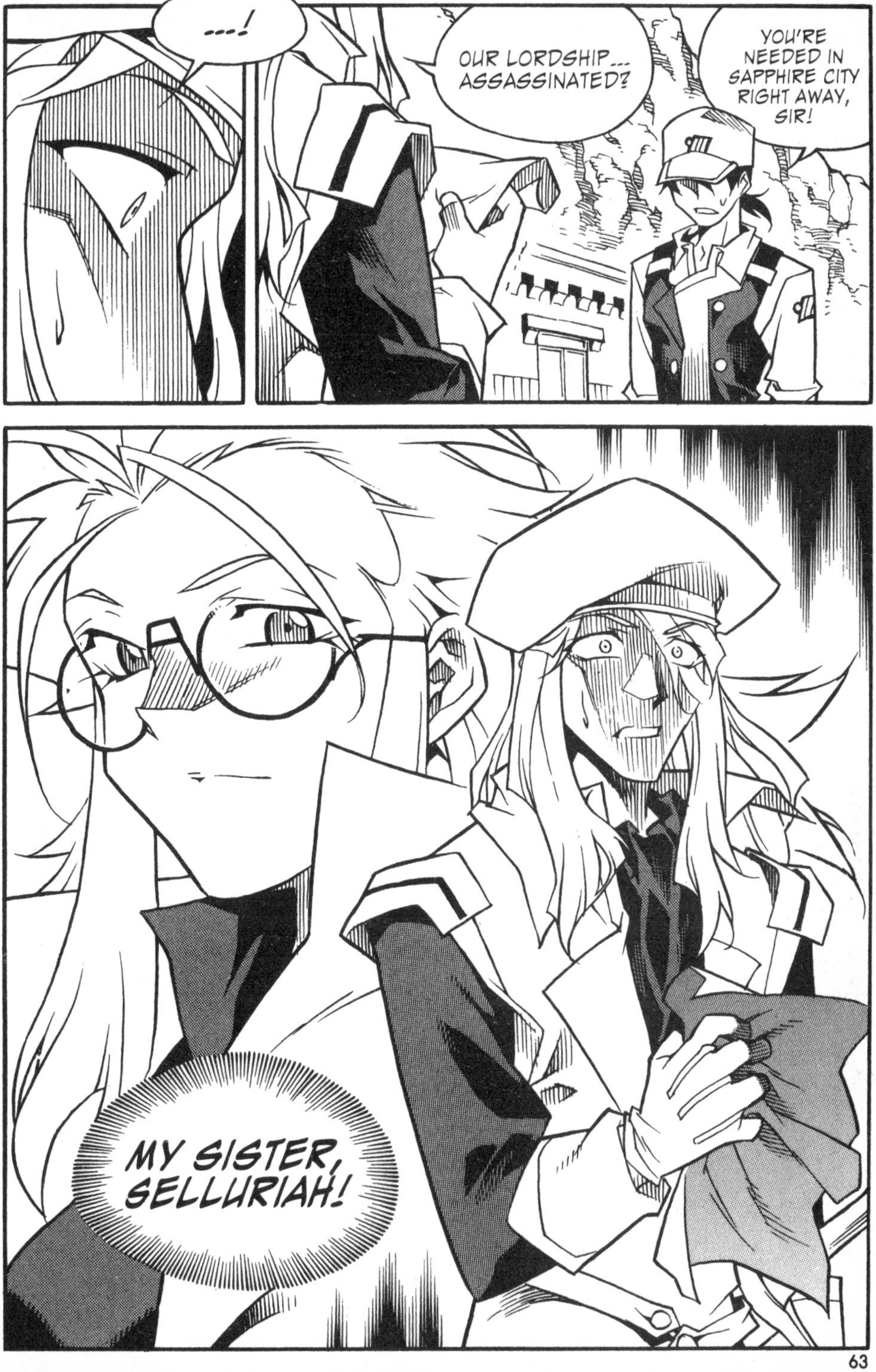
...!
OUR LORDSHIP... ASSASSINATED?
YOU'RE NEEDED IN SAPPHIRE CITY RIGHT AWAY, SIR!
MY SISTER, SELLURIAH!

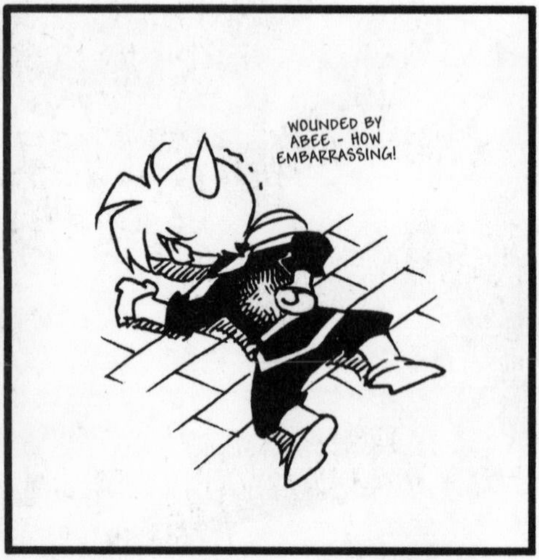
WOUNDED BY
ABEE - HOW
EMBARRASSING!

Step 18 PRISON BREAK

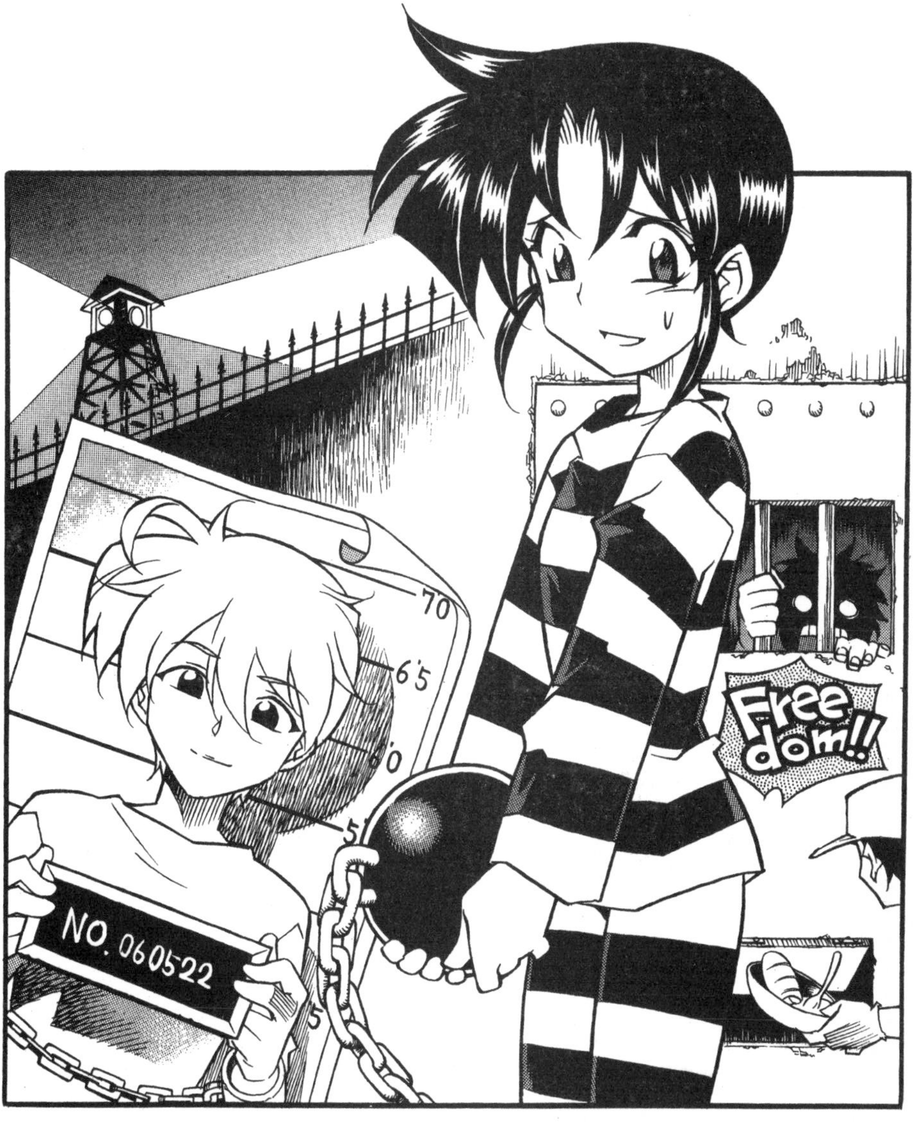
70
65
60
5
NO. 060522
Free dom!!

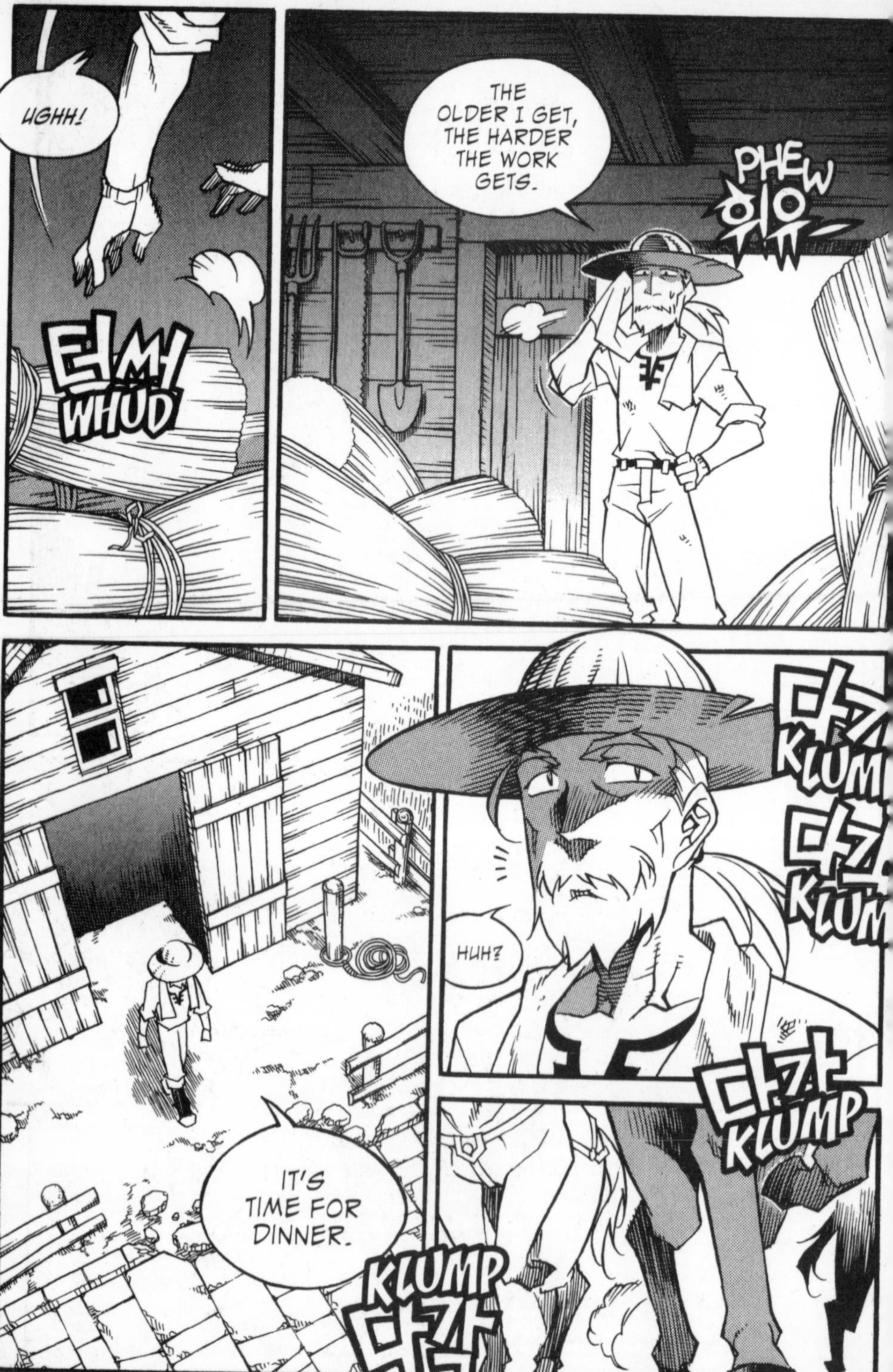
UGHH!
터석
WHUD
THE OLDER I GET, THE HARDER THE WORK GETS.
PHEW
휘유
HUH?
다각
KLUMP
다각
KLUMP
다각
KLUMP
IT'S TIME FOR DINNER.
KLUMP
다각

KLUMP

KLUMP

HBBT

WHAT ARMY ARE THEY WITH?

CAN I ASK YOU SOMETHING, MR.?

O-OKAY.

HOW DO I GET TO THE ROCK BASE FROM HERE?

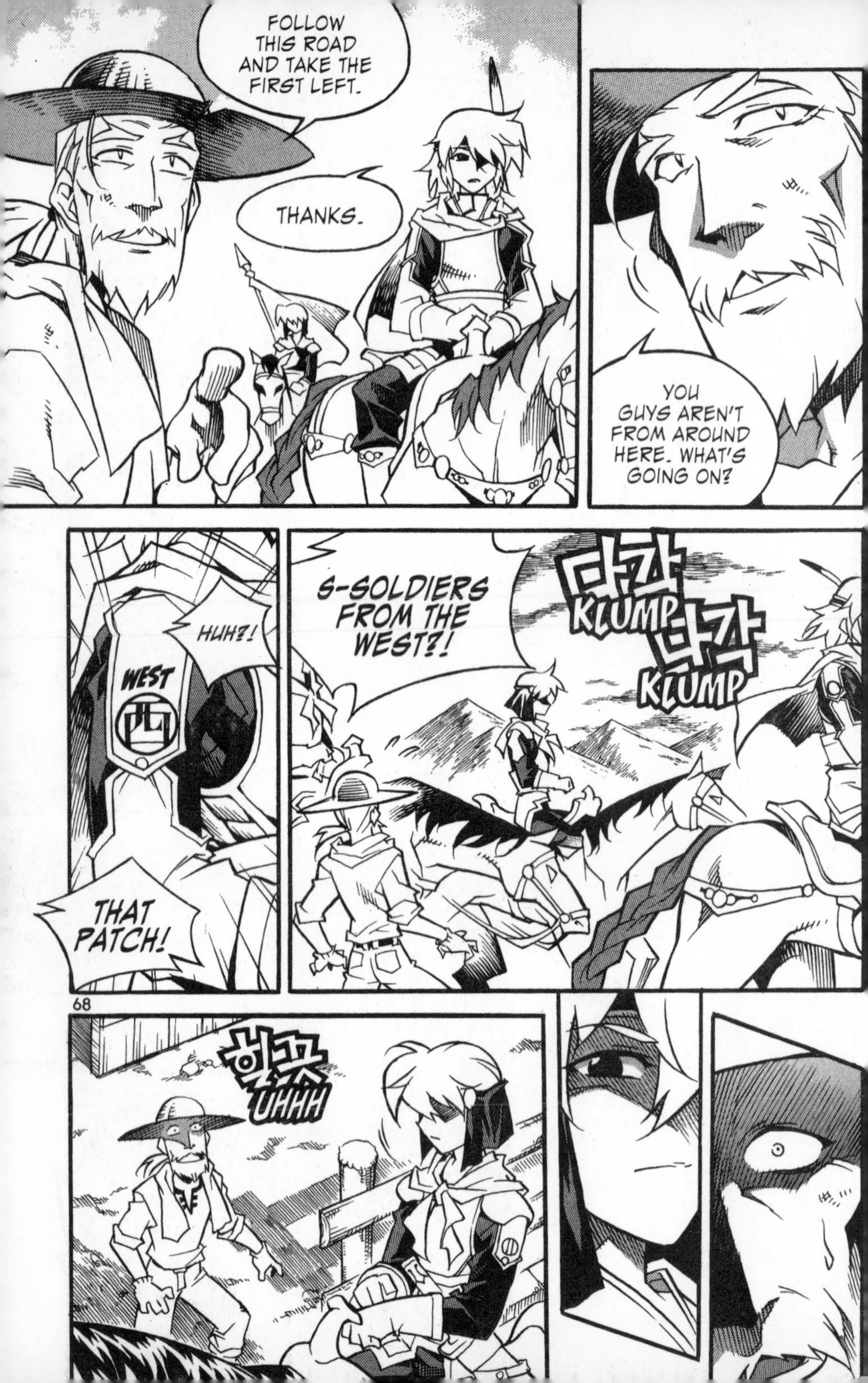
FOLLOW THIS ROAD AND TAKE THE FIRST LEFT.
THANKS.
YOU GUYS AREN'T FROM AROUND HERE. WHAT'S GOING ON?
WEST
HUH?!
THAT PATCH!
S-SOLDIERS FROM THE WEST?!
KLUMP
KLUMP
UHHH

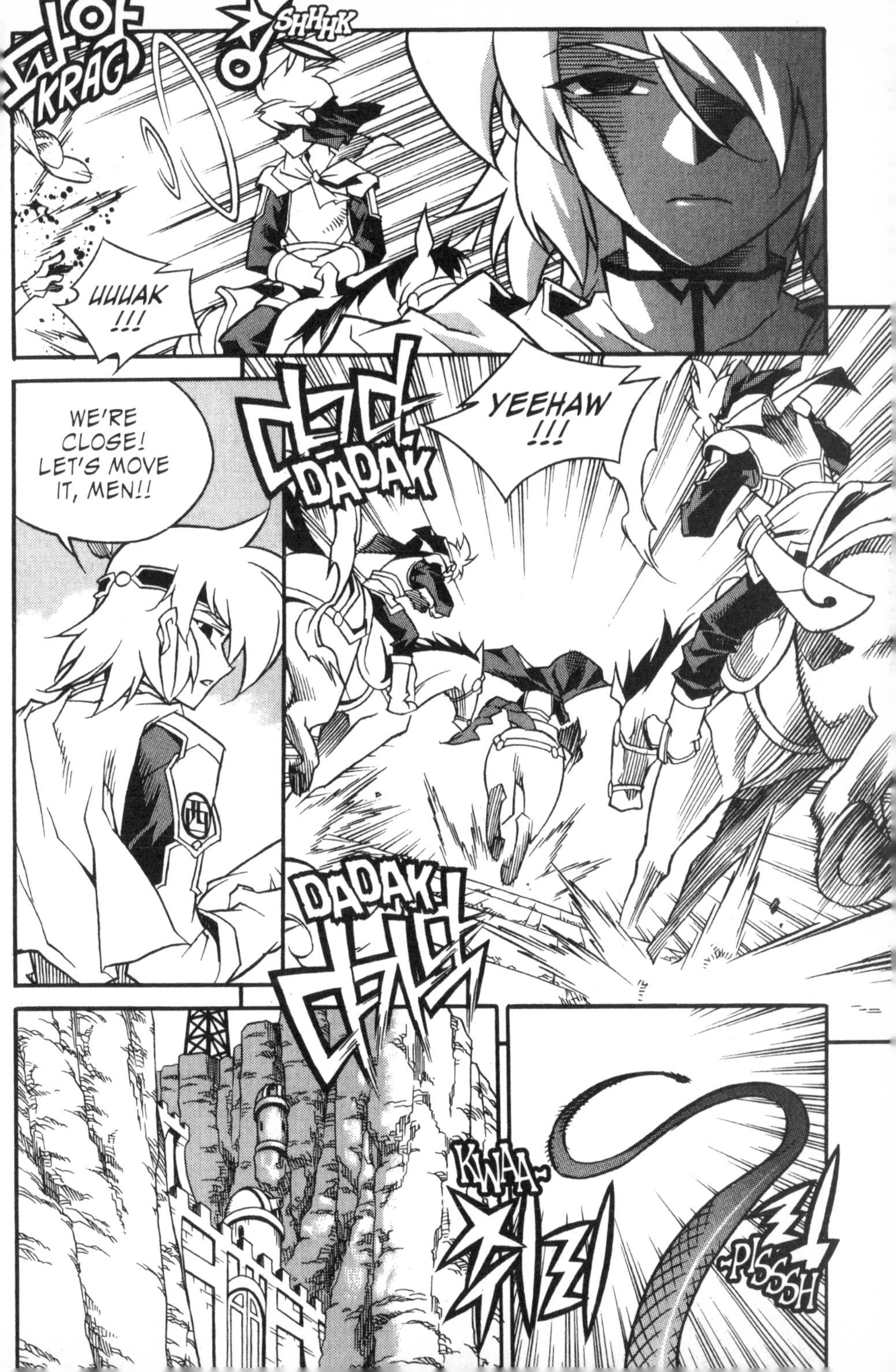
KRAG
SHHHK
UUUAK !!!
WE'RE CLOSE! LET'S MOVE IT, MEN!!
DADAK
YEEHAW !!!
DADAK
KWAA-
PISSSH

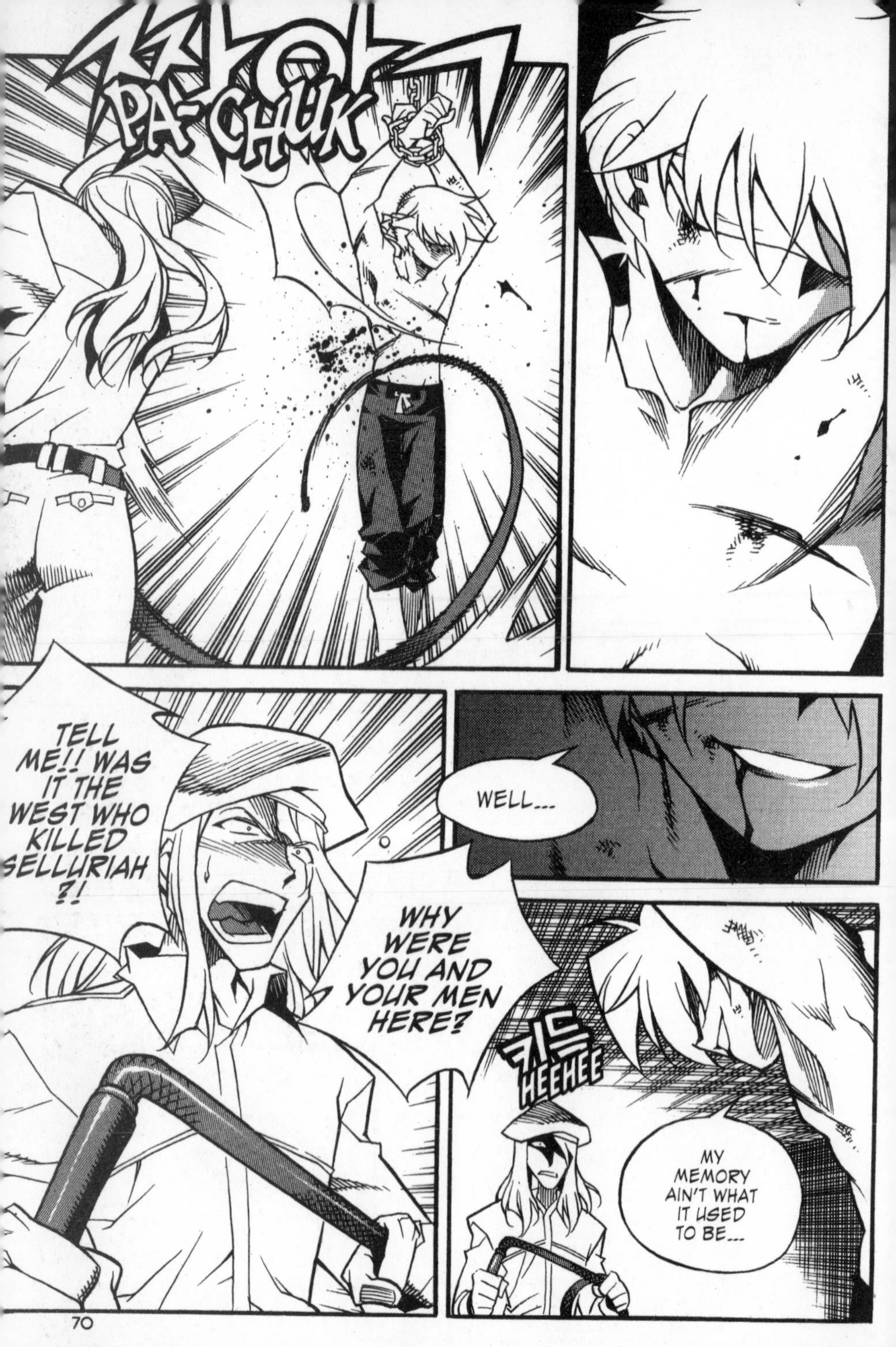
PA-CHUK
TELL ME!! WAS IT THE WEST WHO KILLED SELLURIAH ?!
WELL...
WHY WERE YOU AND YOUR MEN HERE?
HEEHEE
MY MEMORY AIN'T WHAT IT USED TO BE...

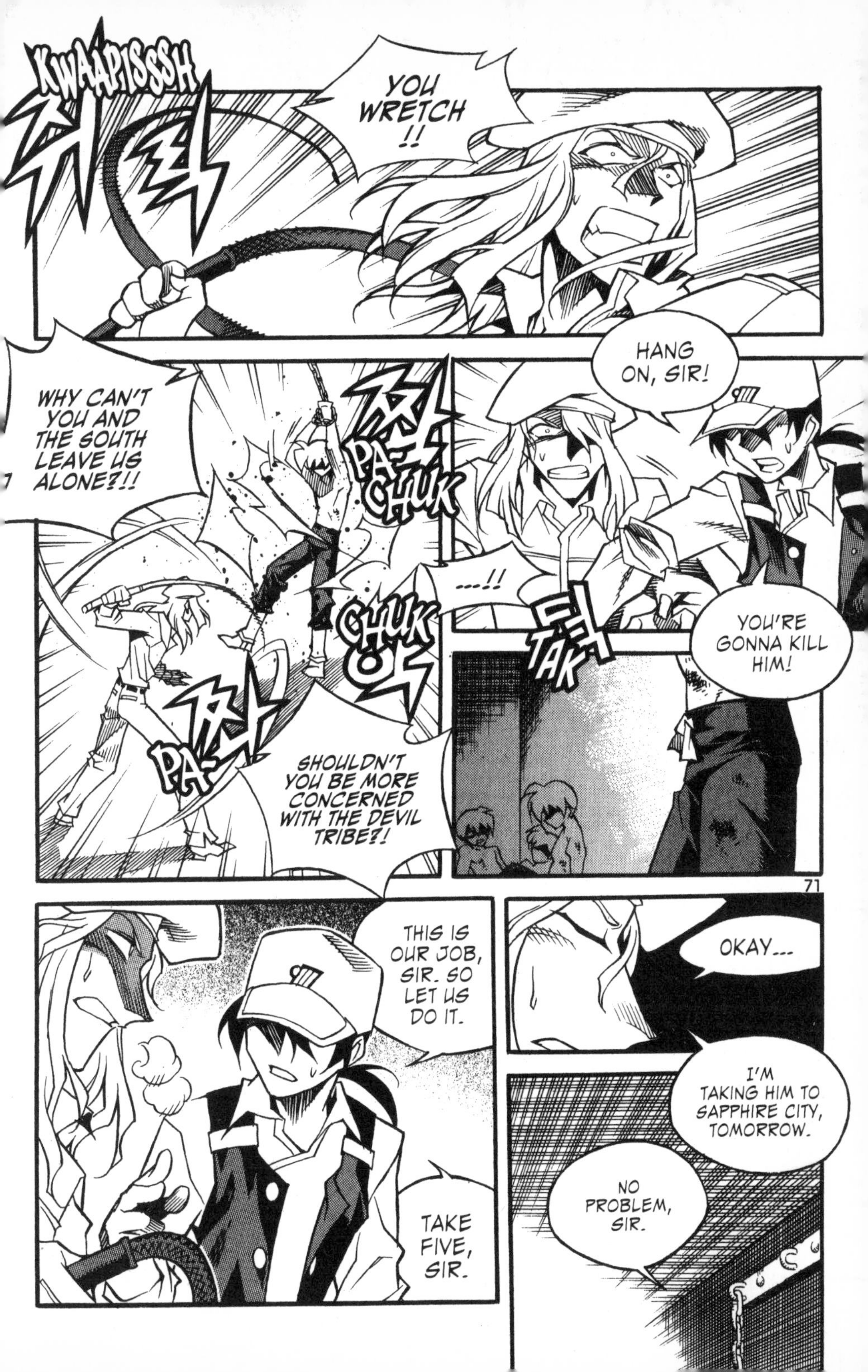
KWAAPISSSH
YOU WRETCH !!
WHY CAN'T YOU AND THE SOUTH LEAVE US ALONE?!!
PA-CHUK
CHUK
PA
SHOULDN'T YOU BE MORE CONCERNED WITH THE DEVIL TRIBE?!
HANG ON, SIR!
...!!
TAK
YOU'RE GONNA KILL HIM!
THIS IS OUR JOB, SIR. SO LET US DO IT.
TAKE FIVE, SIR.
OKAY...
I'M TAKING HIM TO SAPPHIRE CITY, TOMORROW.
NO PROBLEM, SIR.

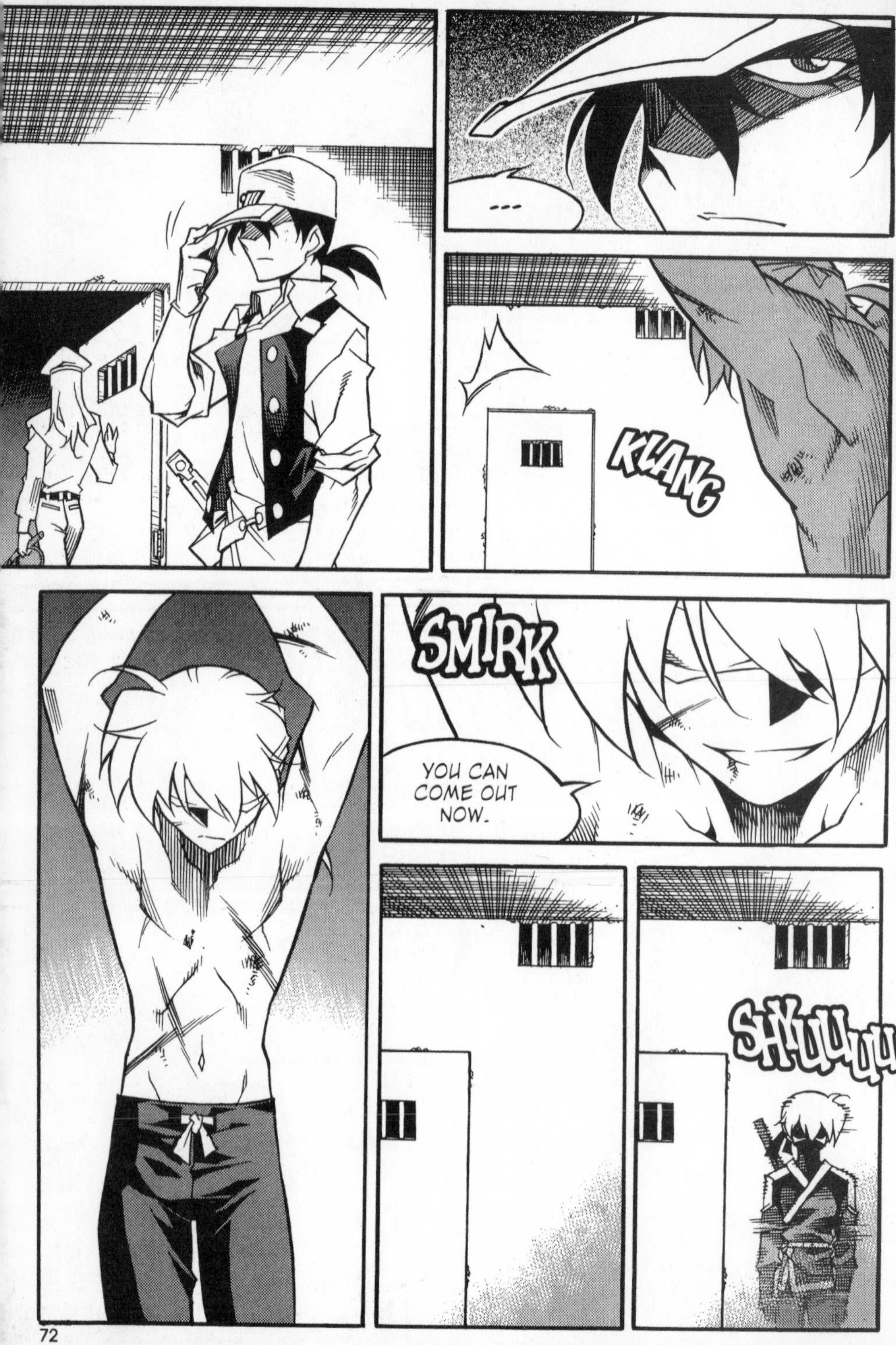
...
KLANG
SMIRK
YOU CAN COME OUT NOW.
SHYUUUU

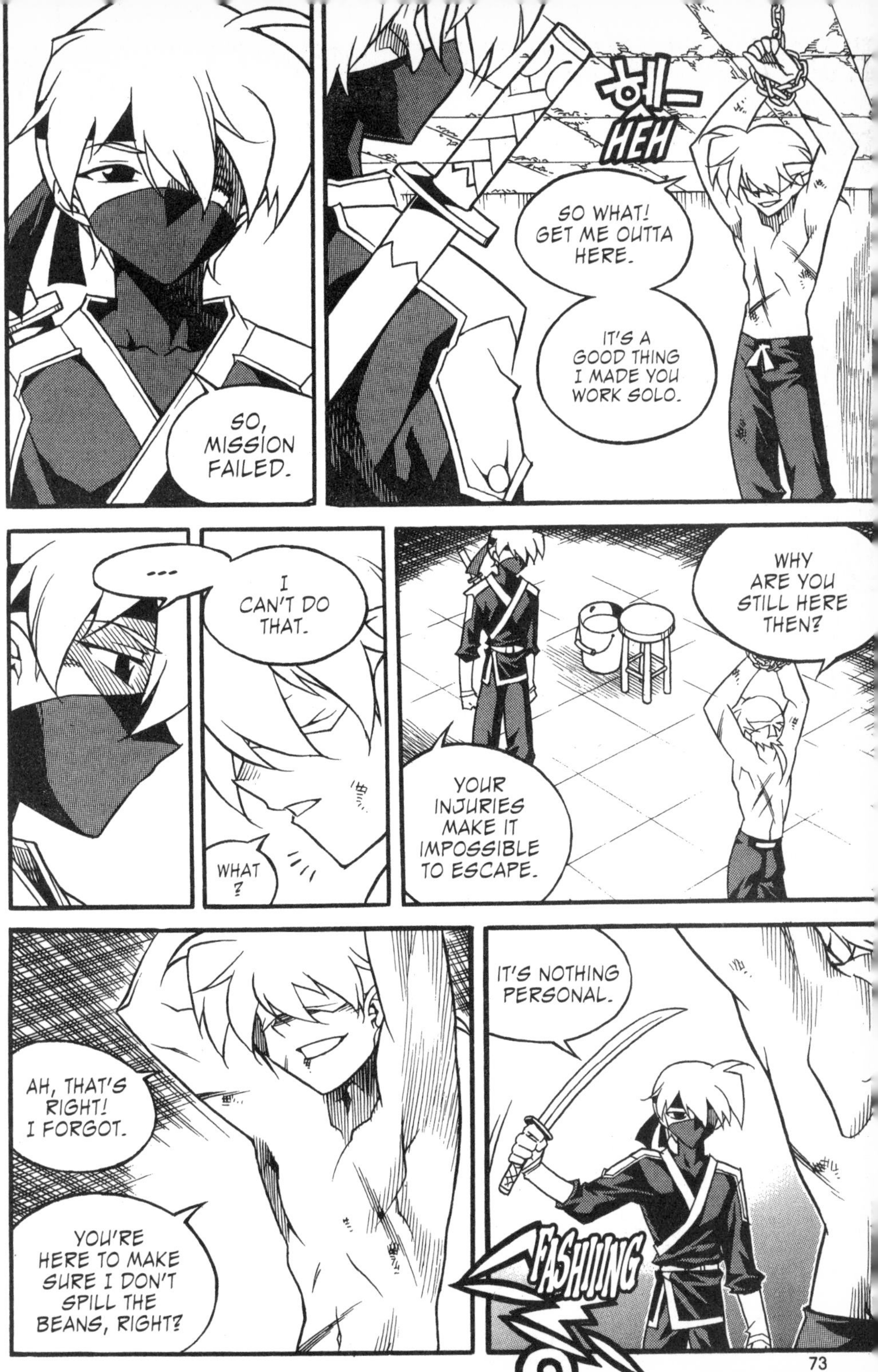
SO, MISSION FAILED.
헤-
HEH
SO WHAT! GET ME OUTTA HERE.
IT'S A GOOD THING I MADE YOU WORK SOLO.
...
I CAN'T DO THAT.
WHAT?
WHY ARE YOU STILL HERE THEN?
YOUR INJURIES MAKE IT IMPOSSIBLE TO ESCAPE.
AH, THAT'S RIGHT! I FORGOT.
YOU'RE HERE TO MAKE SURE I DON'T SPILL THE BEANS, RIGHT?
IT'S NOTHING PERSONAL.
FASHIIING

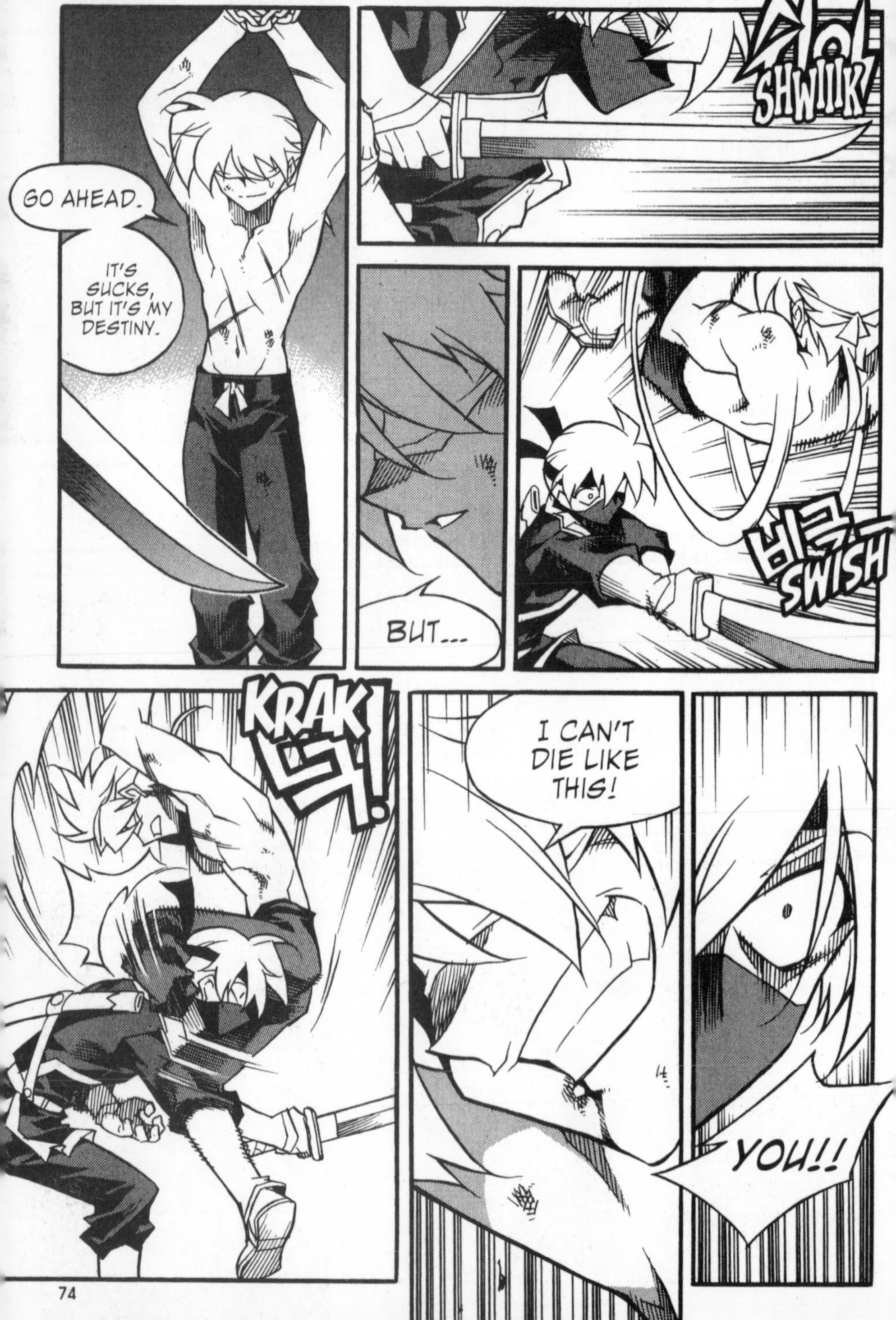
GO AHEAD.
IT'S SUCKS, BUT IT'S MY DESTINY.
쉬익
SHWIIK
BUT...
비크
SWISH
KRAK!
I CAN'T DIE LIKE THIS!
YOU!!

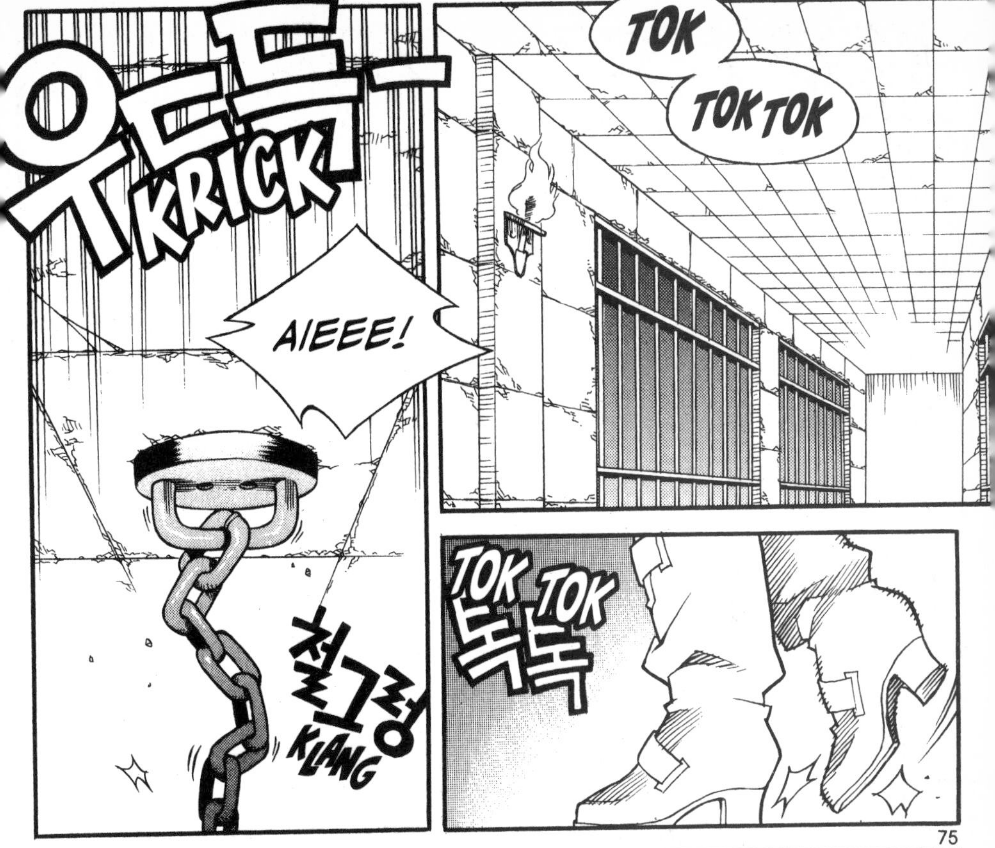
으드득
KRICK
AIEEE!
철그렁
KLANG
TOK
TOK TOK
TOK TOK
톡톡

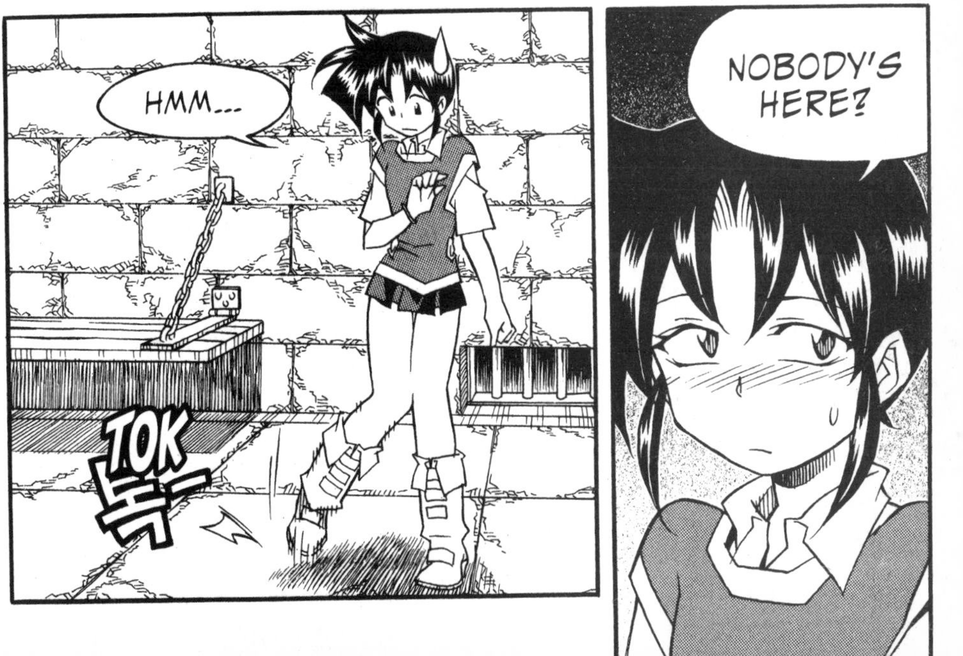
HMM...
TOK
톡-
NOBODY'S HERE?

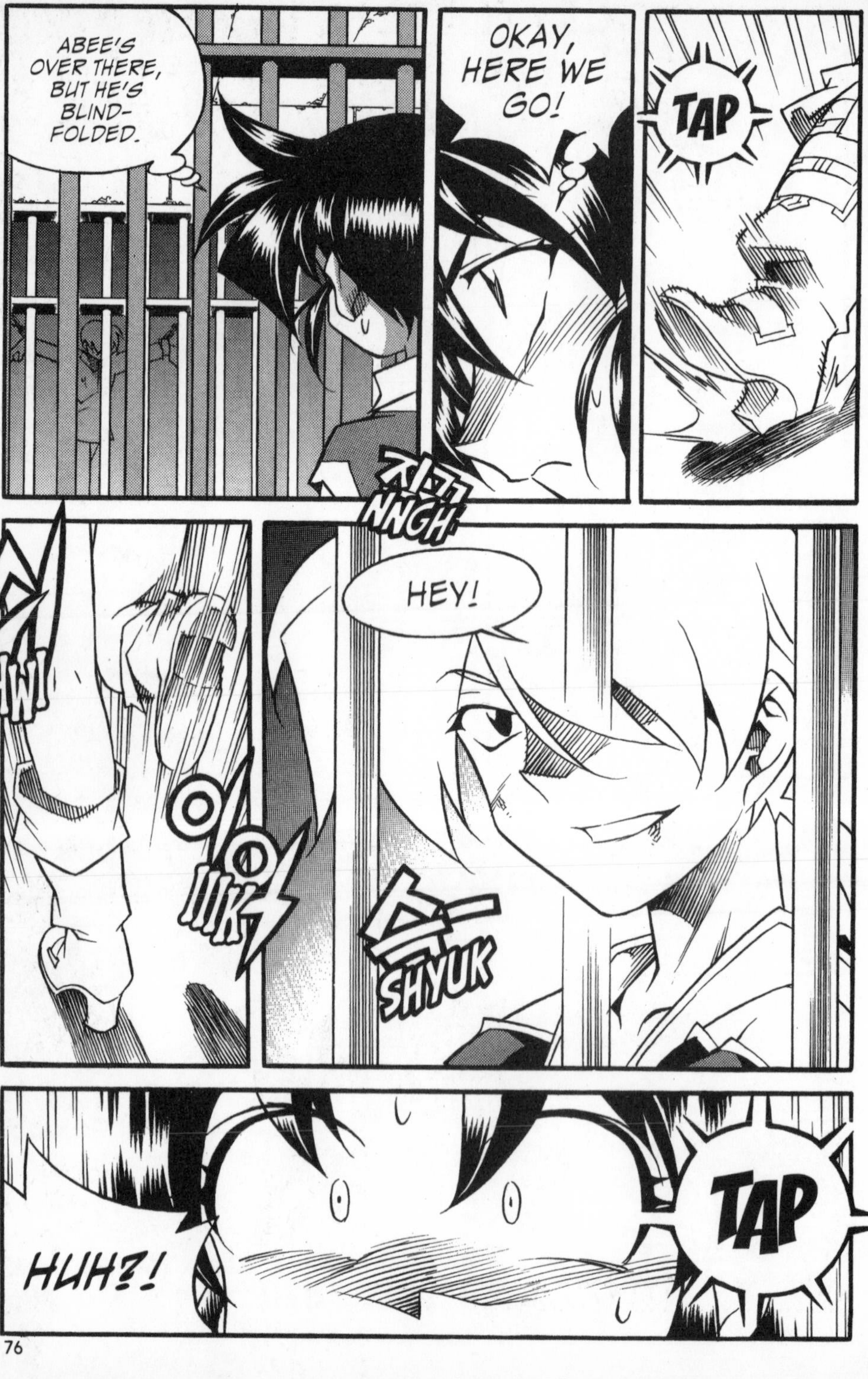
ABEE'S OVER THERE, BUT HE'S BLIND-FOLDED.
OKAY, HERE WE GO!
NNGH
TAP
SHWI
IIIK
HEY!
SHYUK
HUH?!
TAP

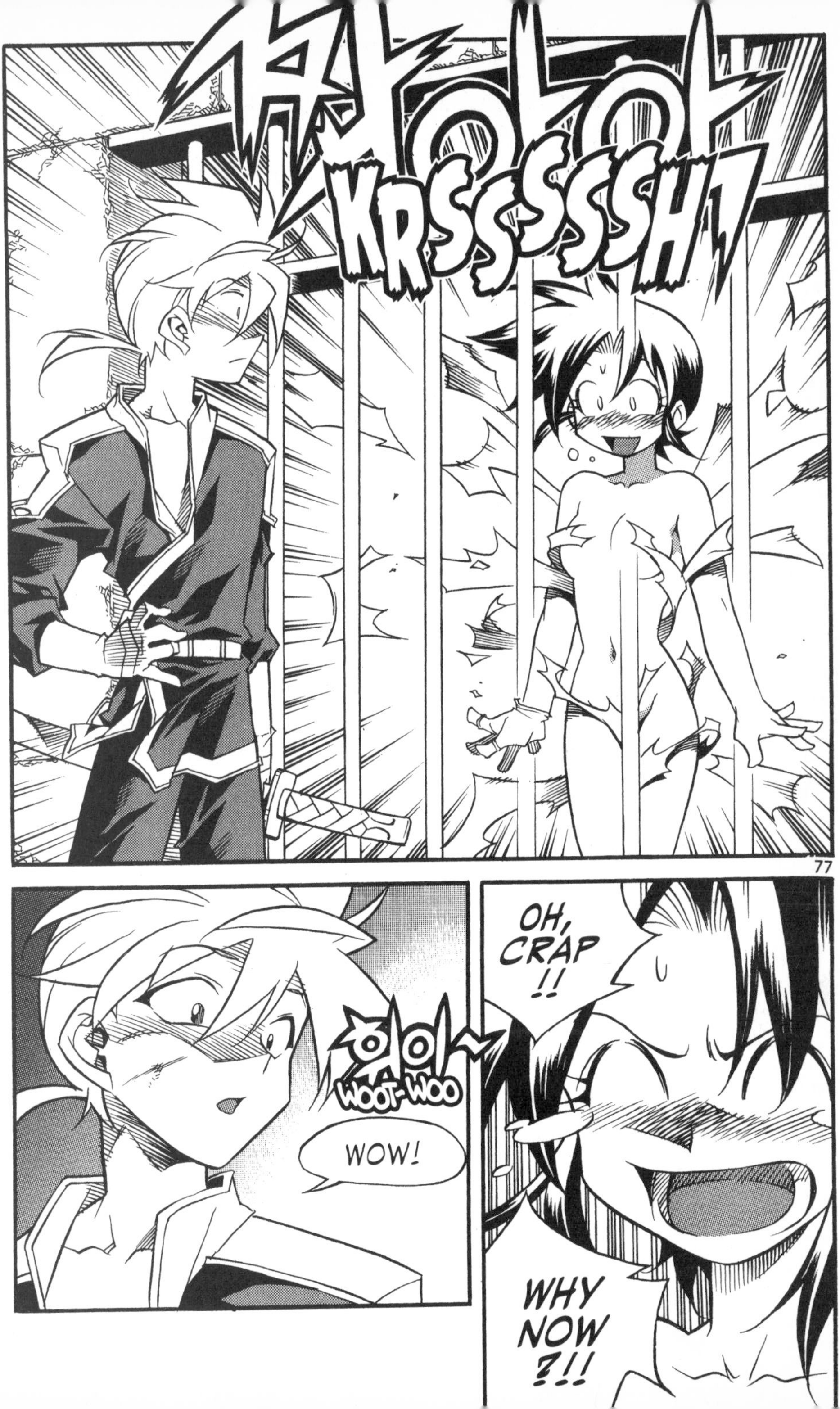
KRSSSSSH
히이~
WOOT-WOO
WOW!
OH, CRAP !!
WHY NOW ?!!

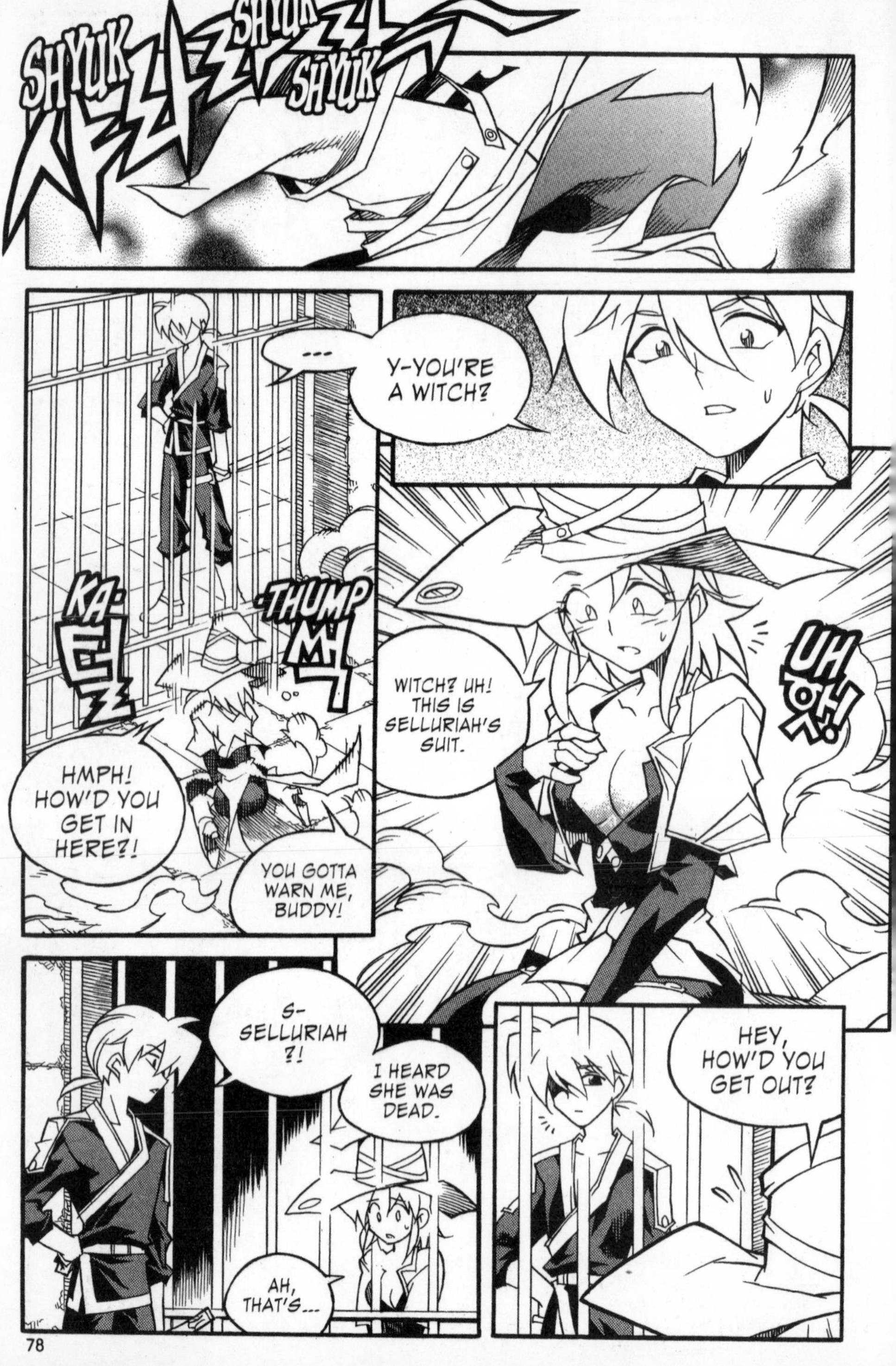
SHYUK
SHYUK
SHYUK
...
KA-THUMP
HMPH! HOW'D YOU GET IN HERE?!
YOU GOTTA WARN ME, BUDDY!
Y-YOU'RE A WITCH?
WITCH? UH! THIS IS SELLURIAH'S SUIT.
UH
S-SELLURIAH?!
I HEARD SHE WAS DEAD.
AH, THAT'S...
HEY, HOW'D YOU GET OUT?

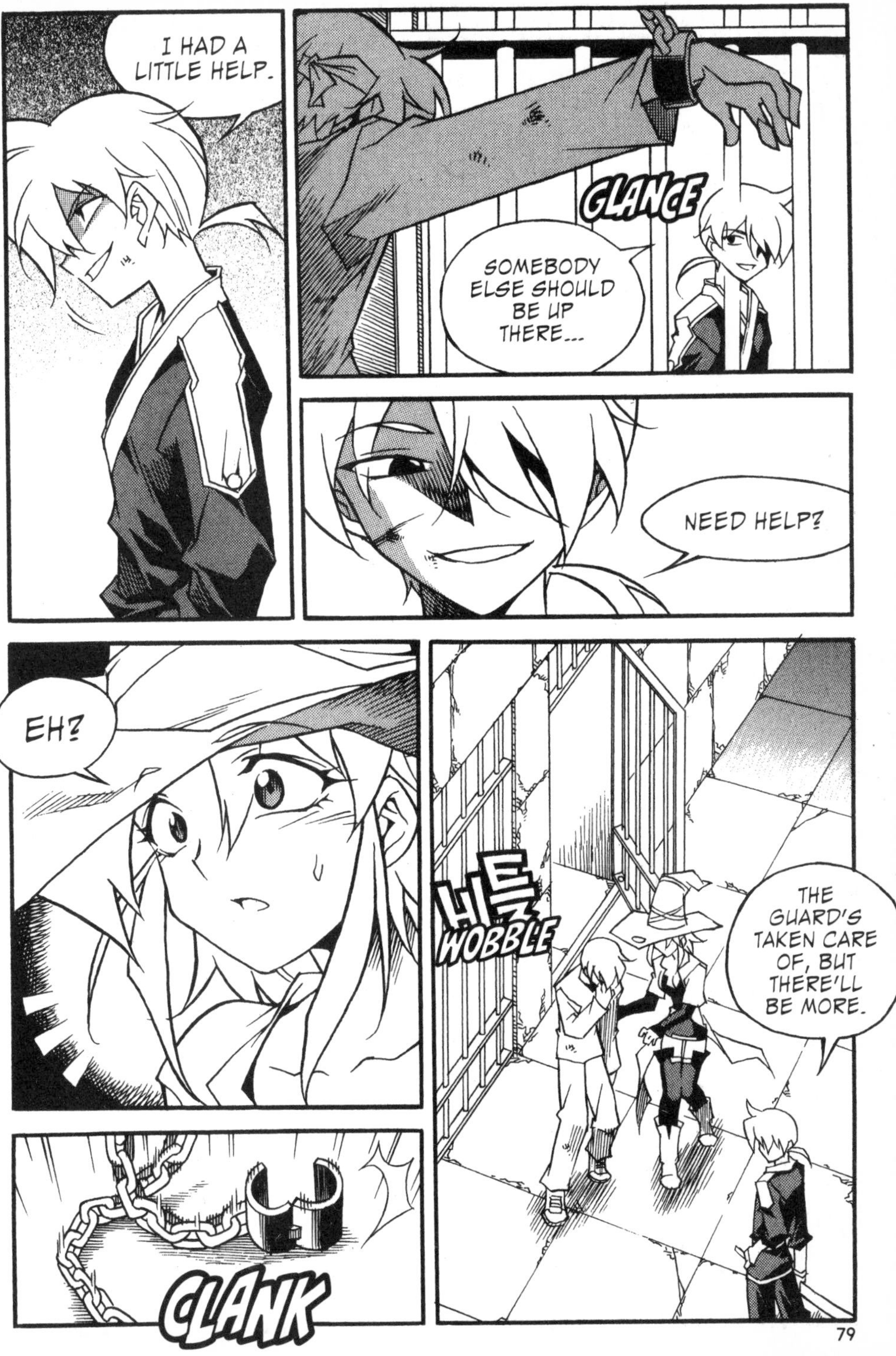
I HAD A LITTLE HELP.
GLANCE
SOMEBODY ELSE SHOULD BE UP THERE...
NEED HELP?
EH?
CLANK
비틀
WOBBLE
THE GUARD'S TAKEN CARE OF, BUT THERE'LL BE MORE.

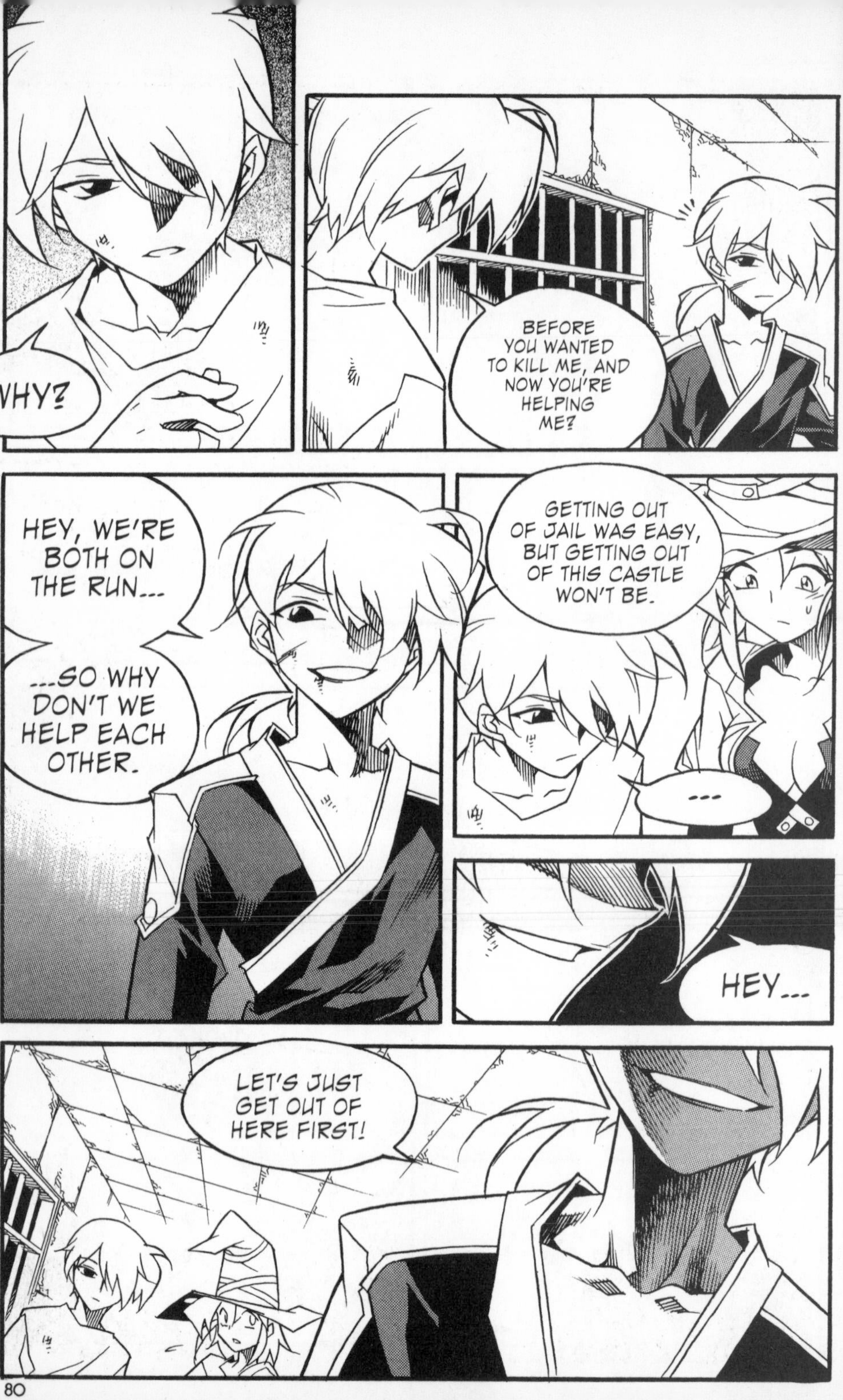
WHY?
BEFORE YOU WANTED TO KILL ME, AND NOW YOU'RE HELPING ME?
HEY, WE'RE BOTH ON THE RUN...
...SO WHY DON'T WE HELP EACH OTHER.
GETTING OUT OF JAIL WAS EASY, BUT GETTING OUT OF THIS CASTLE WON'T BE.
...
HEY...
LET'S JUST GET OUT OF HERE FIRST!

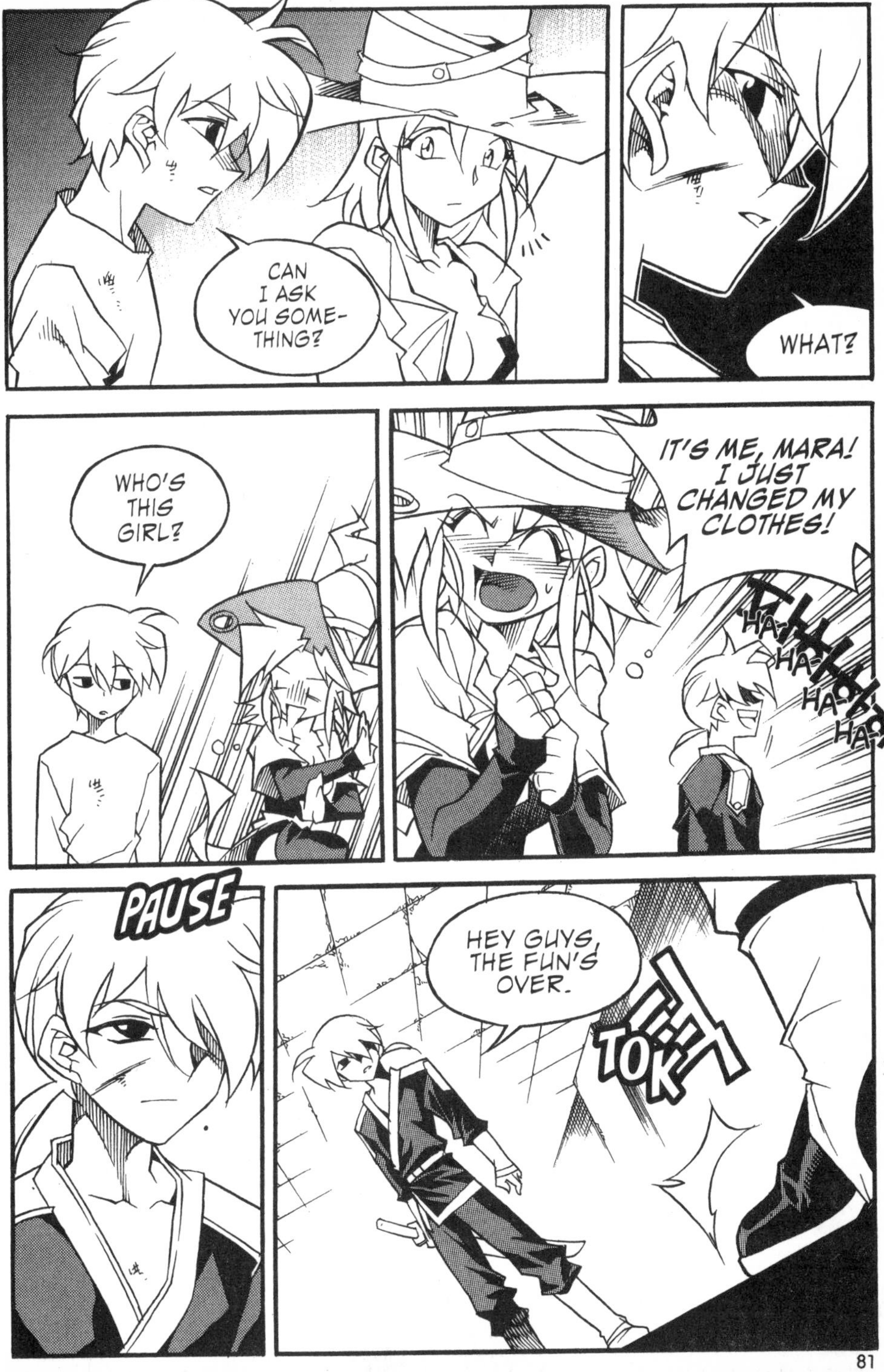
CAN I ASK YOU SOME-THING?
WHAT?
WHO'S THIS GIRL?
IT'S ME, MARA! I JUST CHANGED MY CLOTHES!
HA-HA-HA-HA-
PAUSE
HEY GUYS, THE FUN'S OVER.
TOK

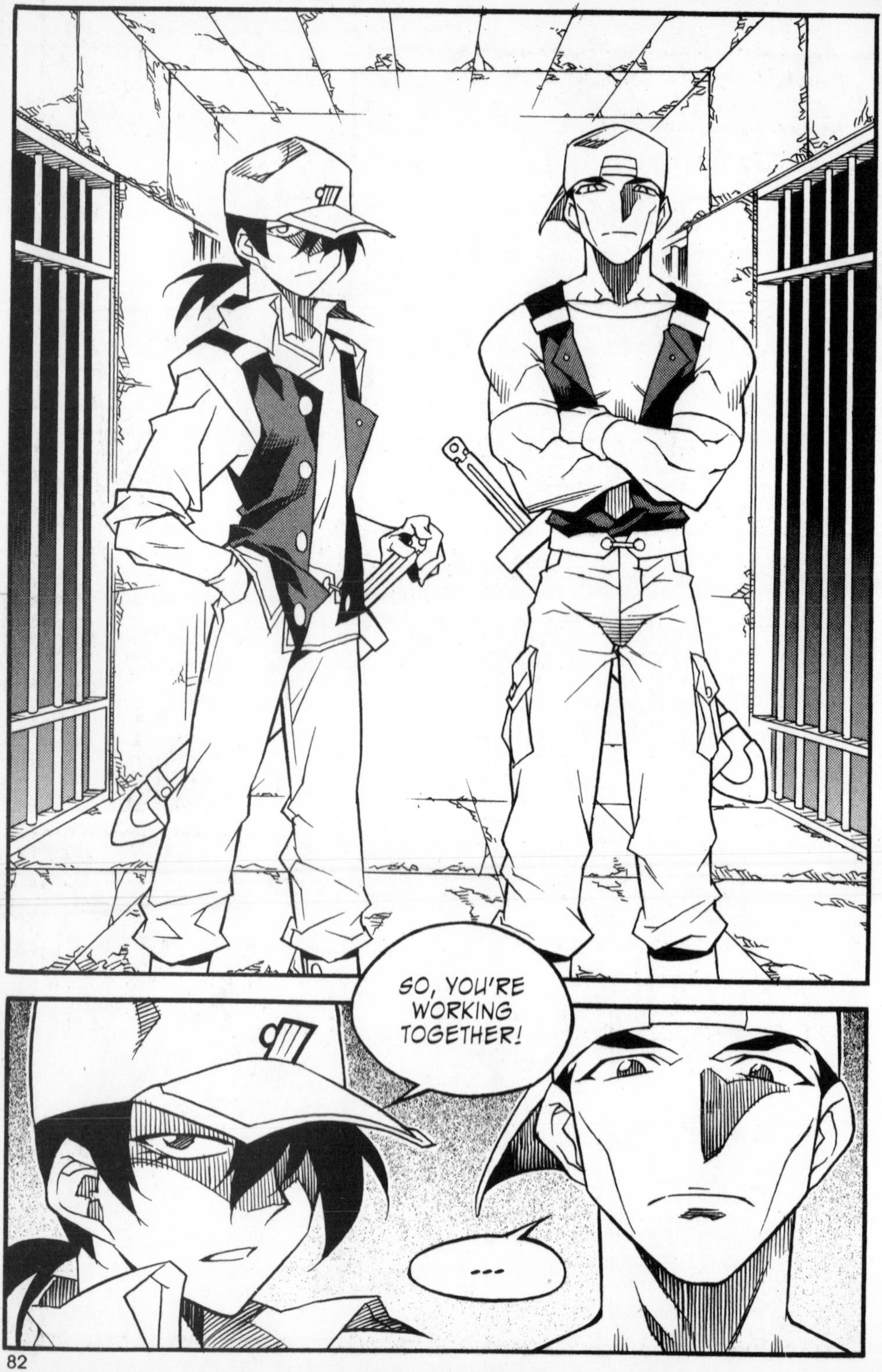
SO, YOU'RE WORKING TOGETHER!
...

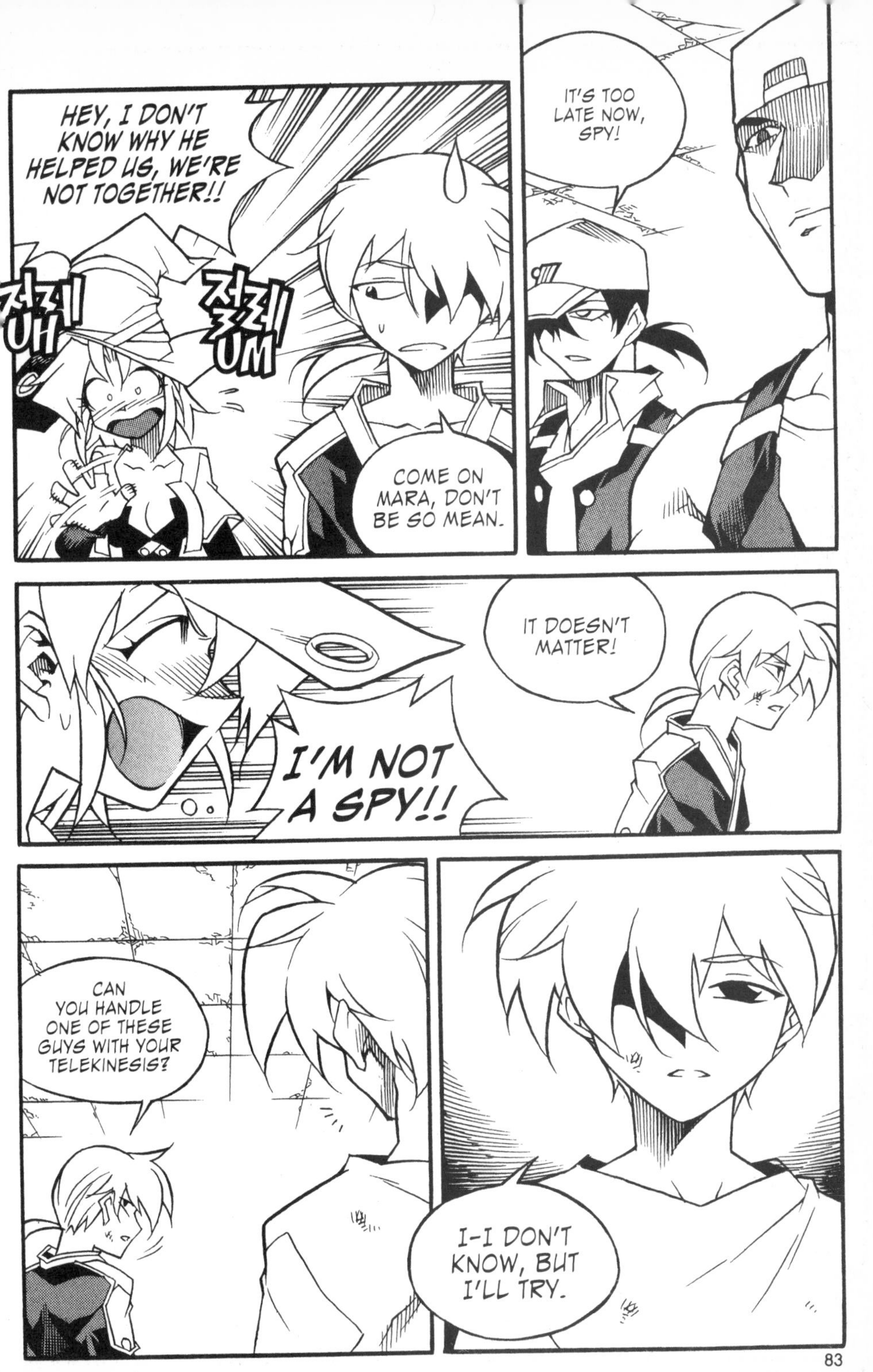
HEY, I DON'T KNOW WHY HE HELPED US, WE'RE NOT TOGETHER!!
UH
절레 UM
COME ON MARA, DON'T BE SO MEAN.
IT'S TOO LATE NOW, SPY!
I'M NOT A SPY!!
IT DOESN'T MATTER!
CAN YOU HANDLE ONE OF THESE GUYS WITH YOUR TELEKINESIS?
I-I DON'T KNOW, BUT I'LL TRY.

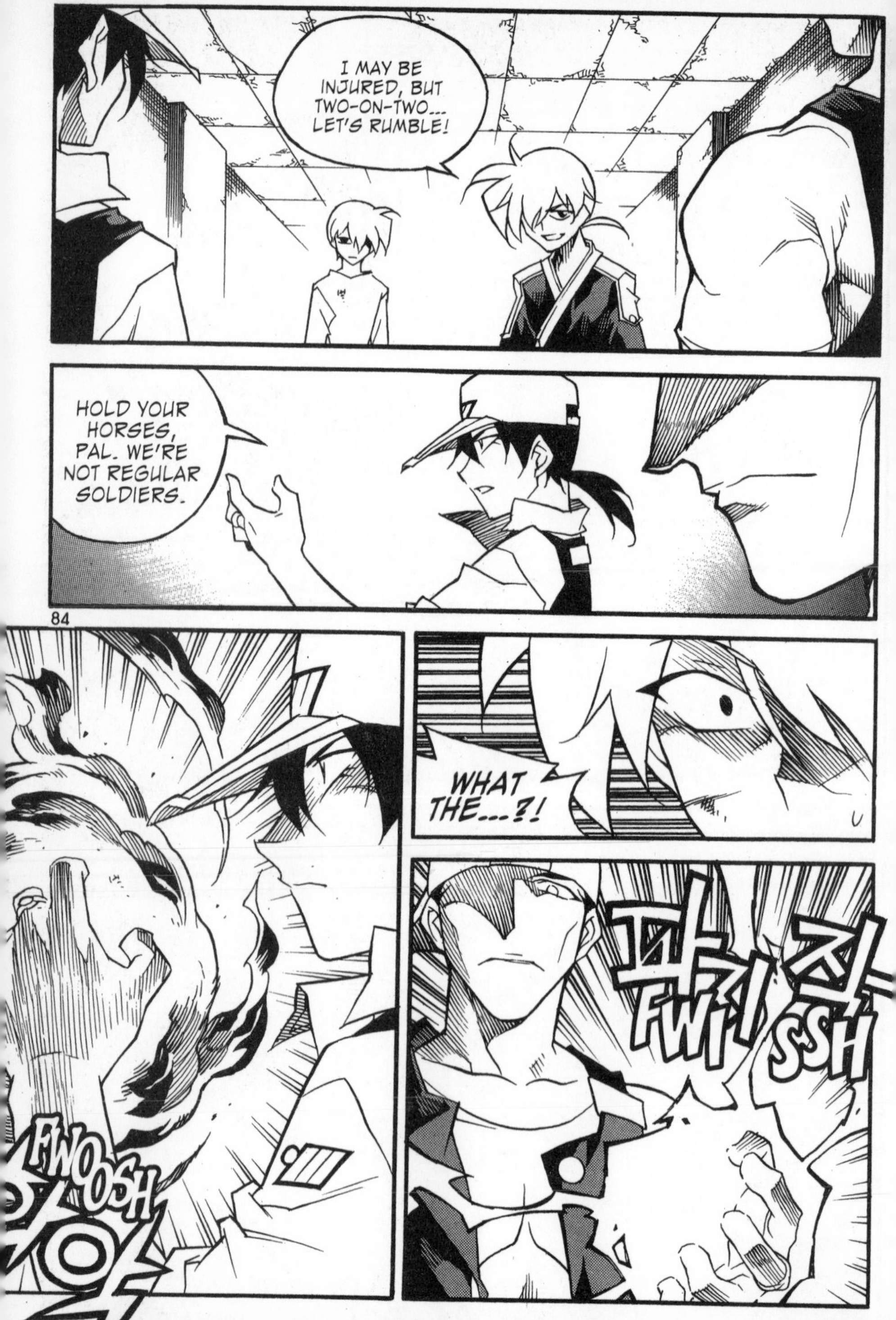
I MAY BE INJURED, BUT TWO-ON-TWO... LET'S RUMBLE!
HOLD YOUR HORSES, PAL. WE'RE NOT REGULAR SOLDIERS.
FWOOSH
WHAT THE...?!
FWISSH

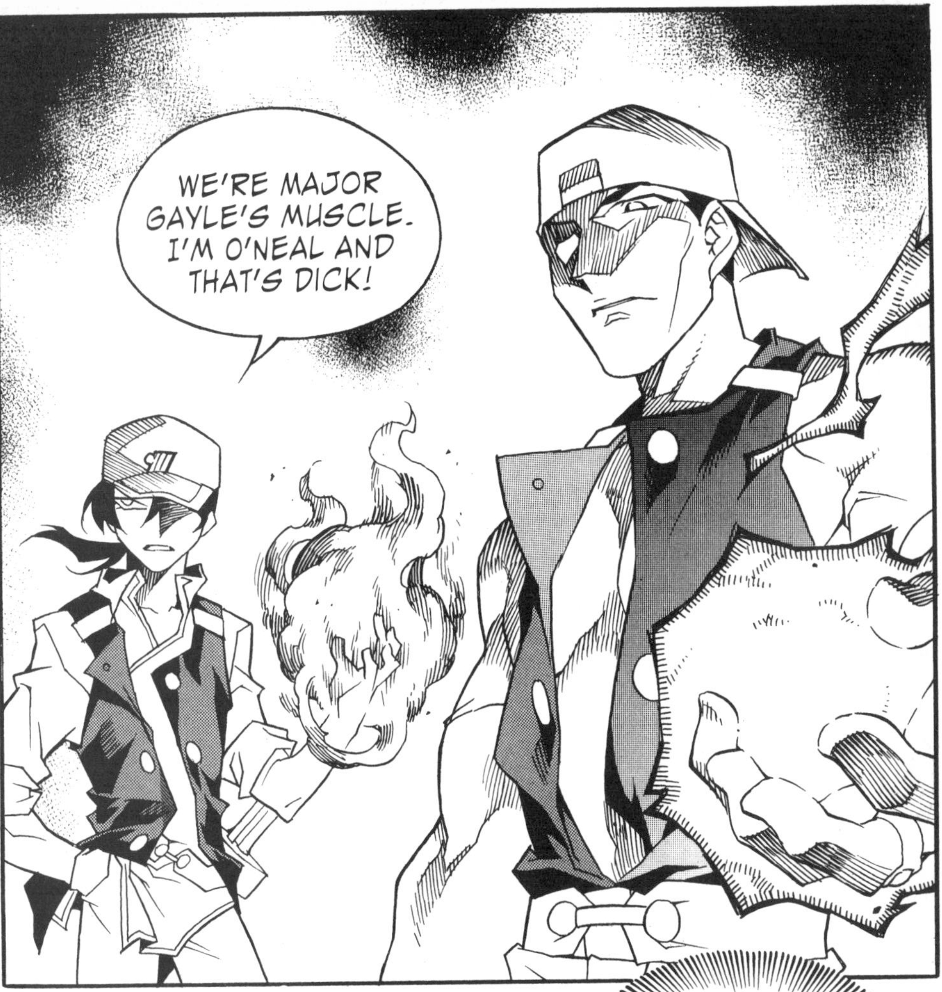
WE'RE MAJOR GAYLE'S MUSCLE. I'M O'NEAL AND THAT'S DICK!

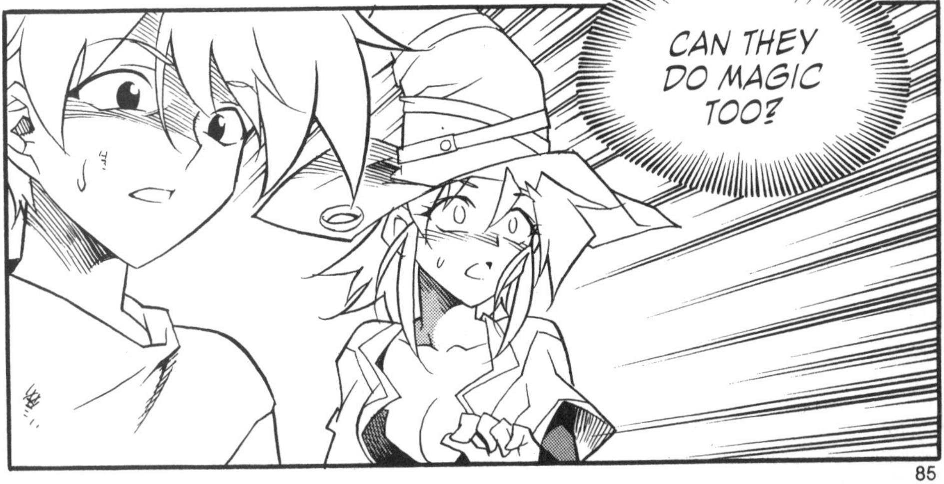
CAN THEY DO MAGIC TOO?

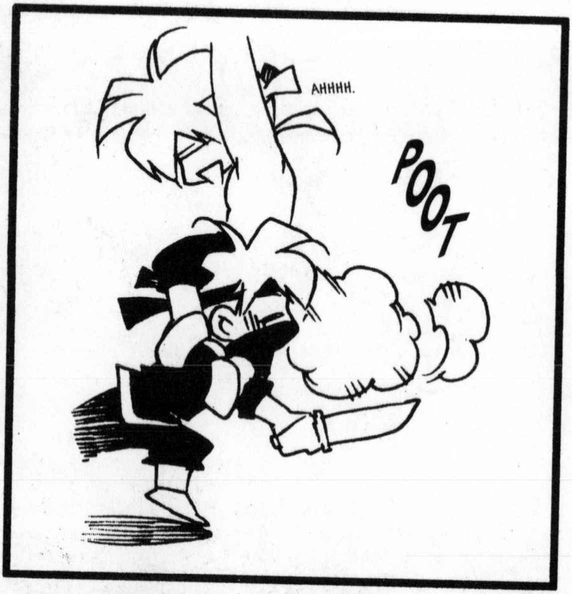
AHHHH.
POOT

Step 19 ON THE SAME WAVELENGTH

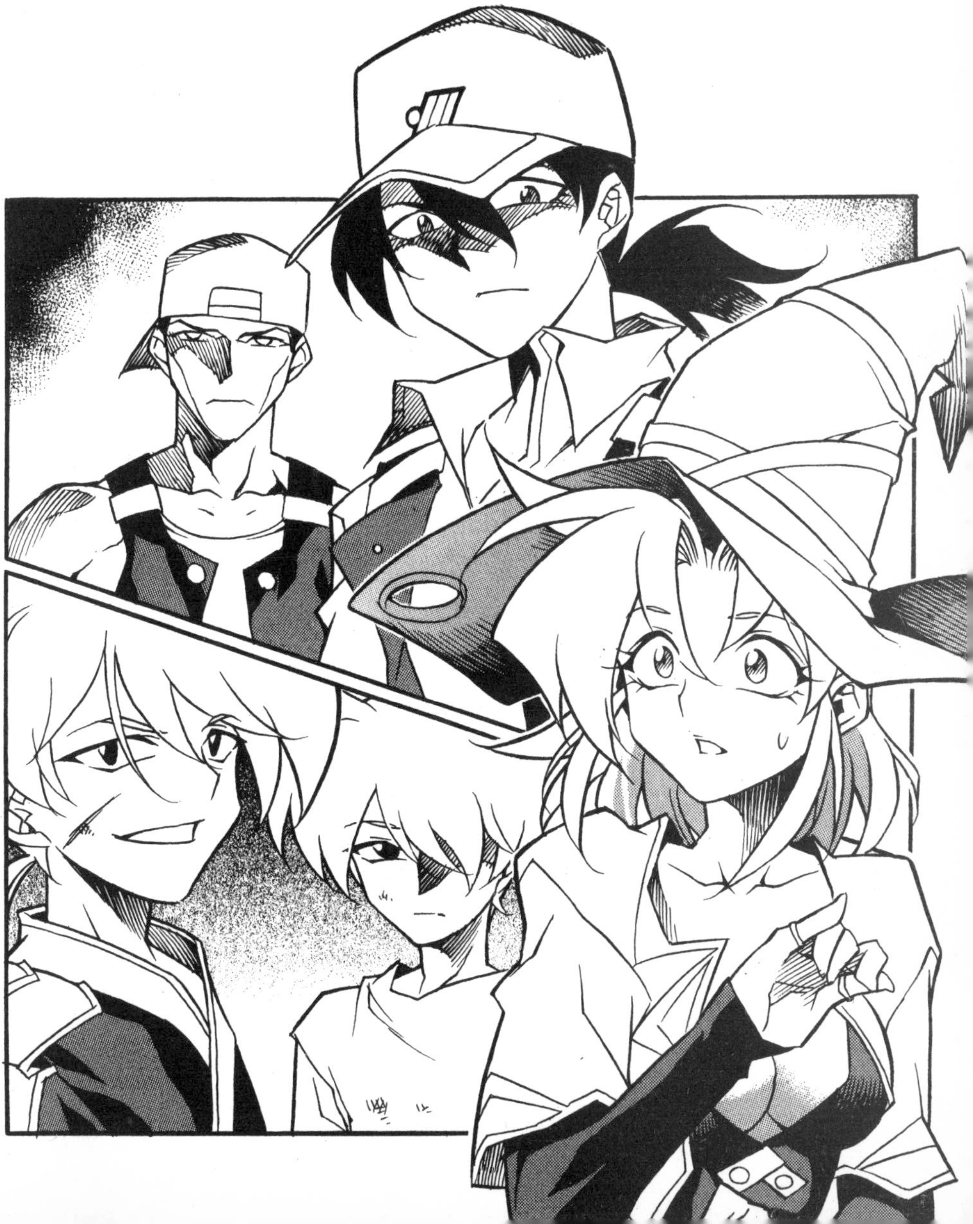

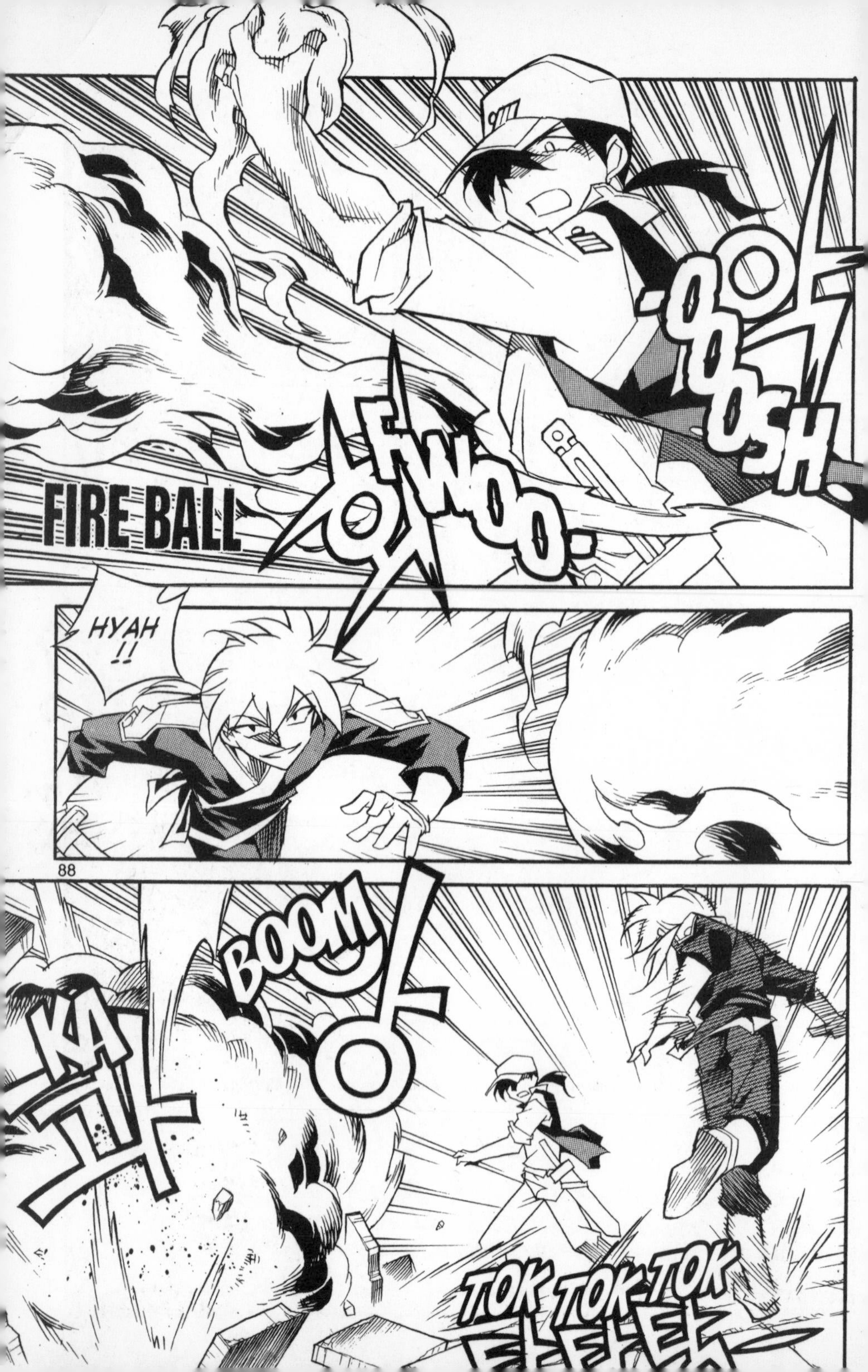
FIRE BALL
FWOO...
-OOOOSH.
HYAH !!
KA
BOOM!
TOK TOK TOK

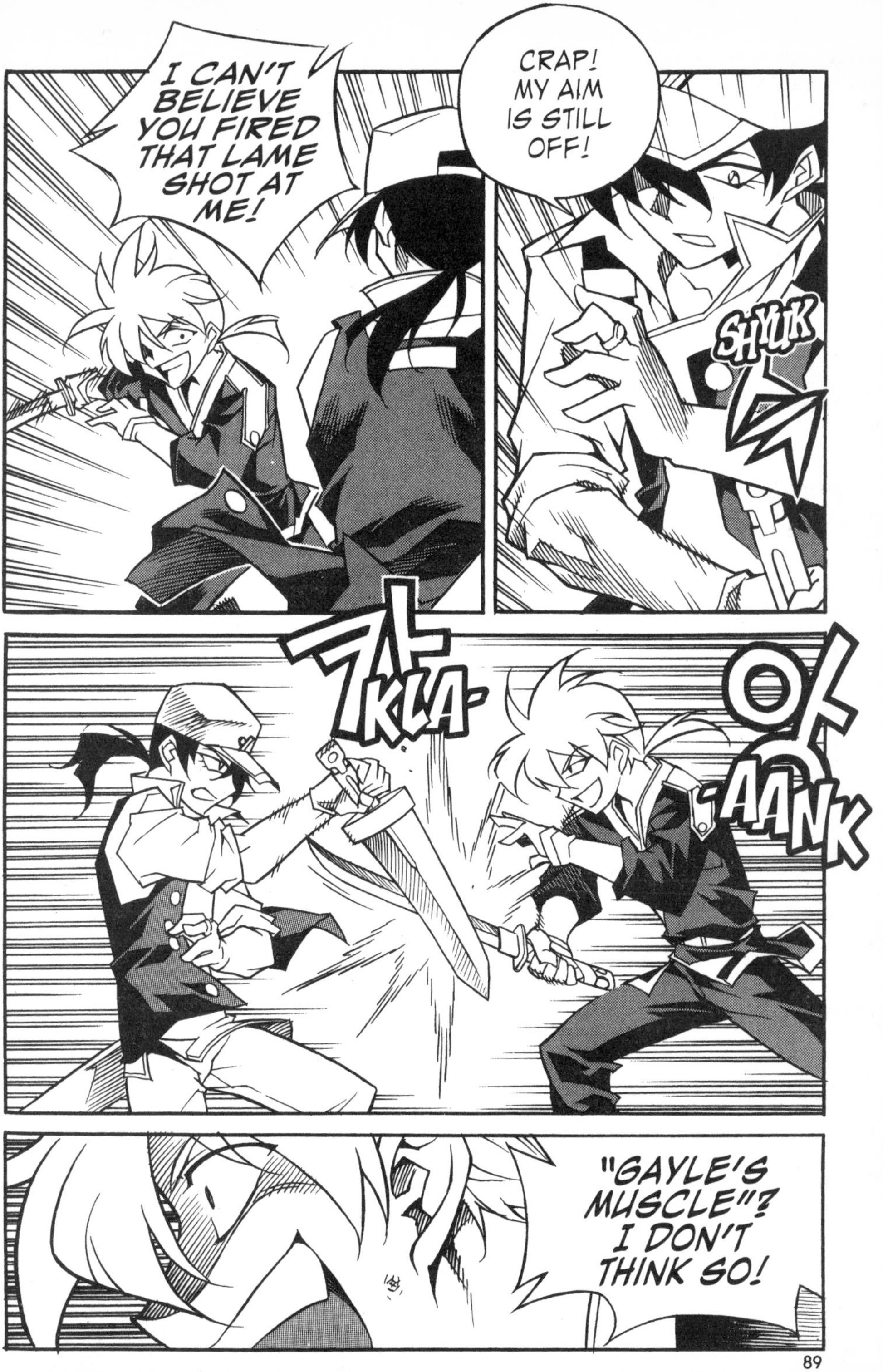
I CAN'T BELIEVE YOU FIRED THAT LAME SHOT AT ME!
CRAP! MY AIM IS STILL OFF!
SHYUK
KLA-
-AANK
"GAYLE'S MUSCLE"? I DON'T THINK SO!

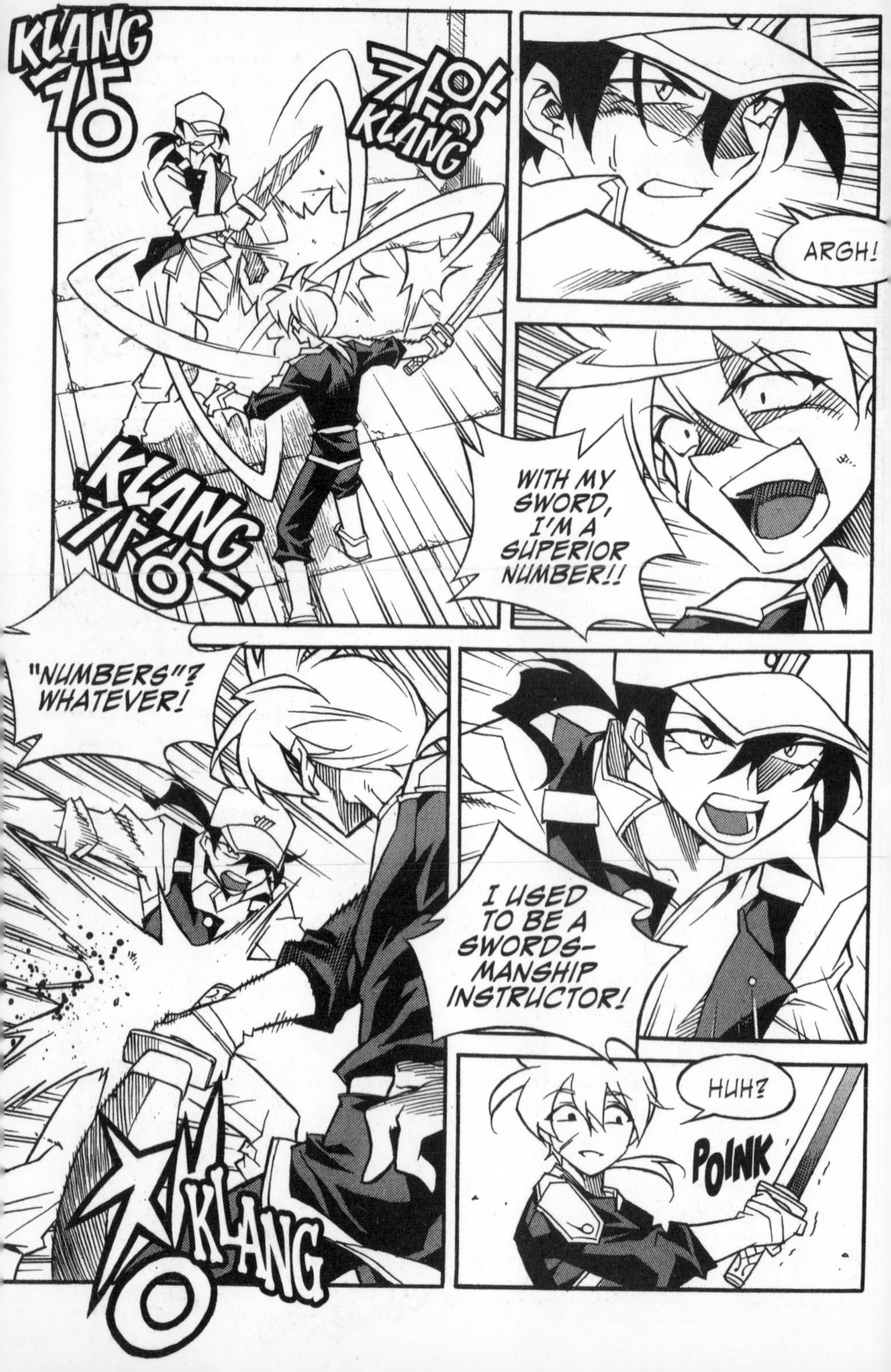
KLANG
KLANG
KLANG
ARGH!
WITH MY SWORD, I'M A SUPERIOR NUMBER!!
"NUMBERS"? WHATEVER!
I USED TO BE A SWORDS-MANSHIP INSTRUCTOR!
HUH?
POINK
KLANG

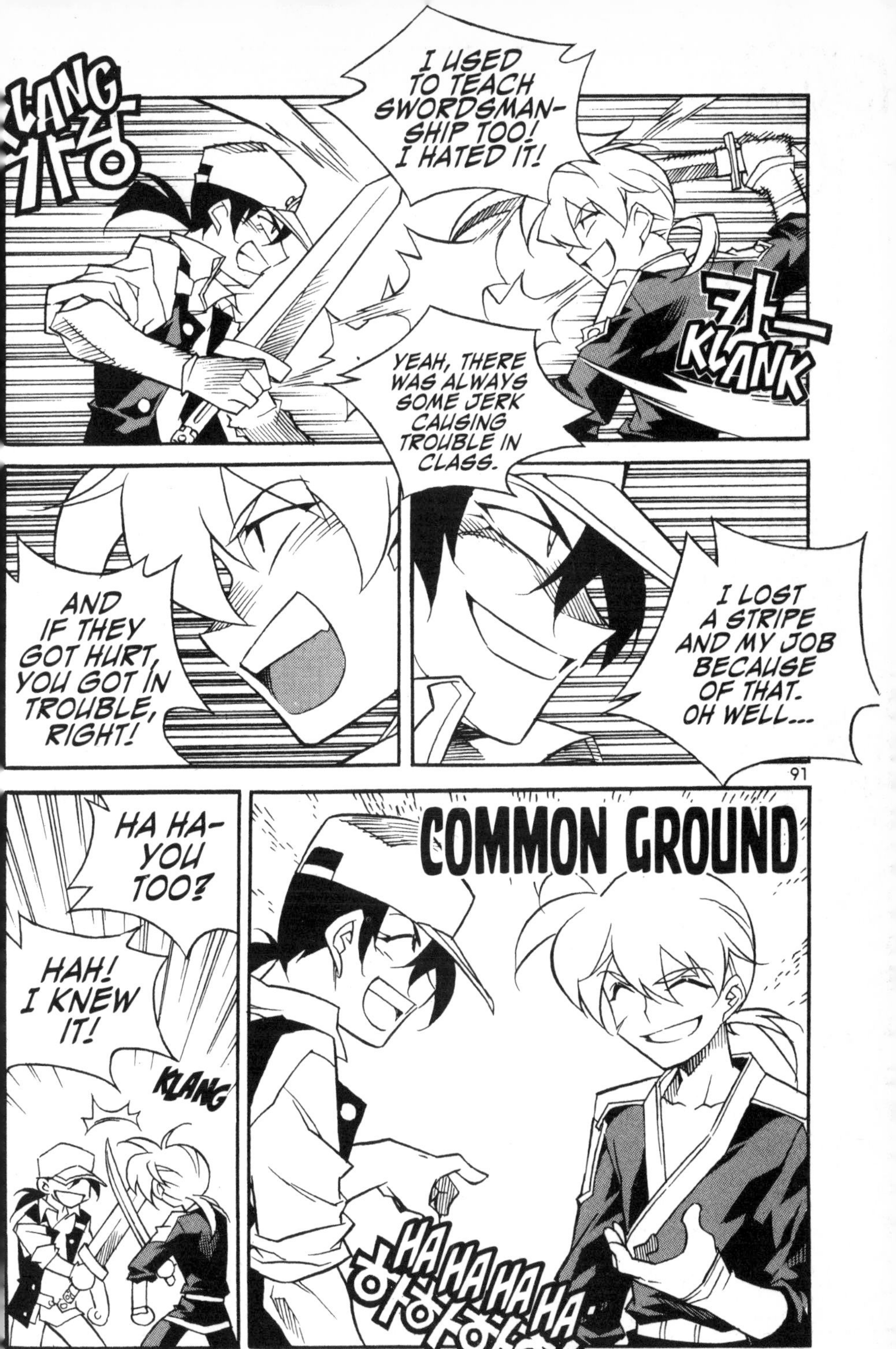
KLANG
I USED TO TEACH SWORDSMANSHIP TOO! I HATED IT!
KLANK
YEAH, THERE WAS ALWAYS SOME JERK CAUSING TROUBLE IN CLASS.
AND IF THEY GOT HURT, YOU GOT IN TROUBLE, RIGHT!
I LOST A STRIPE AND MY JOB BECAUSE OF THAT. OH WELL...
HA HA- YOU TOO?
HAH! I KNEW IT!
KLANG
COMMON GROUND
HA HA HA HA HA

AND THE SAME PONYTAIL...

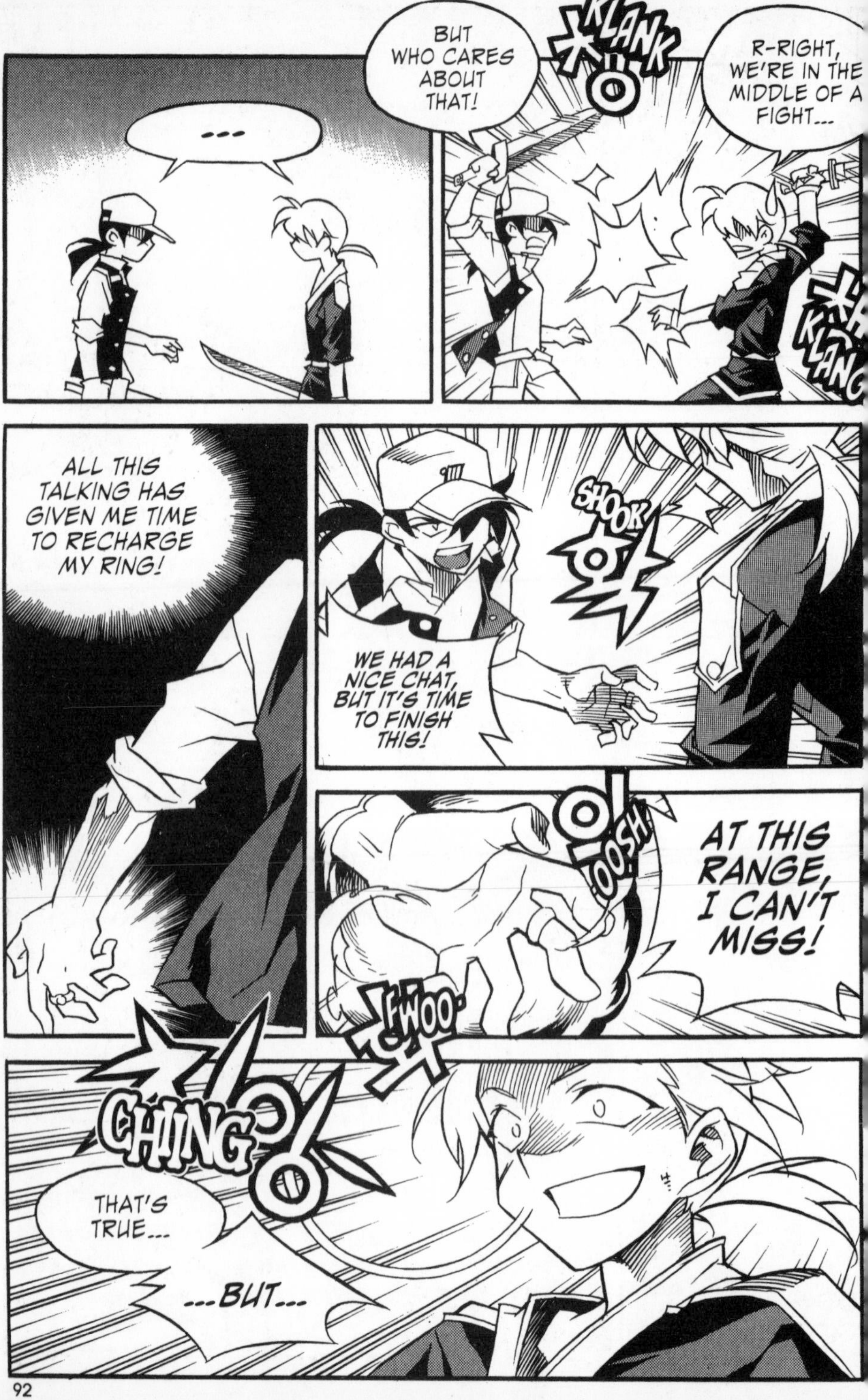
...
BUT WHO CARES ABOUT THAT!
KLANK
R-RIGHT, WE'RE IN THE MIDDLE OF A FIGHT...
KLANG
ALL THIS TALKING HAS GIVEN ME TIME TO RECHARGE MY RING!
SHOOK
WE HAD A NICE CHAT, BUT IT'S TIME TO FINISH THIS!
OOSH
AT THIS RANGE, I CAN'T MISS!
FWOO
CHING
THAT'S TRUE...
...BUT...

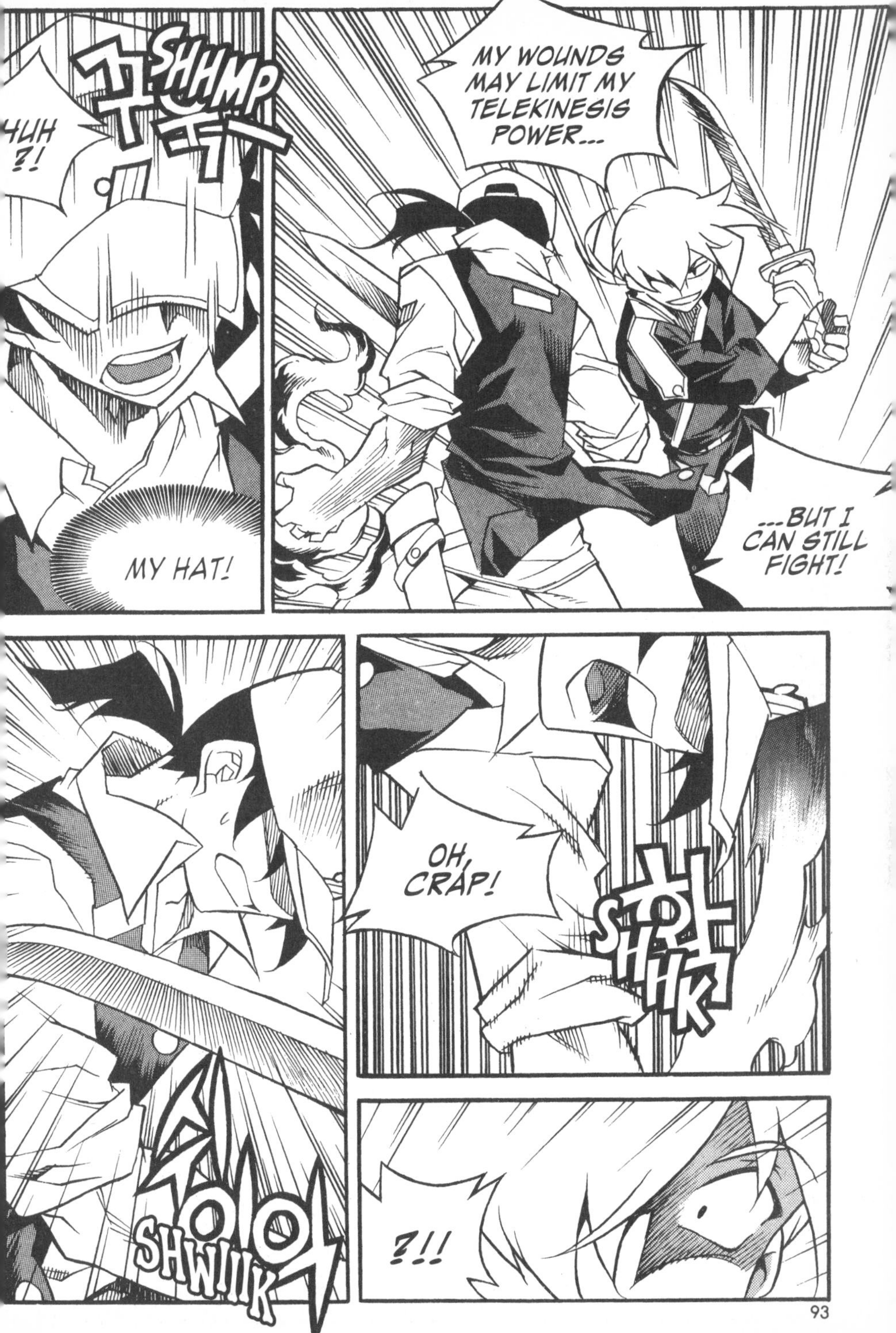
HUH ?!
SHHMP
MY HAT!
MY WOUNDS MAY LIMIT MY TELEKINESIS POWER...
...BUT I CAN STILL FIGHT!
SHWIIIK
OH, CRAP!
SHHK
?!!

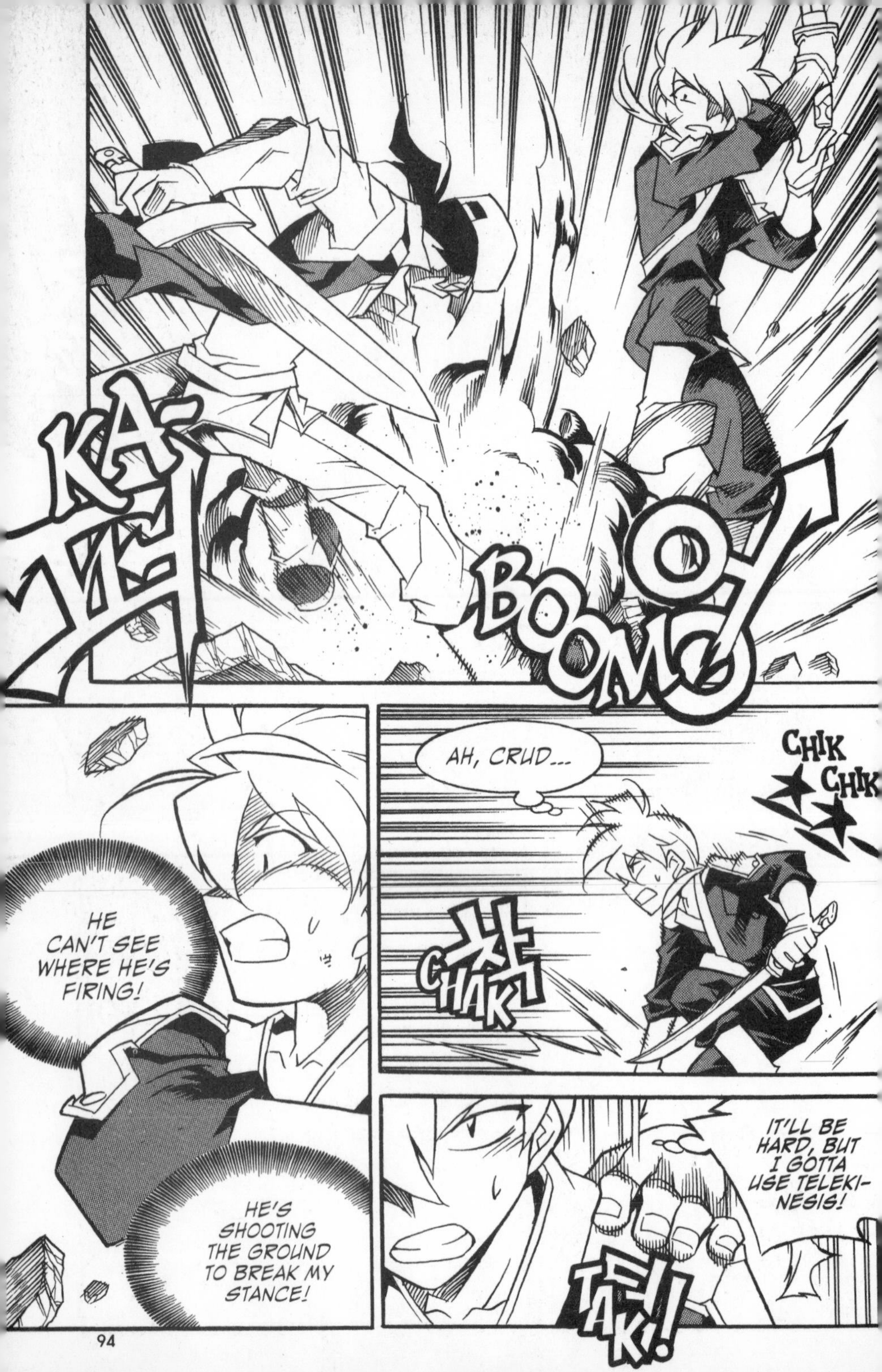
KA-VEM
BOOM
ΦΟΦ
HE CAN'T SEE WHERE HE'S FIRING!
HE'S SHOOTING THE GROUND TO BREAK MY STANCE!
AH, CRUD...
CHIK CHIK
CHAK
IT'LL BE HARD, BUT I GOTTA USE TELEKI-NESIS!
TAK!

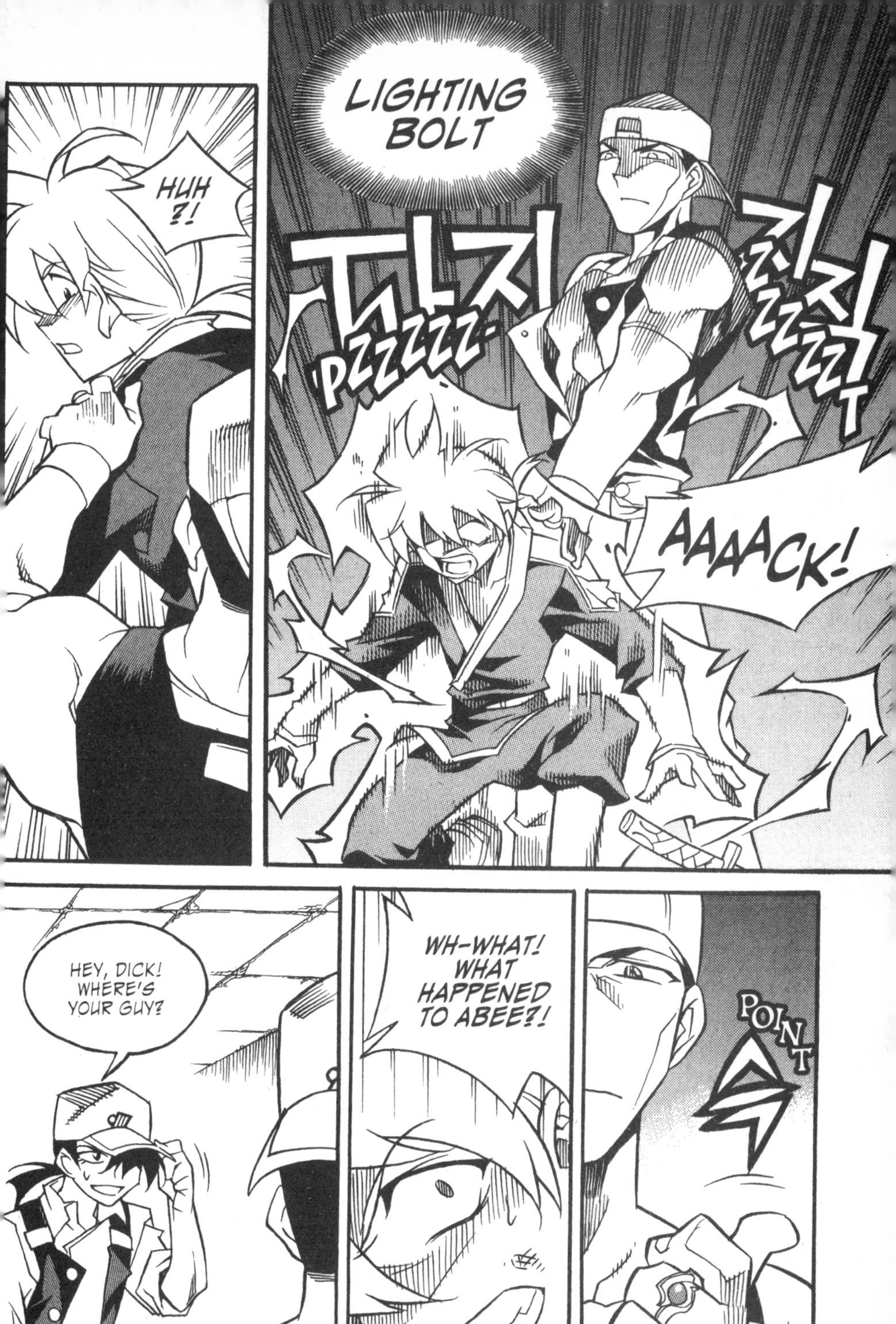
HUH ?!
LIGHTING BOLT
'PZZZZZZ-
ZZZZZZZT
AAAACK!
HEY, DICK! WHERE'S YOUR GUY?
WH-WHAT! WHAT HAPPENED TO ABEE?!
POINT

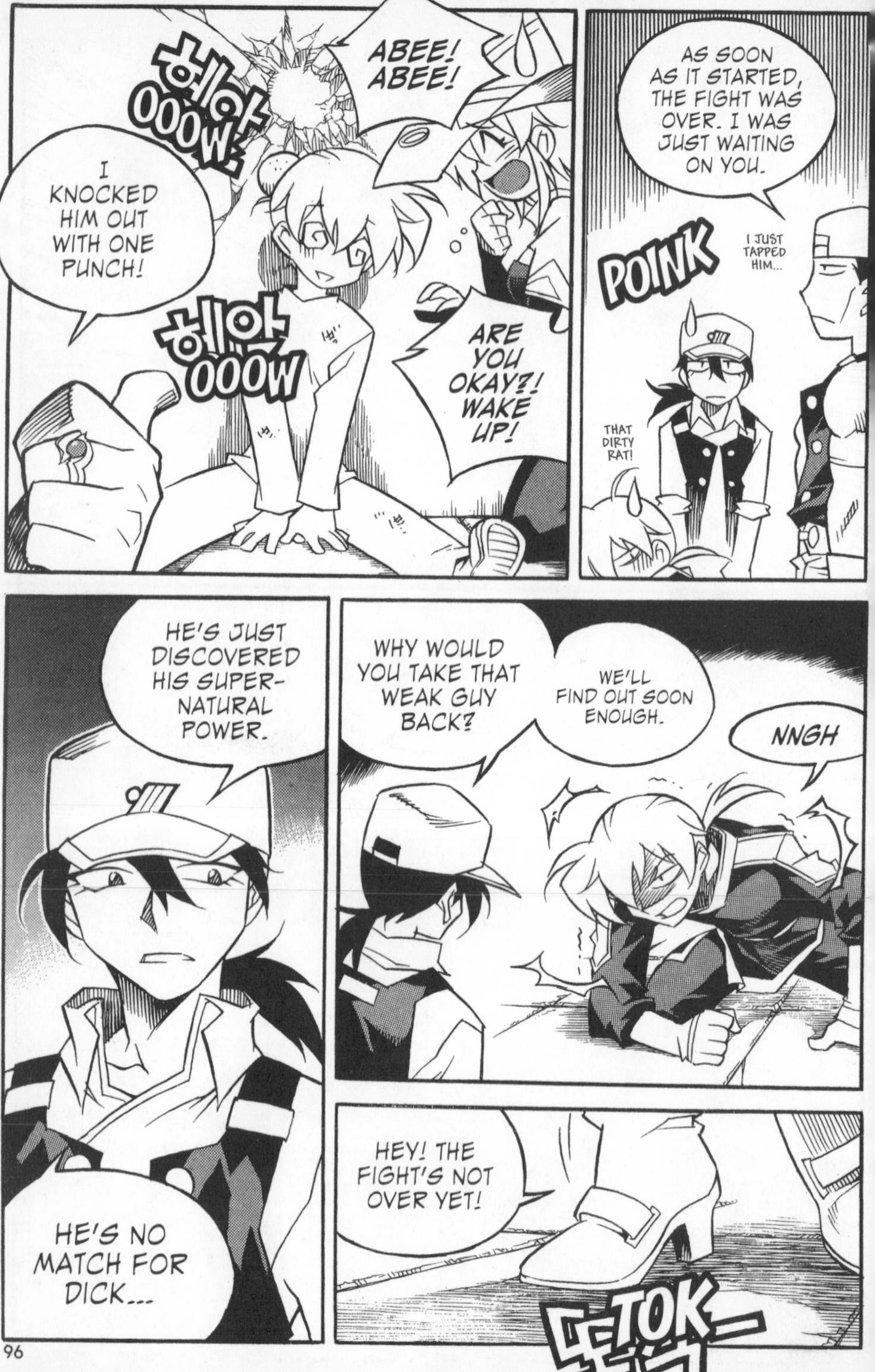

헤야 OOOW
ABEE! ABEE!
I KNOCKED HIM OUT WITH ONE PUNCH!
헤야 OOOW
ARE YOU OKAY?! WAKE UP!
AS SOON AS IT STARTED, THE FIGHT WAS OVER. I WAS JUST WAITING ON YOU.
POINK
I JUST TAPPED HIM...
THAT DIRTY RAT!
HE'S JUST DISCOVERED HIS SUPER-NATURAL POWER.
HE'S NO MATCH FOR DICK...
WHY WOULD YOU TAKE THAT WEAK GUY BACK?
WE'LL FIND OUT SOON ENOUGH.
NNGH
HEY! THE FIGHT'S NOT OVER YET!
TOK

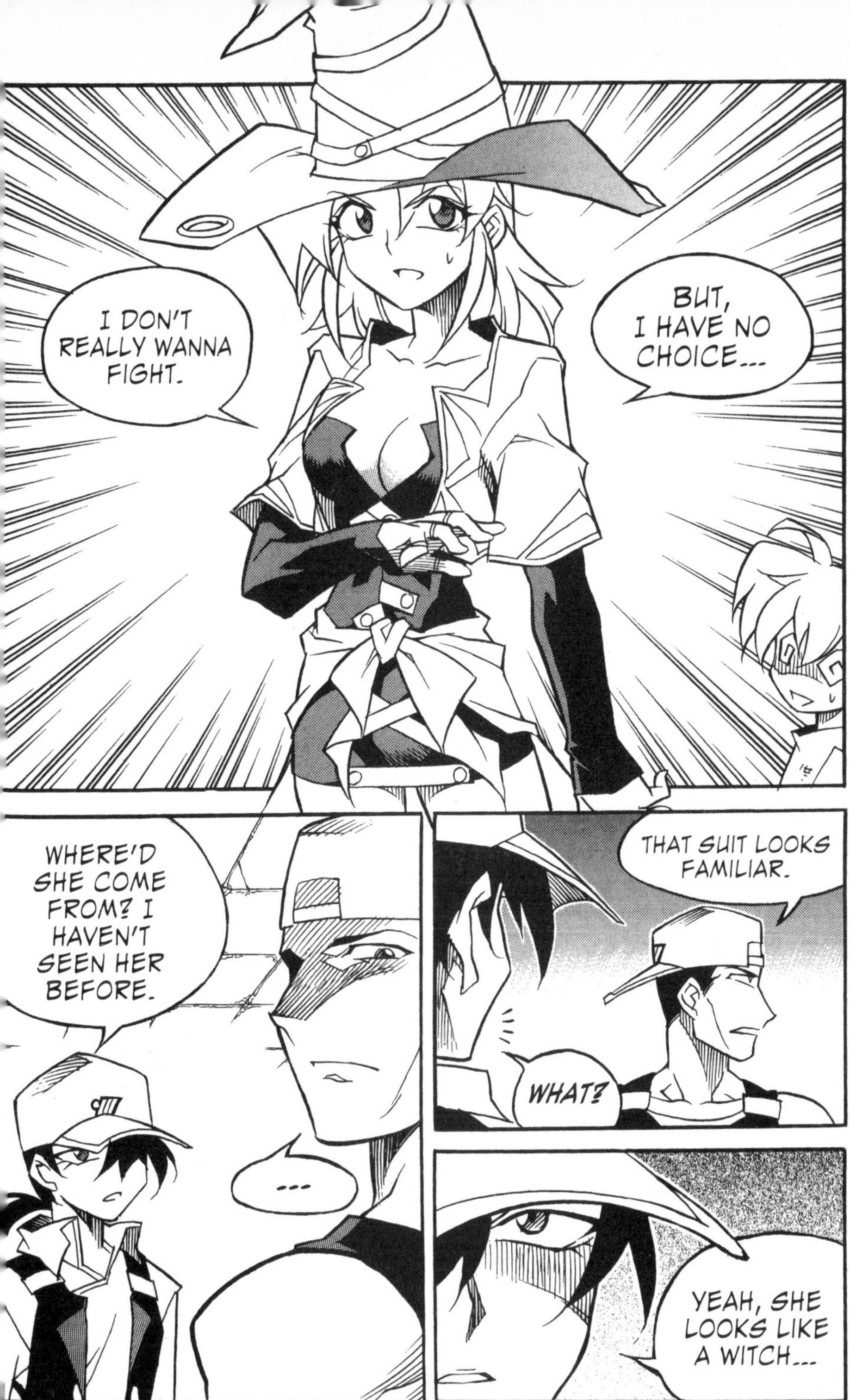

I DON'T REALLY WANNA FIGHT.
BUT, I HAVE NO CHOICE...
WHERE'D SHE COME FROM? I HAVEN'T SEEN HER BEFORE.
...
THAT SUIT LOOKS FAMILIAR.
WHAT?
YEAH, SHE LOOKS LIKE A WITCH...

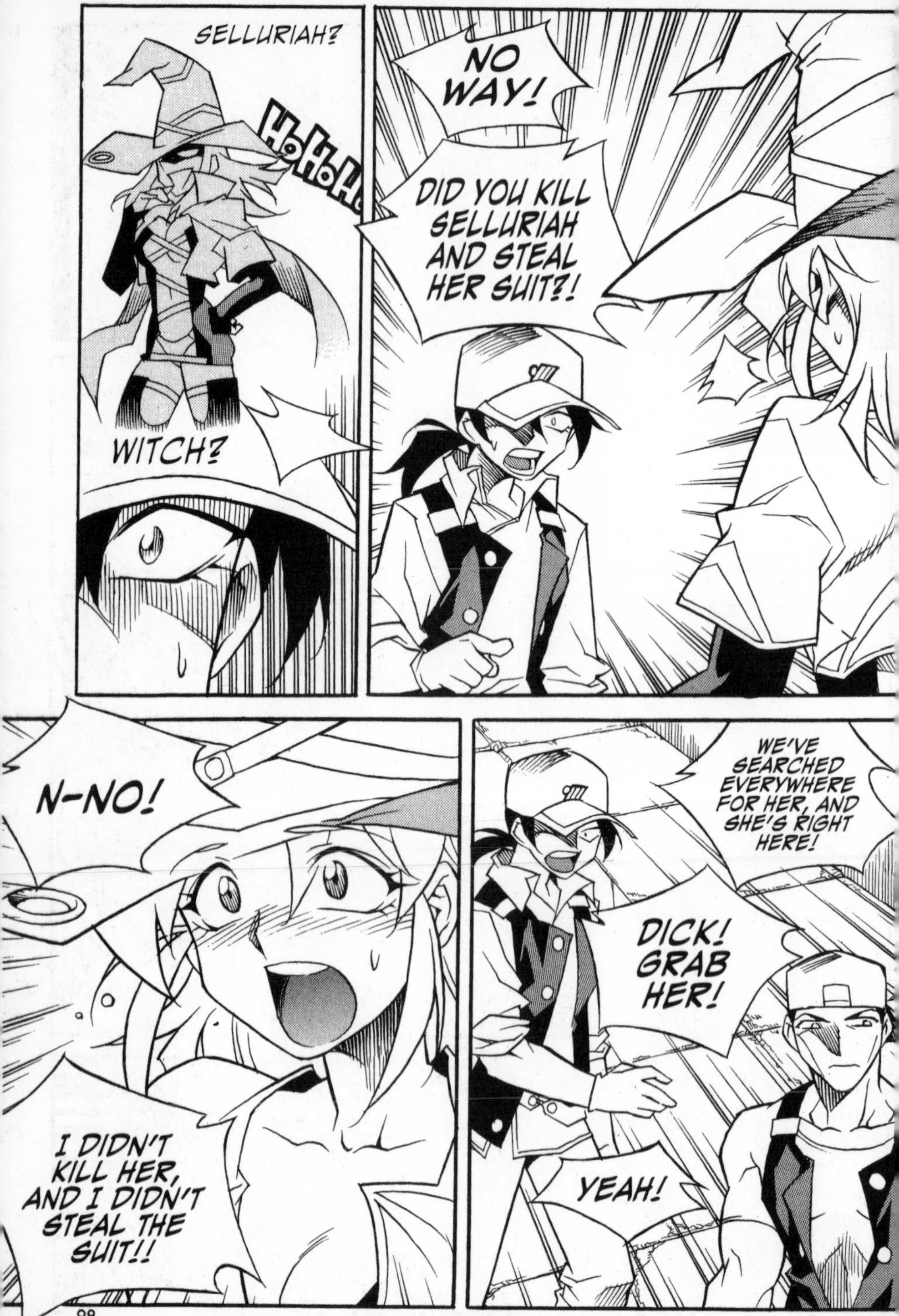
SELLURIAH?
WITCH?
NO WAY!
DID YOU KILL SELLURIAH AND STEAL HER SUIT?!
N-NO!
I DIDN'T KILL HER, AND I DIDN'T STEAL THE SUIT!!
WE'VE SEARCHED EVERYWHERE FOR HER, AND SHE'S RIGHT HERE!
DICK! GRAB HER!
YEAH!

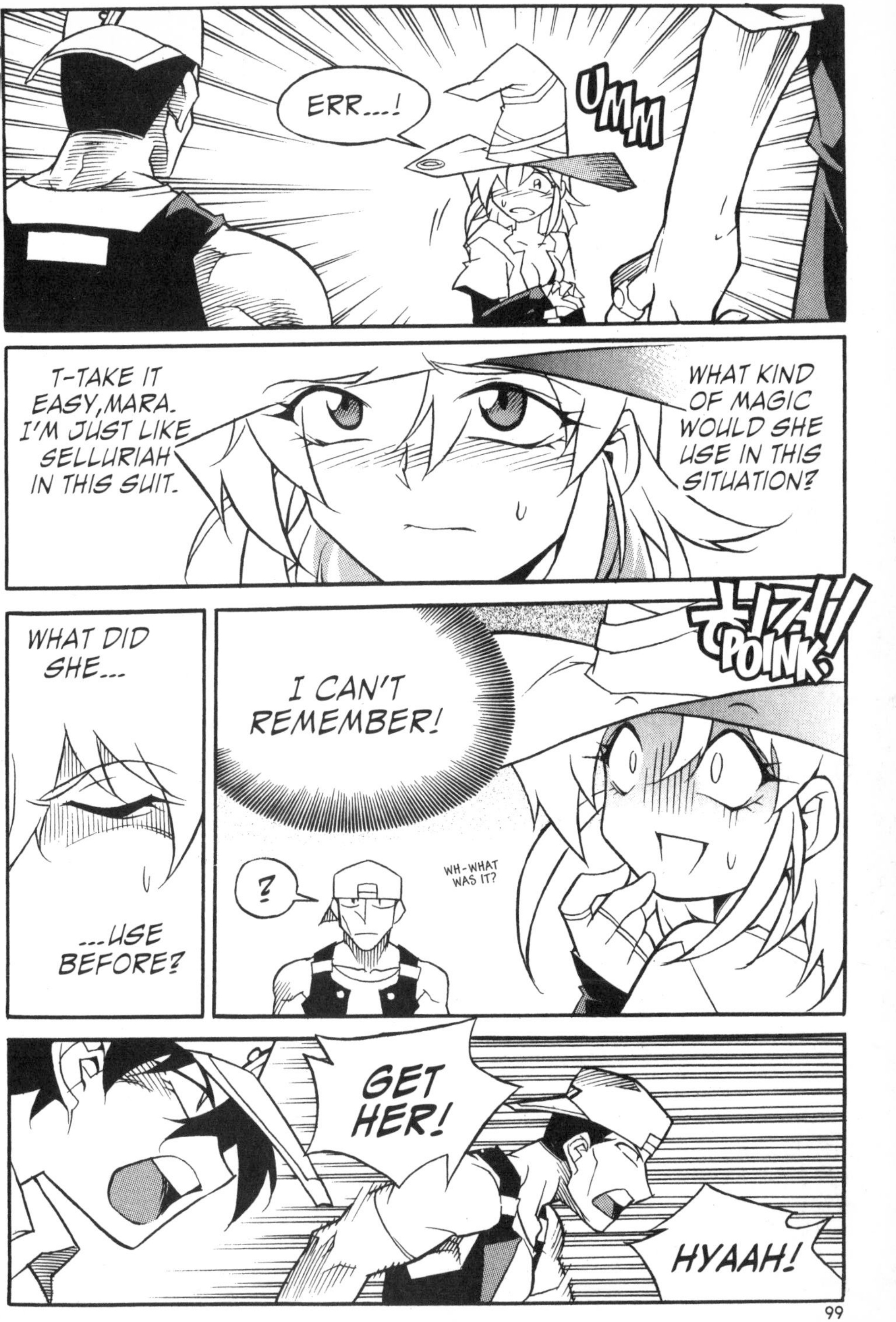
ERR...!
UMM
T-TAKE IT EASY, MARA. I'M JUST LIKE SELLURIAH IN THIS SUIT.
WHAT KIND OF MAGIC WOULD SHE USE IN THIS SITUATION?
WHAT DID SHE...
...USE BEFORE?
I CAN'T REMEMBER!
POINK!
?
WH-WHAT WAS IT?
GET HER!
HYAAH!

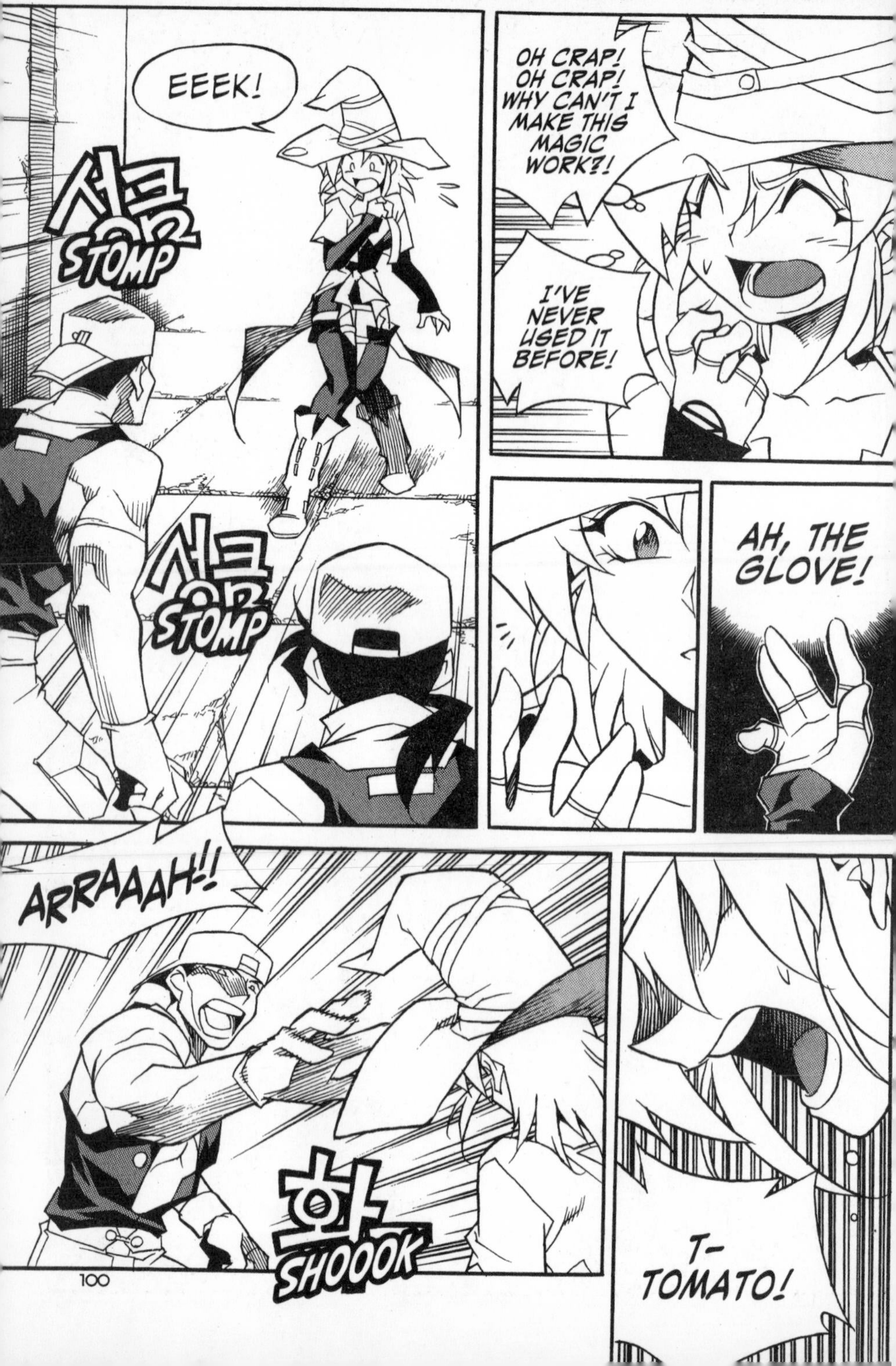
EEEK!
STOMP
STOMP
OH CRAP! OH CRAP! WHY CAN'T I MAKE THIS MAGIC WORK?!
I'VE NEVER USED IT BEFORE!
AH, THE GLOVE!
ARRAAAH!!
SHOOOK
T- TOMATO!

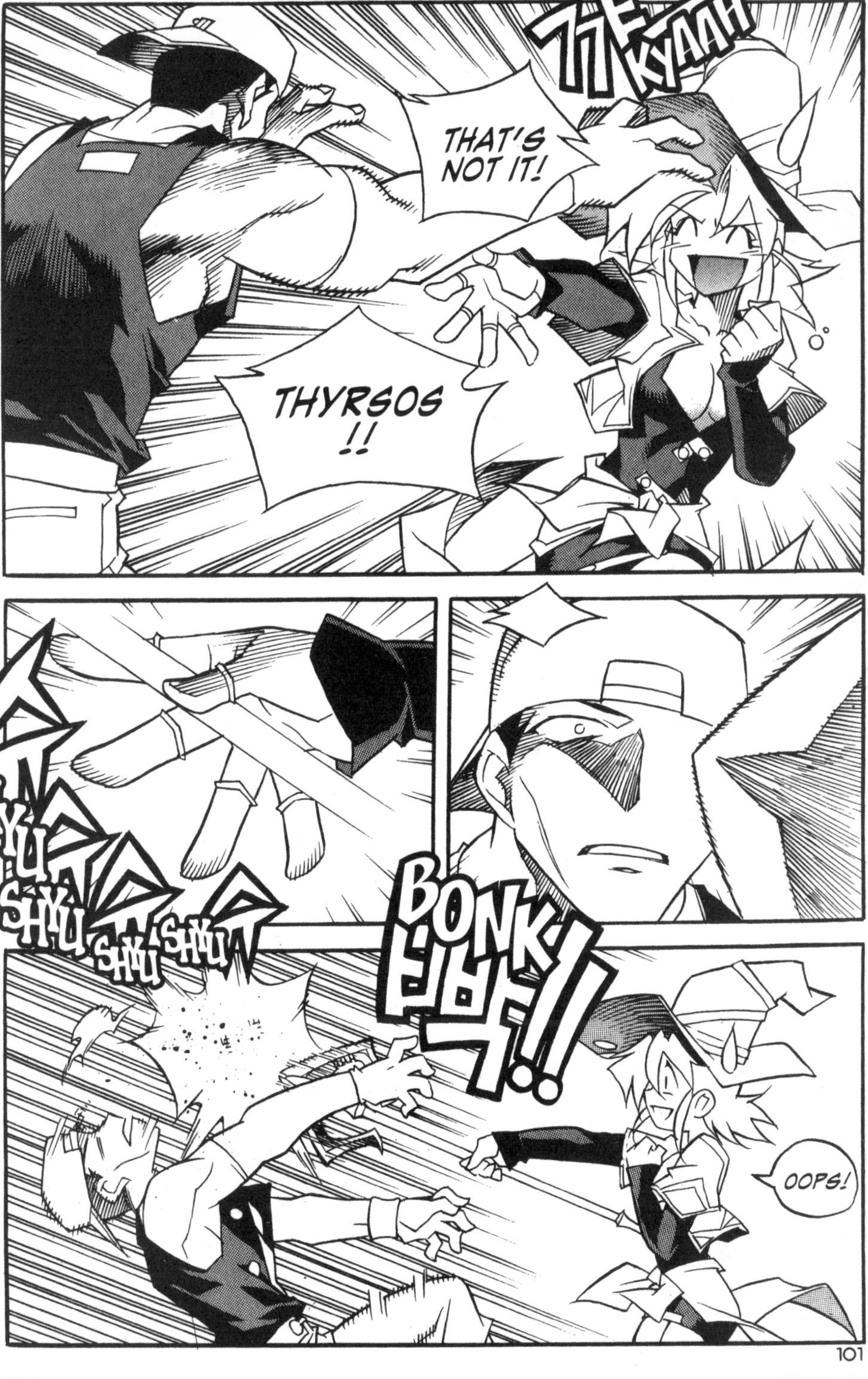
KYAAH
THAT'S NOT IT!
THYRSOS !!
SHYU SHYU SHYU
BONK!!
OOPS!

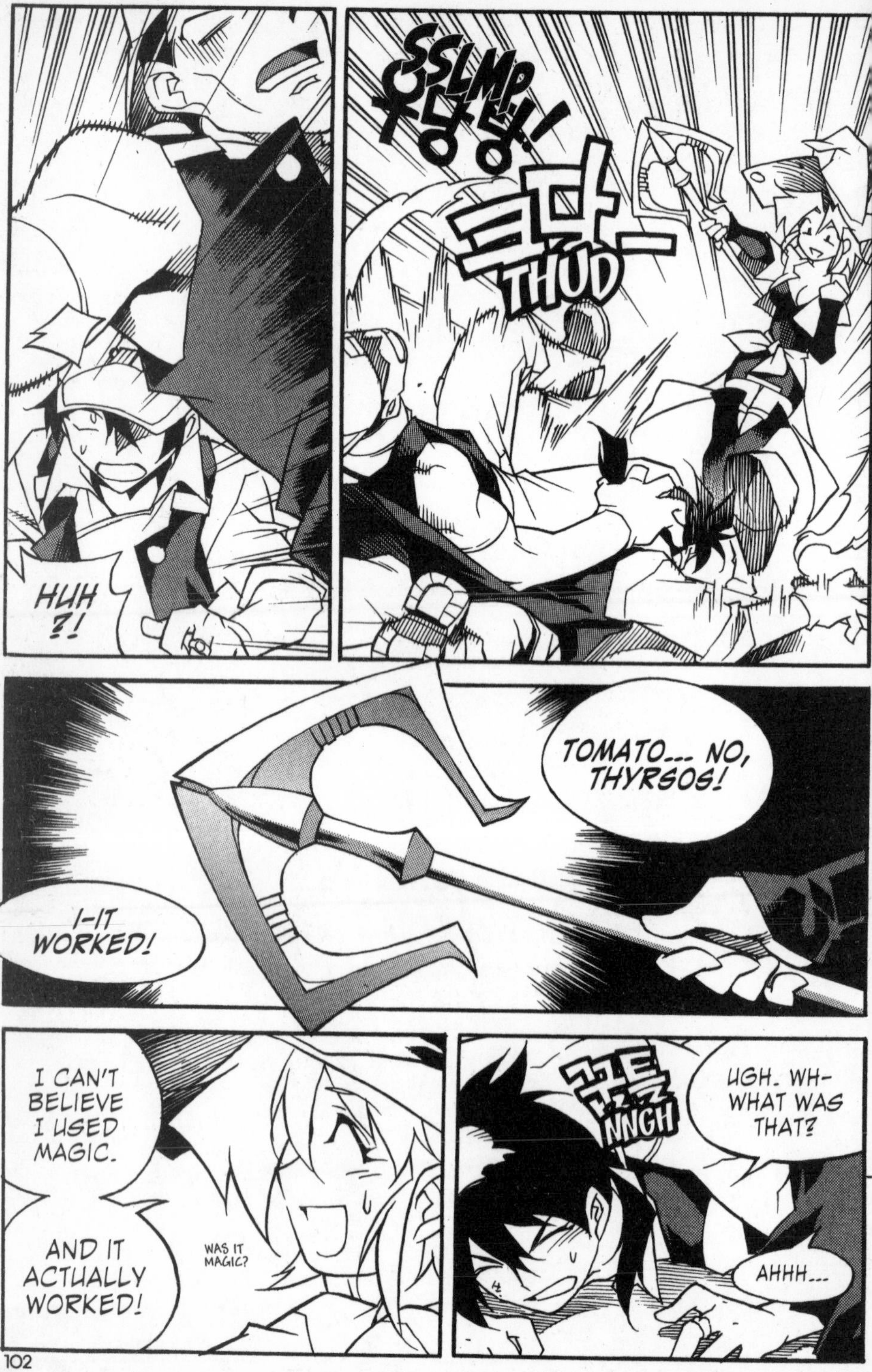
HUH ?!
SSLMP
THUD
TOMATO... NO, THYRSOS!
I-IT WORKED!
I CAN'T BELIEVE I USED MAGIC.
AND IT ACTUALLY WORKED!
WAS IT MAGIC?
NNGH
UGH. WH- WHAT WAS THAT?
AHHH...

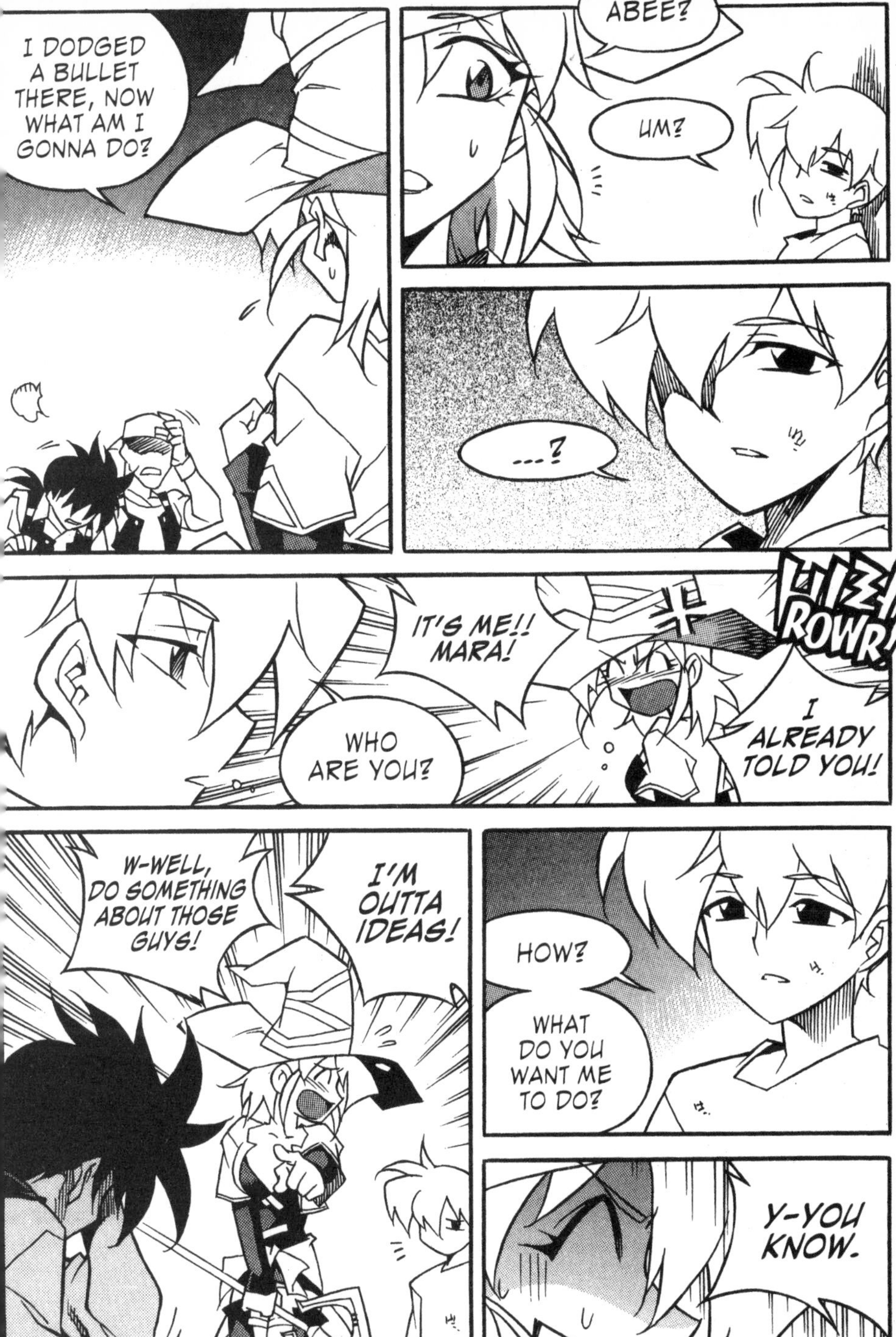
I DODGED A BULLET THERE, NOW WHAT AM I GONNA DO?
ABEE?
UM?
...?
WHO ARE YOU?
IT'S ME!! MARA!
ROWR!
I ALREADY TOLD YOU!
W-WELL, DO SOMETHING ABOUT THOSE GUYS!
I'M OUTTA IDEAS!
HOW?
WHAT DO YOU WANT ME TO DO?
Y-YOU KNOW.
AH, THIS GUY!

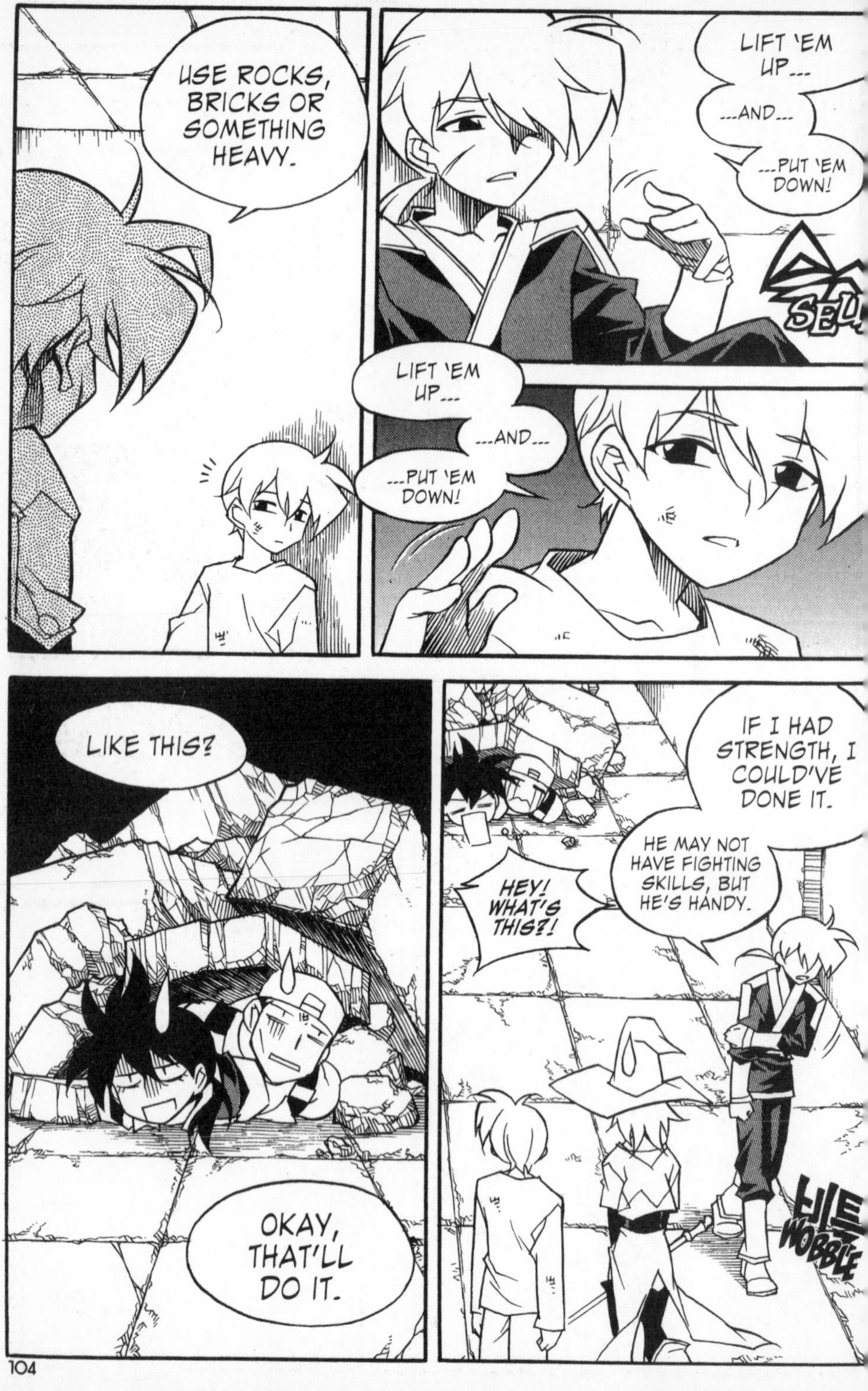
USE ROCKS, BRICKS OR SOMETHING HEAVY.
LIFT 'EM UP...
...AND...
...PUT 'EM DOWN!
SEU
LIFT 'EM UP...
...AND...
...PUT 'EM DOWN!
LIKE THIS?
OKAY, THAT'LL DO IT.
IF I HAD STRENGTH, I COULD'VE DONE IT.
HE MAY NOT HAVE FIGHTING SKILLS, BUT HE'S HANDY.
HEY! WHAT'S THIS?!
WOBBLE

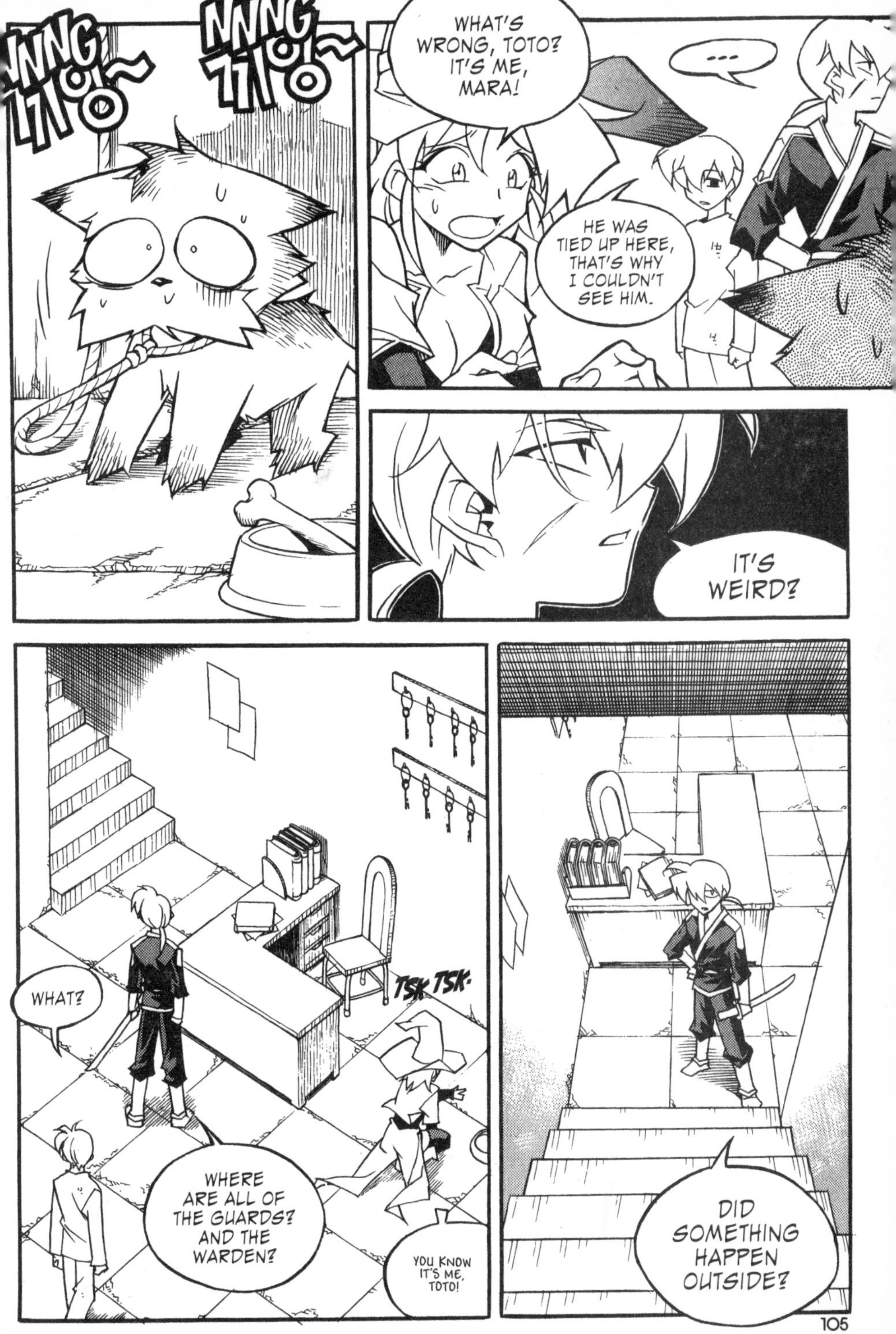
NNNG 끼잉~
NNNG 끼잉~
WHAT'S WRONG, TOTO? IT'S ME, MARA!
...
HE WAS TIED UP HERE, THAT'S WHY I COULDN'T SEE HIM.
IT'S WEIRD?
WHAT?
TSK TSK.
WHERE ARE ALL OF THE GUARDS? AND THE WARDEN?
YOU KNOW IT'S ME, TOTO!
DID SOMETHING HAPPEN OUTSIDE?

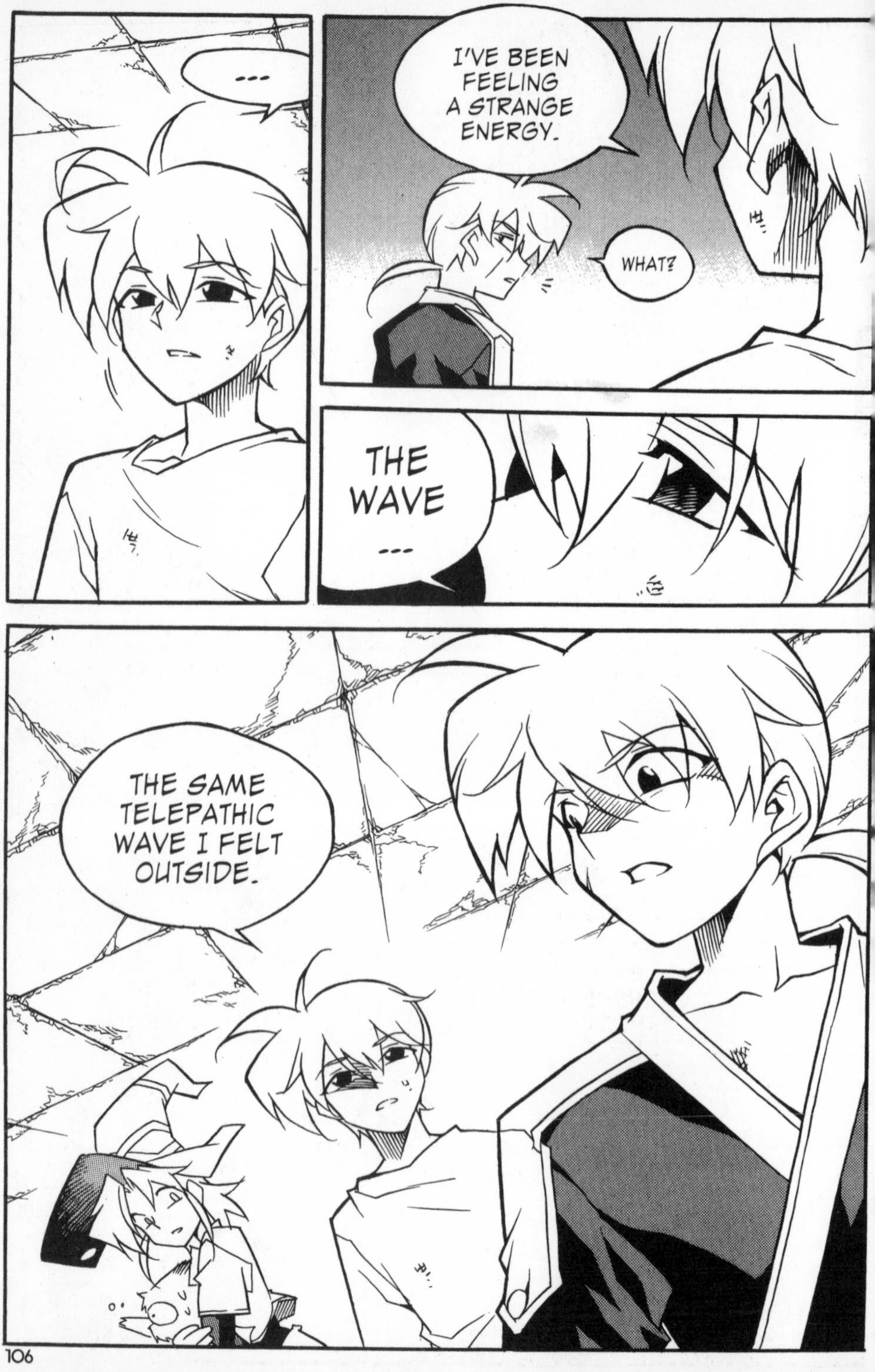
...
I'VE BEEN FEELING A STRANGE ENERGY.
WHAT?
THE WAVE ...
THE SAME TELEPATHIC WAVE I FELT OUTSIDE.

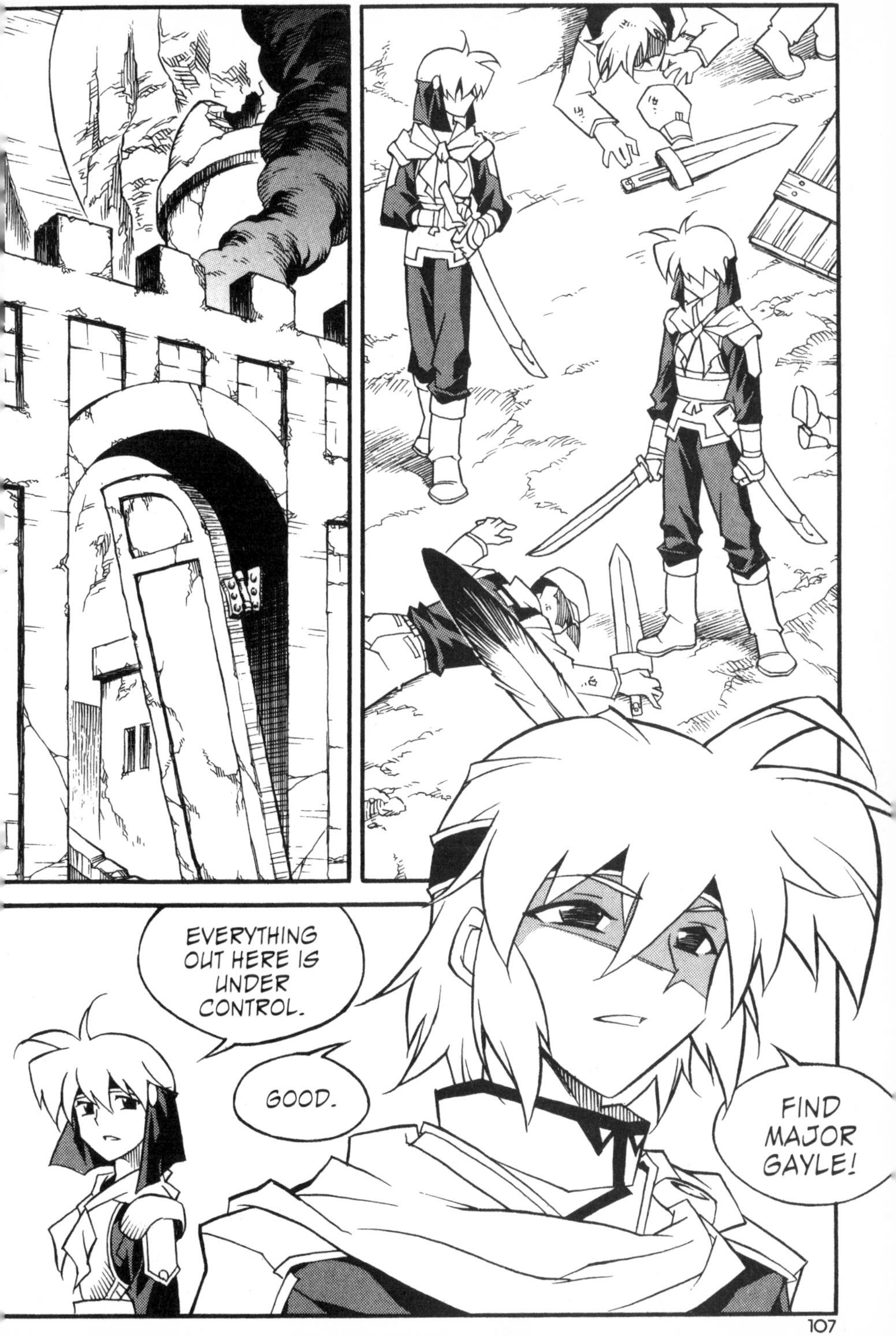
EVERYTHING OUT HERE IS UNDER CONTROL.
GOOD.
FIND MAJOR GAYLE!

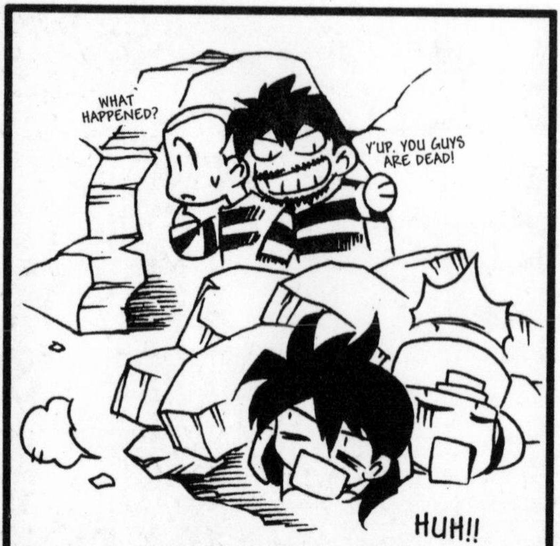
WHAT HAPPENED?
Y'UP, YOU GUYS ARE DEAD!
HUH!!

Step 20 NAME?

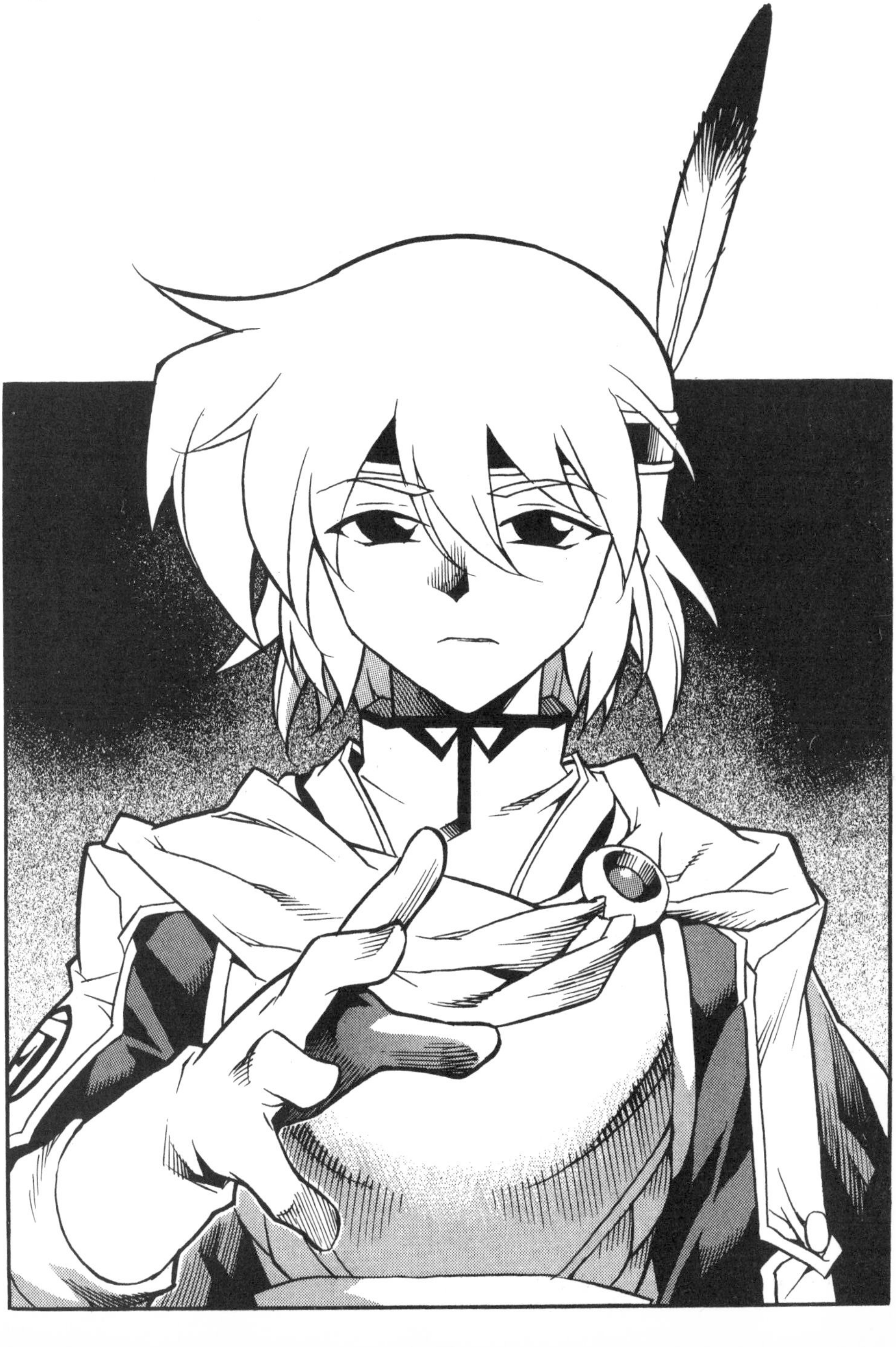

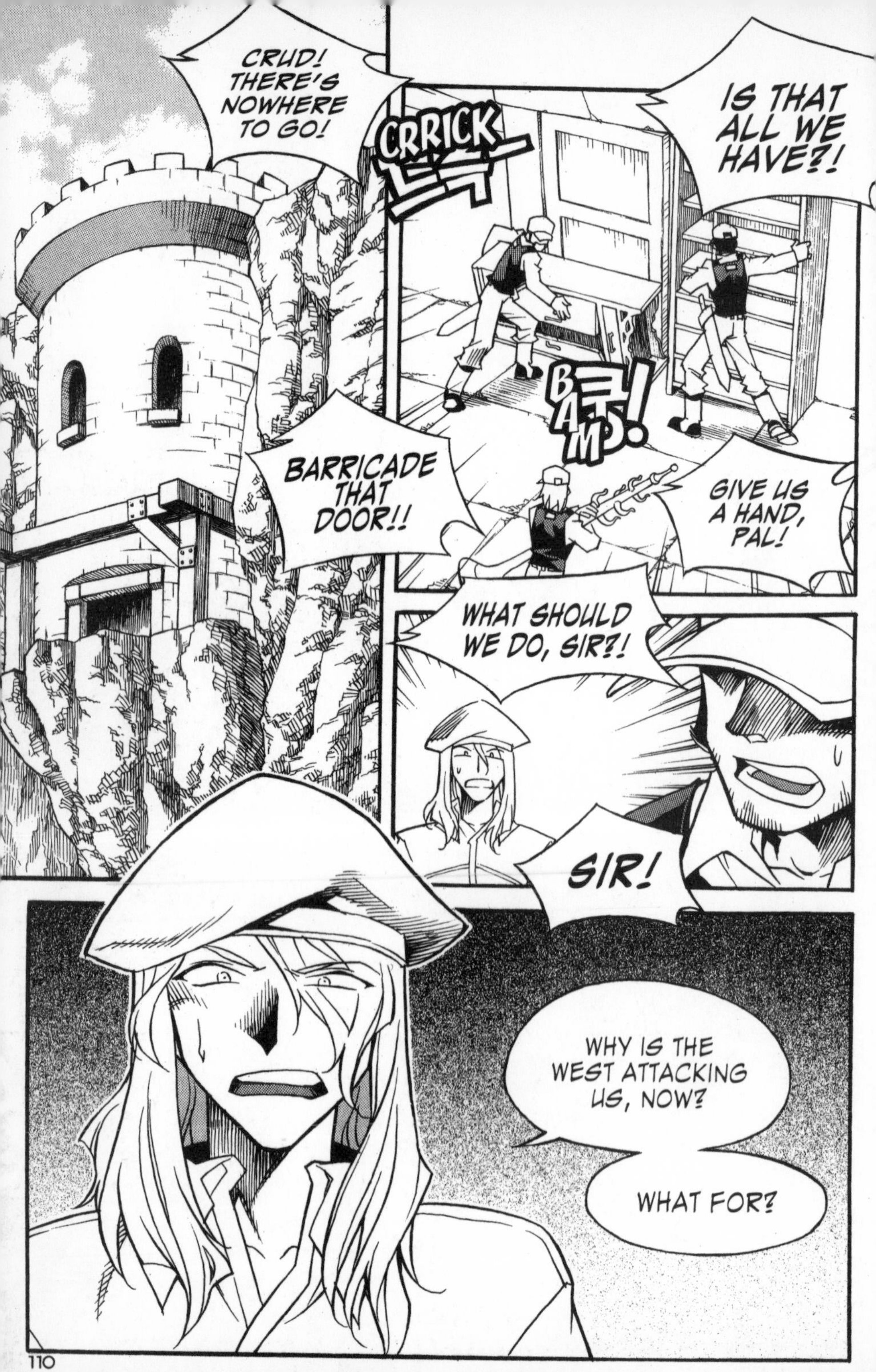
CRUD! THERE'S NOWHERE TO GO!
CRRICK
IS THAT ALL WE HAVE?!
BARRICADE THAT DOOR!!
BAMP!
GIVE US A HAND, PAL!
WHAT SHOULD WE DO, SIR?!
SIR!
WHY IS THE WEST ATTACKING US, NOW?
WHAT FOR?

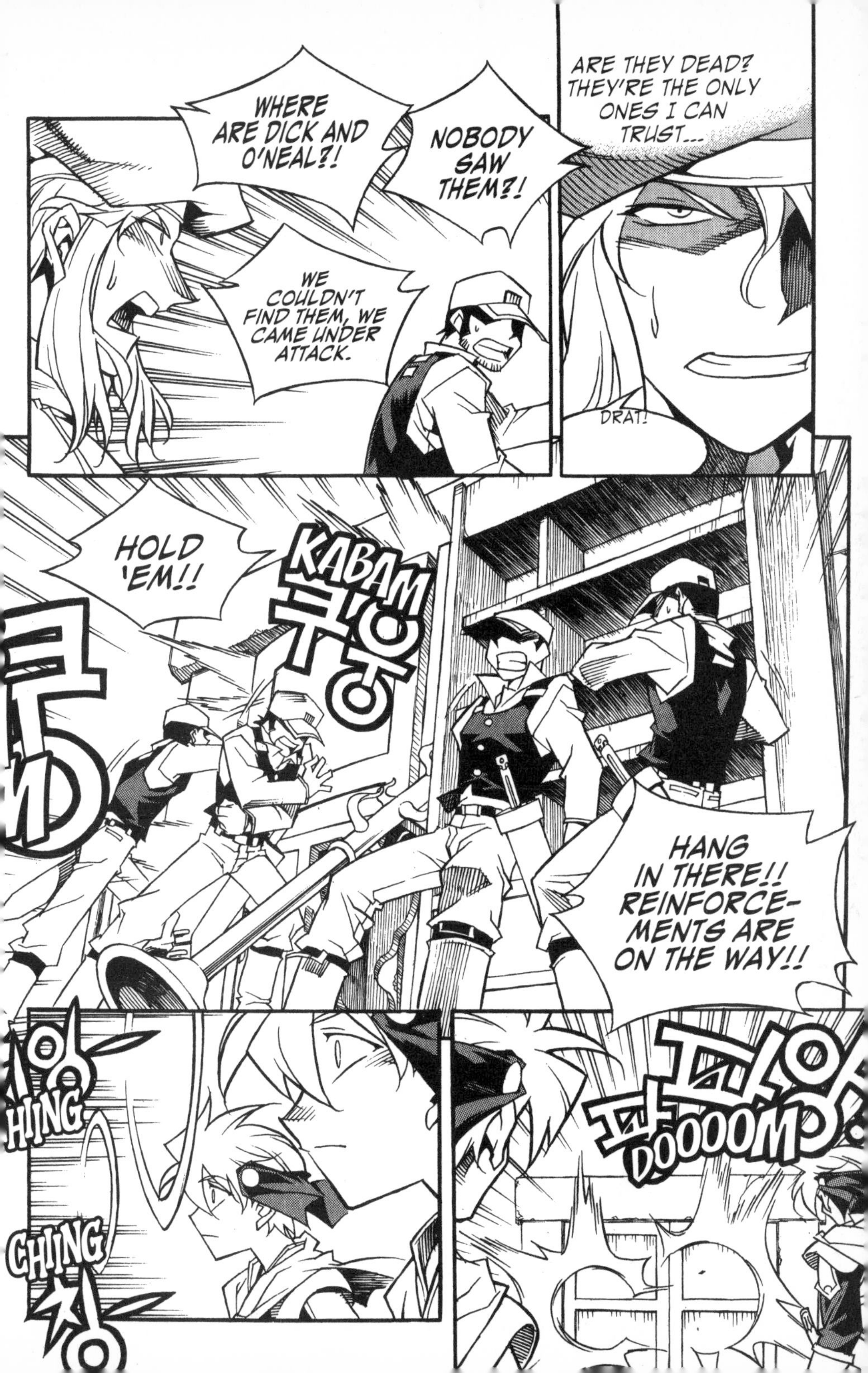
WHERE ARE DICK AND O'NEAL?!
NOBODY SAW THEM?!
WE COULDN'T FIND THEM, WE CAME UNDER ATTACK.
ARE THEY DEAD? THEY'RE THE ONLY ONES I CAN TRUST...
DRAT!
HOLD 'EM!!
KABAM
HANG IN THERE!! REINFORCEMENTS ARE ON THE WAY!!
HIING
CHIING
DOOOOOM

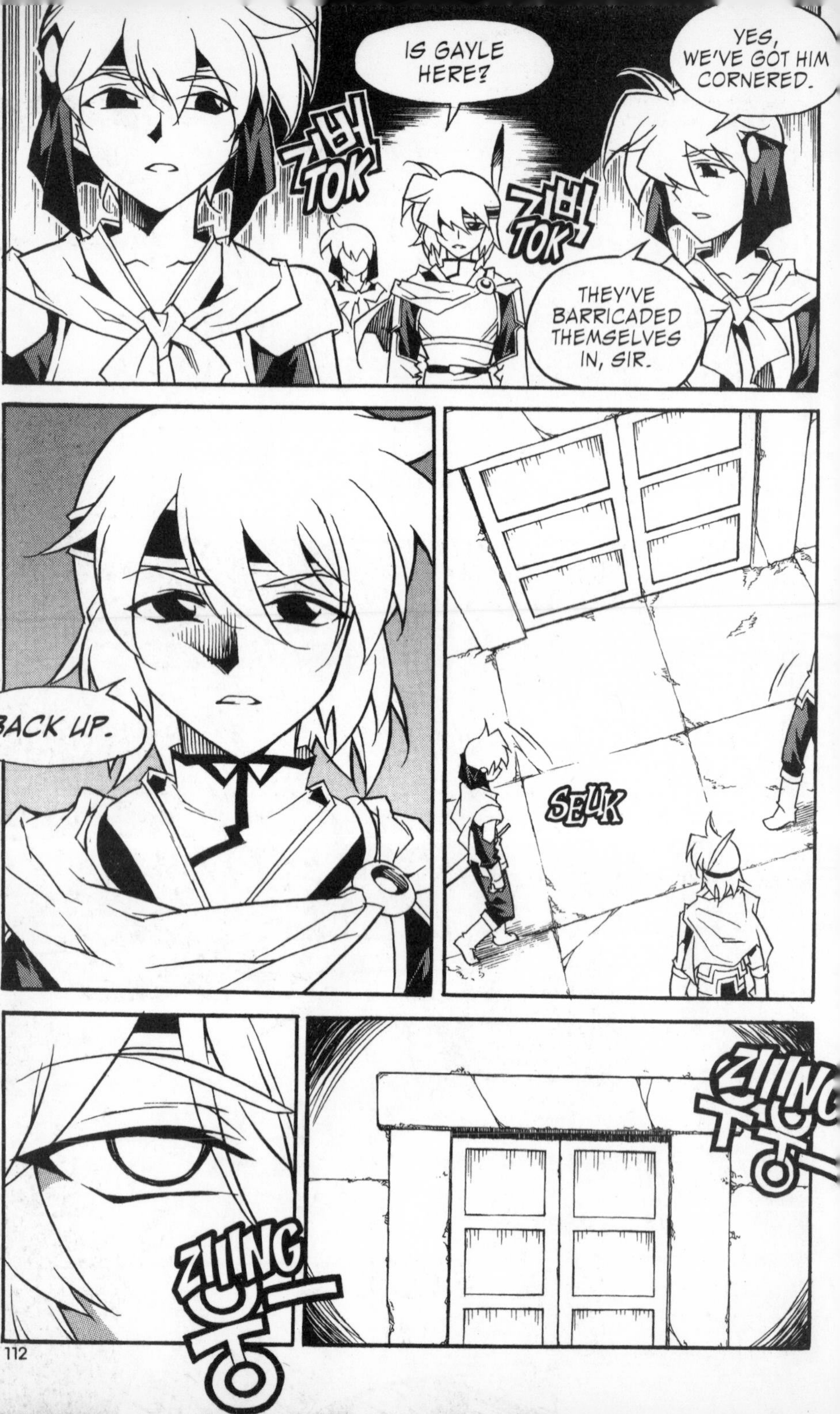
IS GAYLE HERE?
YES, WE'VE GOT HIM CORNERED.
TOK
TOK
THEY'VE BARRICADED THEMSELVES IN, SIR.
BACK UP.
SEUK
ZIIING
ZIIING

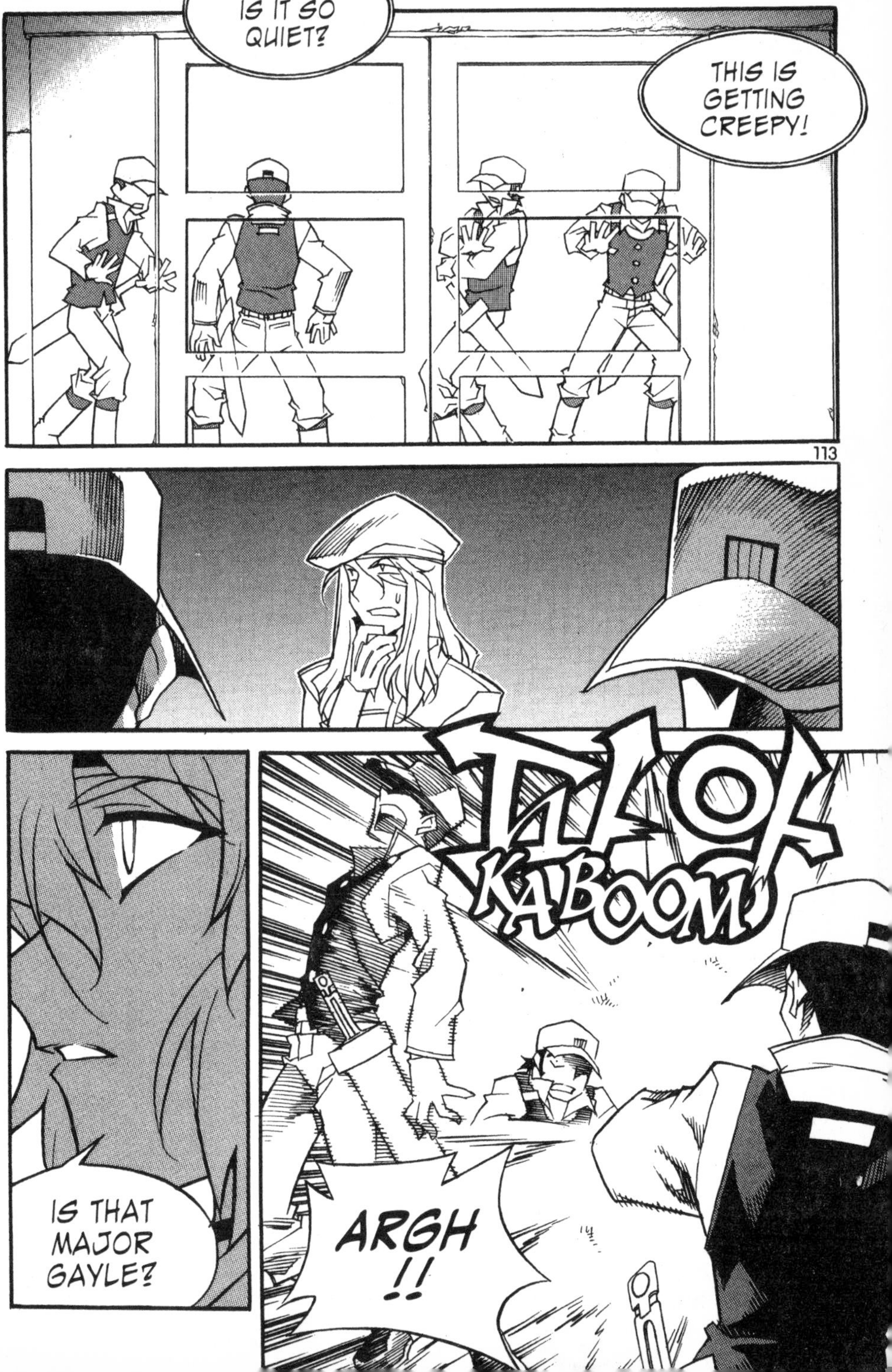
WHY IS IT SO QUIET?
THIS IS GETTING CREEPY!
IS THAT MAJOR GAYLE?
KABOOM
ARGH !!

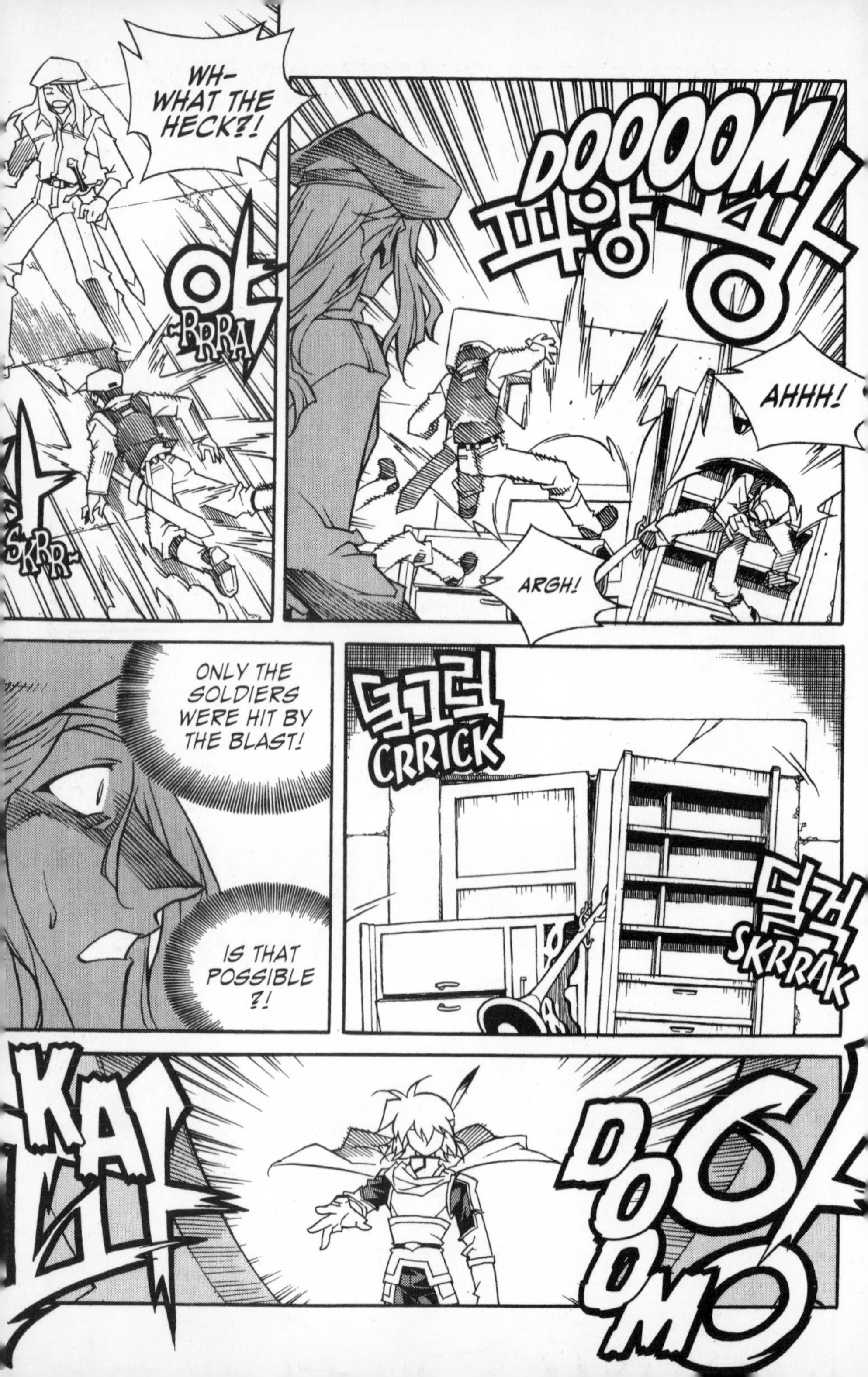
WH- WHAT THE HECK?!
RRRA
SKRR-
DOOOOM!
AHHH!
ARGH!
ONLY THE SOLDIERS WERE HIT BY THE BLAST!
IS THAT POSSIBLE ?!
CRRICK
SKRRAK
DOOOM

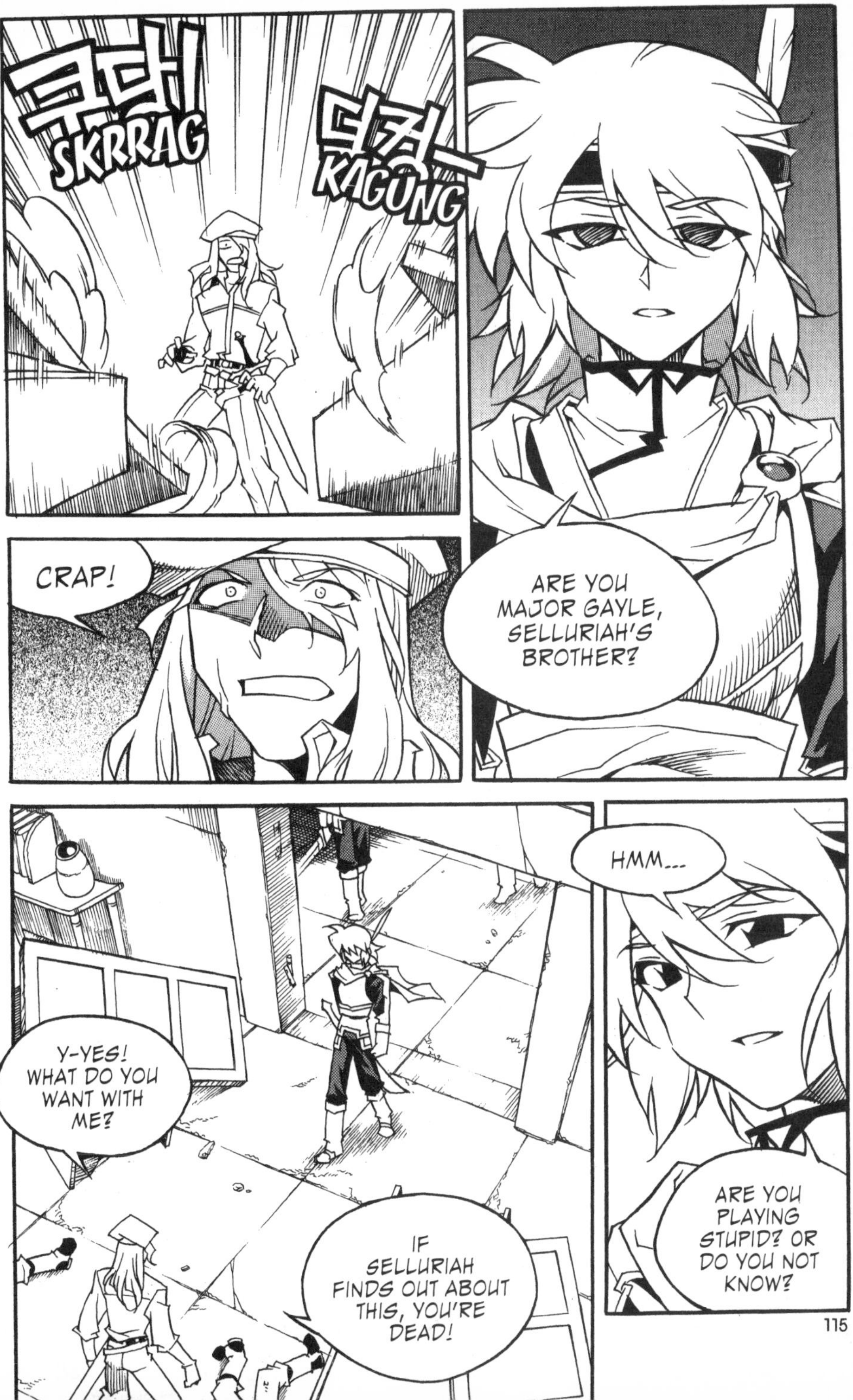
쿠당!
SKRRAG
덜컥
KAGUNG
ARE YOU MAJOR GAYLE, SELLURIAH'S BROTHER?
CRAP!
HMM...
Y-YES! WHAT DO YOU WANT WITH ME?
ARE YOU PLAYING STUPID? OR DO YOU NOT KNOW?
IF SELLURIAH FINDS OUT ABOUT THIS, YOU'RE DEAD!

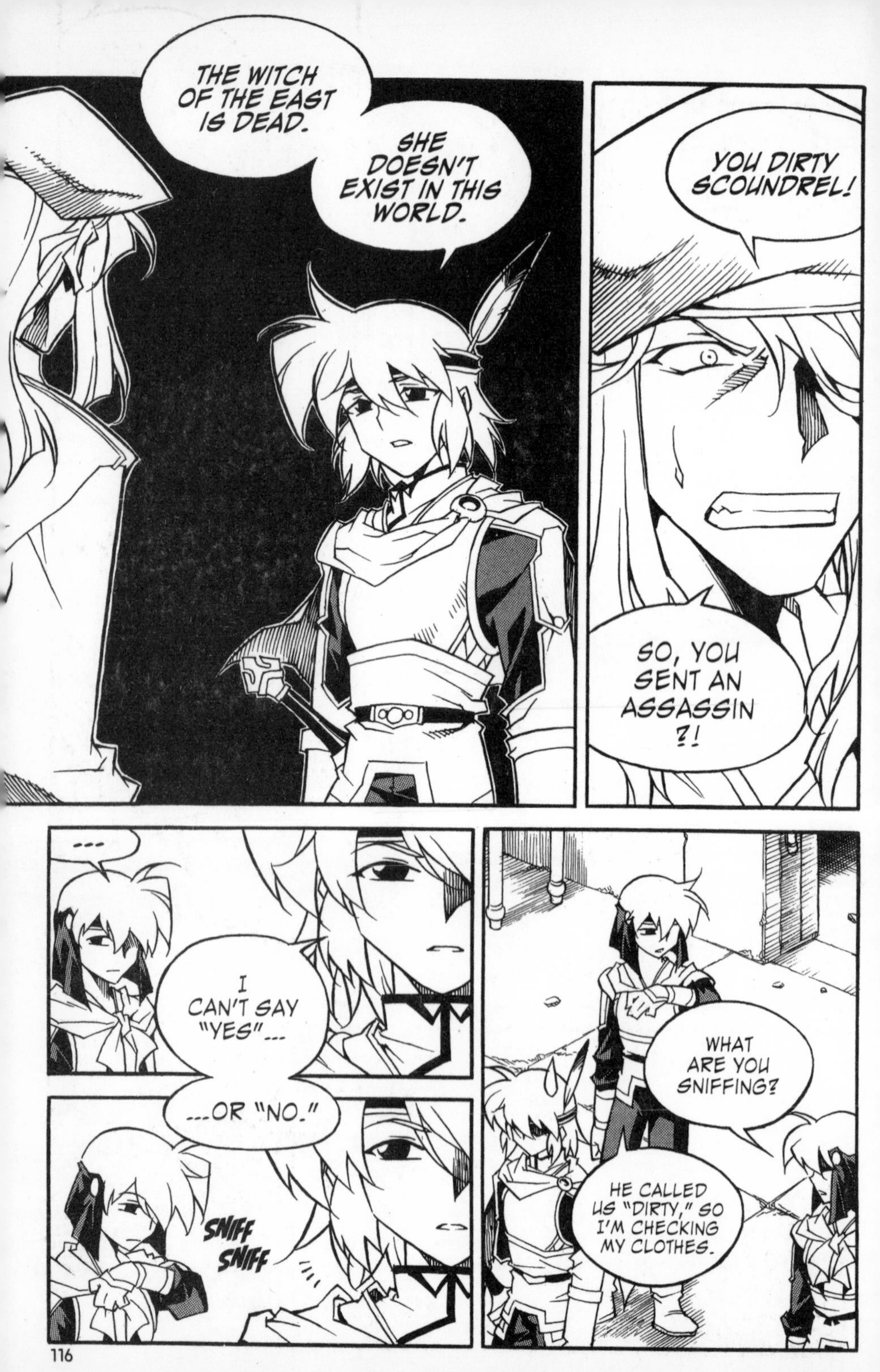
THE WITCH OF THE EAST IS DEAD.
SHE DOESN'T EXIST IN THIS WORLD.
YOU DIRTY SCOUNDREL!
SO, YOU SENT AN ASSASSIN ?!
...
I CAN'T SAY "YES"...
...OR "NO."
SNIFF SNIFF
WHAT ARE YOU SNIFFING?
HE CALLED US "DIRTY," SO I'M CHECKING MY CLOTHES.

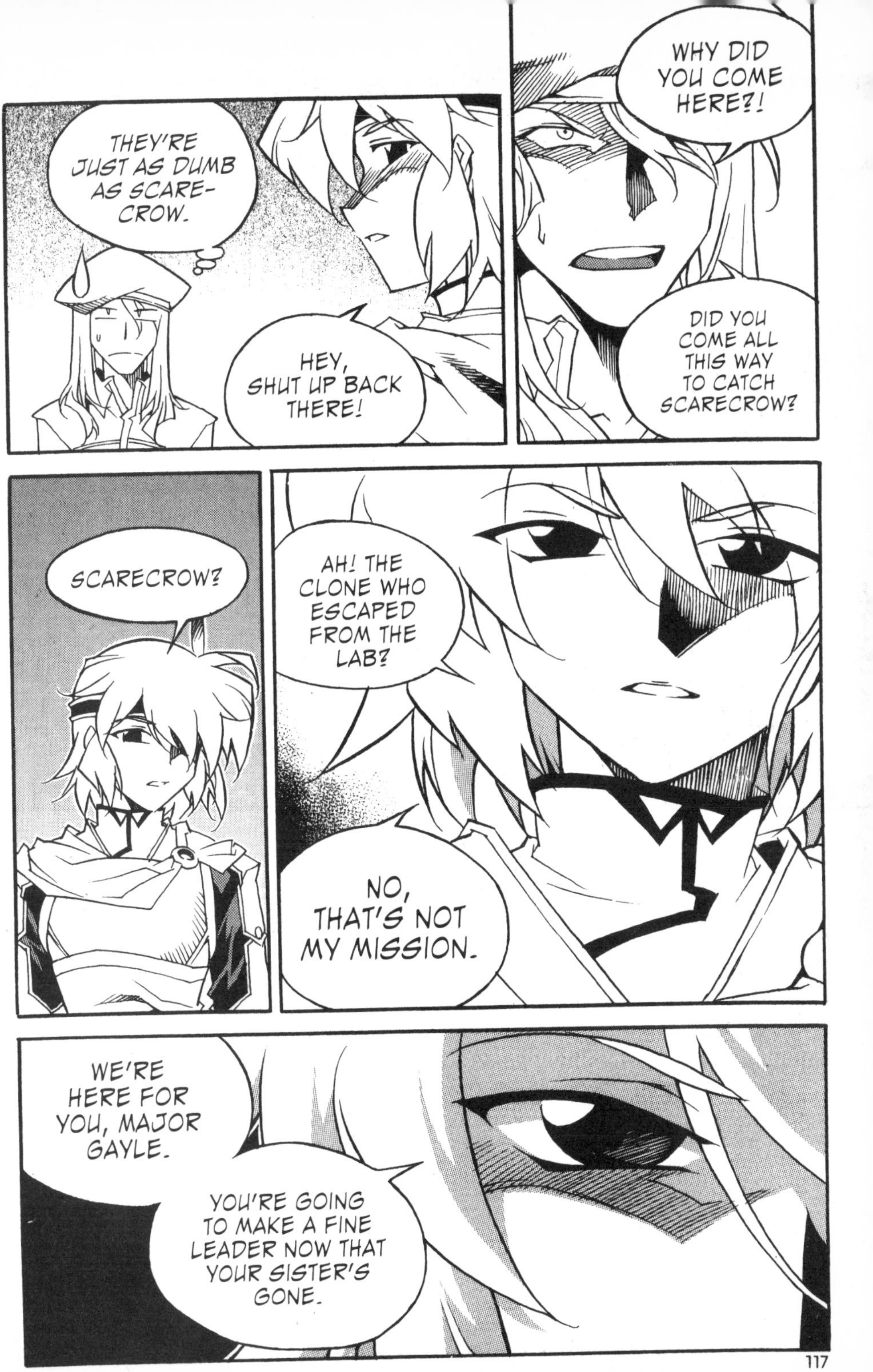
THEY'RE JUST AS DUMB AS SCARE-CROW.
HEY, SHUT UP BACK THERE!
WHY DID YOU COME HERE?!
DID YOU COME ALL THIS WAY TO CATCH SCARECROW?
SCARECROW?
AH! THE CLONE WHO ESCAPED FROM THE LAB?
NO, THAT'S NOT MY MISSION.
WE'RE HERE FOR YOU, MAJOR GAYLE.
YOU'RE GOING TO MAKE A FINE LEADER NOW THAT YOUR SISTER'S GONE.

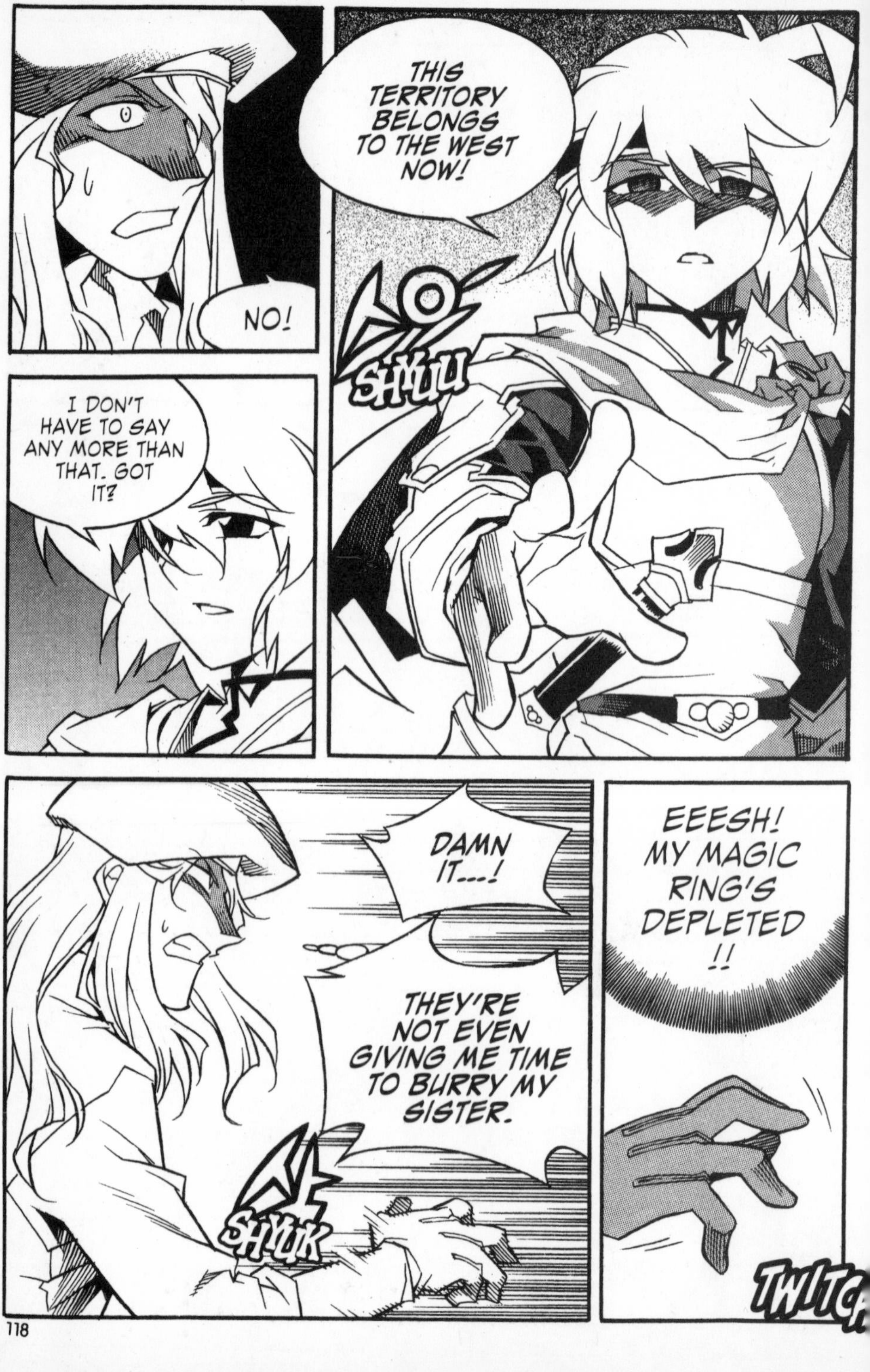
NO!
I DON'T HAVE TO SAY ANY MORE THAN THAT. GOT IT?
THIS TERRITORY BELONGS TO THE WEST NOW!
SHYUU
DAMN IT...!
THEY'RE NOT EVEN GIVING ME TIME TO BURRY MY SISTER.
SHYUK
EEESH! MY MAGIC RING'S DEPLETED !!
TWITCH

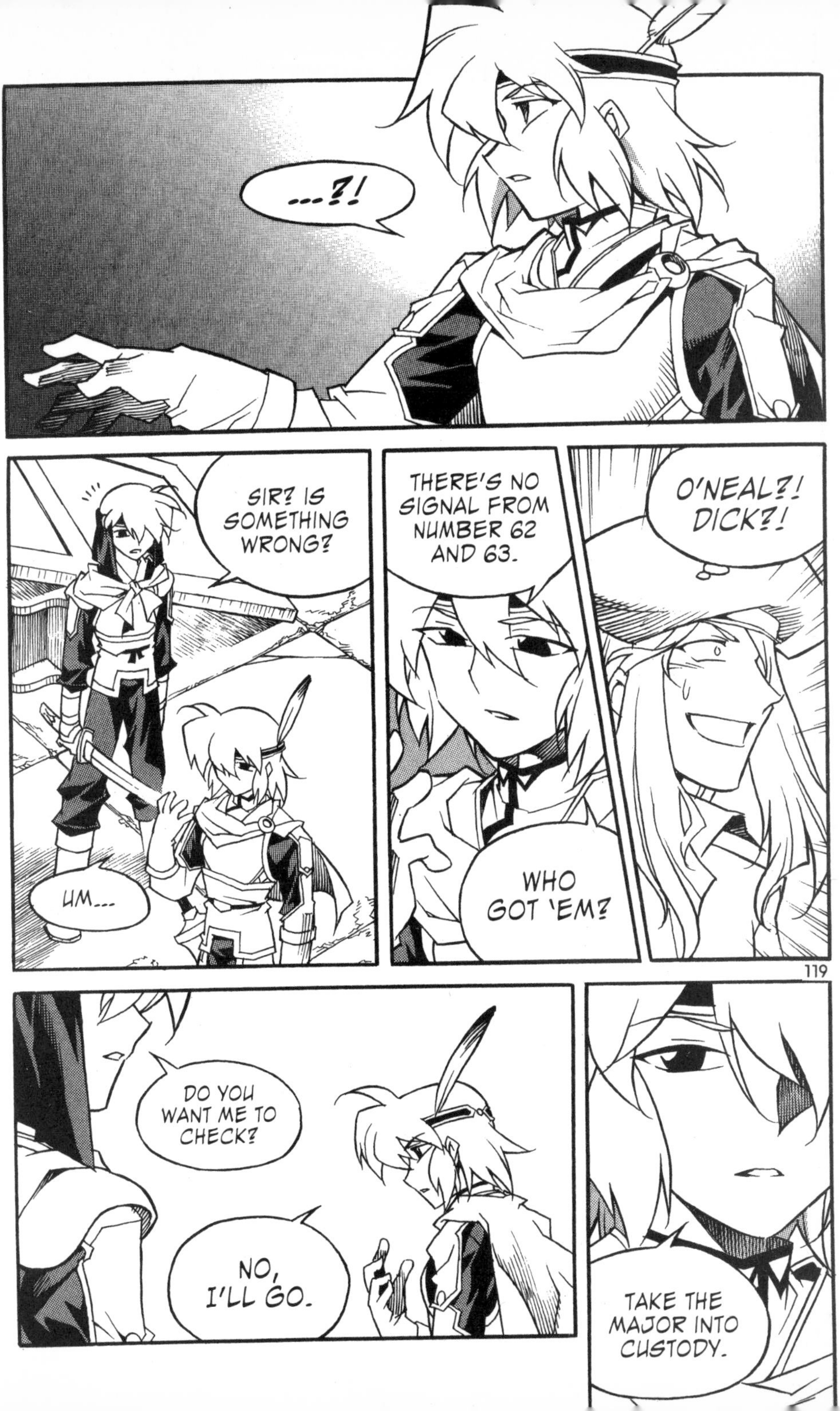
...?!
SIR? IS SOMETHING WRONG?
UM...
THERE'S NO SIGNAL FROM NUMBER 62 AND 63.
WHO GOT 'EM?
O'NEAL?! DICK?!
DO YOU WANT ME TO CHECK?
NO, I'LL GO.
TAKE THE MAJOR INTO CUSTODY.

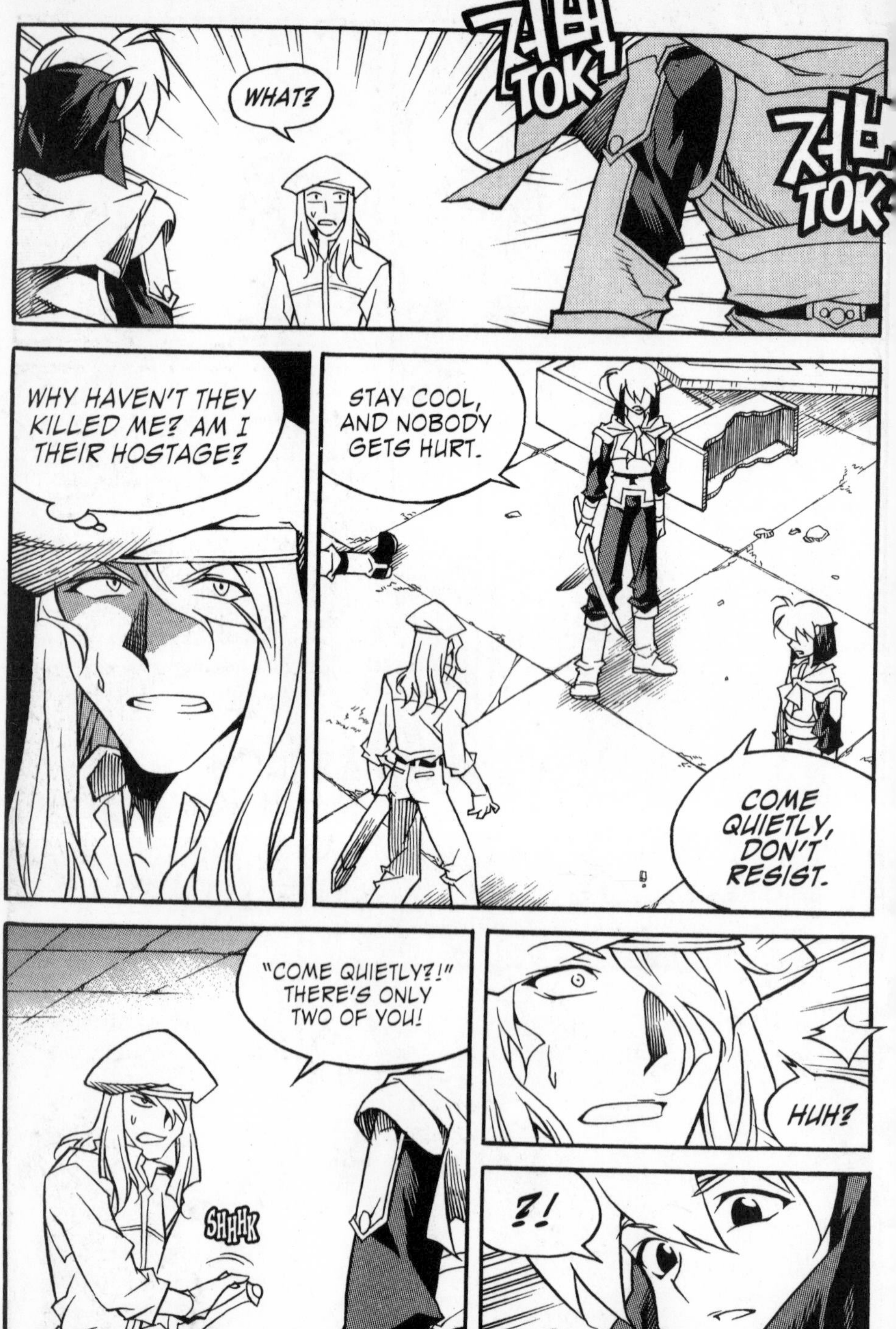
WHAT?
TOK
TOK
WHY HAVEN'T THEY KILLED ME? AM I THEIR HOSTAGE?
STAY COOL, AND NOBODY GETS HURT.
COME QUIETLY, DON'T RESIST.
"COME QUIETLY?!" THERE'S ONLY TWO OF YOU!
SHHHK
HUH?
?!

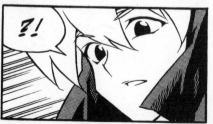

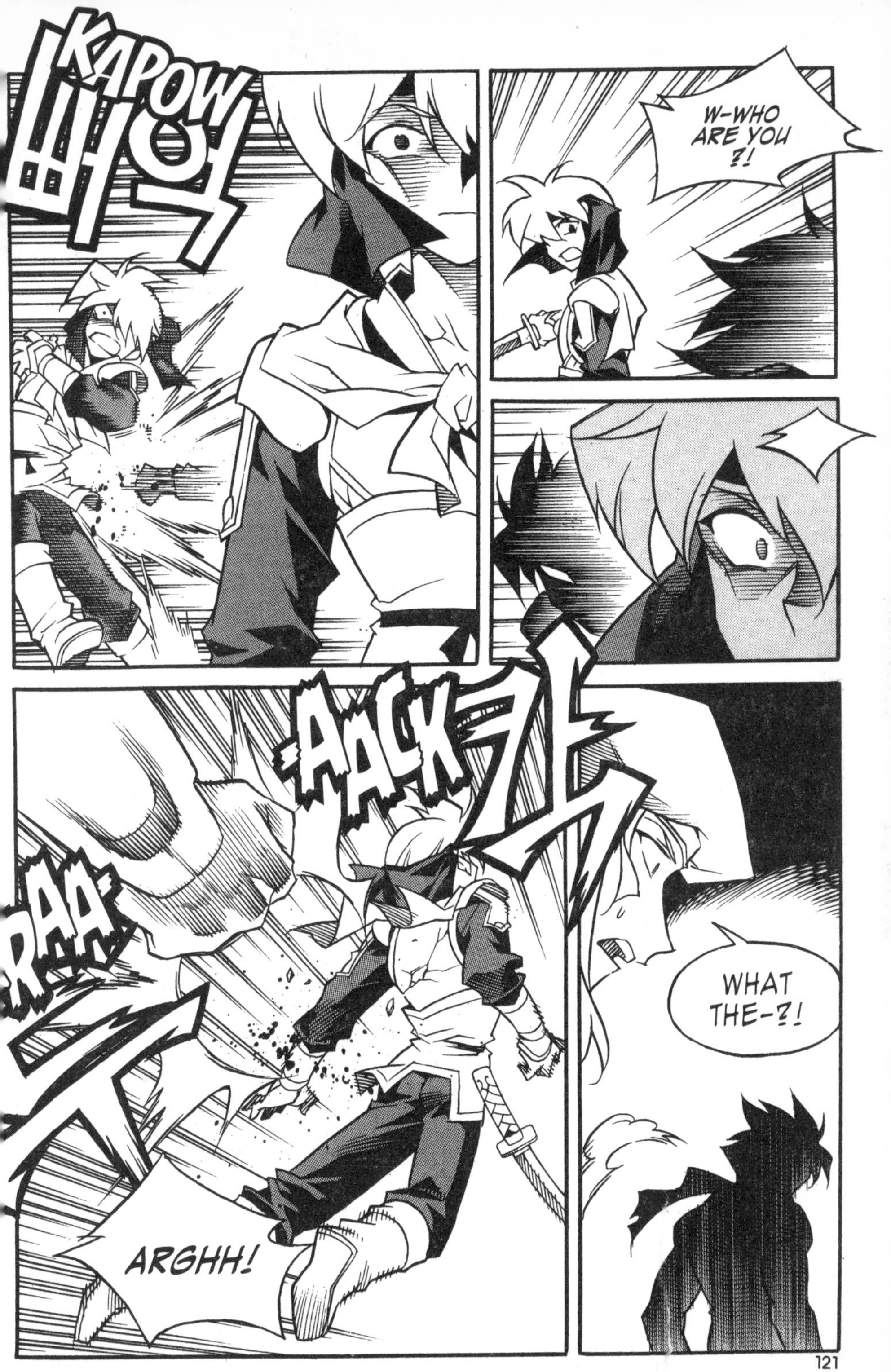
KAPOW!!!
W-WHO ARE YOU ?!
AACK
RAA
ARGHH!
WHAT THE-?!

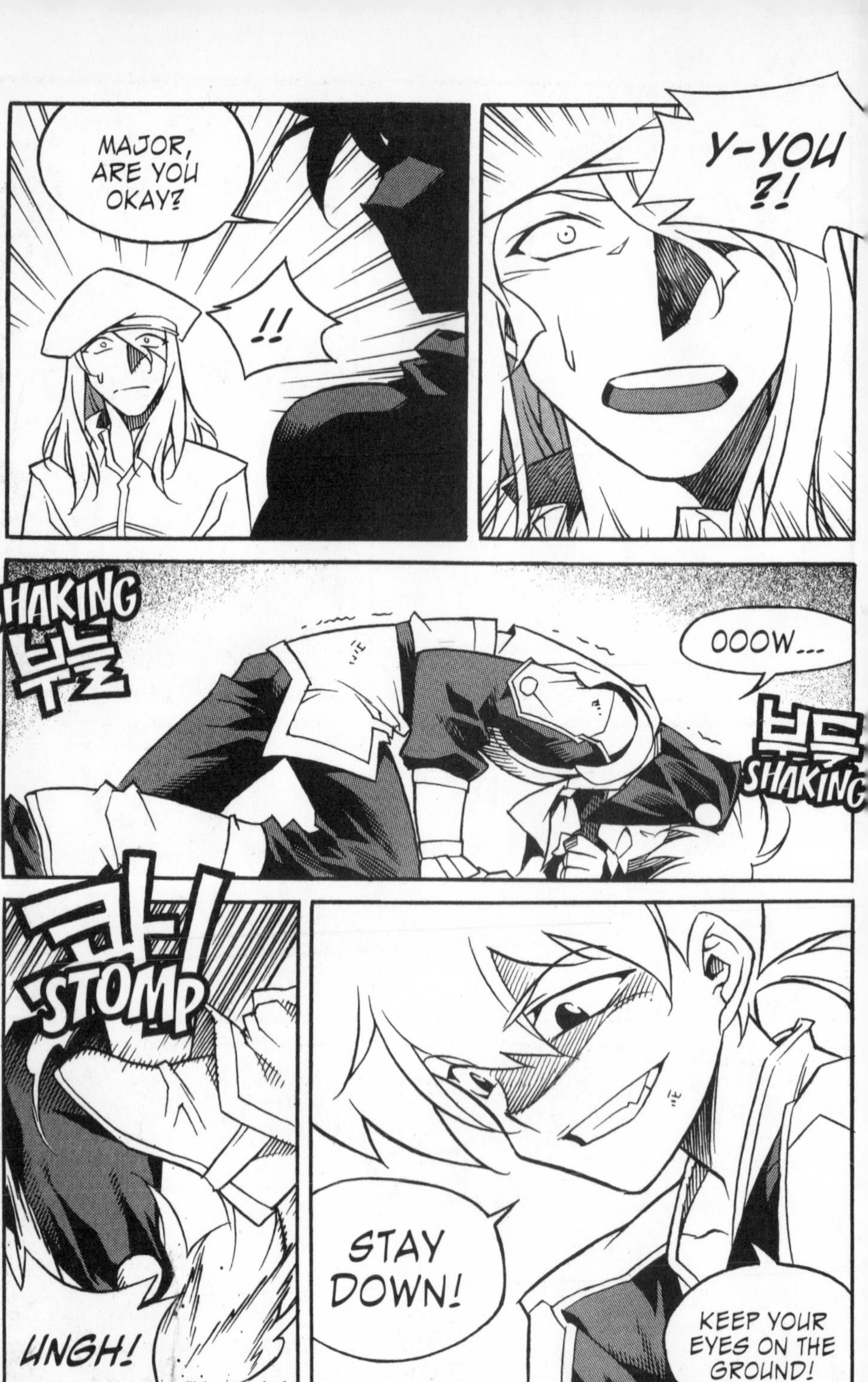
MAJOR, ARE YOU OKAY?
!!
Y-YOU ?!
SHAKING
OOOW...
SHAKING
STOMP
UNGH!
STAY DOWN!
KEEP YOUR EYES ON THE GROUND!

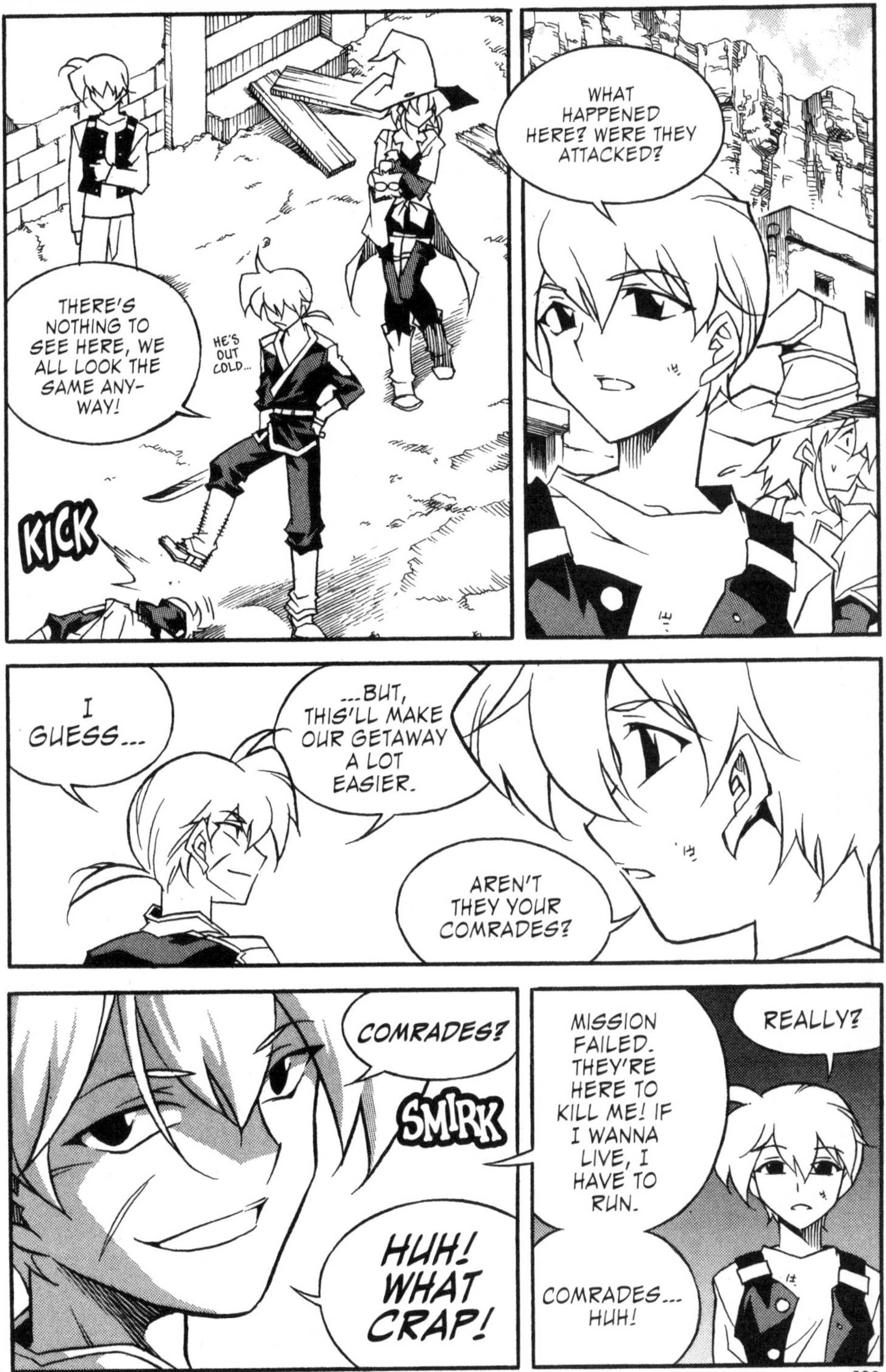
THERE'S NOTHING TO SEE HERE, WE ALL LOOK THE SAME ANY-WAY!
HE'S OUT COLD...
KICK
WHAT HAPPENED HERE? WERE THEY ATTACKED?
I GUESS...
...BUT, THIS'LL MAKE OUR GETAWAY A LOT EASIER.
AREN'T THEY YOUR COMRADES?
COMRADES?
SMIRK
HUH! WHAT CRAP!
MISSION FAILED. THEY'RE HERE TO KILL ME! IF I WANNA LIVE, I HAVE TO RUN.
REALLY?
COMRADES... HUH!

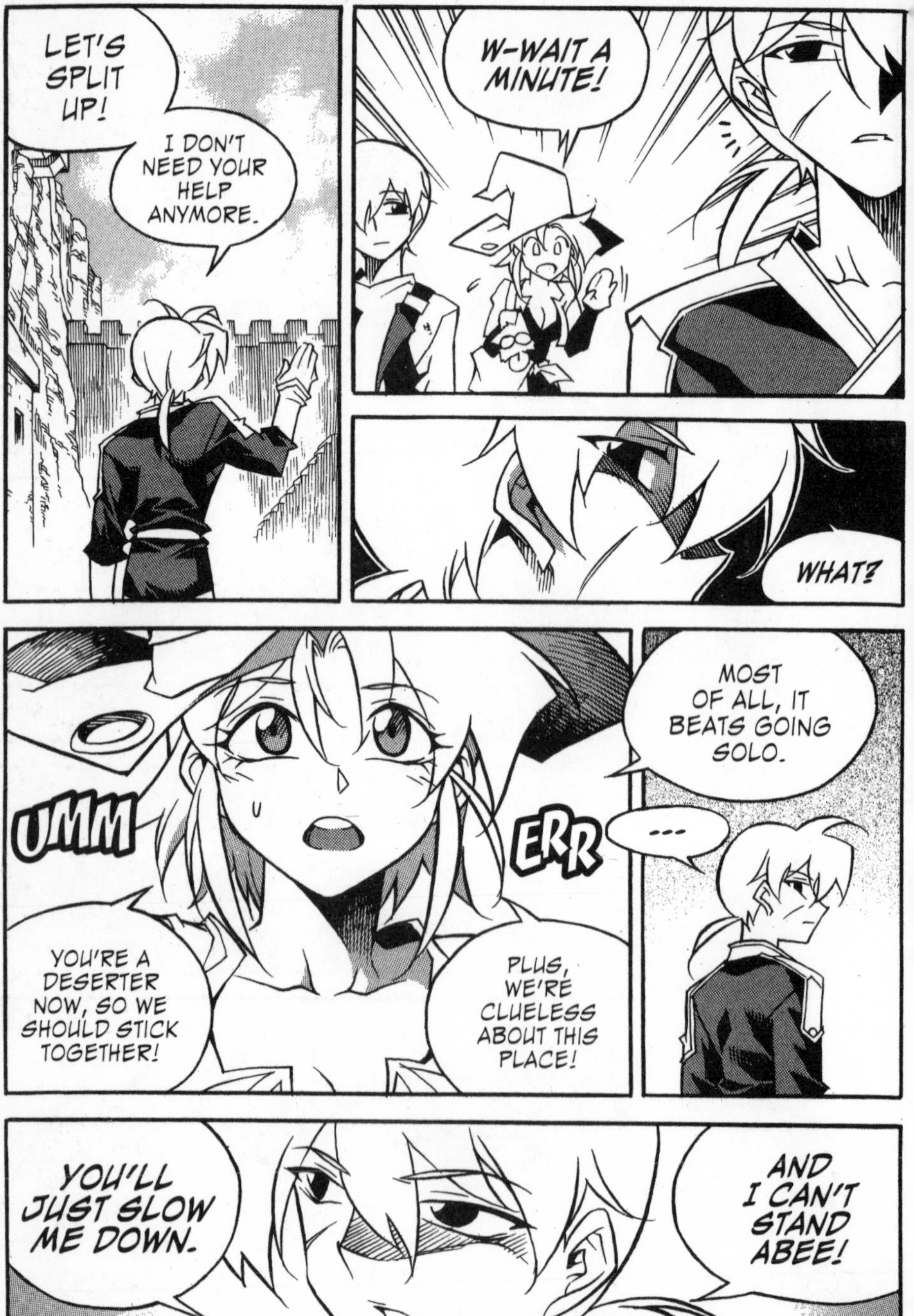
LET'S SPLIT UP!
I DON'T NEED YOUR HELP ANYMORE.
W-WAIT A MINUTE!
WHAT?
UMM
ERR
YOU'RE A DESERTER NOW, SO WE SHOULD STICK TOGETHER!
PLUS, WE'RE CLUELESS ABOUT THIS PLACE!
MOST OF ALL, IT BEATS GOING SOLO.
...
YOU'LL JUST SLOW ME DOWN.
AND I CAN'T STAND ABEE!

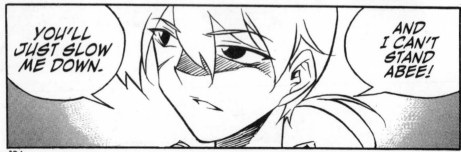

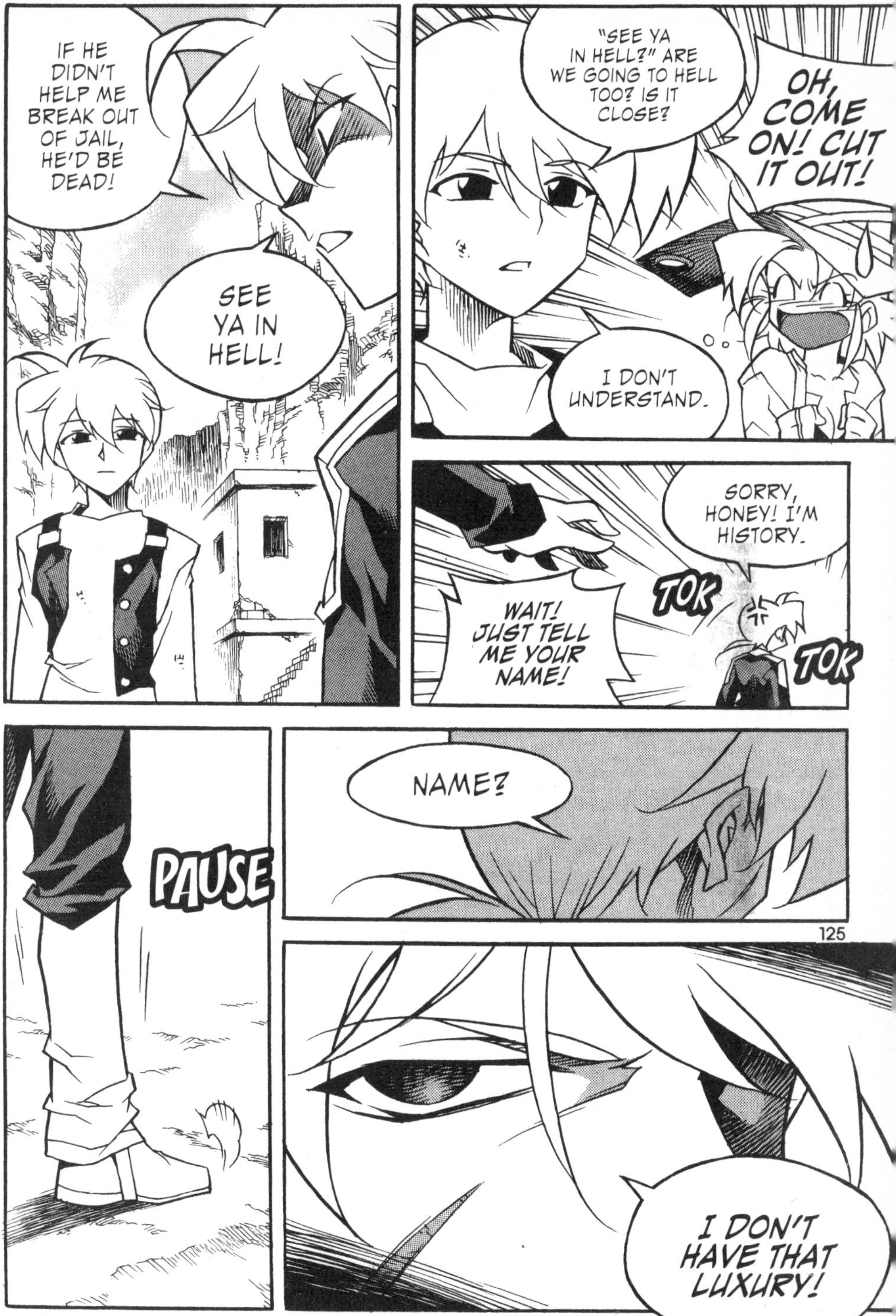
IF HE DIDN'T HELP ME BREAK OUT OF JAIL, HE'D BE DEAD!
SEE YA IN HELL!
"SEE YA IN HELL?" ARE WE GOING TO HELL TOO? IS IT CLOSE?
OH, COME ON! CUT IT OUT!
I DON'T UNDERSTAND.
SORRY, HONEY! I'M HISTORY.
WAIT! JUST TELL ME YOUR NAME!
TOK
TOK
PAUSE
NAME?
I DON'T HAVE THAT LUXURY!

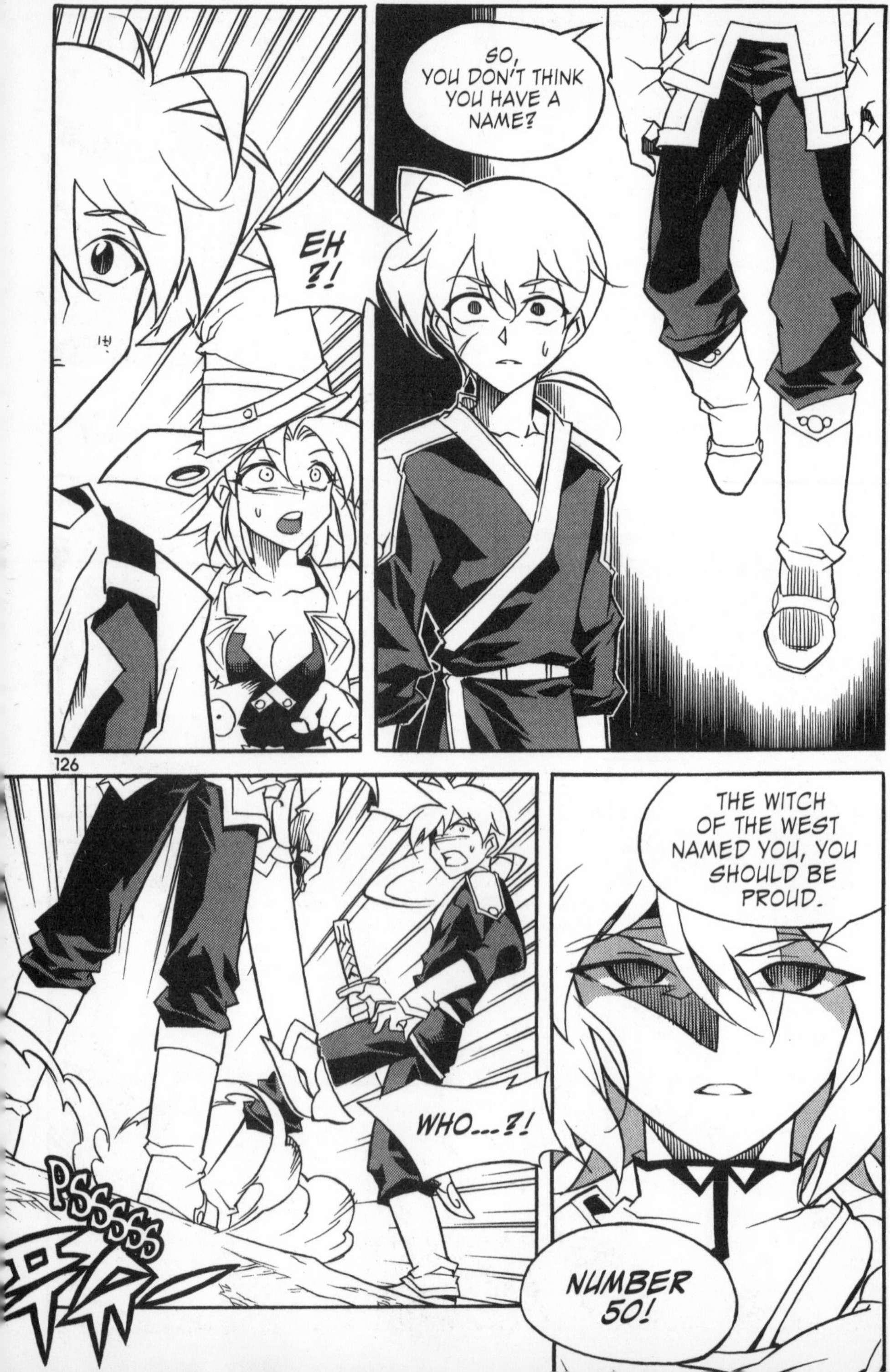
EH ?!
SO, YOU DON'T THINK YOU HAVE A NAME?
PSSSSS
WHO...?!
THE WITCH OF THE WEST NAMED YOU, YOU SHOULD BE PROUD.
NUMBER 50!

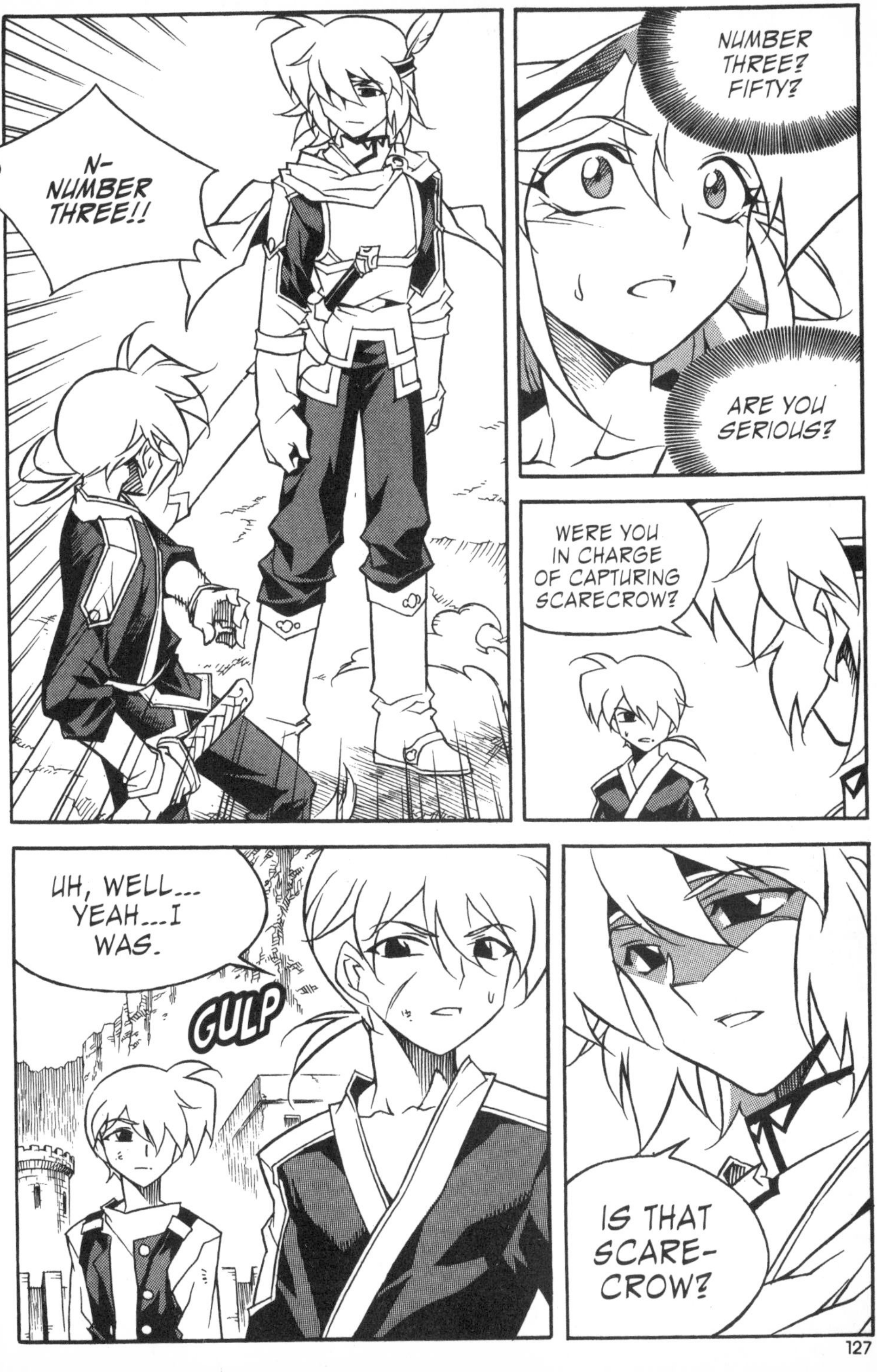
N-NUMBER THREE!!
NUMBER THREE? FIFTY?
ARE YOU SERIOUS?
WERE YOU IN CHARGE OF CAPTURING SCARECROW?
UH, WELL... YEAH...I WAS.
GULP
IS THAT SCARE-CROW?

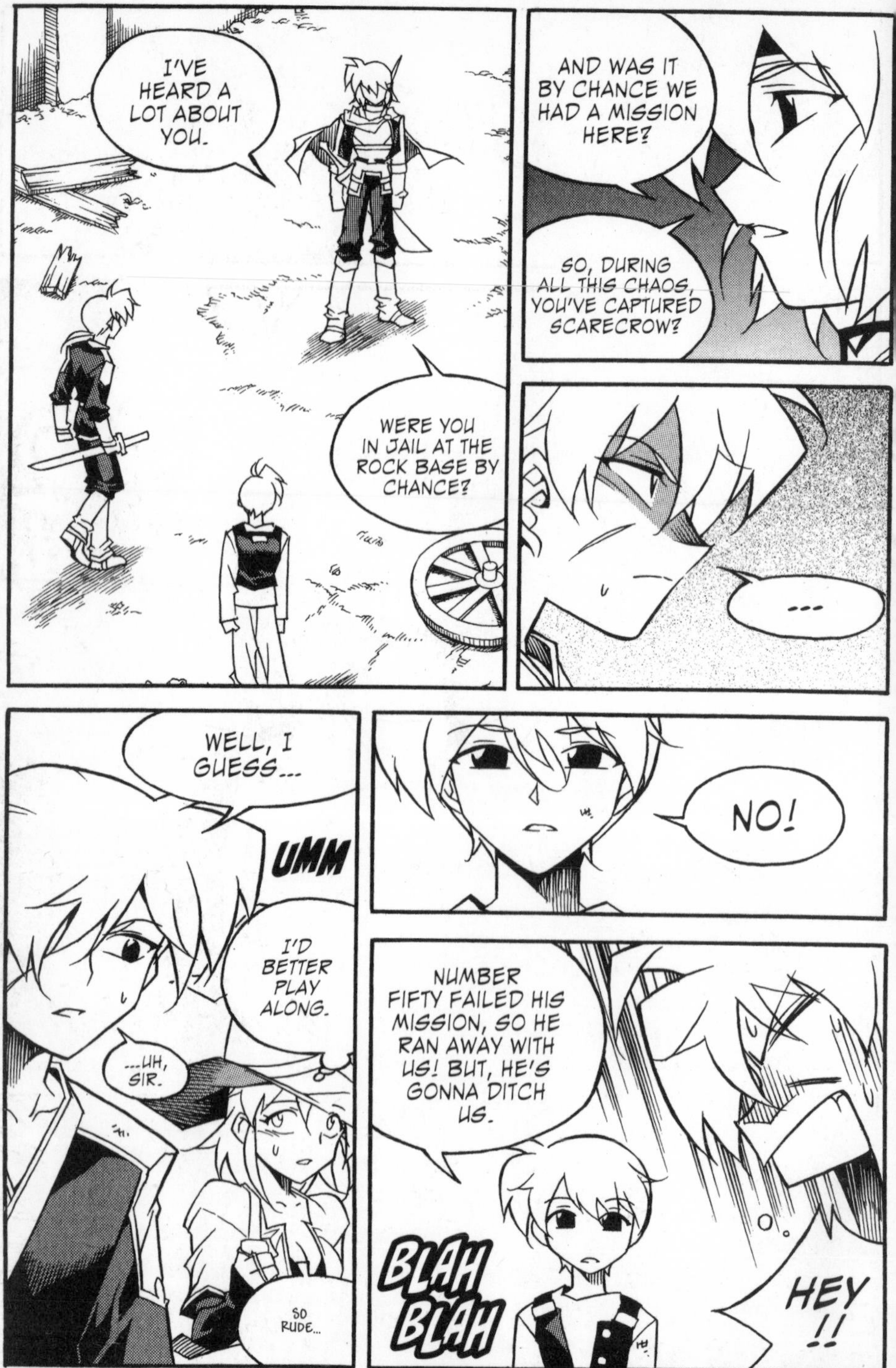
I'VE HEARD A LOT ABOUT YOU.
WERE YOU IN JAIL AT THE ROCK BASE BY CHANCE?
AND WAS IT BY CHANCE WE HAD A MISSION HERE?
SO, DURING ALL THIS CHAOS, YOU'VE CAPTURED SCARECROW?
...
WELL, I GUESS...
UMM
I'D BETTER PLAY ALONG.
...UH, SIR.
SO RUDE...
NO!
NUMBER FIFTY FAILED HIS MISSION, SO HE RAN AWAY WITH US! BUT, HE'S GONNA DITCH US.
BLAH BLAH
HEY !!

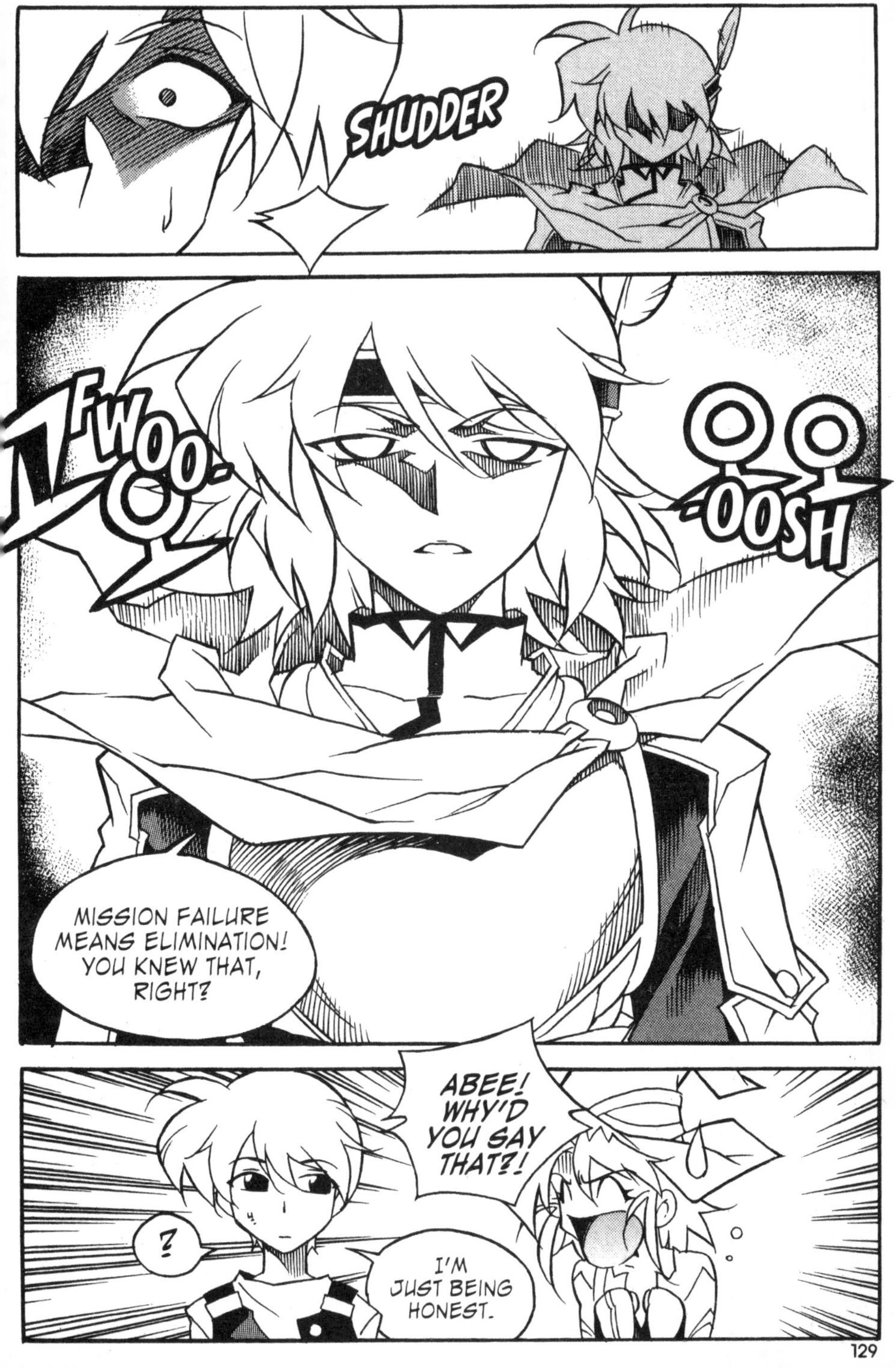
SHUDDER
FWOO-
-OOSH
MISSION FAILURE MEANS ELIMINATION! YOU KNEW THAT, RIGHT?
ABEE! WHY'D YOU SAY THAT?!
?
I'M JUST BEING HONEST.

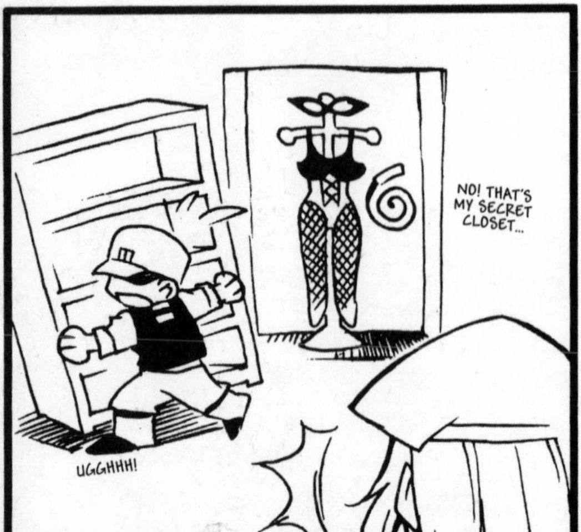
NO! THAT'S MY SECRET CLOSET...
UGGHHH!

Step 21 TELEKINETIC BATTLE

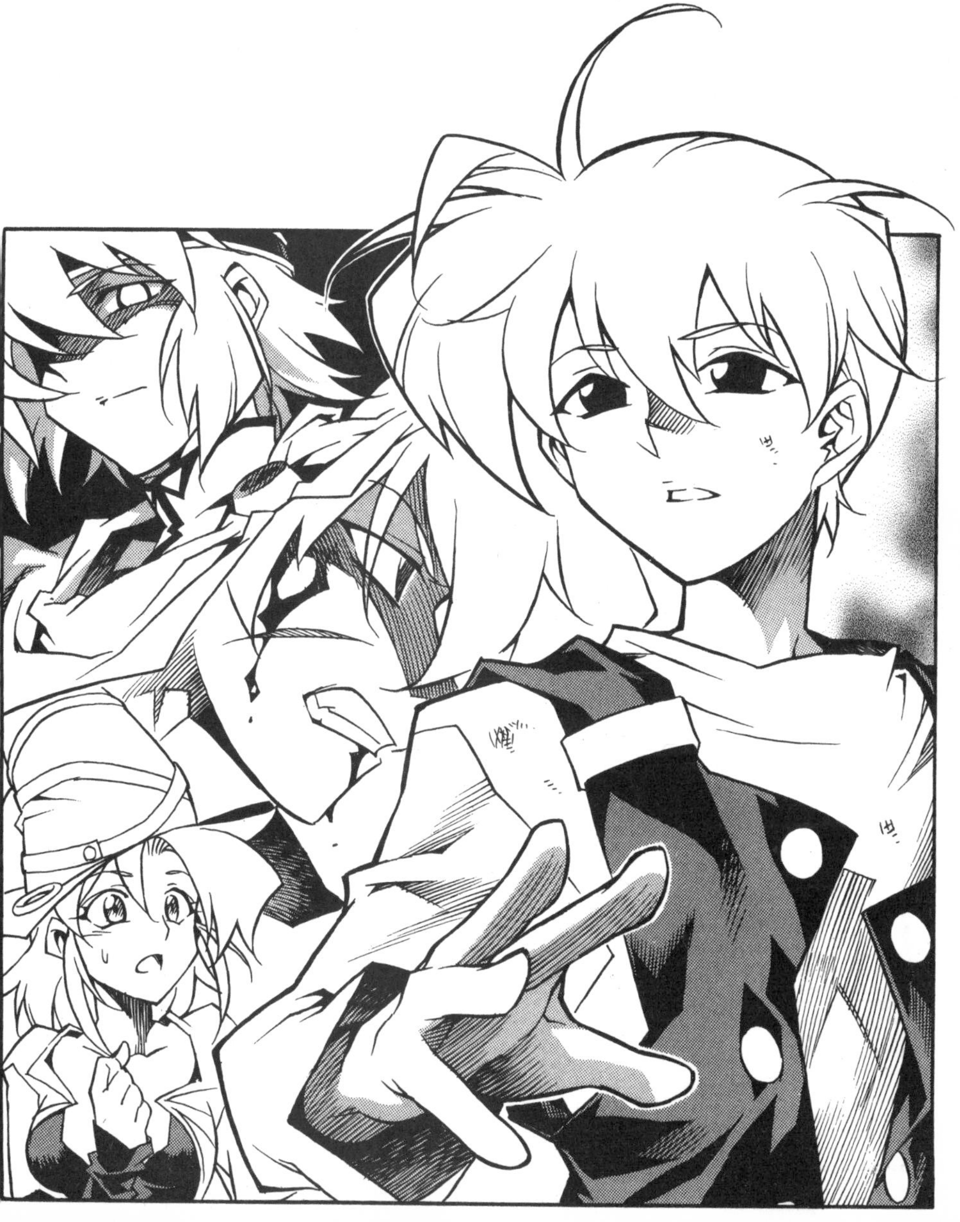

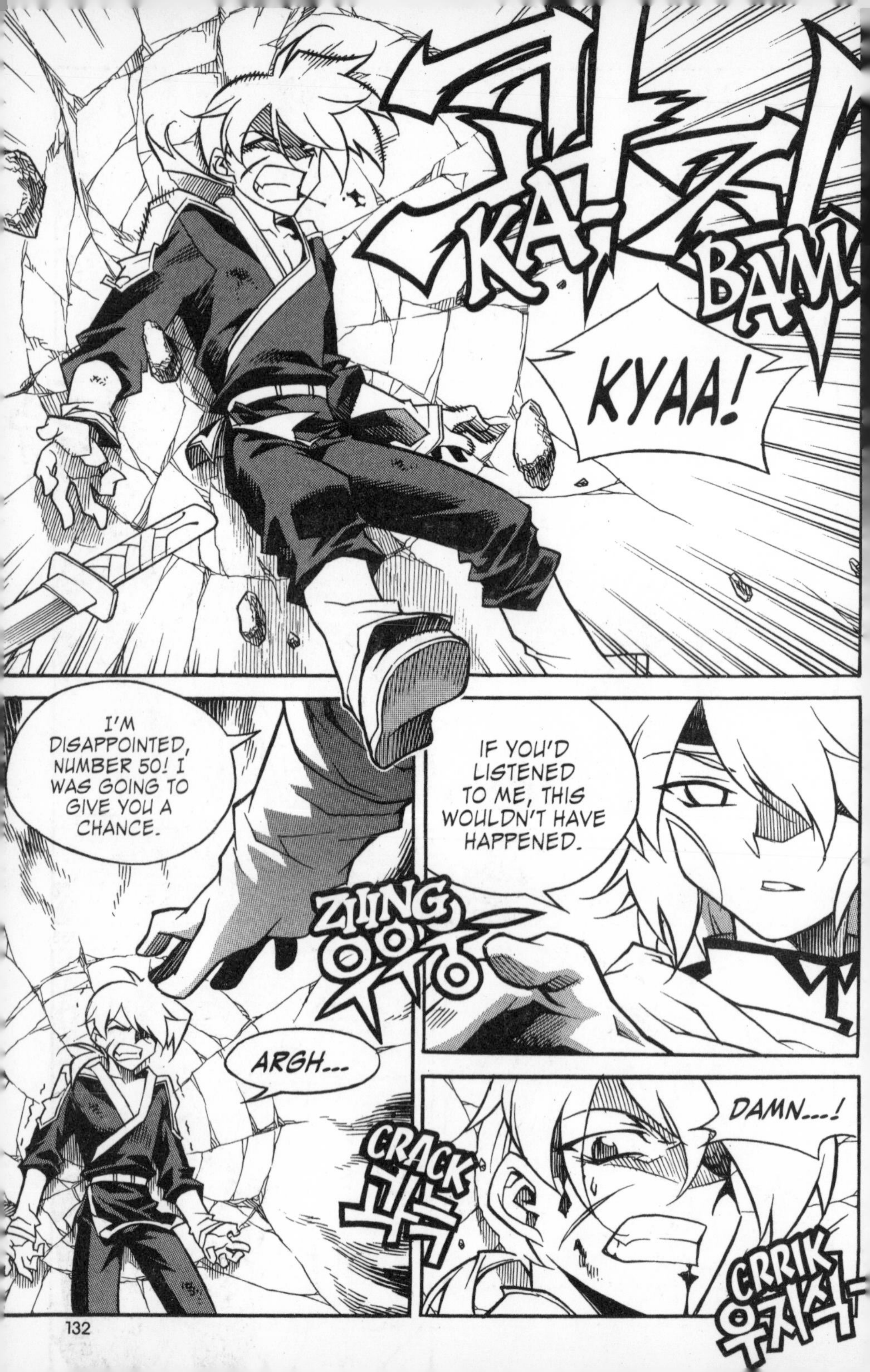
KA-BAM
KYAA!
I'M DISAPPOINTED, NUMBER 50! I WAS GOING TO GIVE YOU A CHANCE.
ZIING
ARGH...
CRACK
IF YOU'D LISTENED TO ME, THIS WOULDN'T HAVE HAPPENED.
DAMN...!
CRRIK

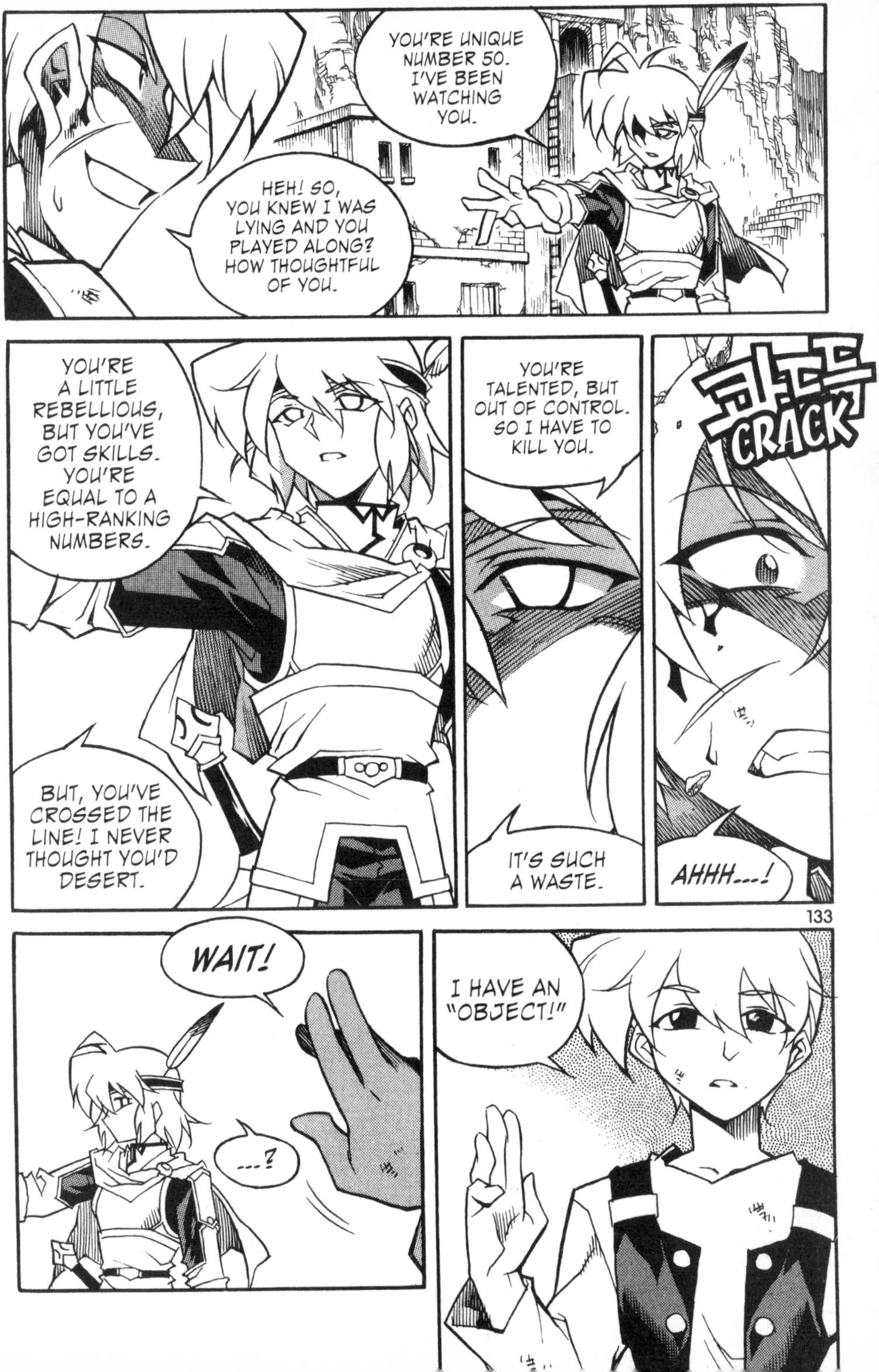
YOU'RE UNIQUE NUMBER 50. I'VE BEEN WATCHING YOU.
HEH! SO, YOU KNEW I WAS LYING AND YOU PLAYED ALONG? HOW THOUGHTFUL OF YOU.
YOU'RE A LITTLE REBELLIOUS, BUT YOU'VE GOT SKILLS. YOU'RE EQUAL TO A HIGH-RANKING NUMBERS.
BUT, YOU'VE CROSSED THE LINE! I NEVER THOUGHT YOU'D DESERT.
YOU'RE TALENTED, BUT OUT OF CONTROL. SO I HAVE TO KILL YOU.
IT'S SUCH A WASTE.
CRACK
AHHH...!
WAIT!
...?
I HAVE AN "OBJECT!"

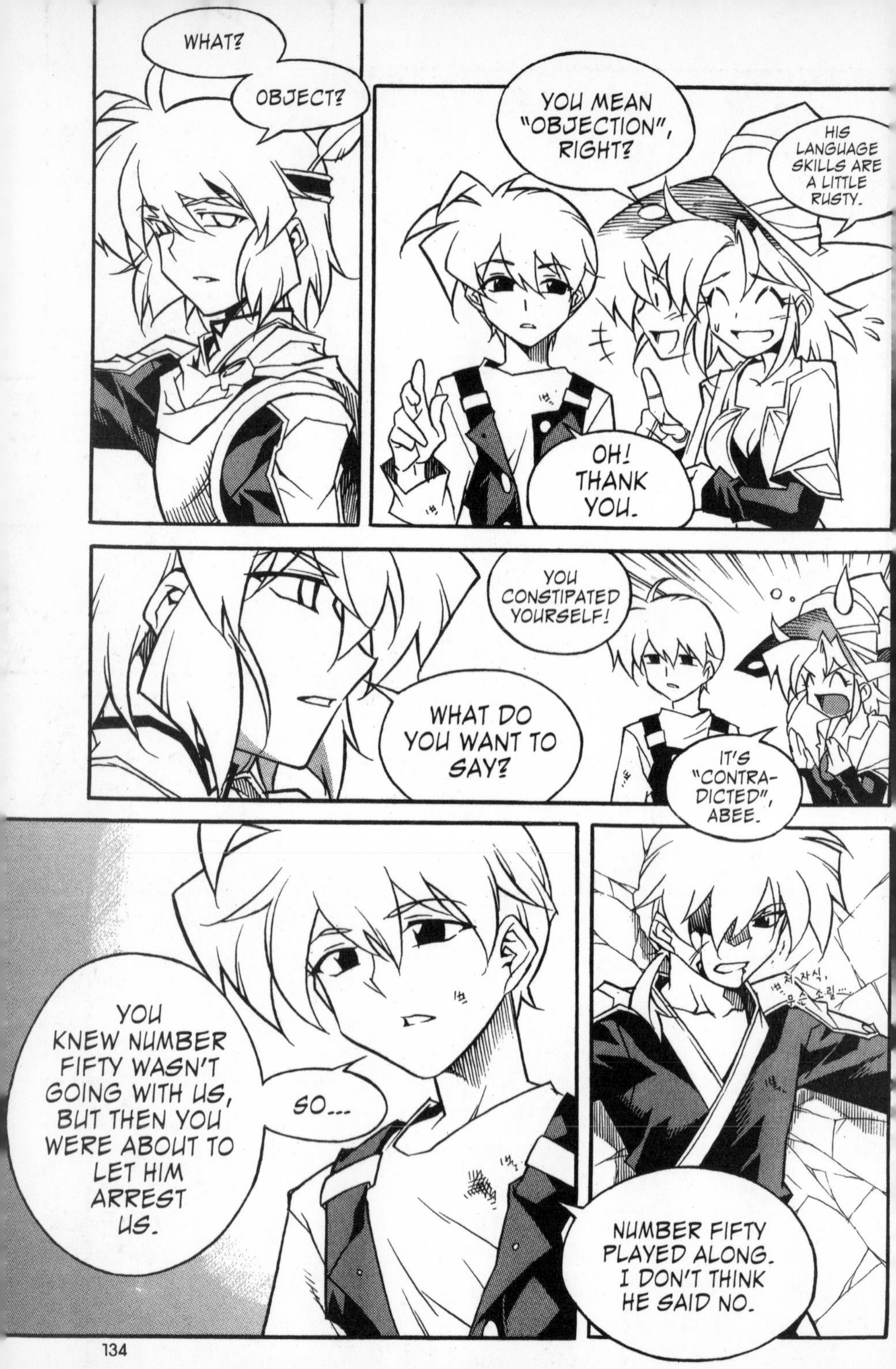
WHAT?
OBJECT?
YOU MEAN "OBJECTION", RIGHT?
HIS LANGUAGE SKILLS ARE A LITTLE RUSTY.
OH! THANK YOU.
WHAT DO YOU WANT TO SAY?
YOU CONSTIPATED YOURSELF!
IT'S "CONTRA-DICTED", ABEE.
SO...
YOU KNEW NUMBER FIFTY WASN'T GOING WITH US, BUT THEN YOU WERE ABOUT TO LET HIM ARREST US.
저 자식, 무슨 소릴...
NUMBER FIFTY PLAYED ALONG. I DON'T THINK HE SAID NO.

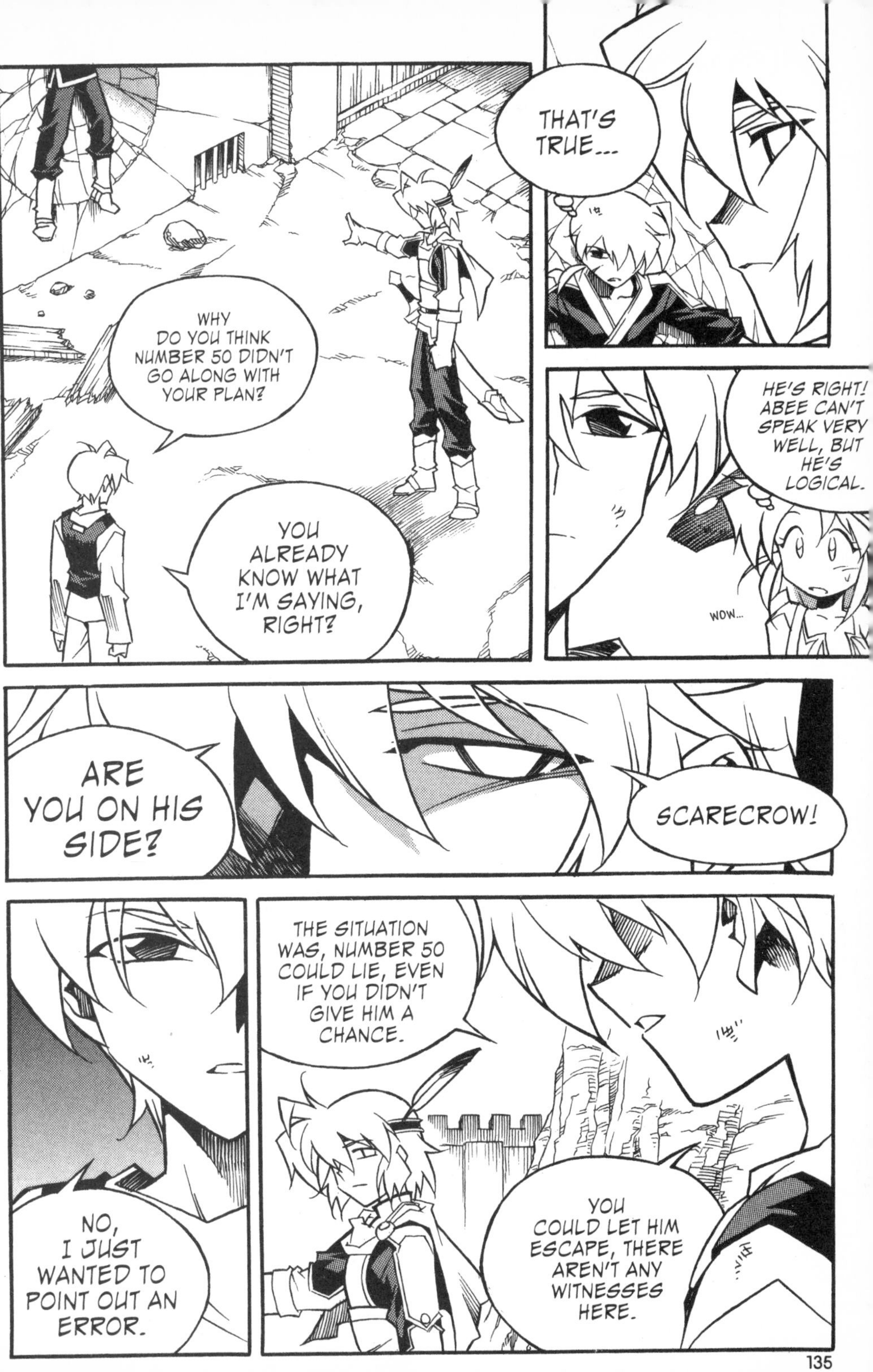
WHY DO YOU THINK NUMBER 50 DIDN'T GO ALONG WITH YOUR PLAN?
YOU ALREADY KNOW WHAT I'M SAYING, RIGHT?
THAT'S TRUE...
HE'S RIGHT! ABEE CAN'T SPEAK VERY WELL, BUT HE'S LOGICAL.
WOW...
ARE YOU ON HIS SIDE?
SCARECROW!
NO, I JUST WANTED TO POINT OUT AN ERROR.
THE SITUATION WAS, NUMBER 50 COULD LIE, EVEN IF YOU DIDN'T GIVE HIM A CHANCE.
YOU COULD LET HIM ESCAPE, THERE AREN'T ANY WITNESSES HERE.

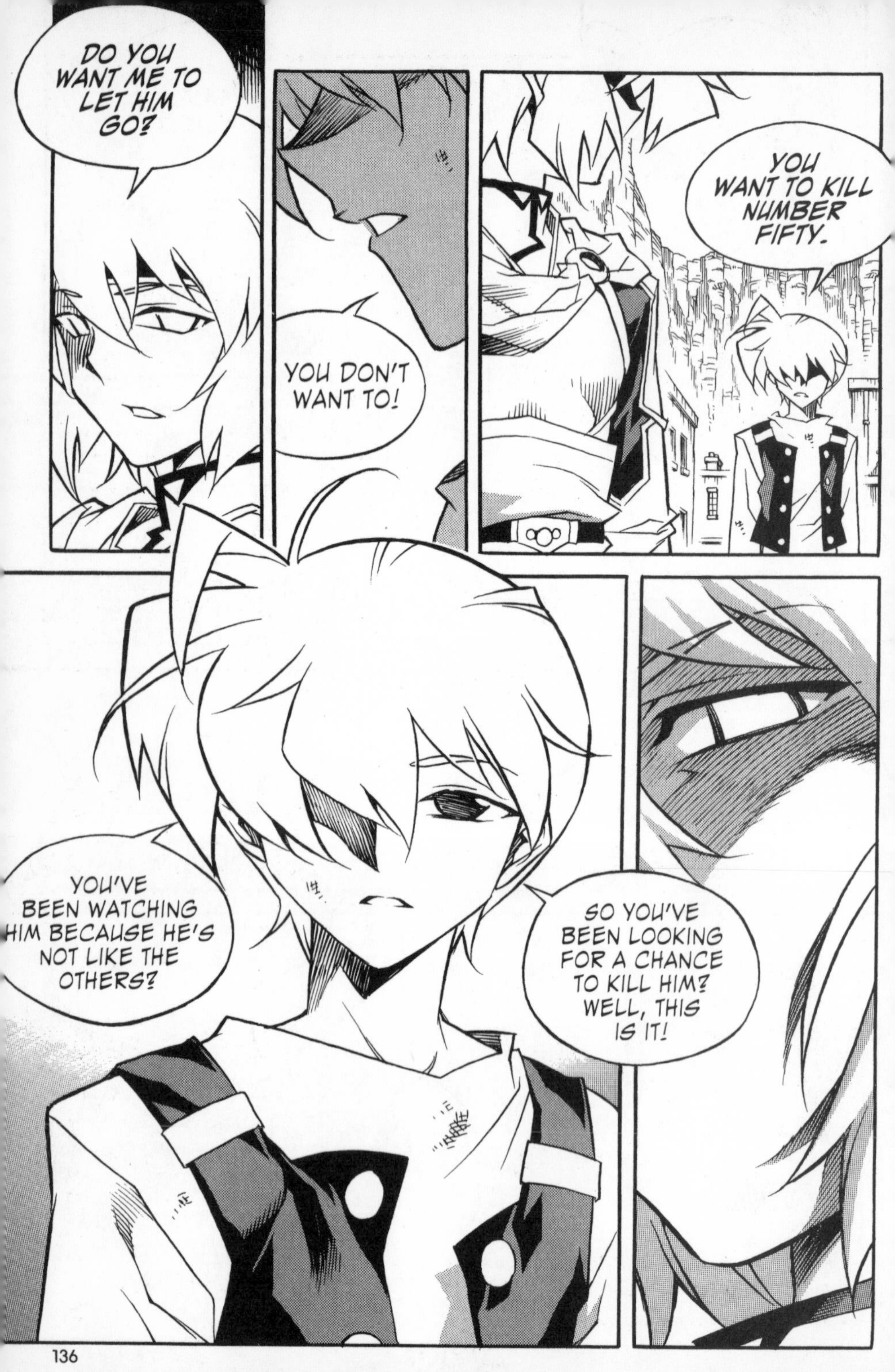

DO YOU WANT ME TO LET HIM GO?
YOU DON'T WANT TO!
YOU WANT TO KILL NUMBER FIFTY.
YOU'VE BEEN WATCHING HIM BECAUSE HE'S NOT LIKE THE OTHERS?
SO YOU'VE BEEN LOOKING FOR A CHANCE TO KILL HIM? WELL, THIS IS IT!

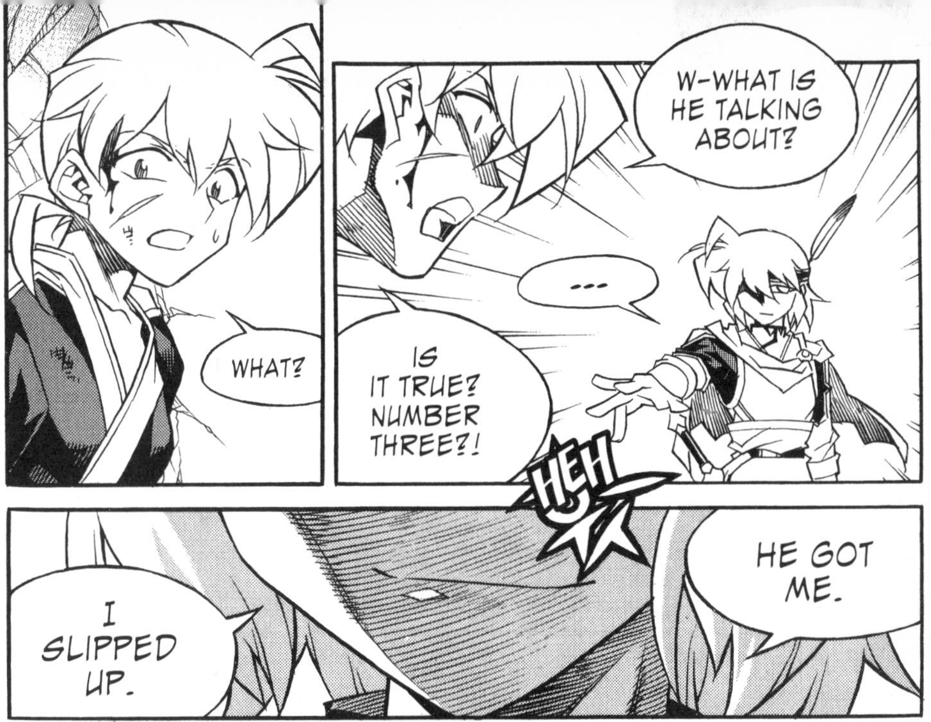
WHAT?
W-WHAT IS HE TALKING ABOUT?
...
IS IT TRUE? NUMBER THREE?!
HEH
I SLIPPED UP.
HE GOT ME.

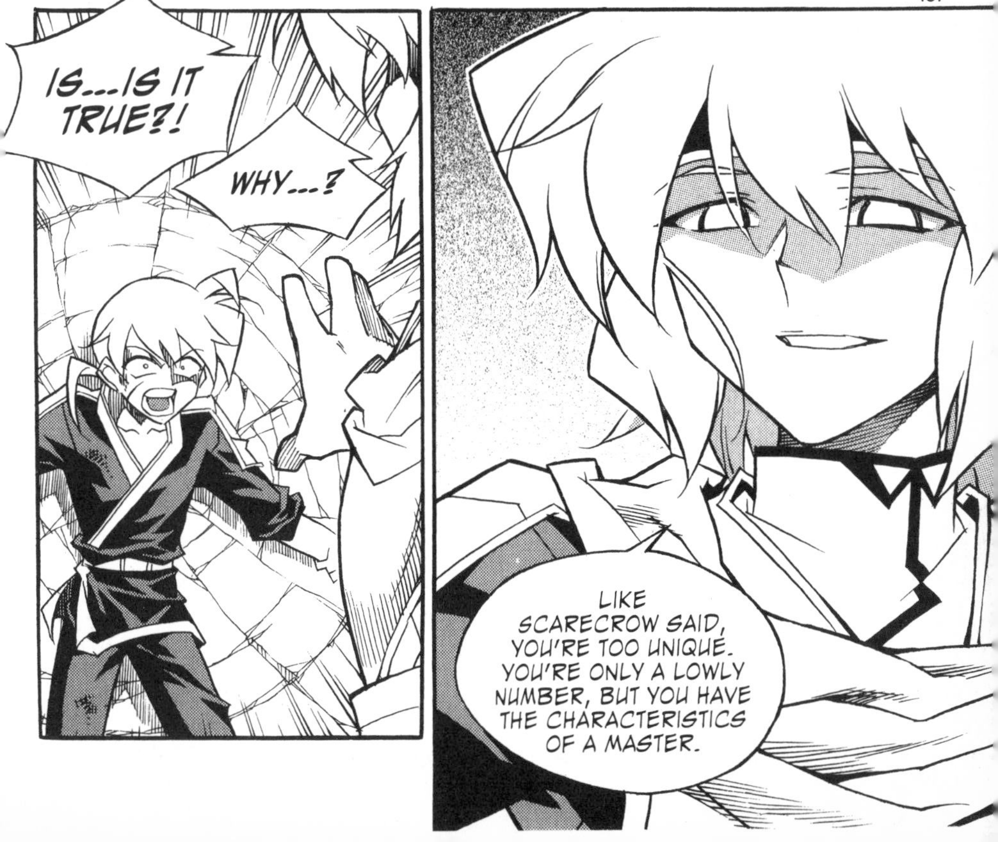
IS...IS IT TRUE?!
WHY...?
LIKE SCARECROW SAID, YOU'RE TOO UNIQUE. YOU'RE ONLY A LOWLY NUMBER, BUT YOU HAVE THE CHARACTERISTICS OF A MASTER.

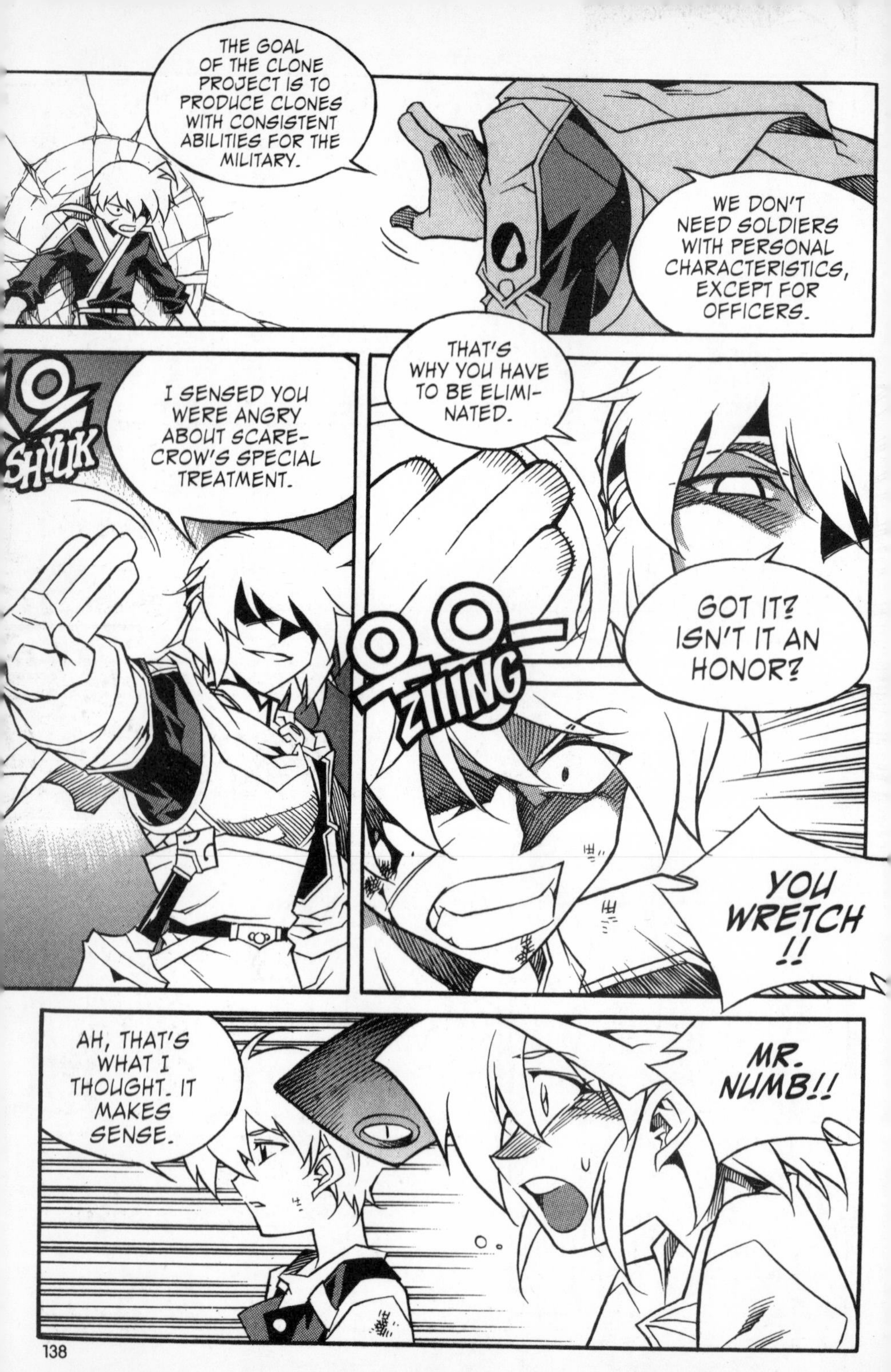
THE GOAL OF THE CLONE PROJECT IS TO PRODUCE CLONES WITH CONSISTENT ABILITIES FOR THE MILITARY.
WE DON'T NEED SOLDIERS WITH PERSONAL CHARACTERISTICS, EXCEPT FOR OFFICERS.
SHYUK
I SENSED YOU WERE ANGRY ABOUT SCARE-CROW'S SPECIAL TREATMENT.
THAT'S WHY YOU HAVE TO BE ELIMI-NATED.
GOT IT? ISN'T IT AN HONOR?
ZIIING
YOU WRETCH !!
AH, THAT'S WHAT I THOUGHT. IT MAKES SENSE.
MR. NUMB!!

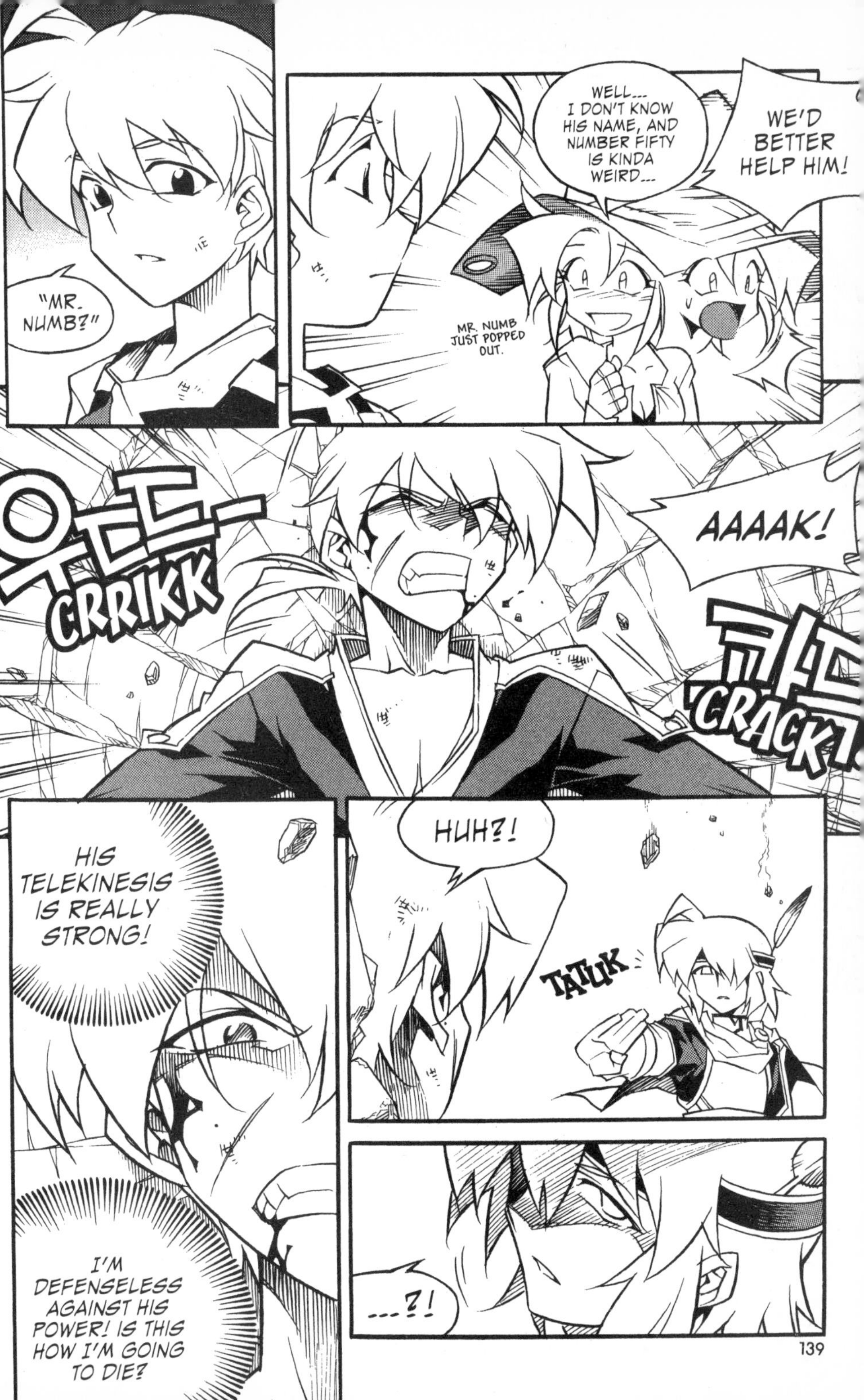
"MR. NUMB?"
WELL... I DON'T KNOW HIS NAME, AND NUMBER FIFTY IS KINDA WEIRD...
MR. NUMB JUST POPPED OUT.
WE'D BETTER HELP HIM!
CRRIKK
AAAAK!
CRACK!
HIS TELEKINESIS IS REALLY STRONG!
I'M DEFENSELESS AGAINST HIS POWER! IS THIS HOW I'M GOING TO DIE?
HUH?!
TATUK
...?!

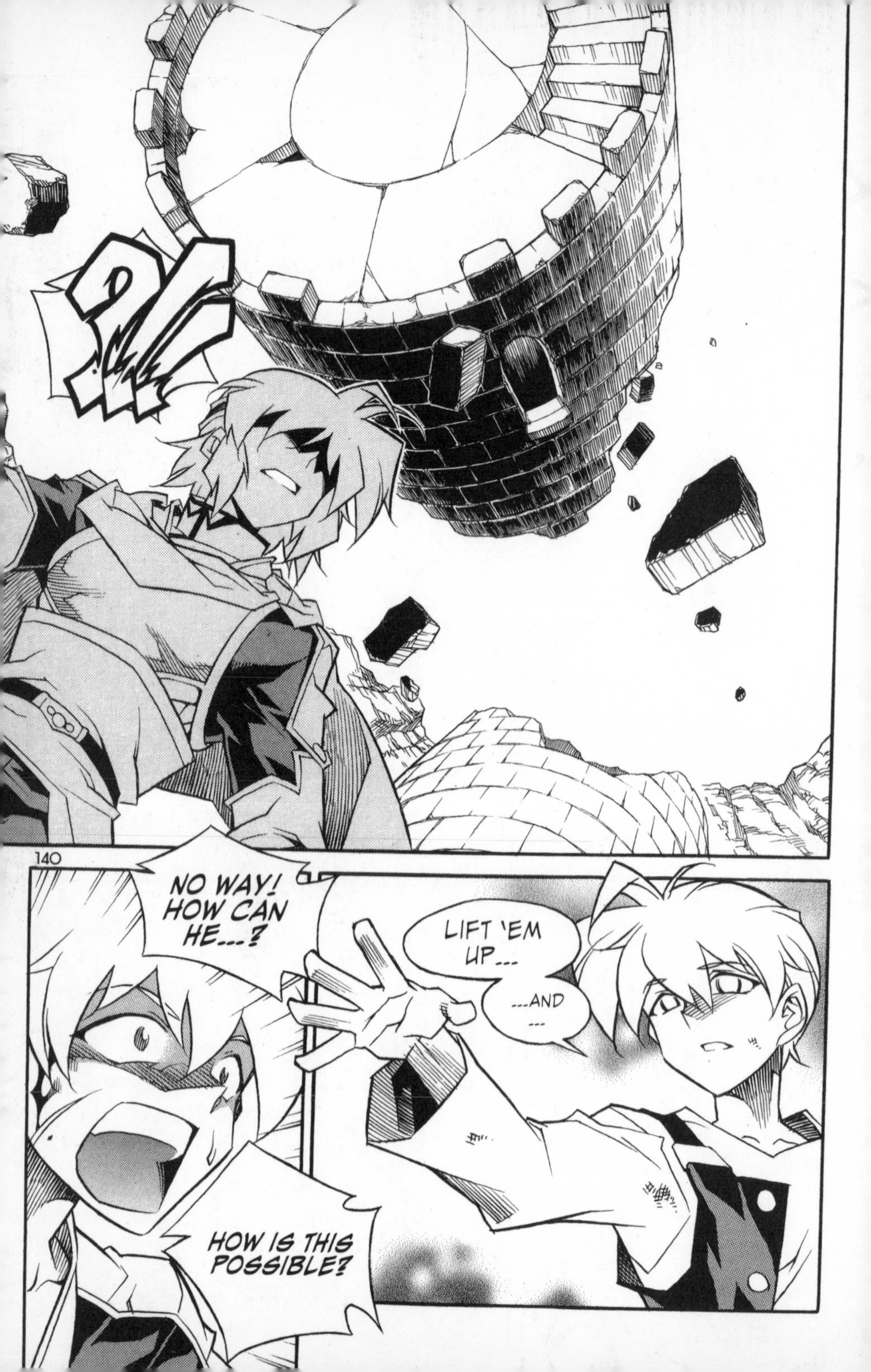
?!
NO WAY! HOW CAN HE...?
HOW IS THIS POSSIBLE?
LIFT 'EM UP...
...AND ...

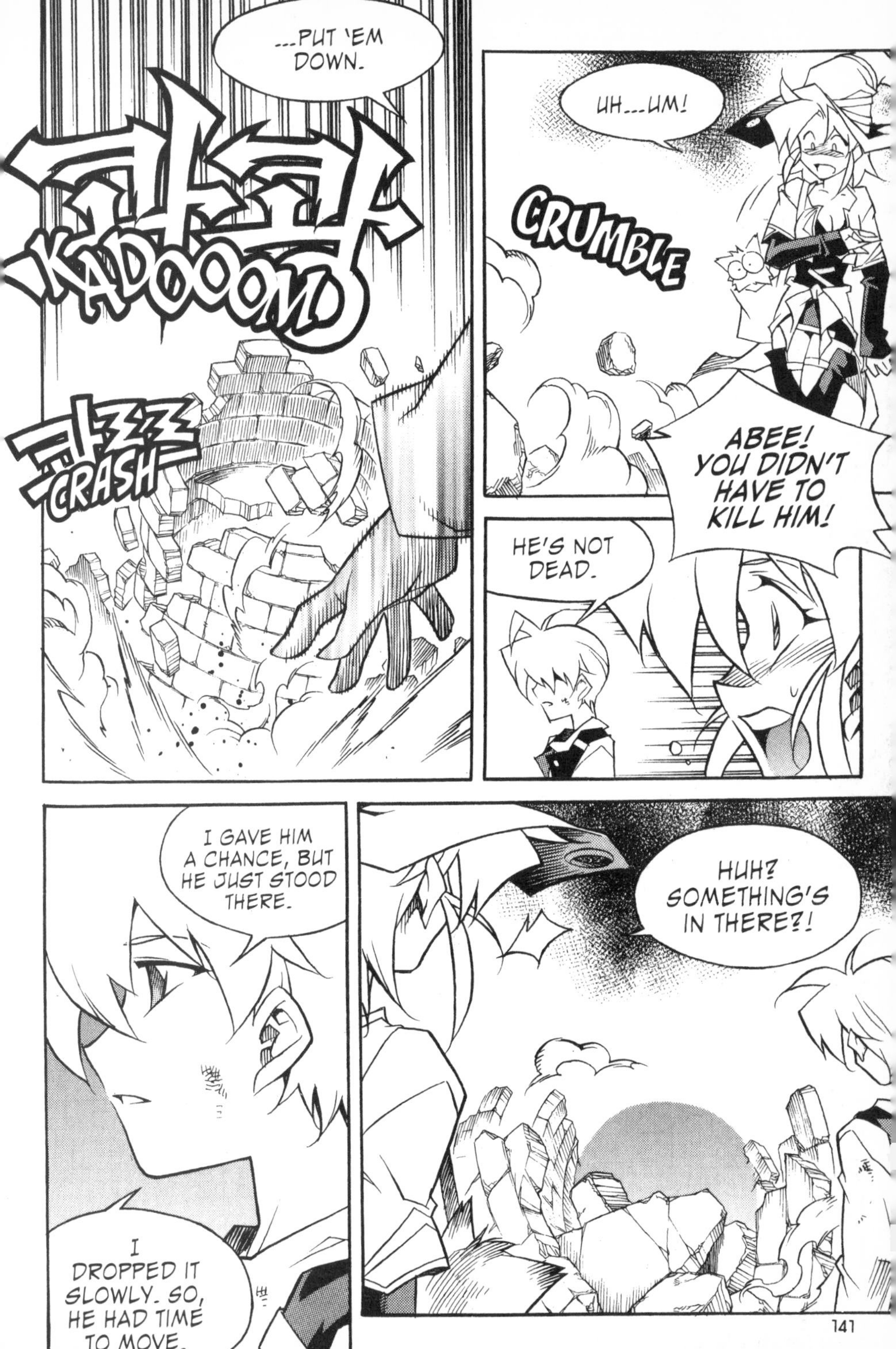
...PUT 'EM DOWN.
KADOOOM
CRASH
UH...UM!
CRUMBLE
ABEE! YOU DIDN'T HAVE TO KILL HIM!
HE'S NOT DEAD.
I GAVE HIM A CHANCE, BUT HE JUST STOOD THERE.
I DROPPED IT SLOWLY. SO, HE HAD TIME TO MOVE.
HUH? SOMETHING'S IN THERE?!

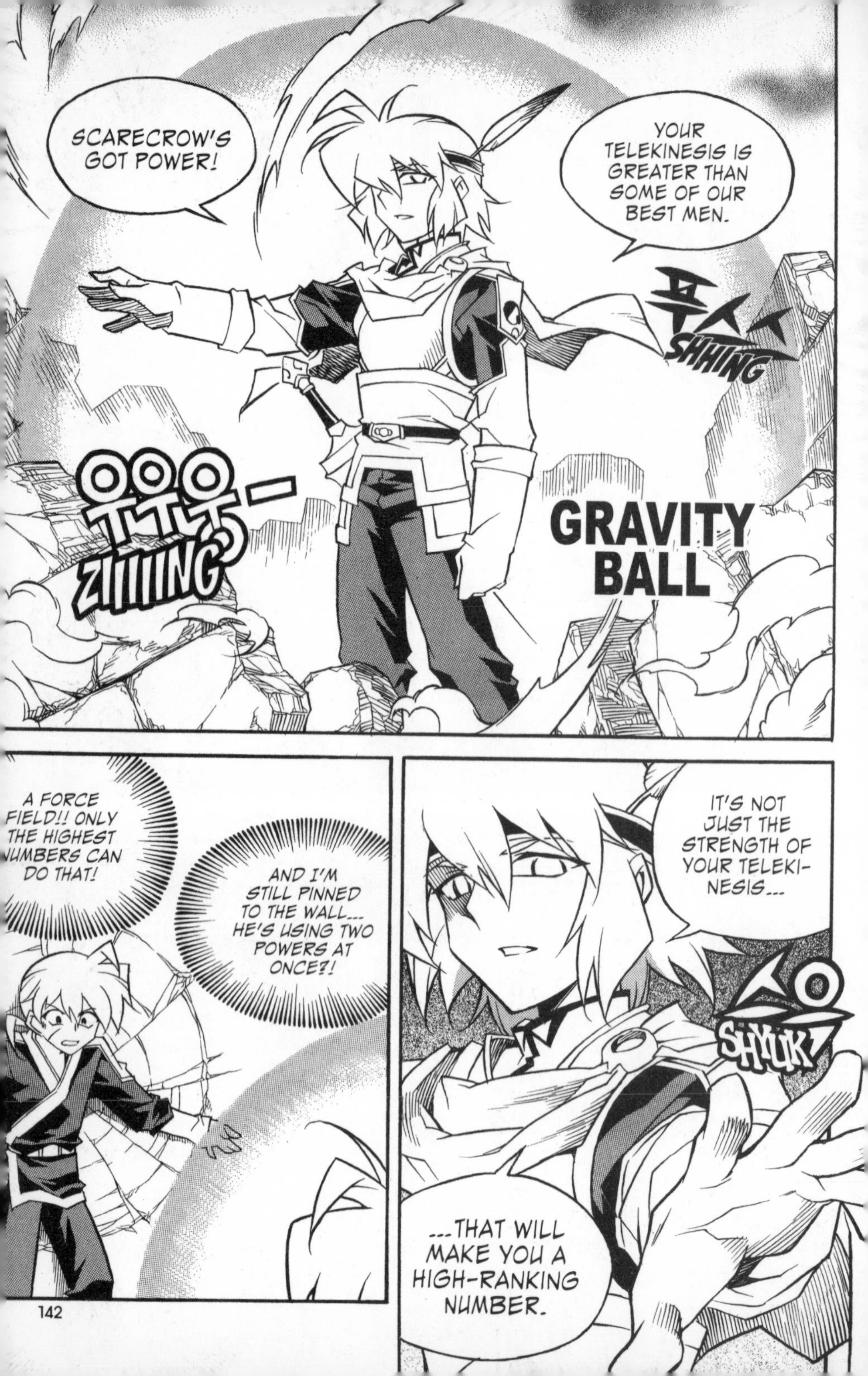
SCARECROW'S GOT POWER!
YOUR TELEKINESIS IS GREATER THAN SOME OF OUR BEST MEN.
SHHING
ZIIIIING
GRAVITY BALL
A FORCE FIELD!! ONLY THE HIGHEST NUMBERS CAN DO THAT!
AND I'M STILL PINNED TO THE WALL... HE'S USING TWO POWERS AT ONCE?!
IT'S NOT JUST THE STRENGTH OF YOUR TELEKI-NESIS...
SHYUK
...THAT WILL MAKE YOU A HIGH-RANKING NUMBER.

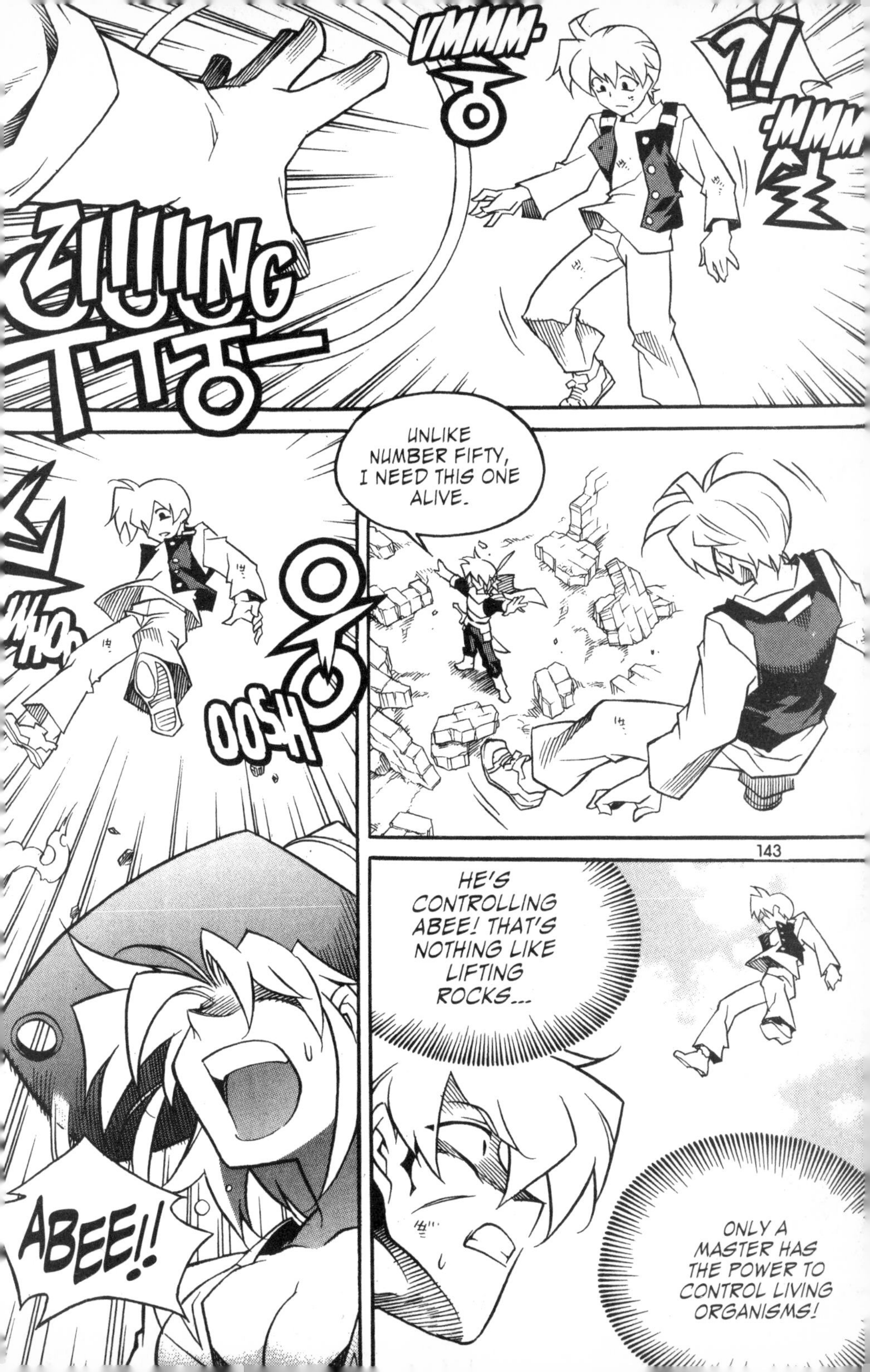

ZIIIING
VMMM-
?!
-MMM
WHO
OOSH
UNLIKE NUMBER FIFTY, I NEED THIS ONE ALIVE.
ABEE!!
HE'S CONTROLLING ABEE! THAT'S NOTHING LIKE LIFTING ROCKS...
ONLY A MASTER HAS THE POWER TO CONTROL LIVING ORGANISMS!

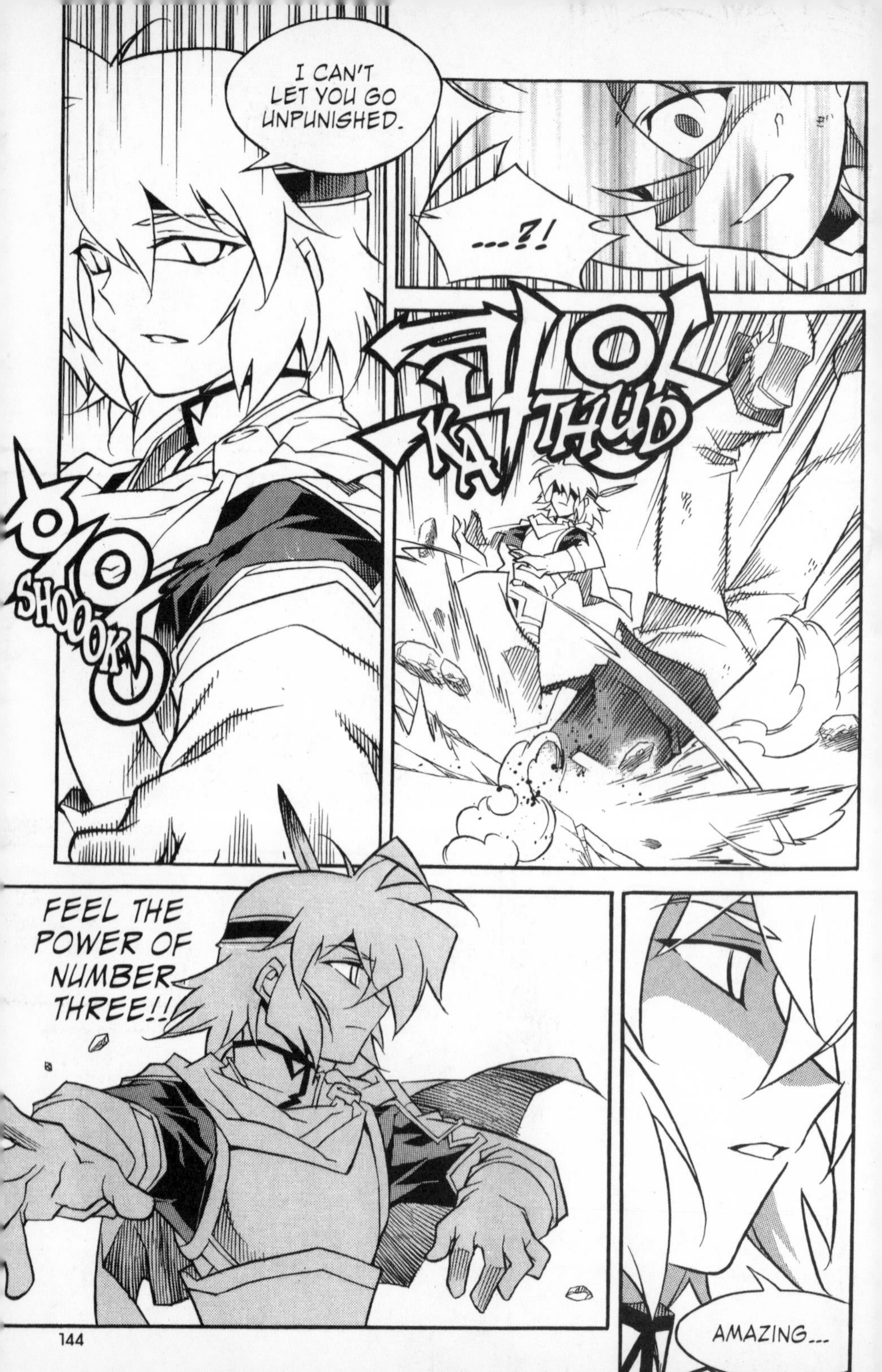
I CAN'T LET YOU GO UNPUNISHED.
...?!
KA THUD
SHOOOOK
FEEL THE POWER OF NUMBER THREE!!
AMAZING...

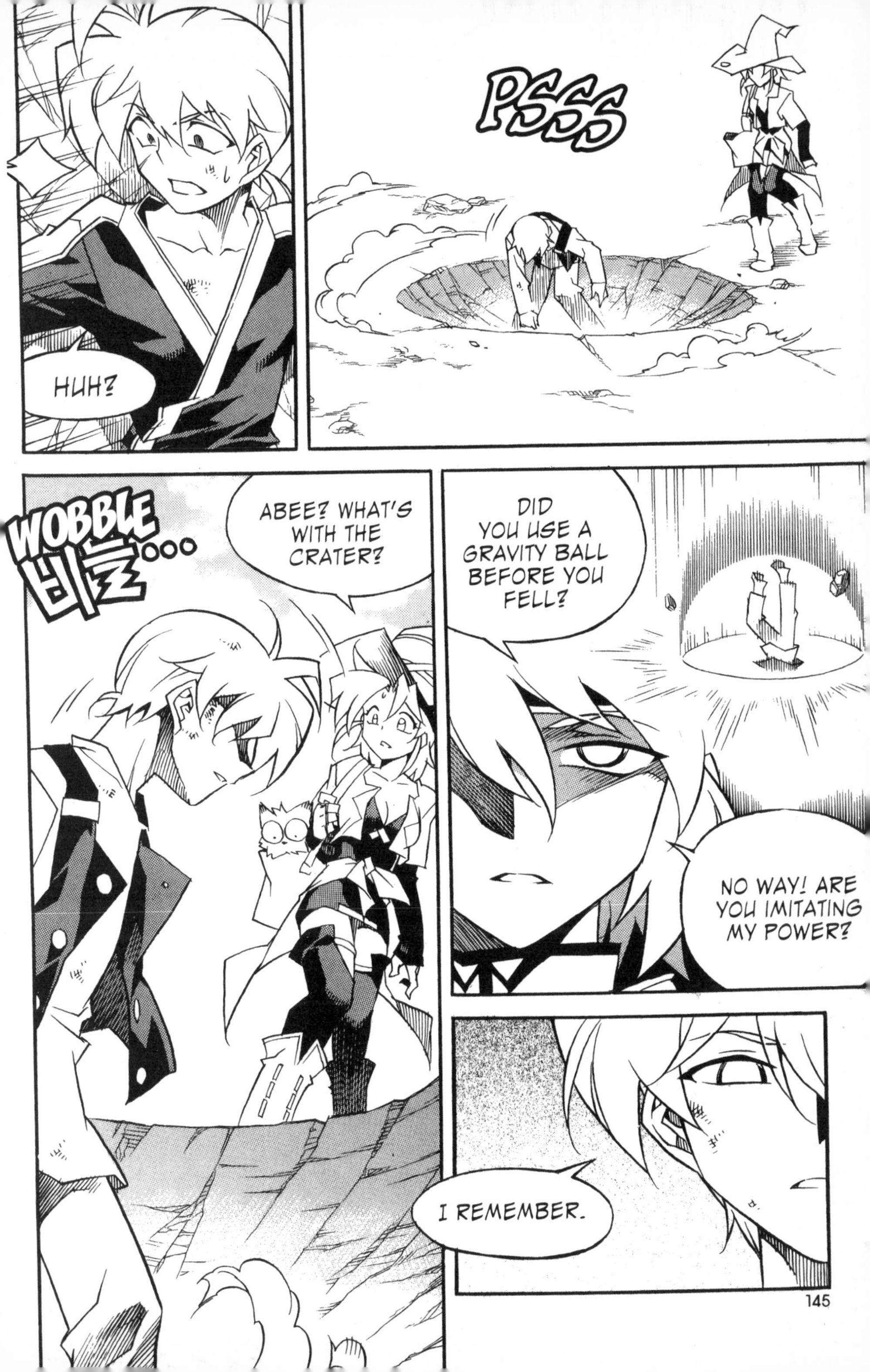
HUH?
PSSS
WOBBLE
비틀
ABEE? WHAT'S WITH THE CRATER?
DID YOU USE A GRAVITY BALL BEFORE YOU FELL?
NO WAY! ARE YOU IMITATING MY POWER?
I REMEMBER.

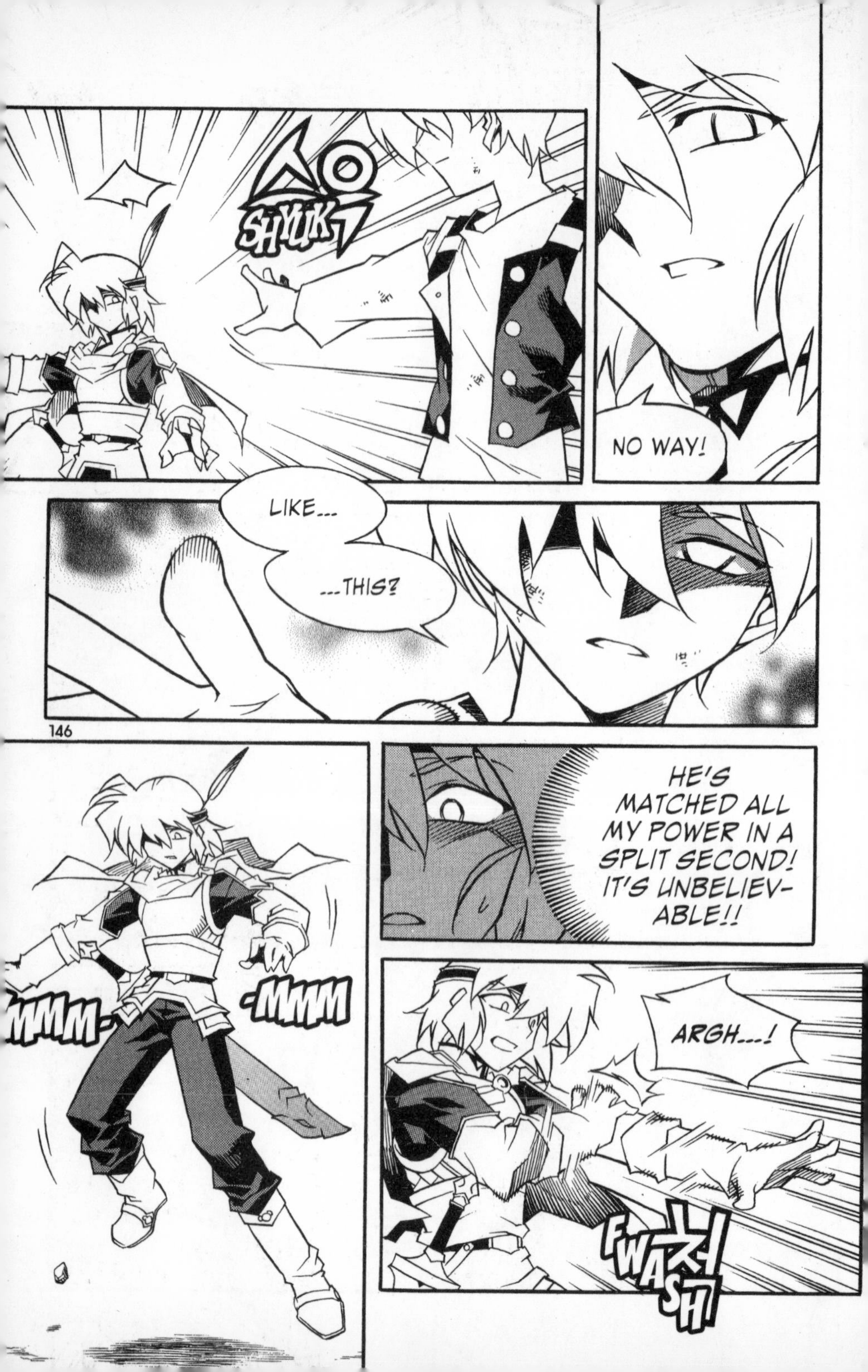
SHYUK
NO WAY!
LIKE...
...THIS?
MMMM-
-MMM
HE'S MATCHED ALL MY POWER IN A SPLIT SECOND! IT'S UNBELIEV-ABLE!!
ARGH...!
FWASH

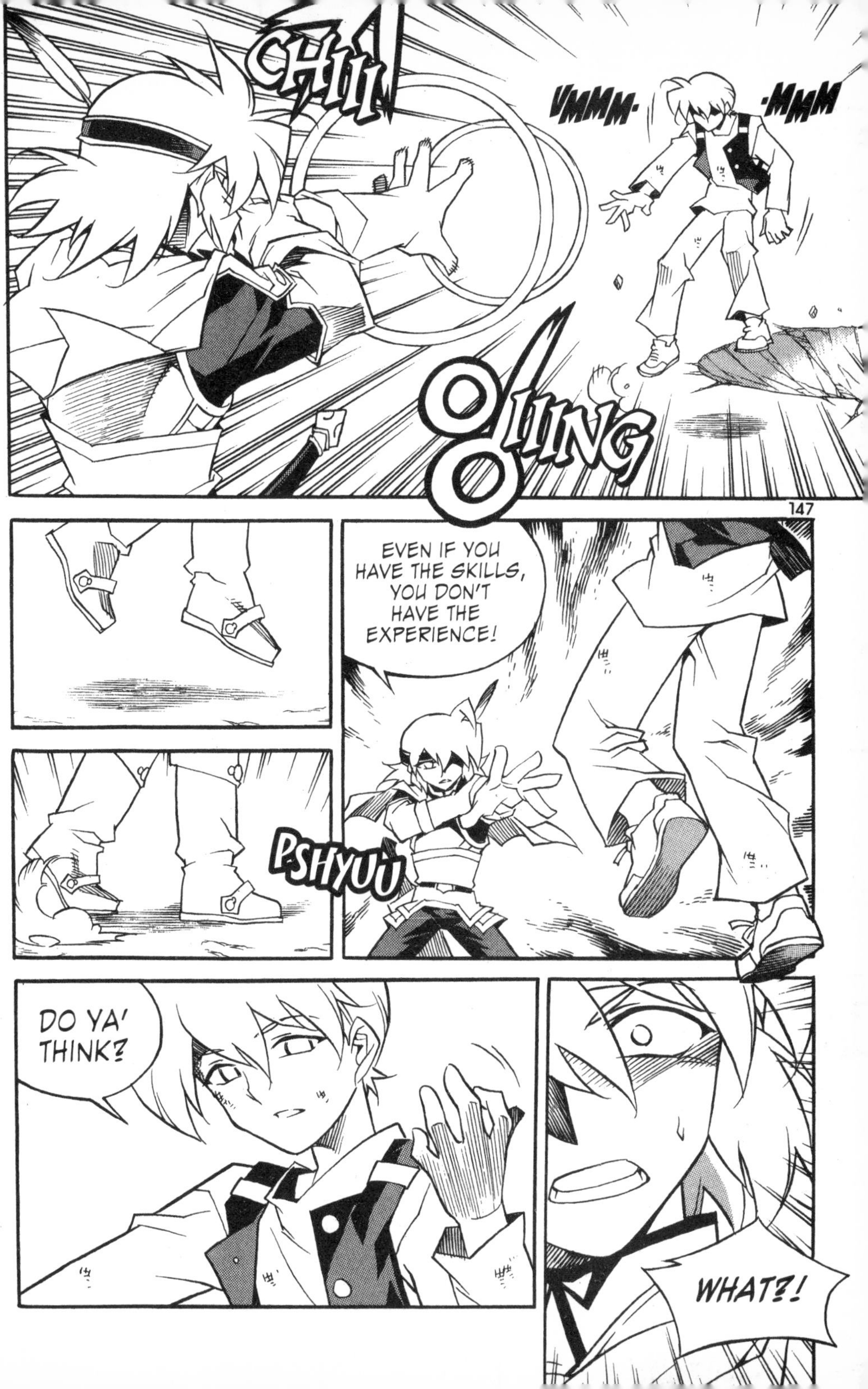
CHII
UMMM-
-MMM
GIIING
EVEN IF YOU HAVE THE SKILLS, YOU DON'T HAVE THE EXPERIENCE!
PSHYUU
DO YA' THINK?
WHAT?!

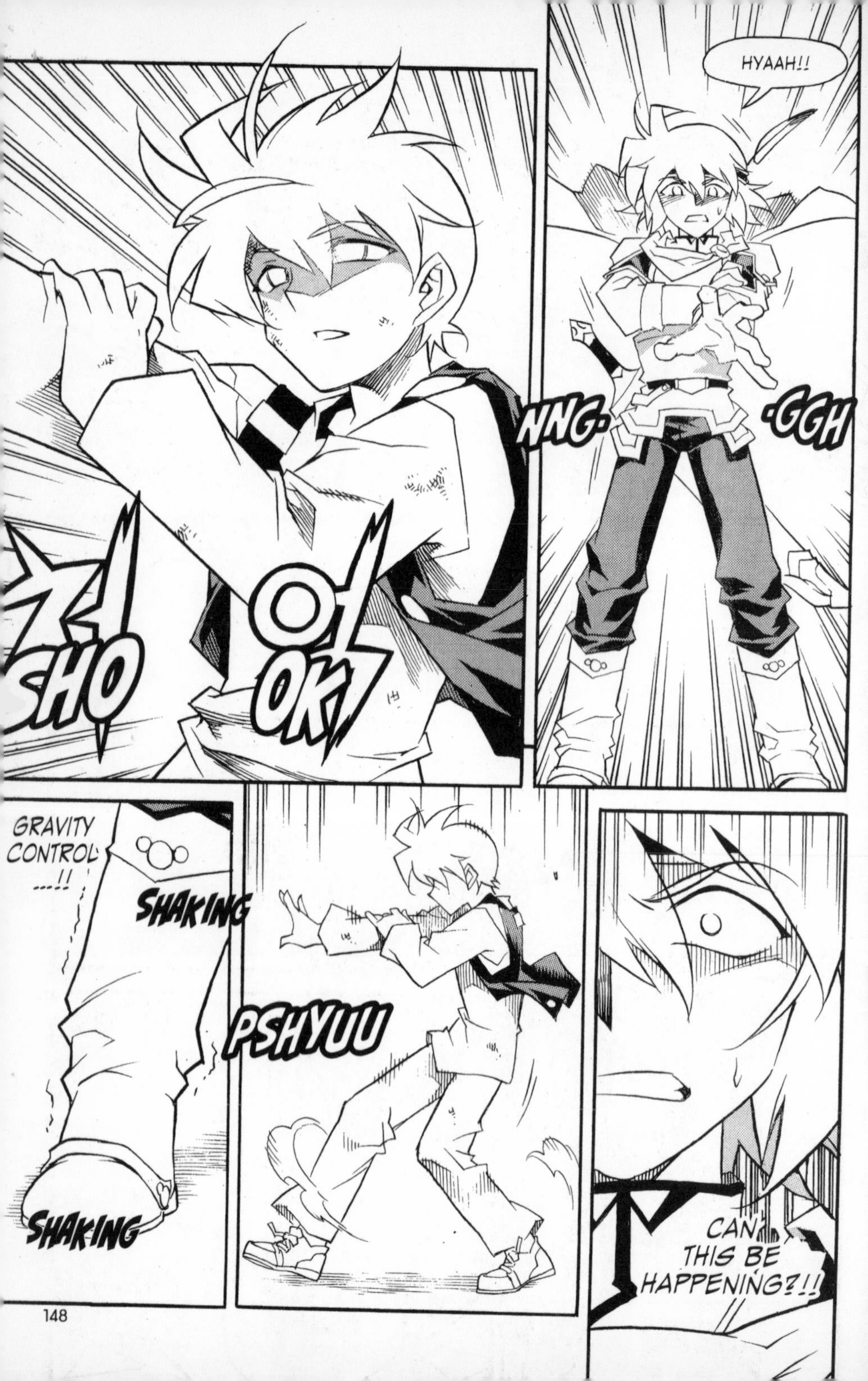
SHO
OK
HYAAH!!
NNG-
-GGH
GRAVITY CONTROL
-----!!
SHAKING
SHAKING
PSHYUU
CAN THIS BE HAPPENING?!!

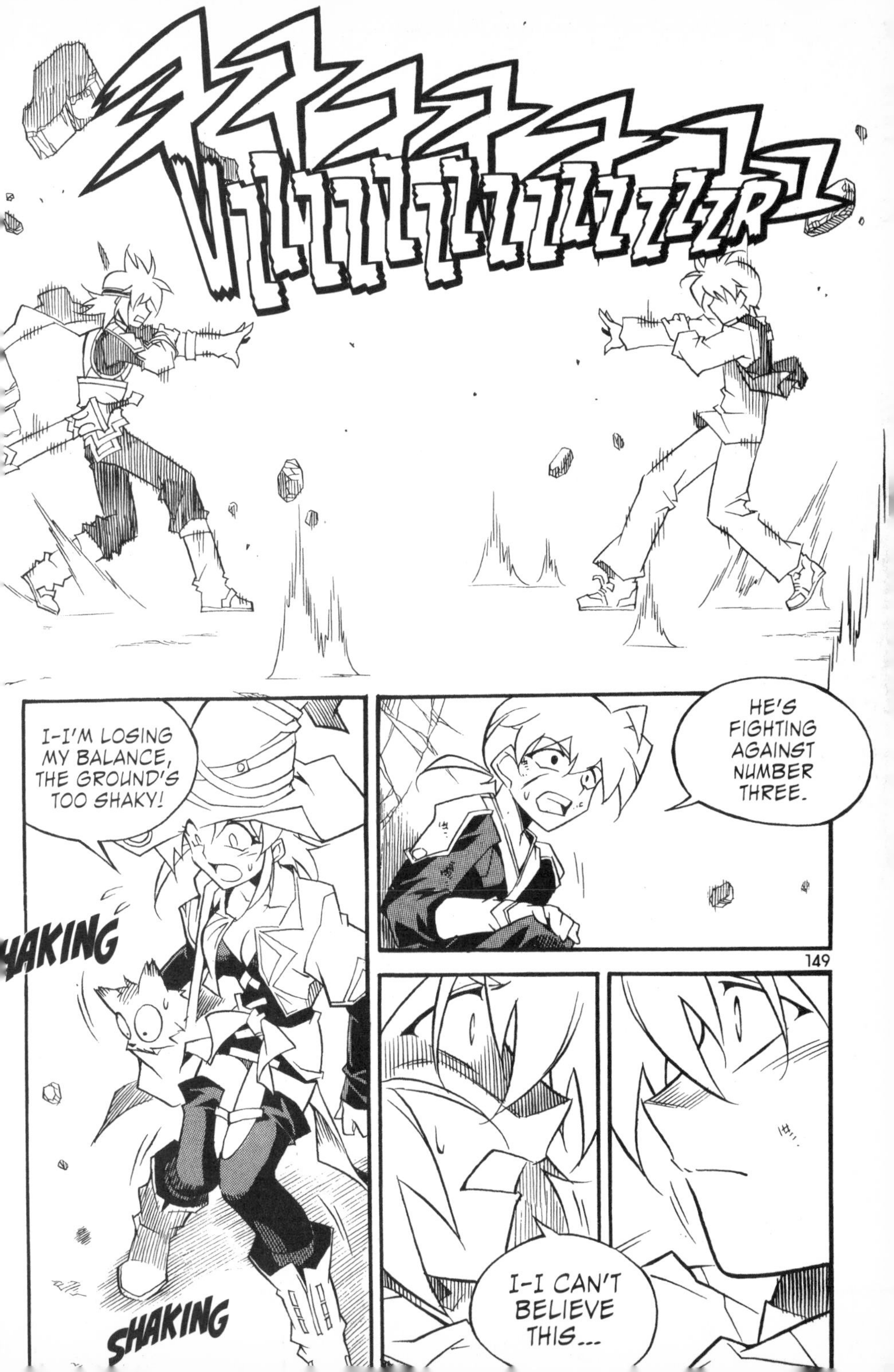
I-I'M LOSING MY BALANCE, THE GROUND'S TOO SHAKY!
SHAKING
SHAKING
HE'S FIGHTING AGAINST NUMBER THREE.
I-I CAN'T BELIEVE THIS...

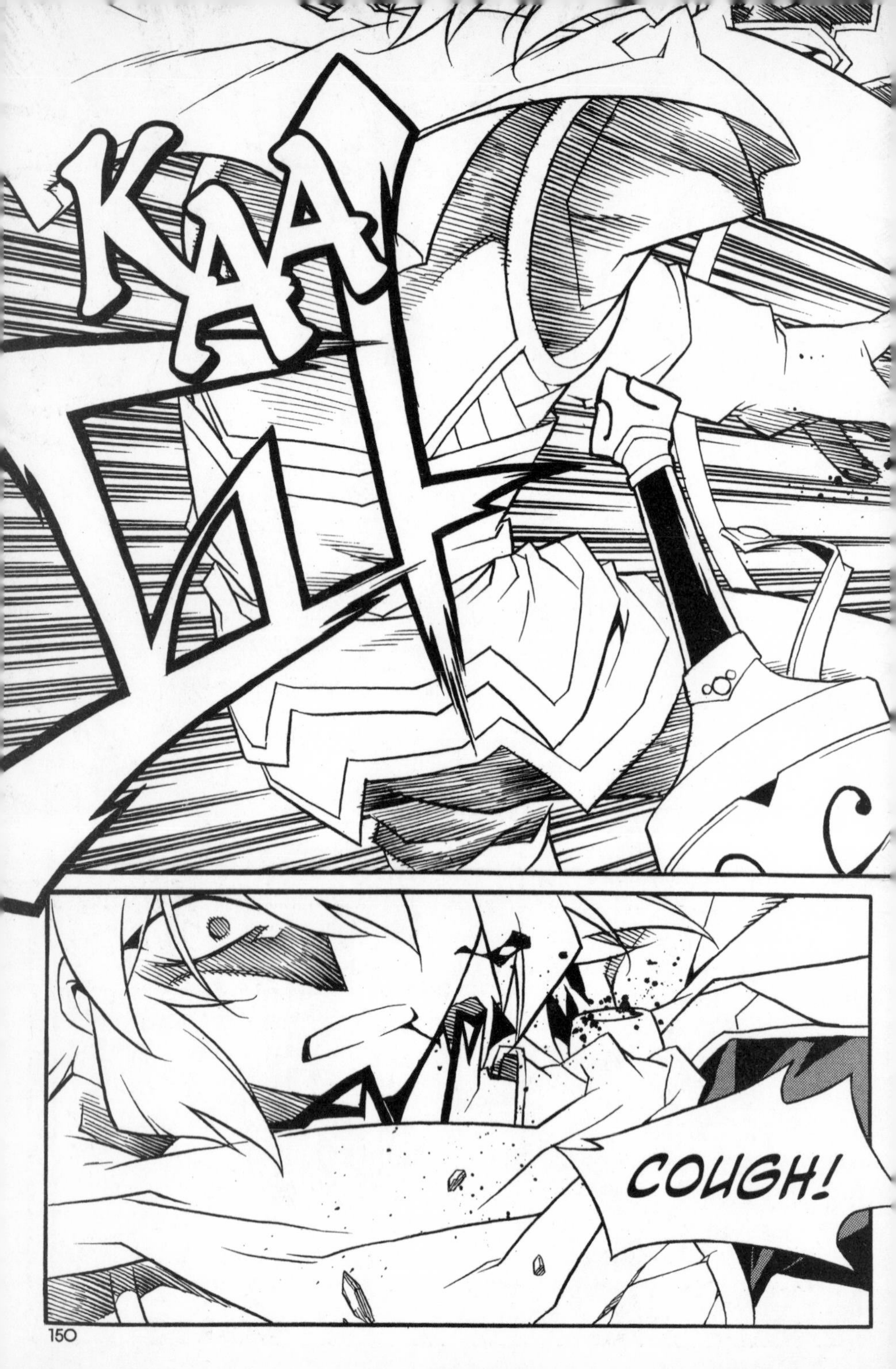
KA-
CHUNK
COUGH!

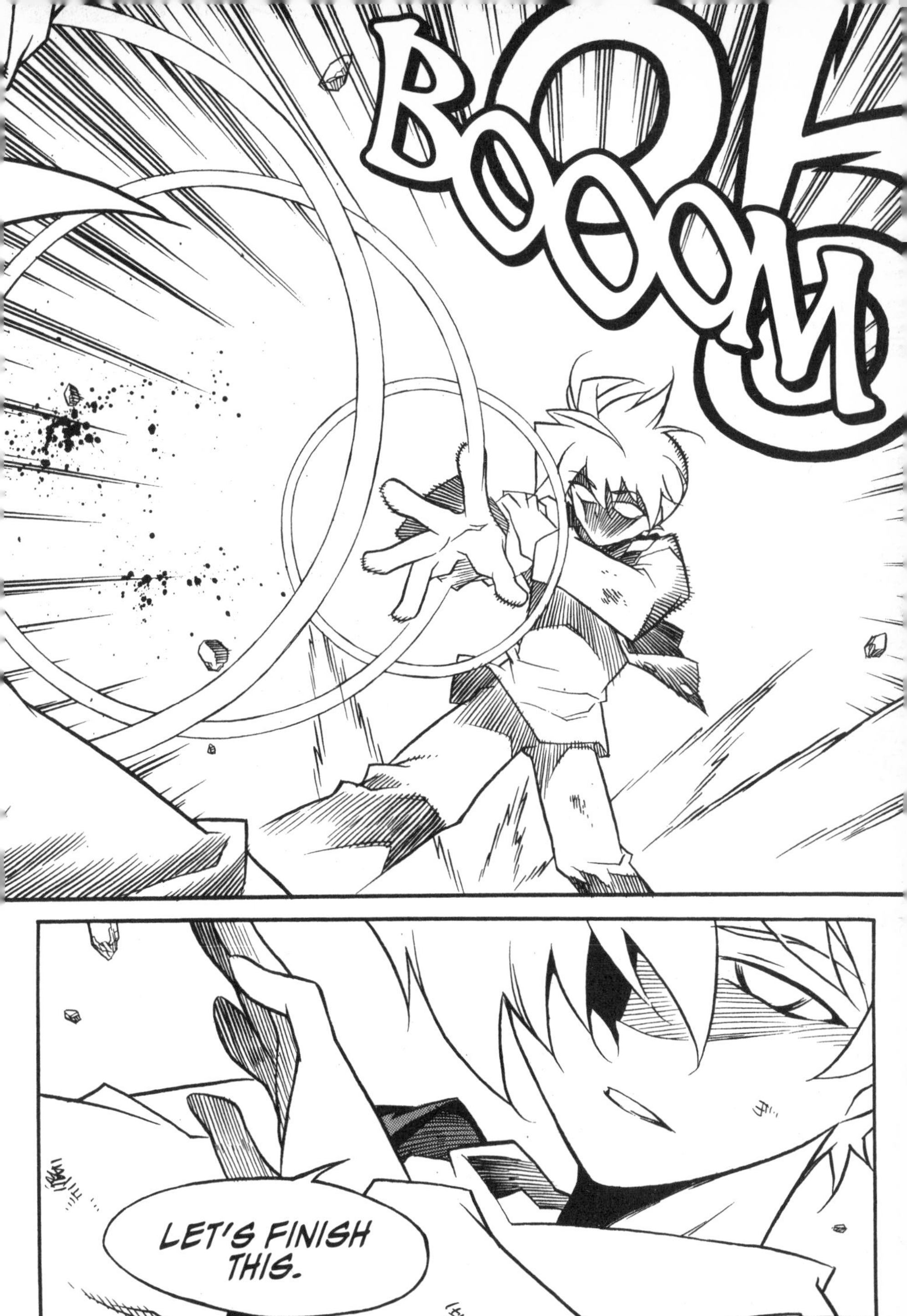
BOOOOOM
LET'S FINISH THIS.

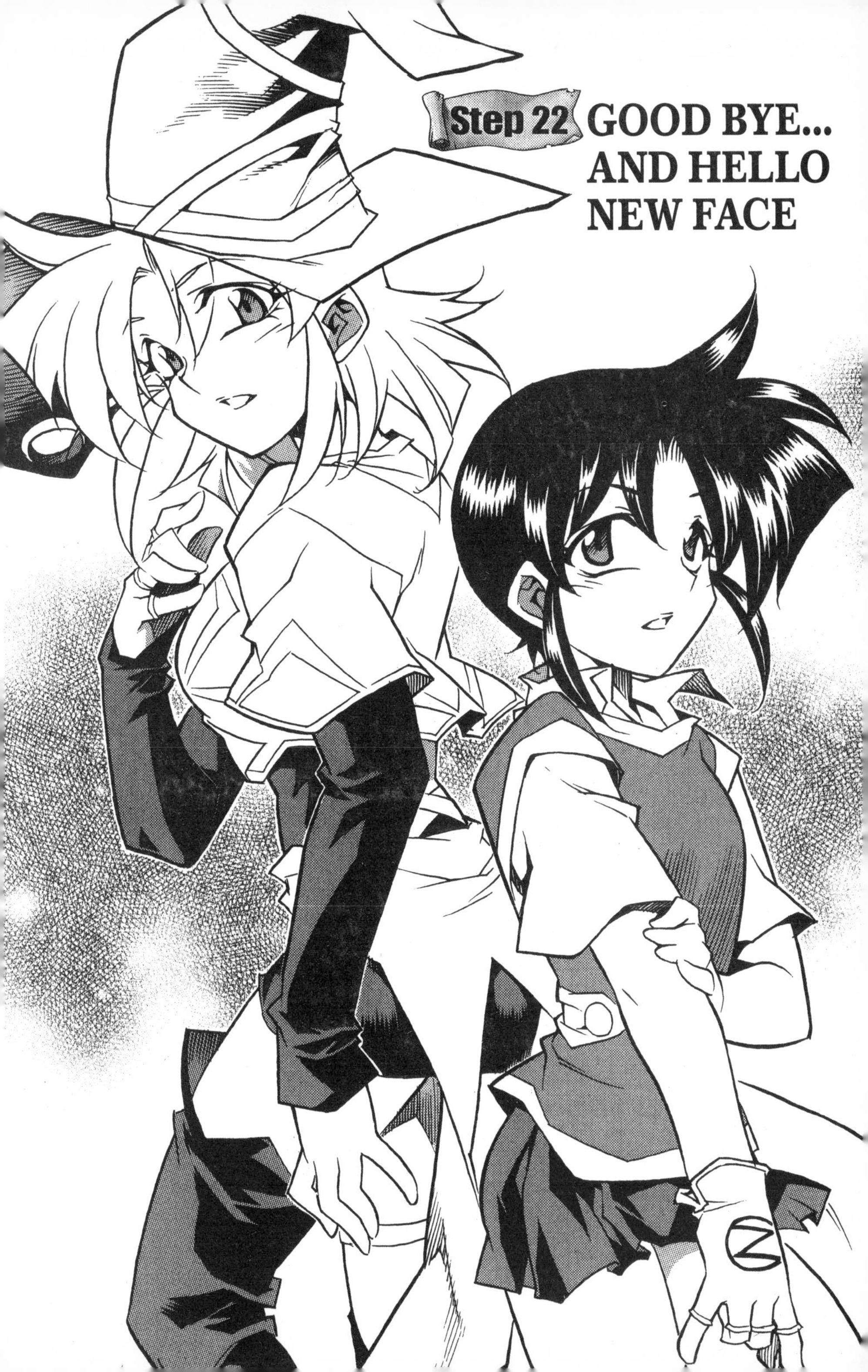
Step 22
GOOD BYE...
AND HELLO
NEW FACE

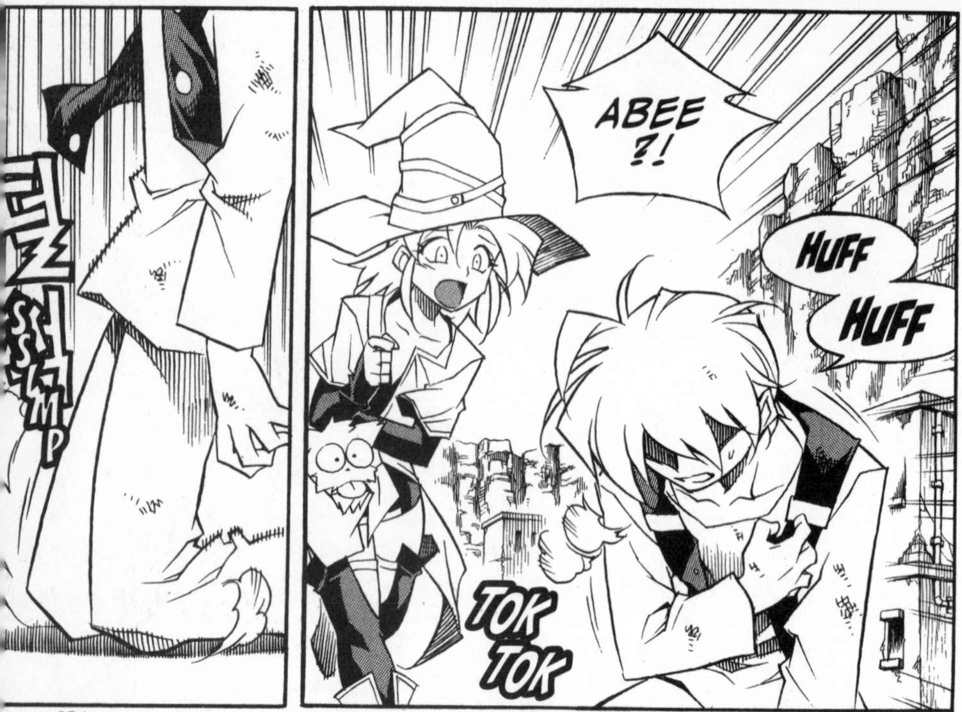
SSLUMP
ABEE ?!
TOK TOK
HUFF HUFF

154

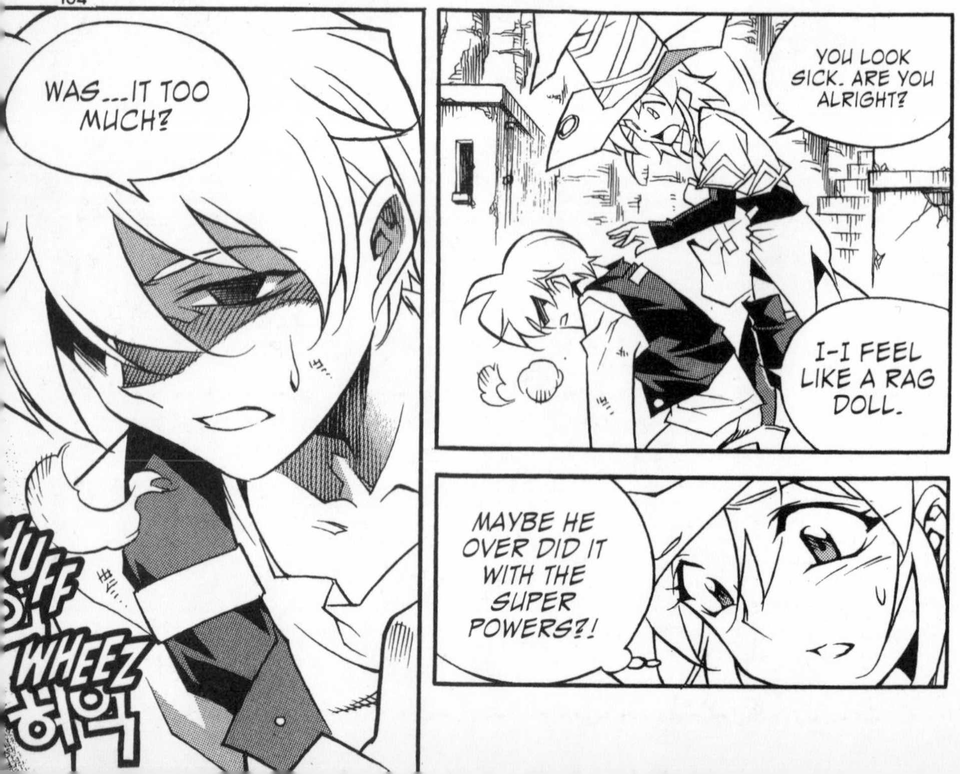
WAS...IT TOO MUCH?
HUFF
WHEEZ
허억
YOU LOOK SICK. ARE YOU ALRIGHT?
I-I FEEL LIKE A RAG DOLL.
MAYBE HE OVER DID IT WITH THE SUPER POWERS?!

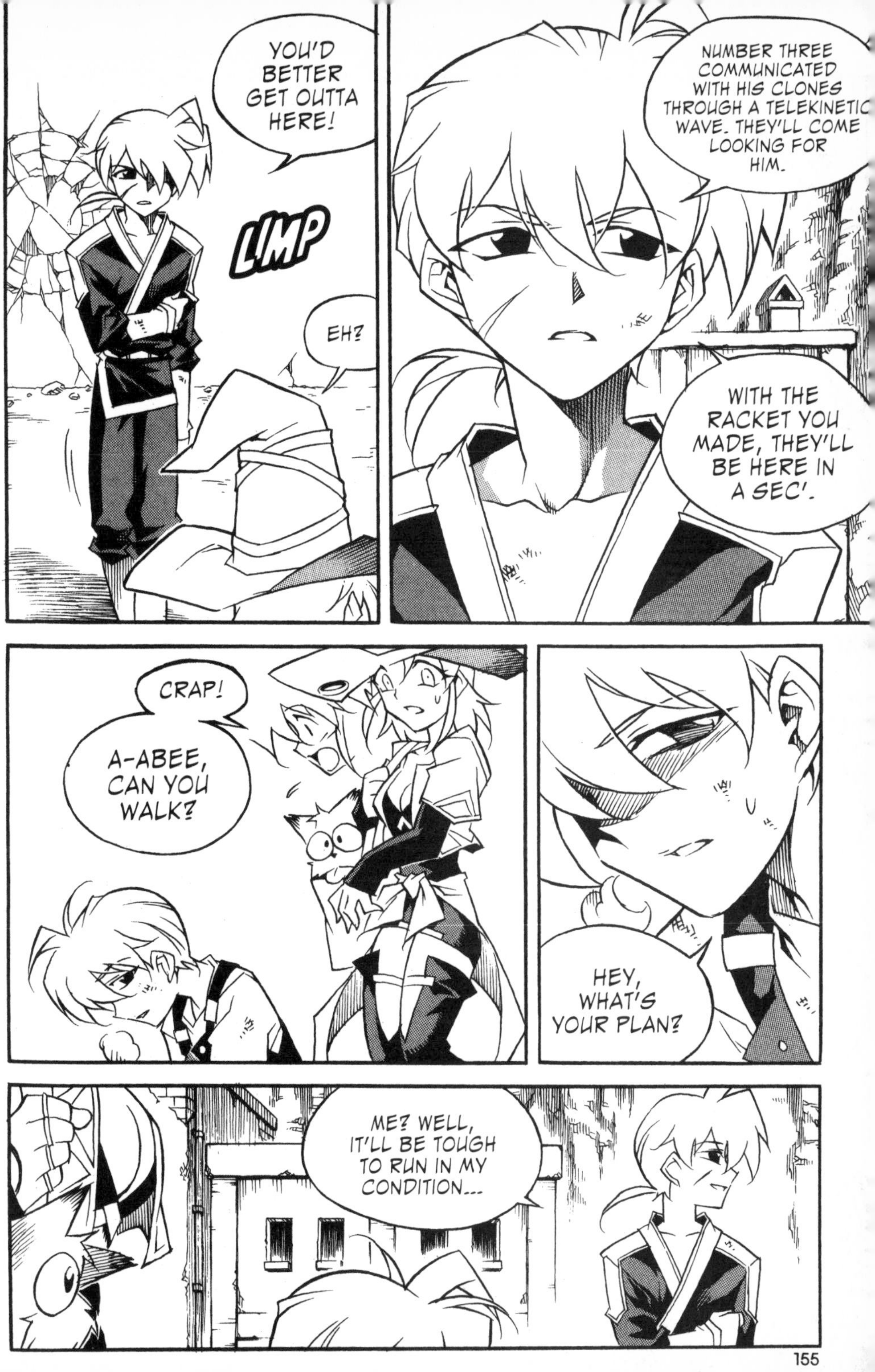
YOU'D BETTER GET OUTTA HERE!
LIMP
EH?
NUMBER THREE COMMUNICATED WITH HIS CLONES THROUGH A TELEKINETIC WAVE. THEY'LL COME LOOKING FOR HIM.
WITH THE RACKET YOU MADE, THEY'LL BE HERE IN A SEC'.
CRAP!
A-ABEE, CAN YOU WALK?
HEY, WHAT'S YOUR PLAN?
ME? WELL, IT'LL BE TOUGH TO RUN IN MY CONDITION...

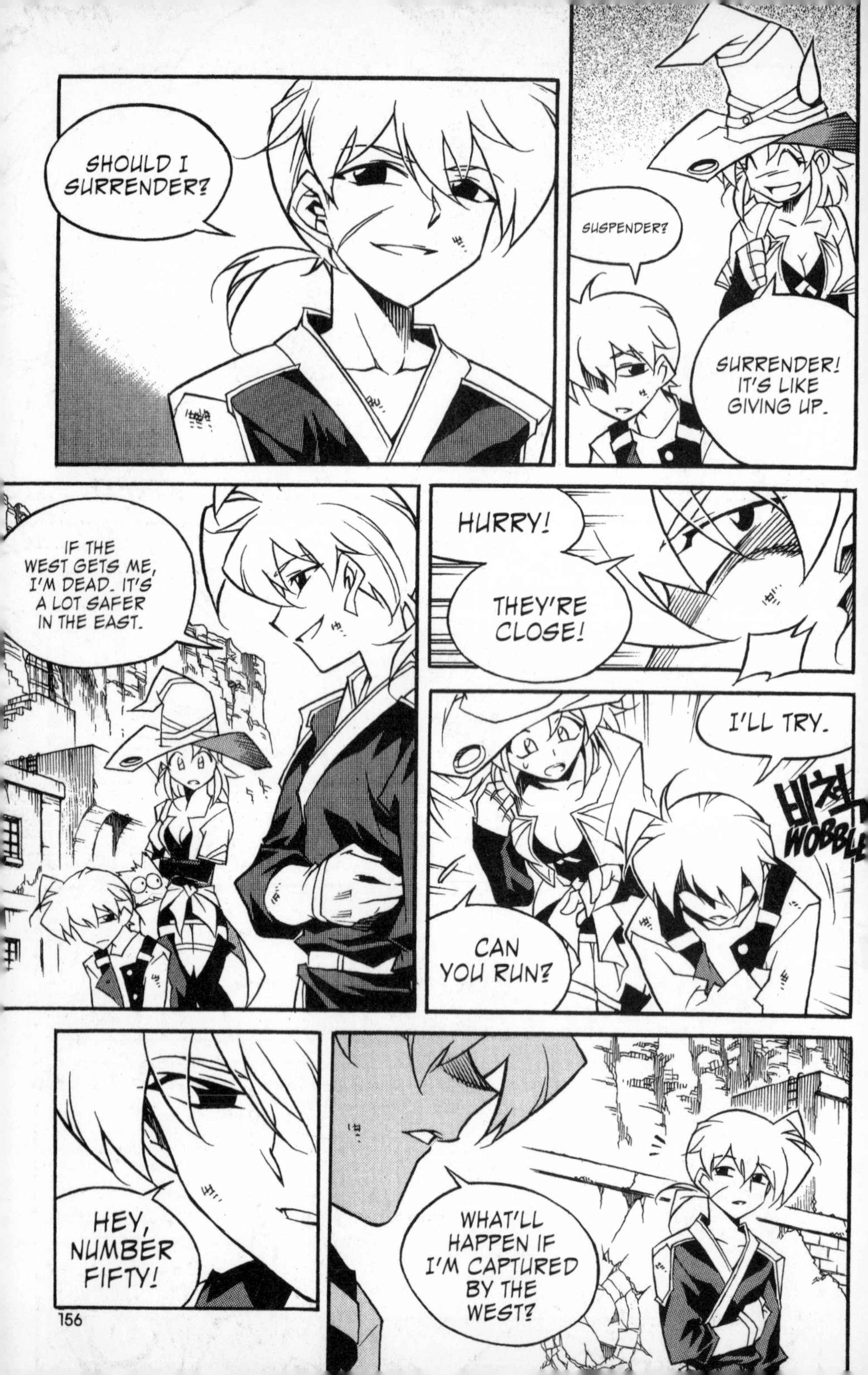
SHOULD I SURRENDER?
SUSPENDER?
SURRENDER! IT'S LIKE GIVING UP.
IF THE WEST GETS ME, I'M DEAD. IT'S A LOT SAFER IN THE EAST.
HURRY!
THEY'RE CLOSE!
I'LL TRY.
비척
WOBBLE
CAN YOU RUN?
HEY, NUMBER FIFTY!
WHAT'LL HAPPEN IF I'M CAPTURED BY THE WEST?

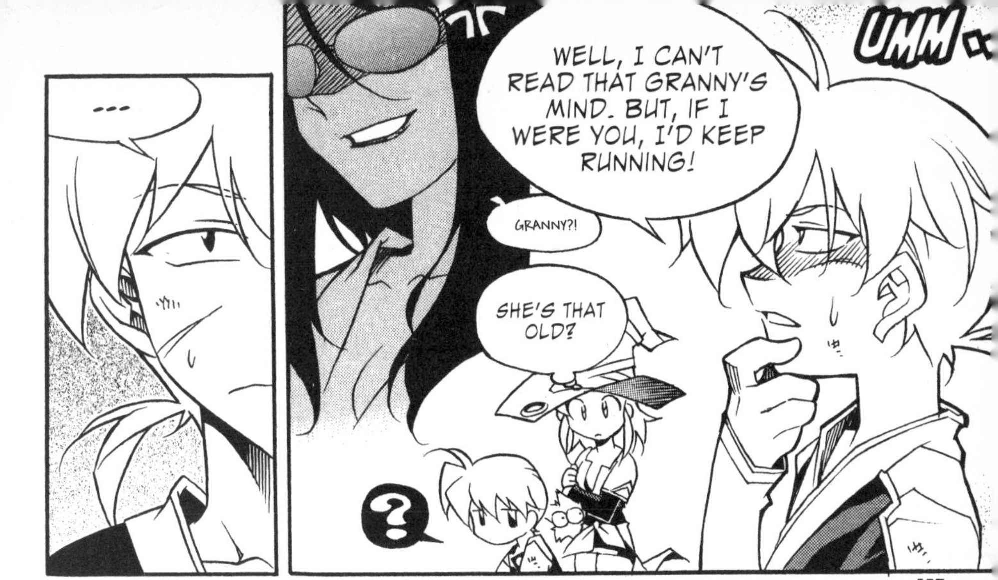
...
WELL, I CAN'T READ THAT GRANNY'S MIND. BUT, IF I WERE YOU, I'D KEEP RUNNING!
GRANNY?!
SHE'S THAT OLD?
?
UMM

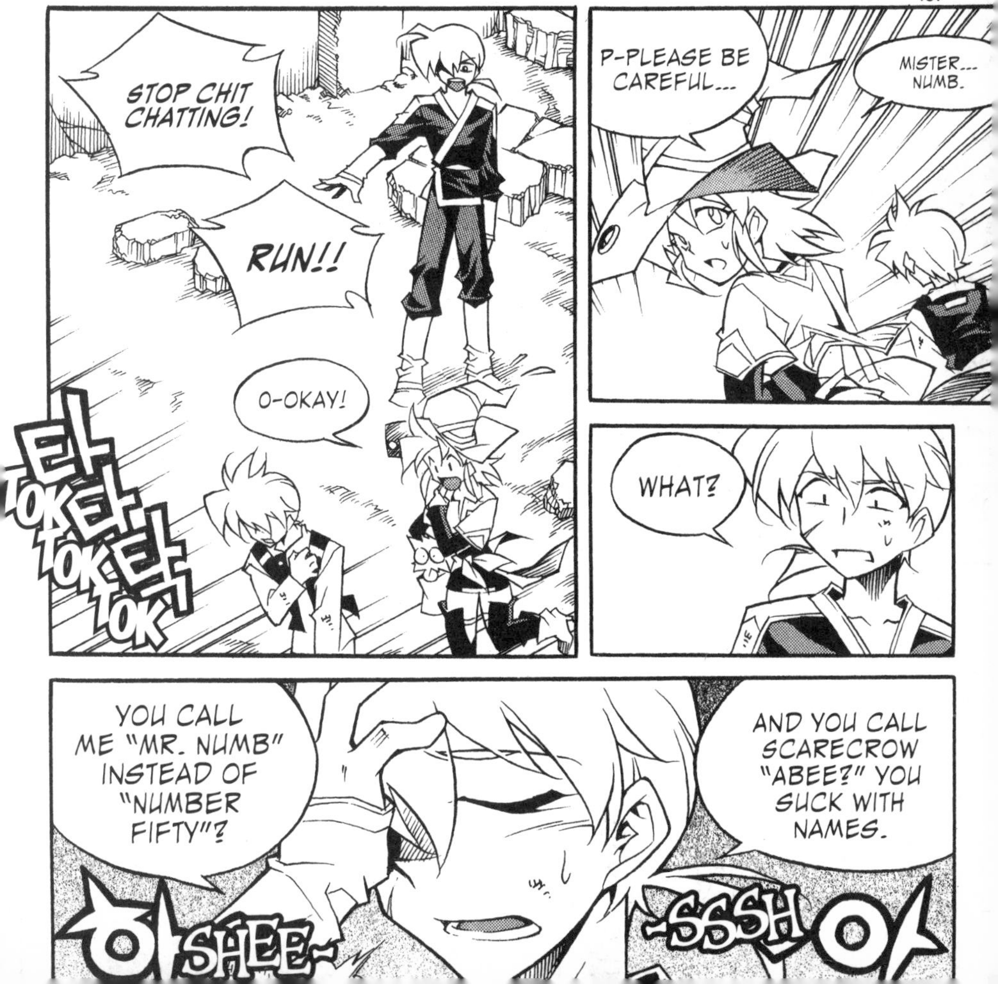
STOP CHIT CHATTING!
RUN!!
O-OKAY!
타 TOK 타 TOK 타 TOK
P-PLEASE BE CAREFUL...
MISTER... NUMB.
WHAT?
YOU CALL ME "MR. NUMB" INSTEAD OF "NUMBER FIFTY"?
AND YOU CALL SCARECROW "ABEE?" YOU SUCK WITH NAMES.
SHEE-
-SSSH

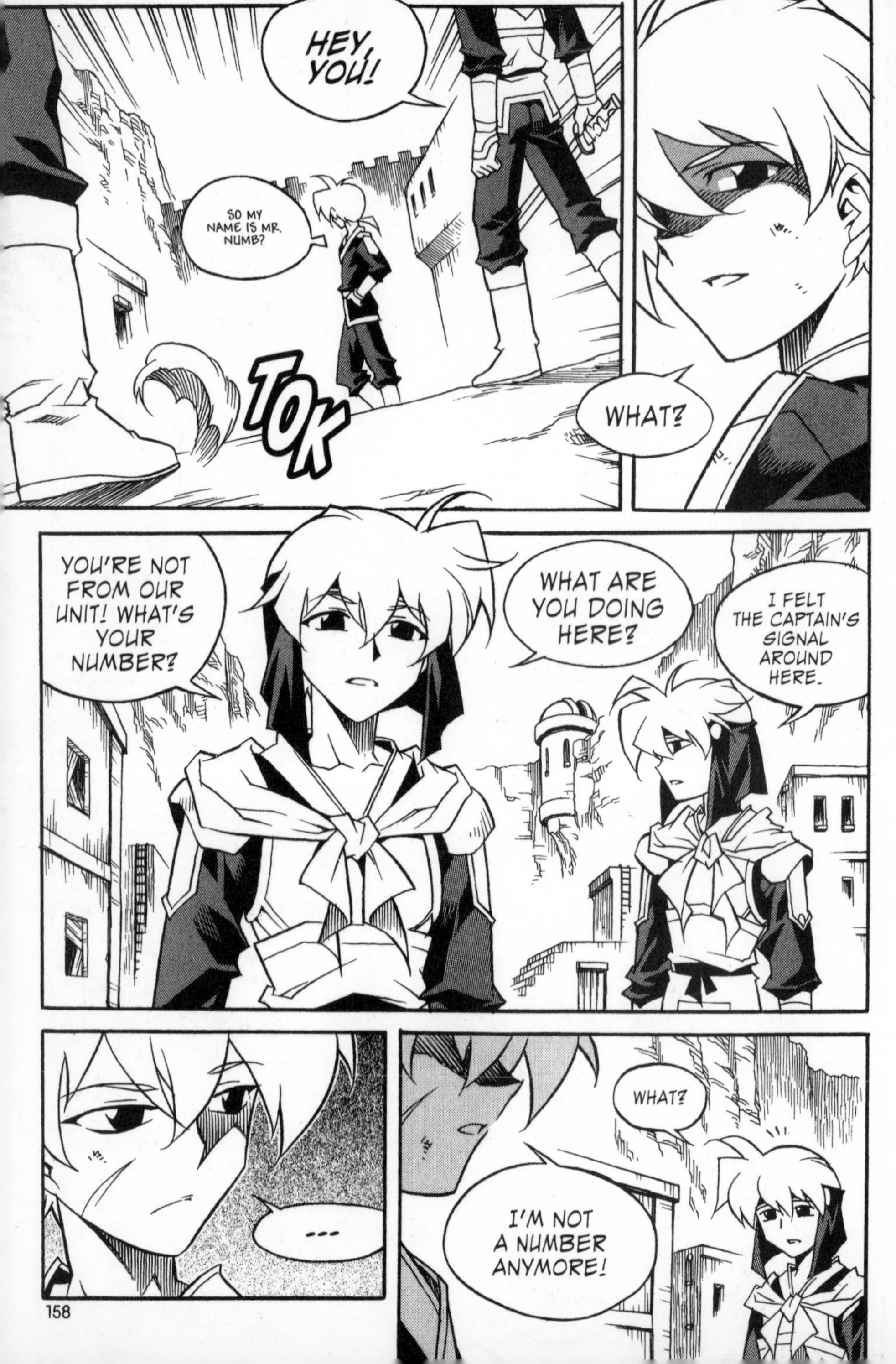

HEY, YOU!
SO MY NAME IS MR. NUMB?
TOK
WHAT?
YOU'RE NOT FROM OUR UNIT! WHAT'S YOUR NUMBER?
WHAT ARE YOU DOING HERE?
I FELT THE CAPTAIN'S SIGNAL AROUND HERE.
...
WHAT?
I'M NOT A NUMBER ANYMORE!

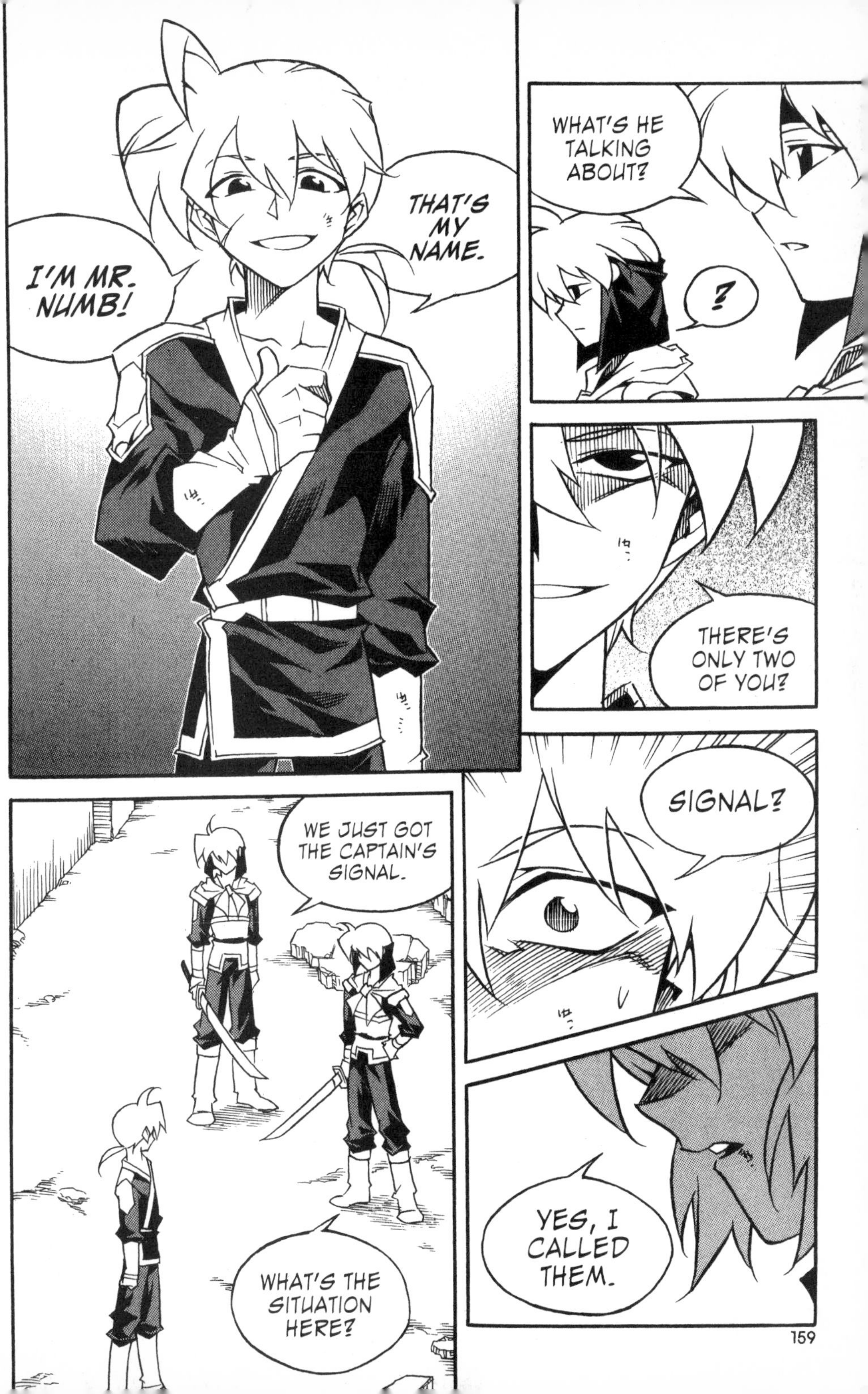
I'M MR. NUMB!
THAT'S MY NAME.
WHAT'S HE TALKING ABOUT?
?
THERE'S ONLY TWO OF YOU?
WE JUST GOT THE CAPTAIN'S SIGNAL.
WHAT'S THE SITUATION HERE?
SIGNAL?
YES, I CALLED THEM.

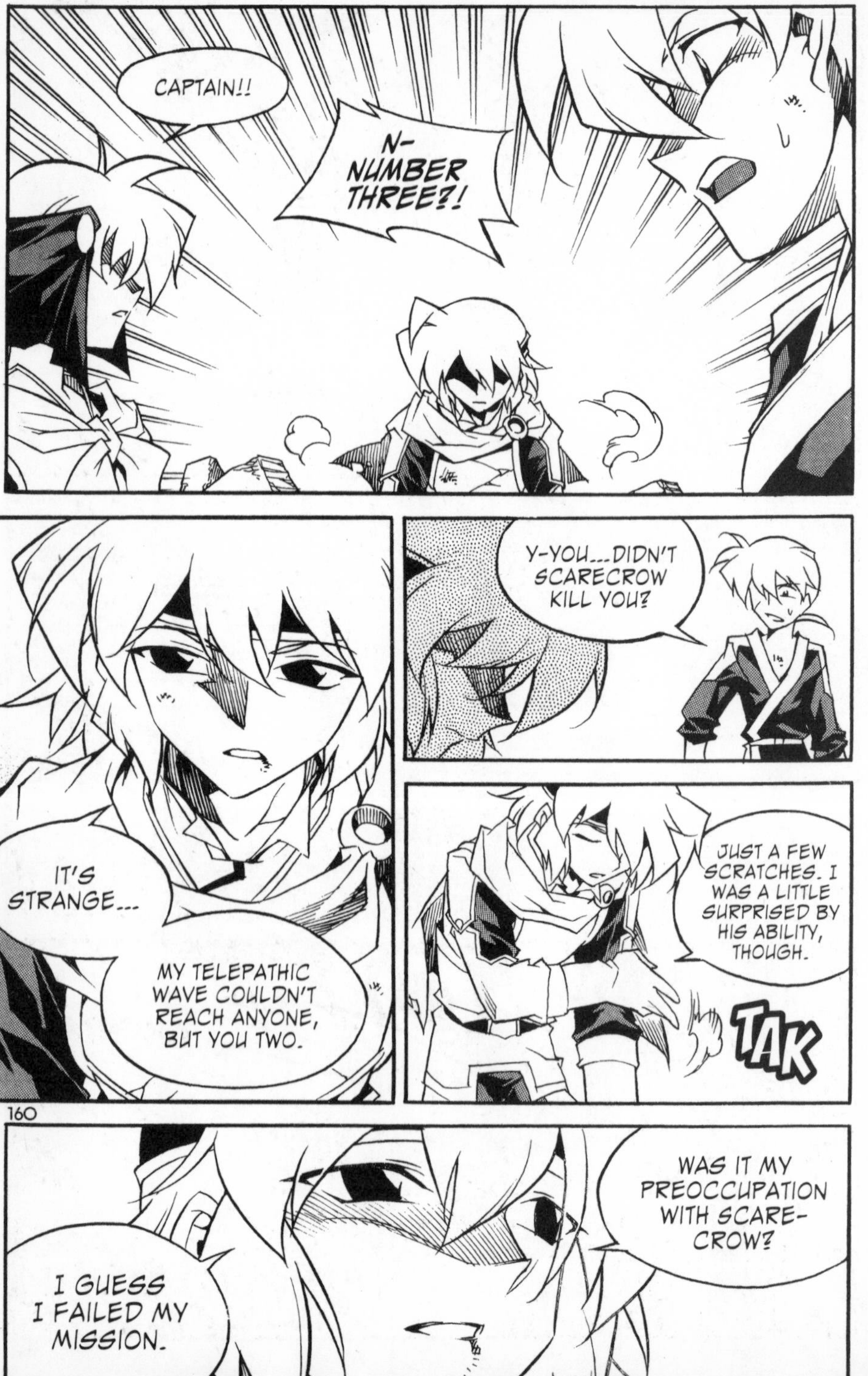
CAPTAIN!!
N-NUMBER THREE?!
IT'S STRANGE...
MY TELEPATHIC WAVE COULDN'T REACH ANYONE, BUT YOU TWO.
Y-YOU...DIDN'T SCARECROW KILL YOU?
JUST A FEW SCRATCHES. I WAS A LITTLE SURPRISED BY HIS ABILITY, THOUGH.
TAK
I GUESS I FAILED MY MISSION.
WAS IT MY PREOCCUPATION WITH SCARE-CROW?

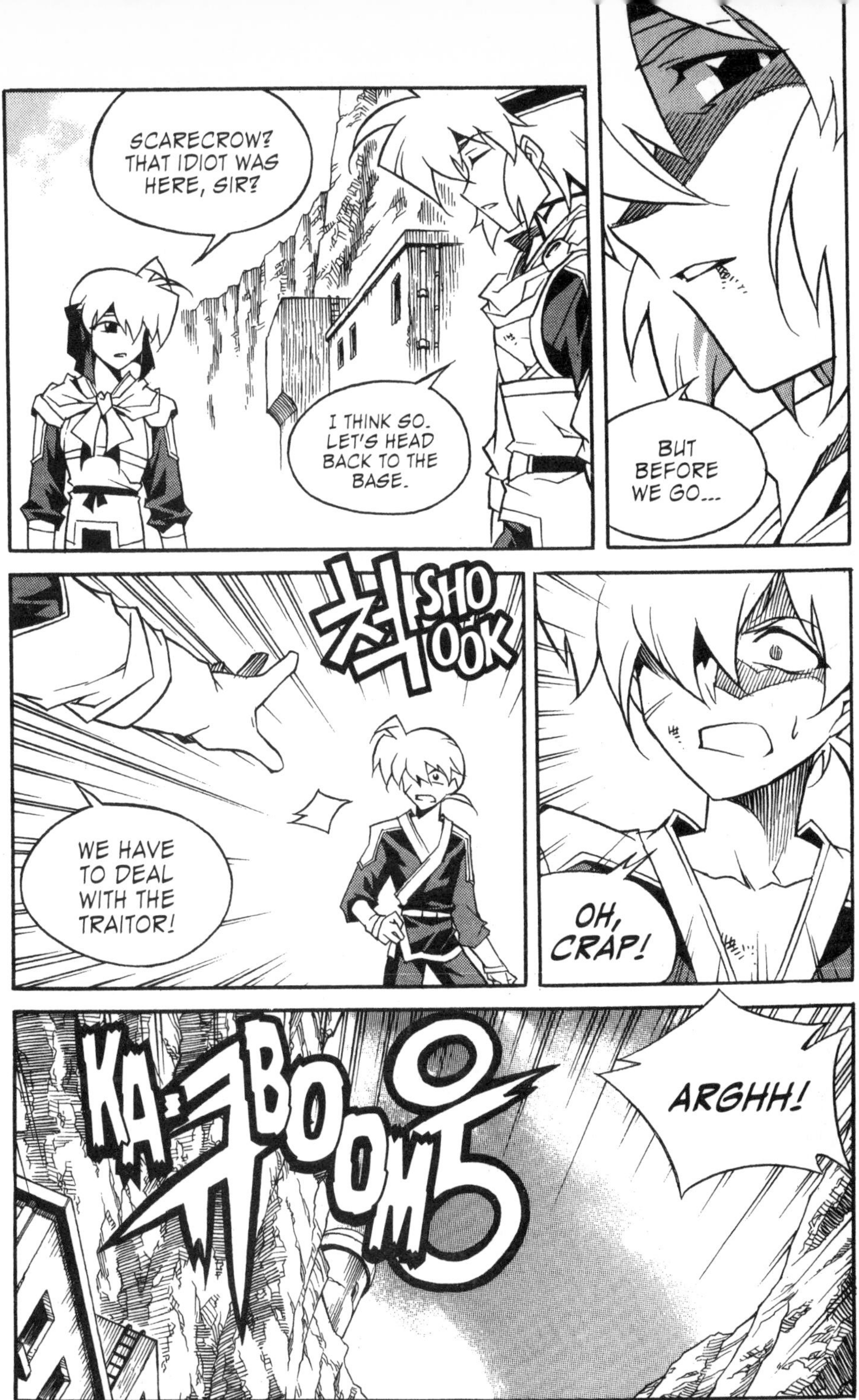
SCARECROW? THAT IDIOT WAS HERE, SIR?
I THINK SO. LET'S HEAD BACK TO THE BASE.
BUT BEFORE WE GO...
SHO OOK
WE HAVE TO DEAL WITH THE TRAITOR!
OH, CRAP!
KA-BOOM
ARGHH!

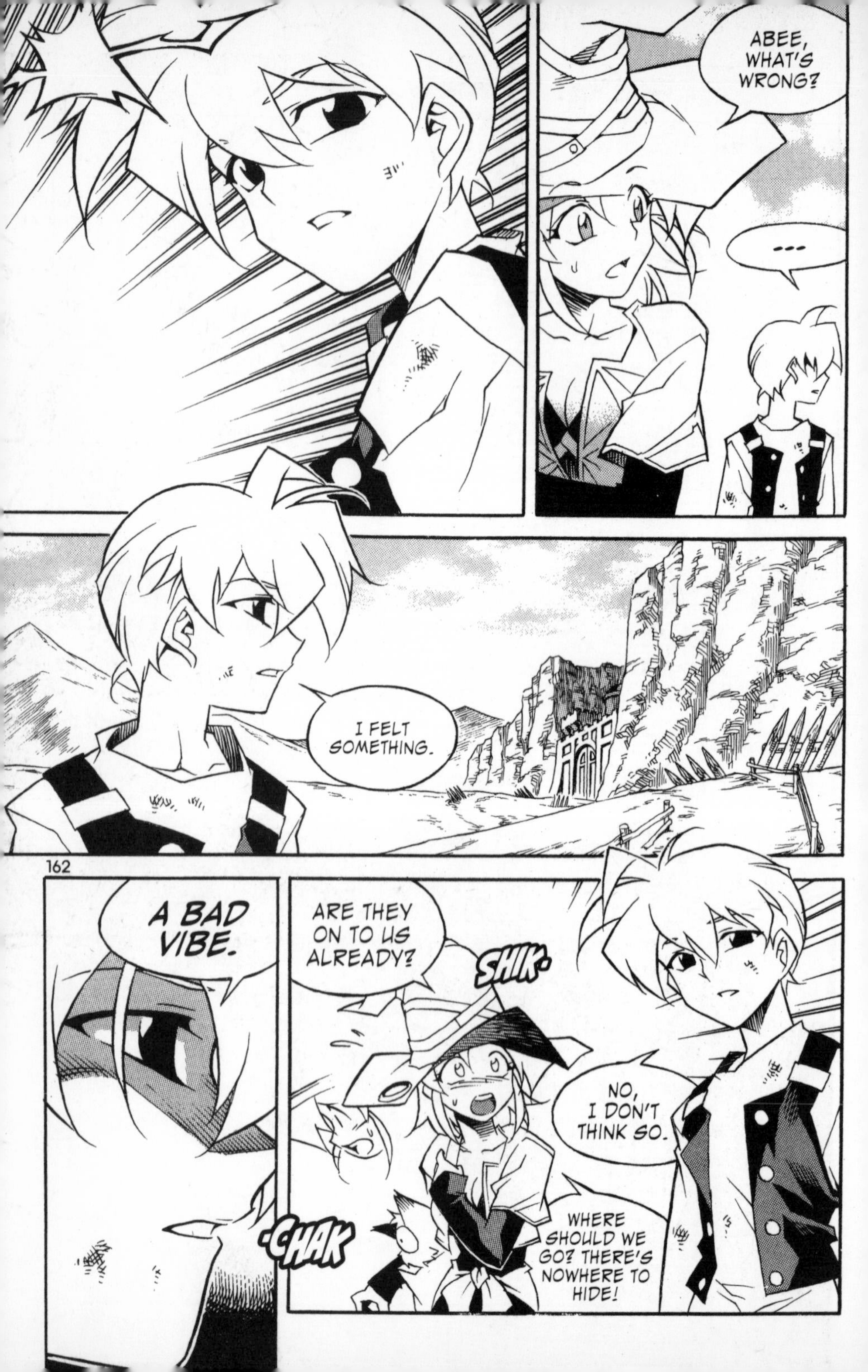
ABEE, WHAT'S WRONG?
...
I FELT SOMETHING.
A BAD VIBE.
ARE THEY ON TO US ALREADY?
SHIK-
NO, I DON'T THINK SO.
-CHAK
WHERE SHOULD WE GO? THERE'S NOWHERE TO HIDE!

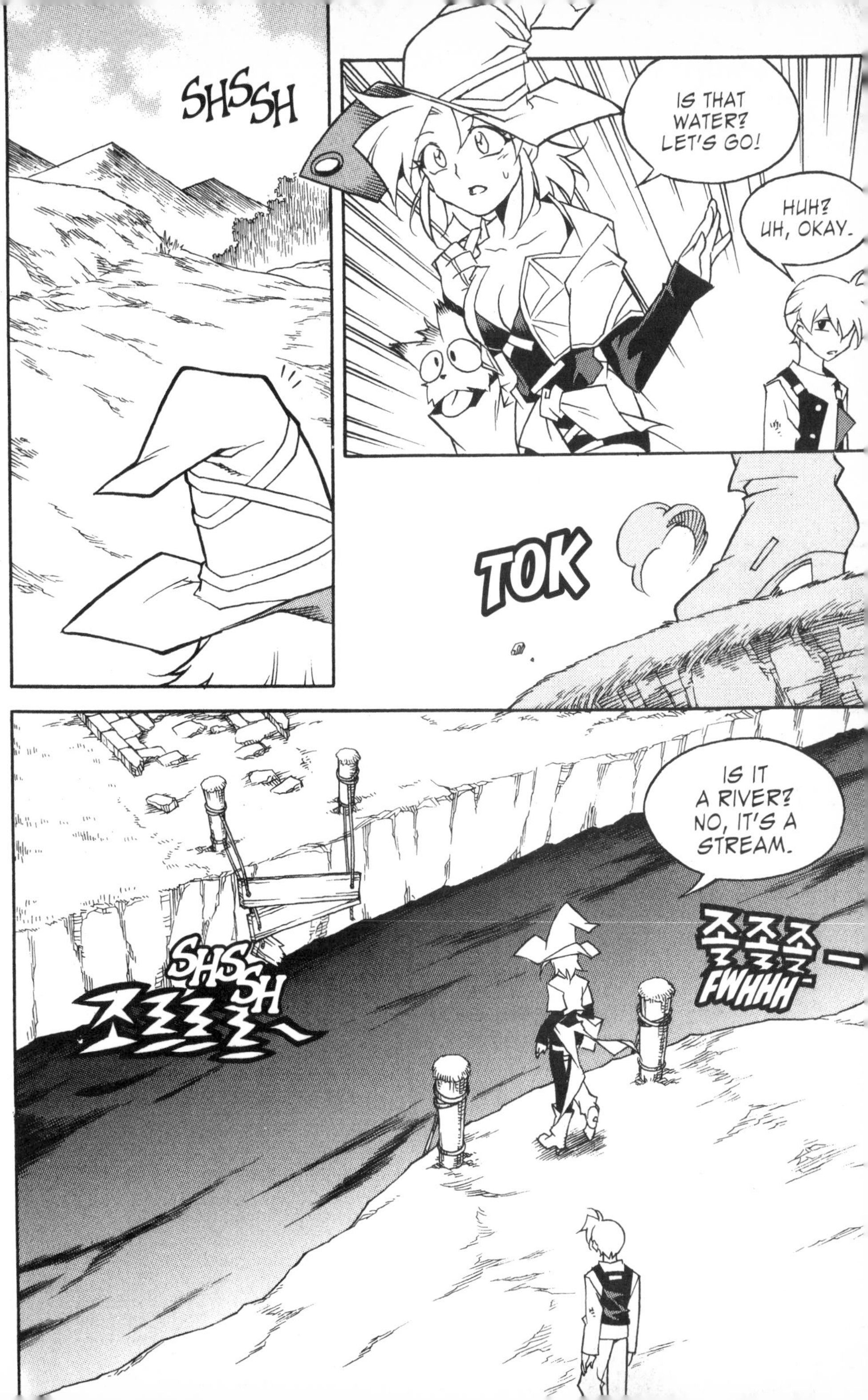
SHSSH
IS THAT WATER? LET'S GO!
HUH? UH, OKAY.
TOK
SHSSH
IS IT A RIVER? NO, IT'S A STREAM.
졸졸졸—
FWHHH

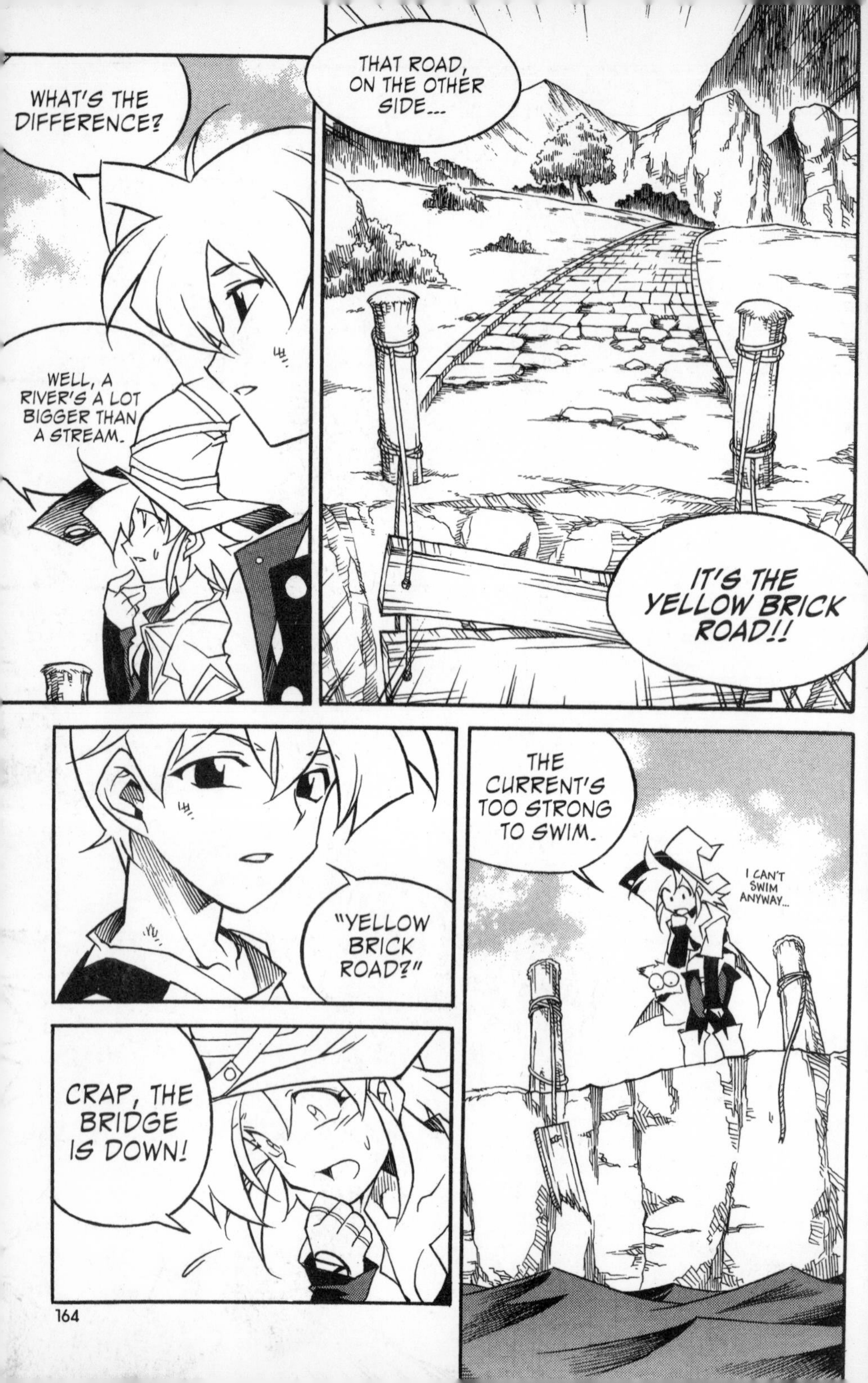
WHAT'S THE DIFFERENCE?
WELL, A RIVER'S A LOT BIGGER THAN A STREAM.
THAT ROAD, ON THE OTHER SIDE...
IT'S THE YELLOW BRICK ROAD!!
"YELLOW BRICK ROAD?"
CRAP, THE BRIDGE IS DOWN!
THE CURRENT'S TOO STRONG TO SWIM.
I CAN'T SWIM ANYWAY...

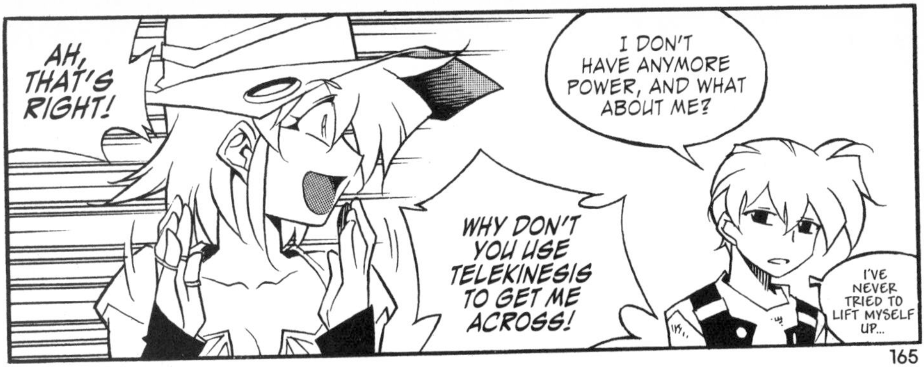
AH, THAT'S RIGHT!
I DON'T HAVE ANYMORE POWER, AND WHAT ABOUT ME?
WHY DON'T YOU USE TELEKINESIS TO GET ME ACROSS!
I'VE NEVER TRIED TO LIFT MYSELF UP...

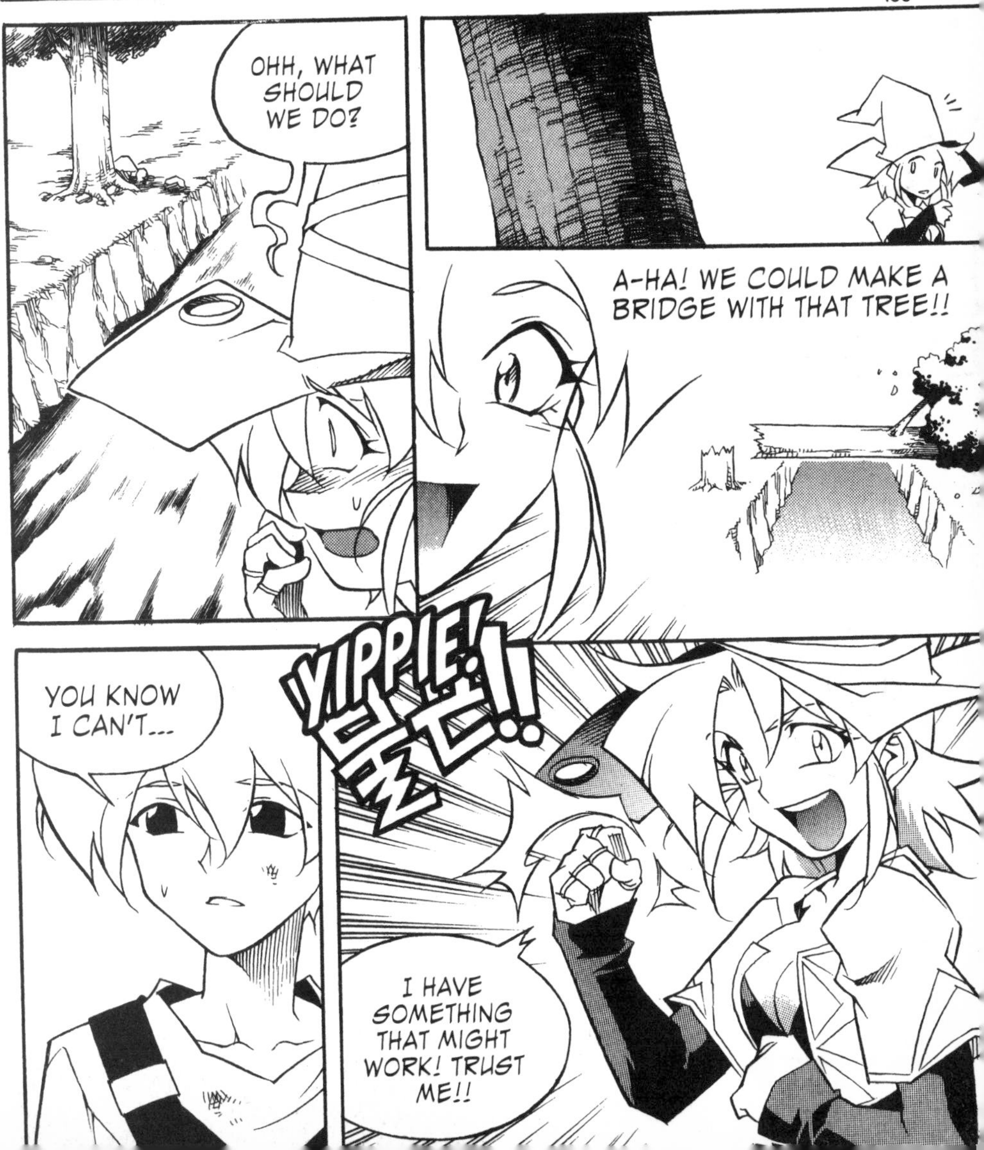
OHH, WHAT SHOULD WE DO?
A-HA! WE COULD MAKE A BRIDGE WITH THAT TREE!!
YOU KNOW I CAN'T...
YIPPIE!
I HAVE SOMETHING THAT MIGHT WORK! TRUST ME!!

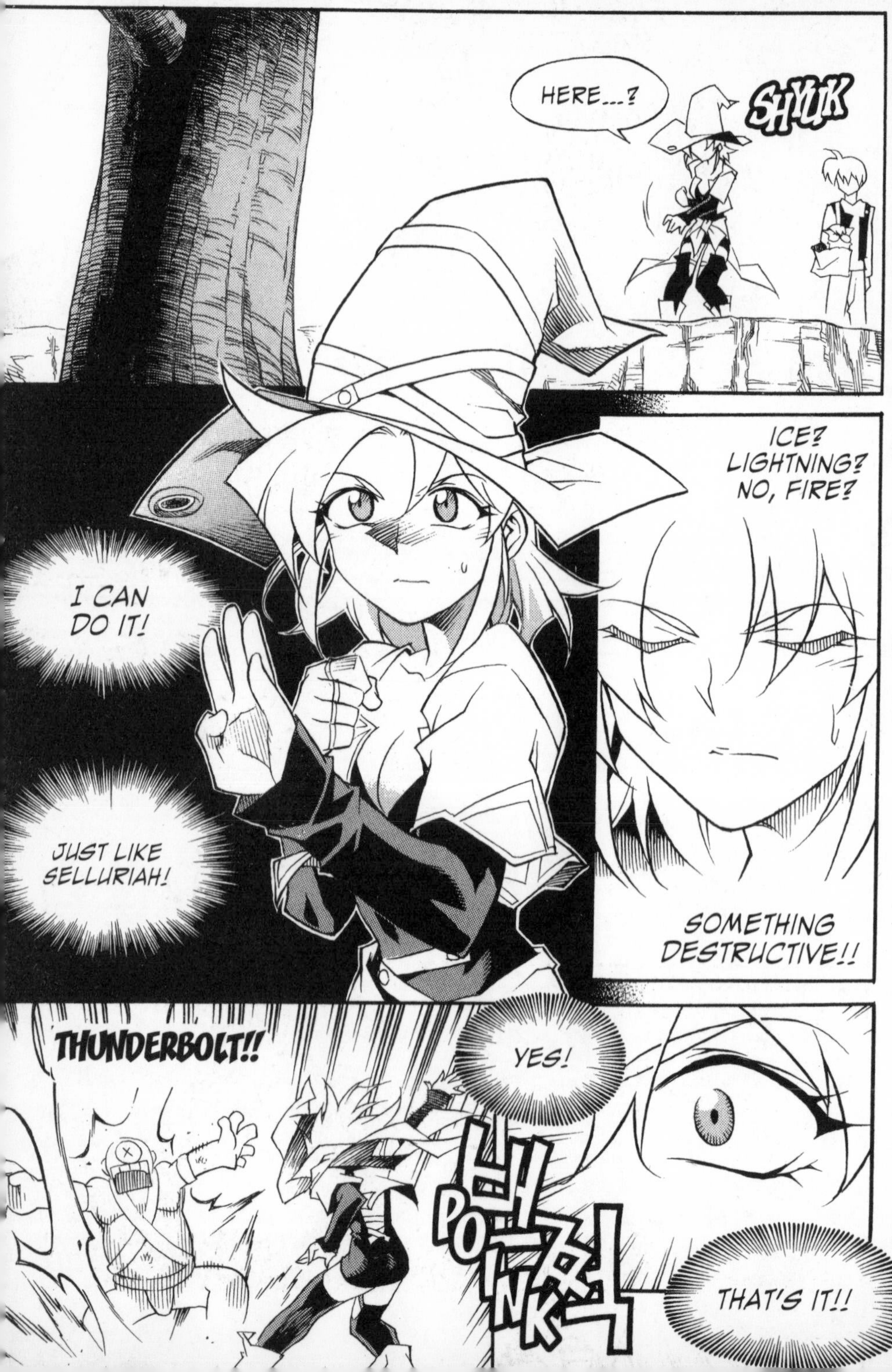
HERE...?
SHYUK
ICE? LIGHTNING? NO, FIRE?
I CAN DO IT!
JUST LIKE SELLURIAH!
SOMETHING DESTRUCTIVE!!
THUNDERBOLT!!
YES!
POINK
THAT'S IT!!

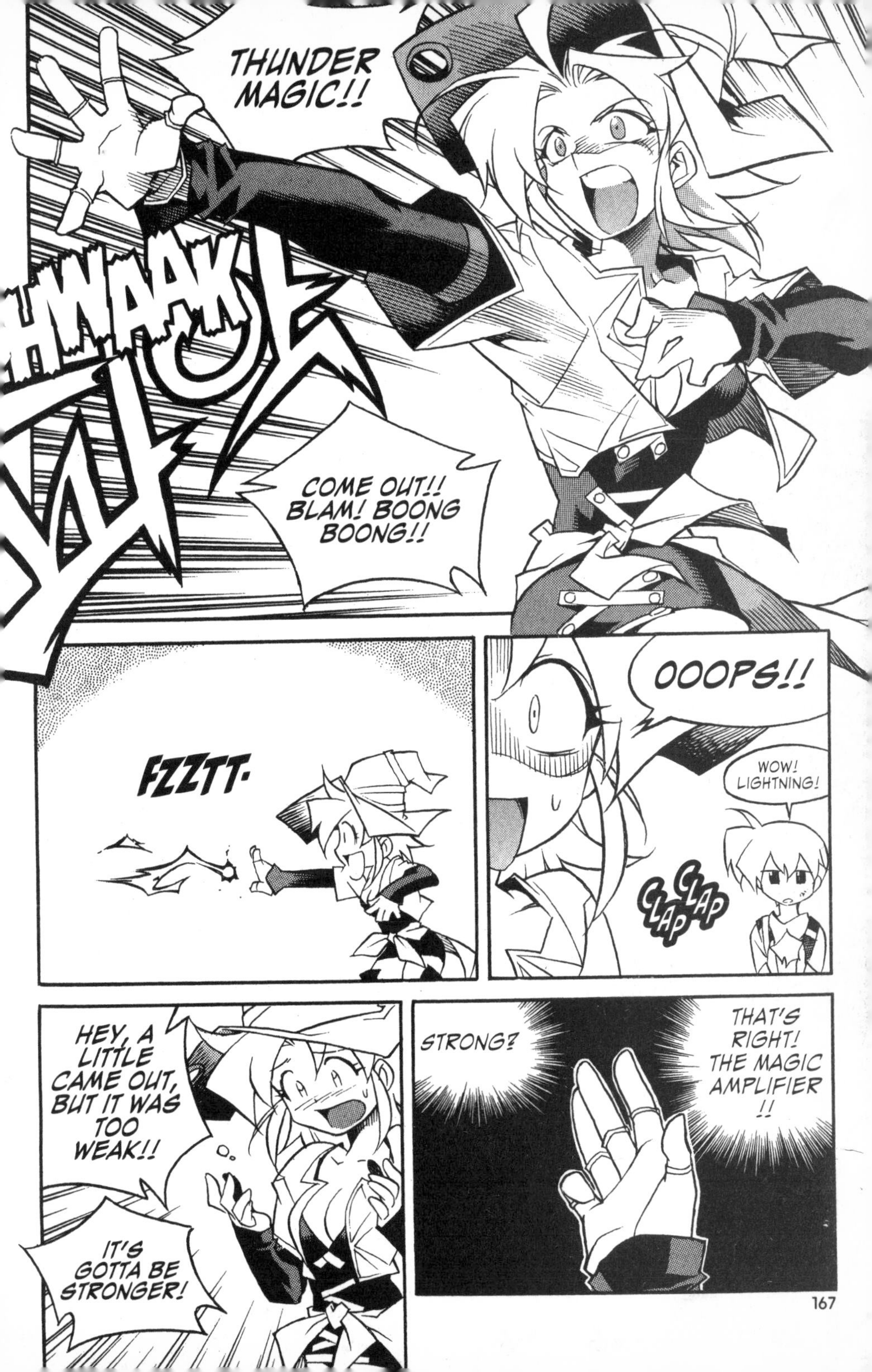
THUNDER MAGIC!!
WHAAK
ZZT
COME OUT!! BLAM! BOONG BOONG!!
FZZTT-
OOOPS!!
WOW! LIGHTNING!
CLAP CLAP CLAP
HEY, A LITTLE CAME OUT, BUT IT WAS TOO WEAK!!
IT'S GOTTA BE STRONGER!
STRONG?
THAT'S RIGHT! THE MAGIC AMPLIFIER !!

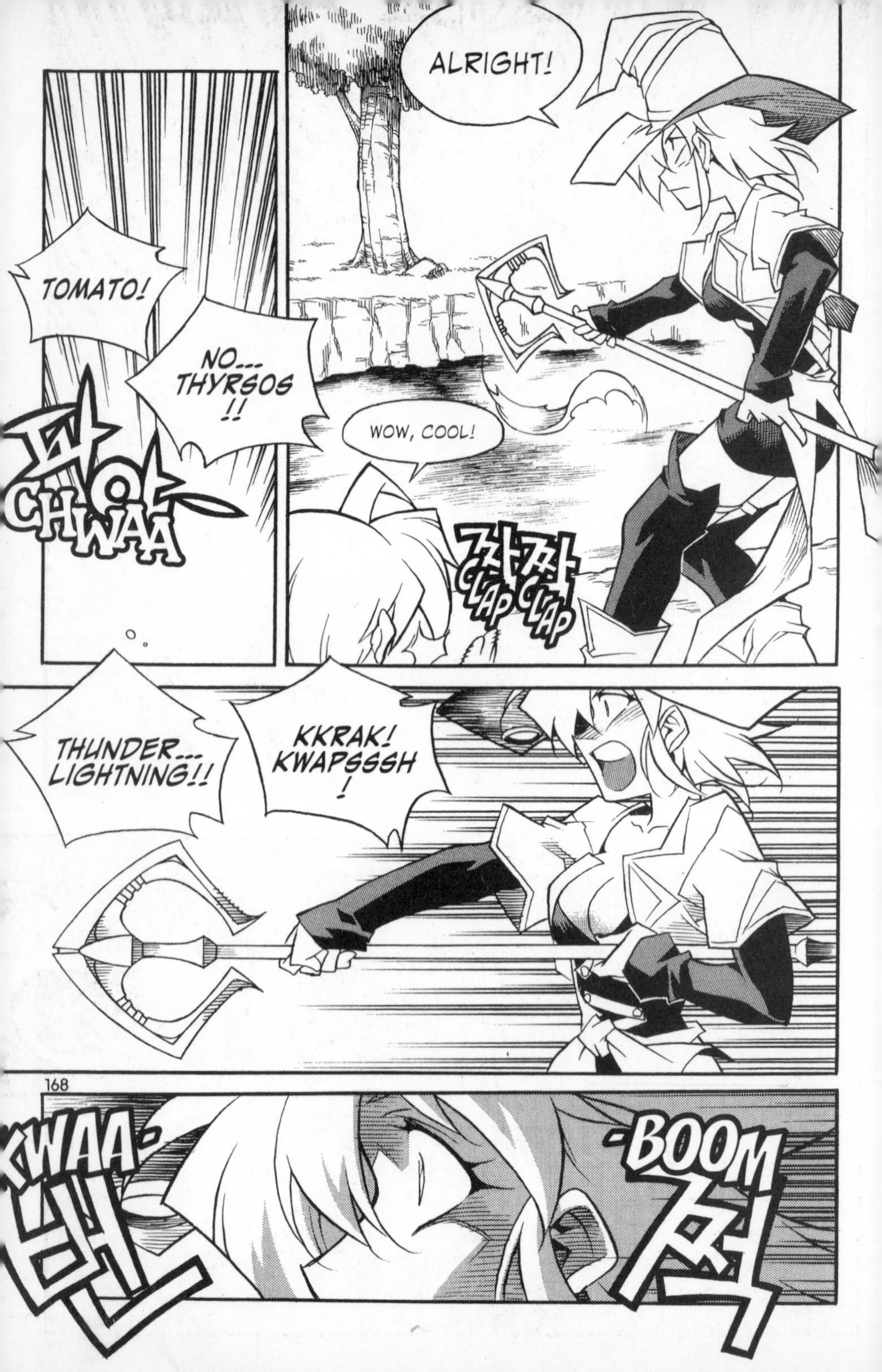
TOMATO!
NO... THYRSOS !!
CHWAA
ALRIGHT!
WOW, COOL!
CLAP CLAP
THUNDER... LIGHTNING!!
KKRAK! KWAPSSSH !
KWAA-
-BOOM

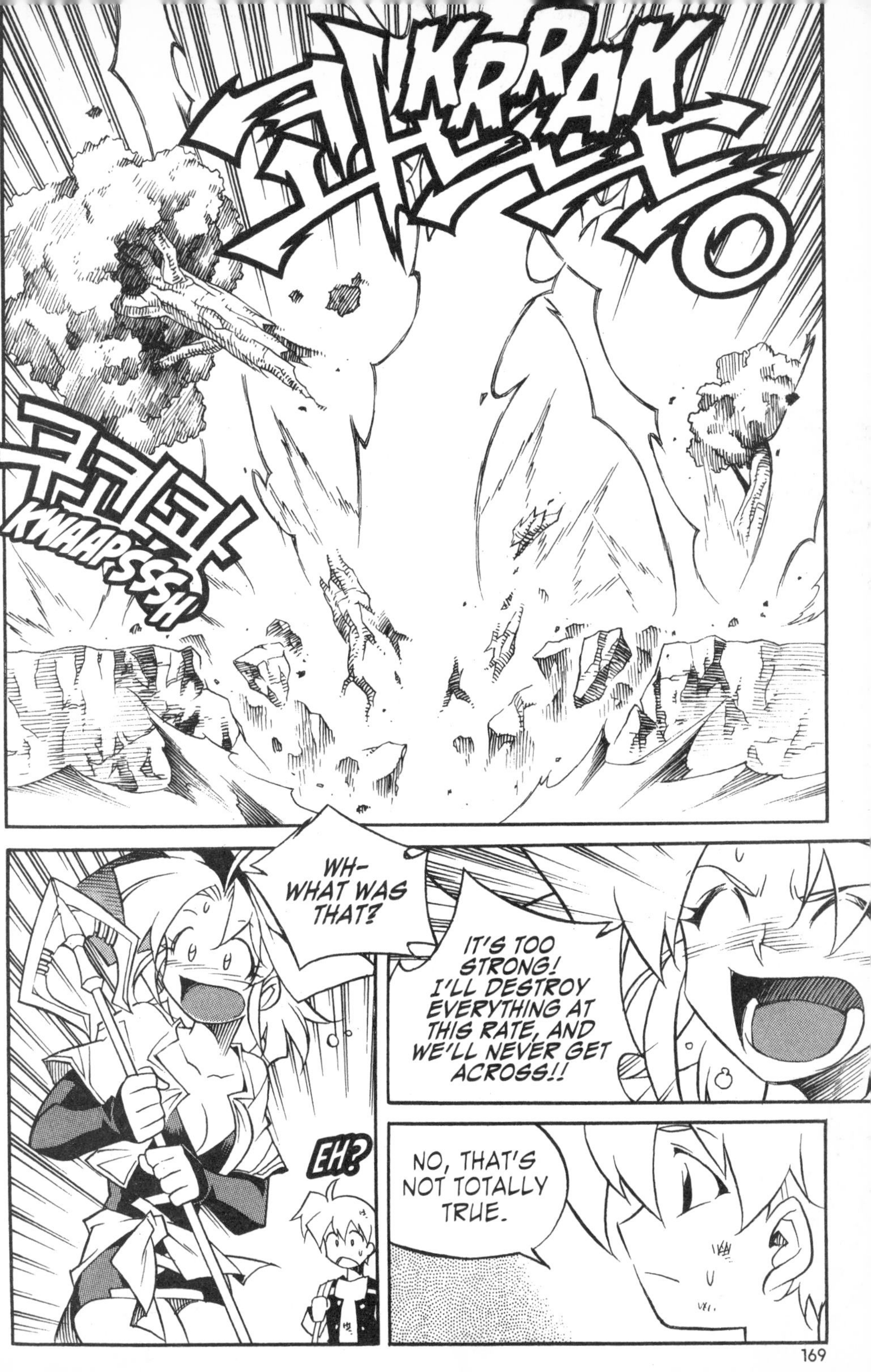
KRAK
KWAAPSSSH
WH- WHAT WAS THAT?
EH?
IT'S TOO STRONG! I'LL DESTROY EVERYTHING AT THIS RATE, AND WE'LL NEVER GET ACROSS!!
NO, THAT'S NOT TOTALLY TRUE.

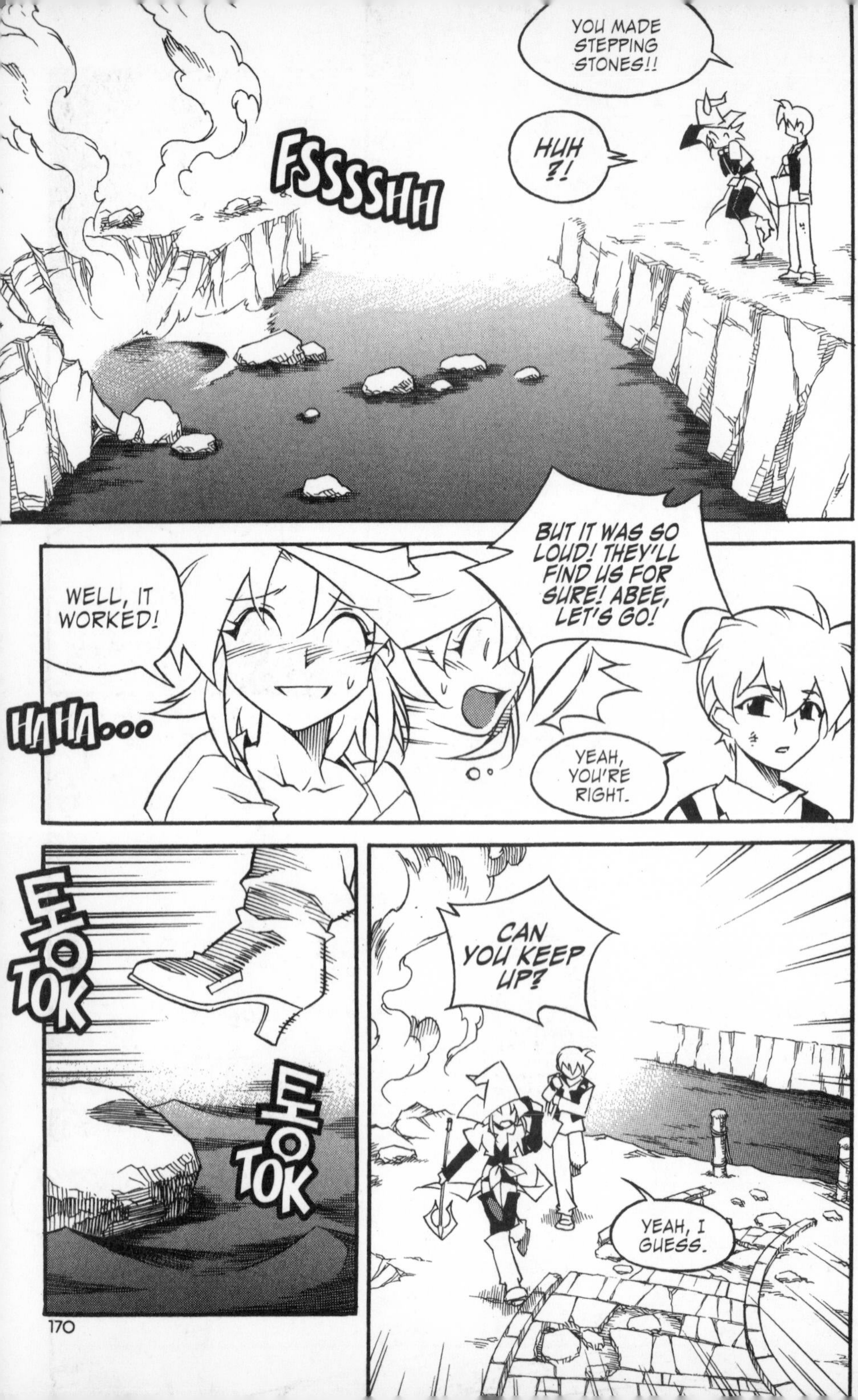
YOU MADE STEPPING STONES!!
FSSSSHH
HUH ?!
WELL, IT WORKED!
HAHA...
BUT IT WAS SO LOUD! THEY'LL FIND US FOR SURE! ABEE, LET'S GO!
YEAH, YOU'RE RIGHT.
TOK
TOK
CAN YOU KEEP UP?
YEAH, I GUESS.

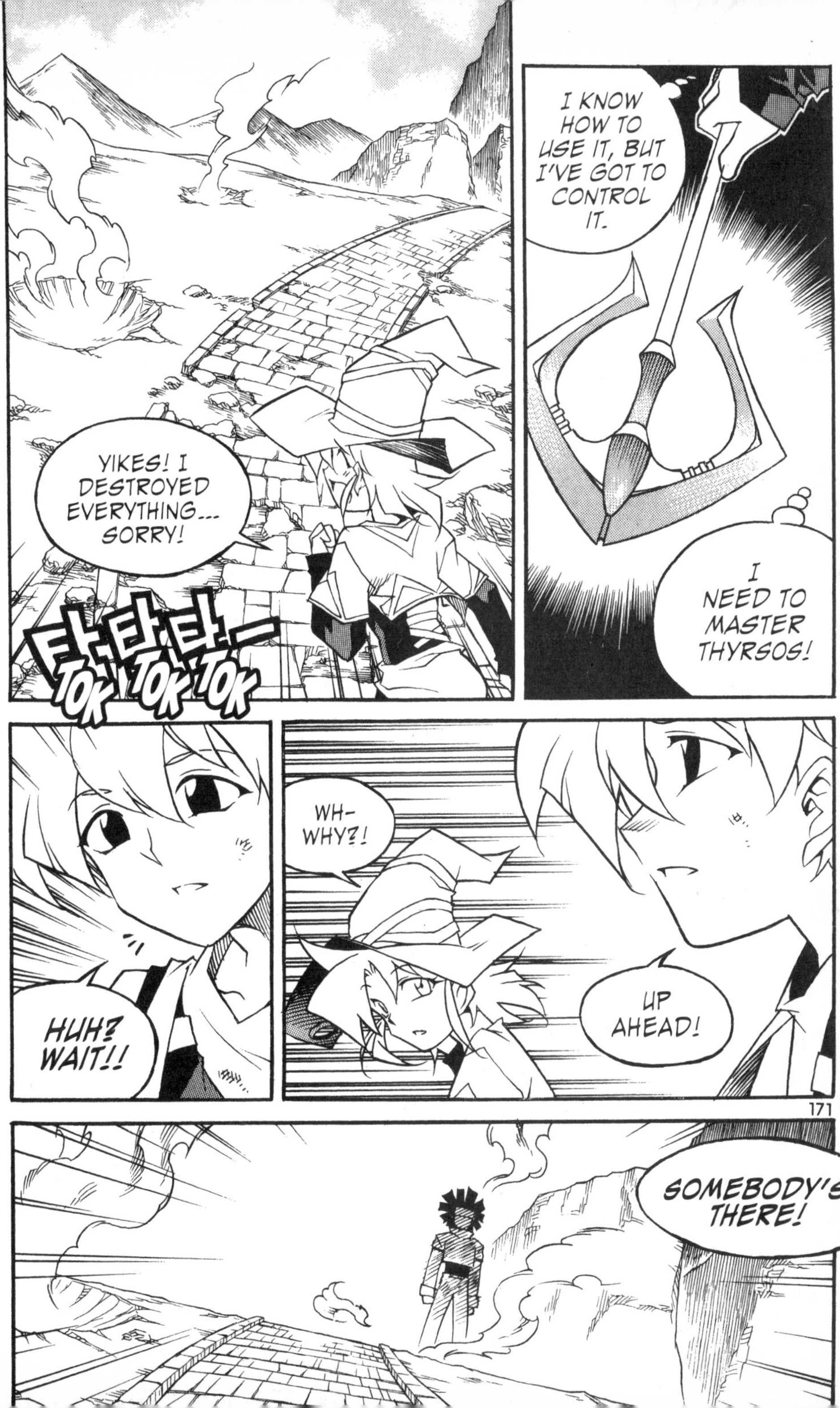
YIKES! I DESTROYED EVERYTHING... SORRY!
타,타,타—
TOK TOK TOK
I KNOW HOW TO USE IT, BUT I'VE GOT TO CONTROL IT.
I NEED TO MASTER THYRSOS!
HUH? WAIT!!
WH- WHY?!
UP AHEAD!
SOMEBODY'S THERE!

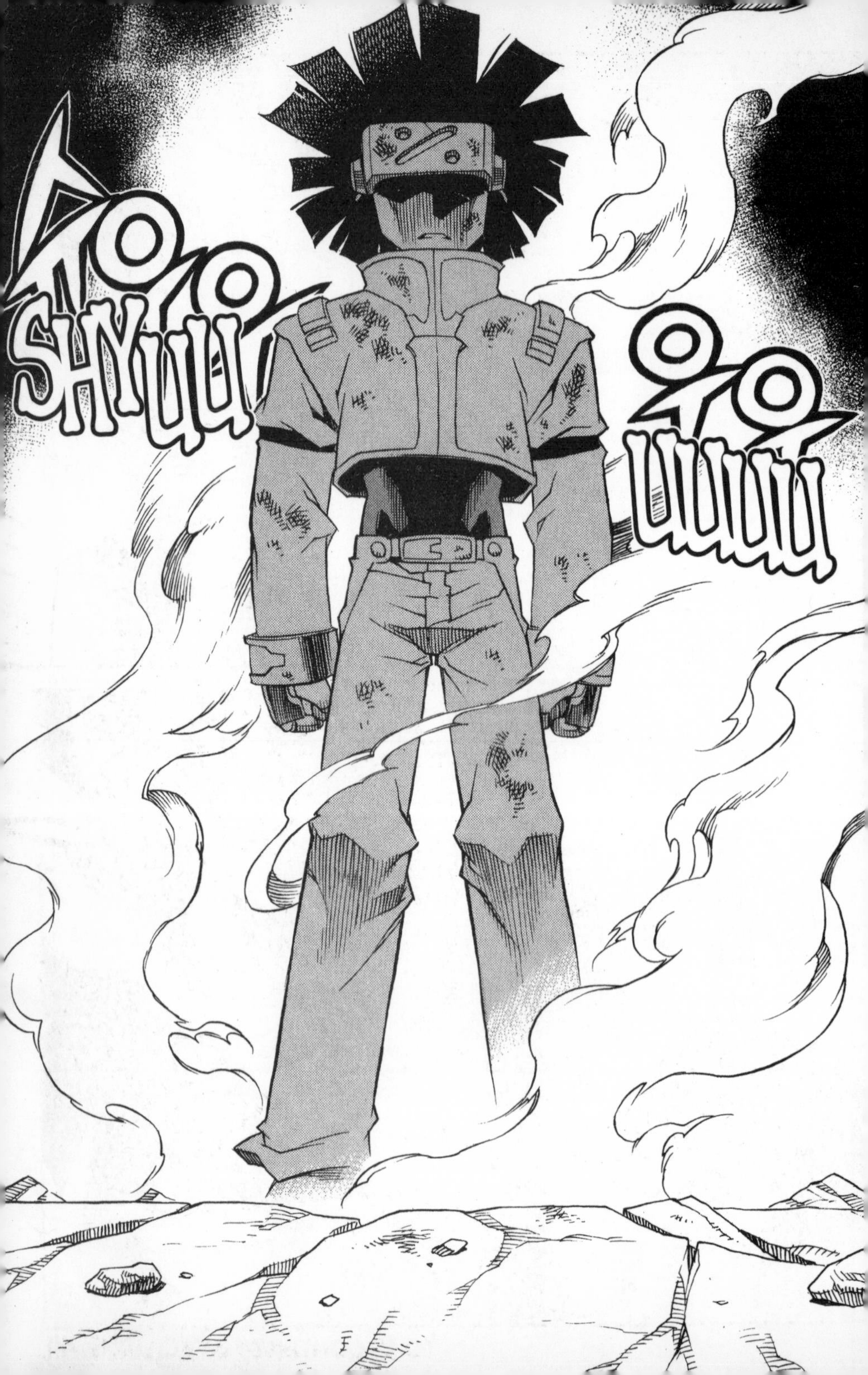
SHYUU
UUUUU

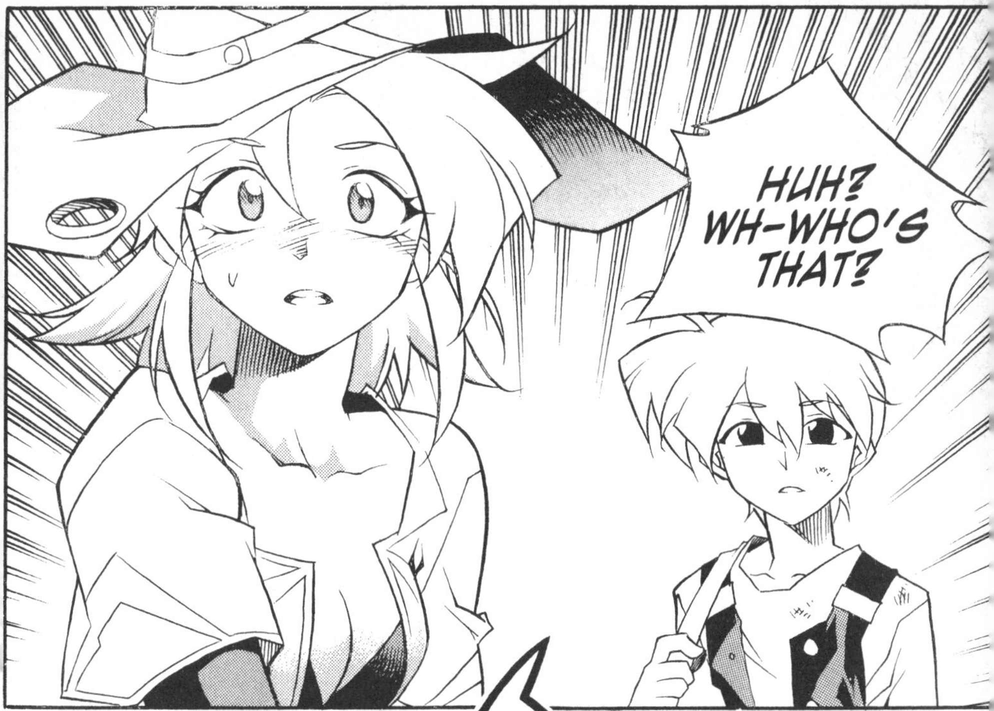
HUH? WH-WHO'S THAT?

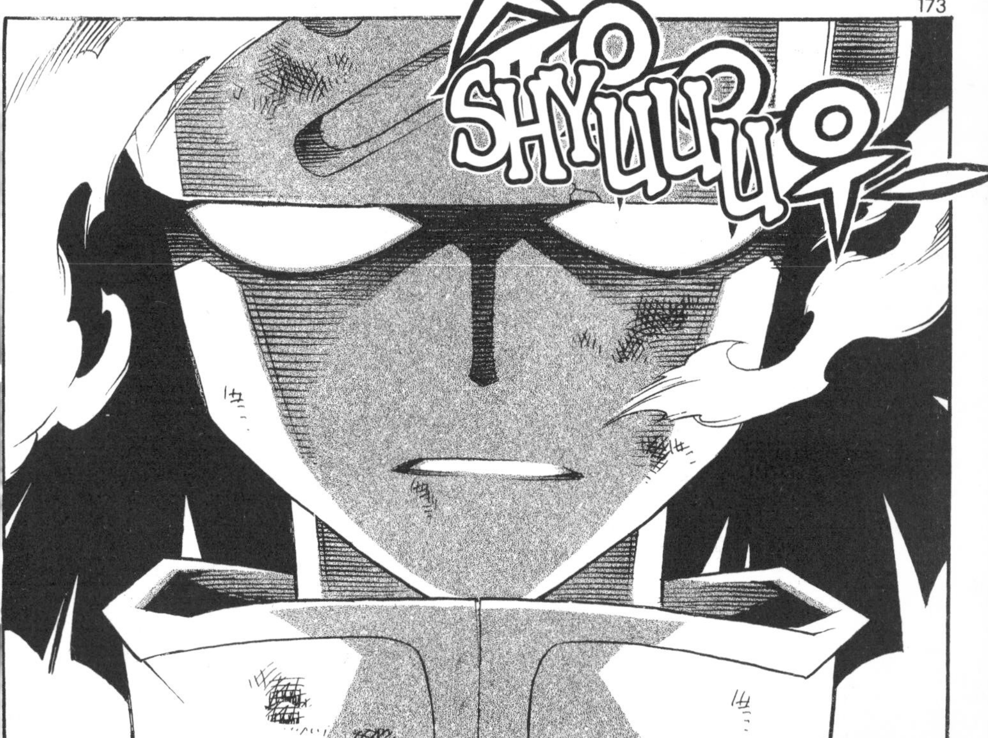
SHYUURU

TO BE CONTINUED IN **VOLUME 4!!**

DEADLINE BLUES

데드라인 블루스

BATTLER

REGRET

SAGA <DEAD SONG>

NEAN

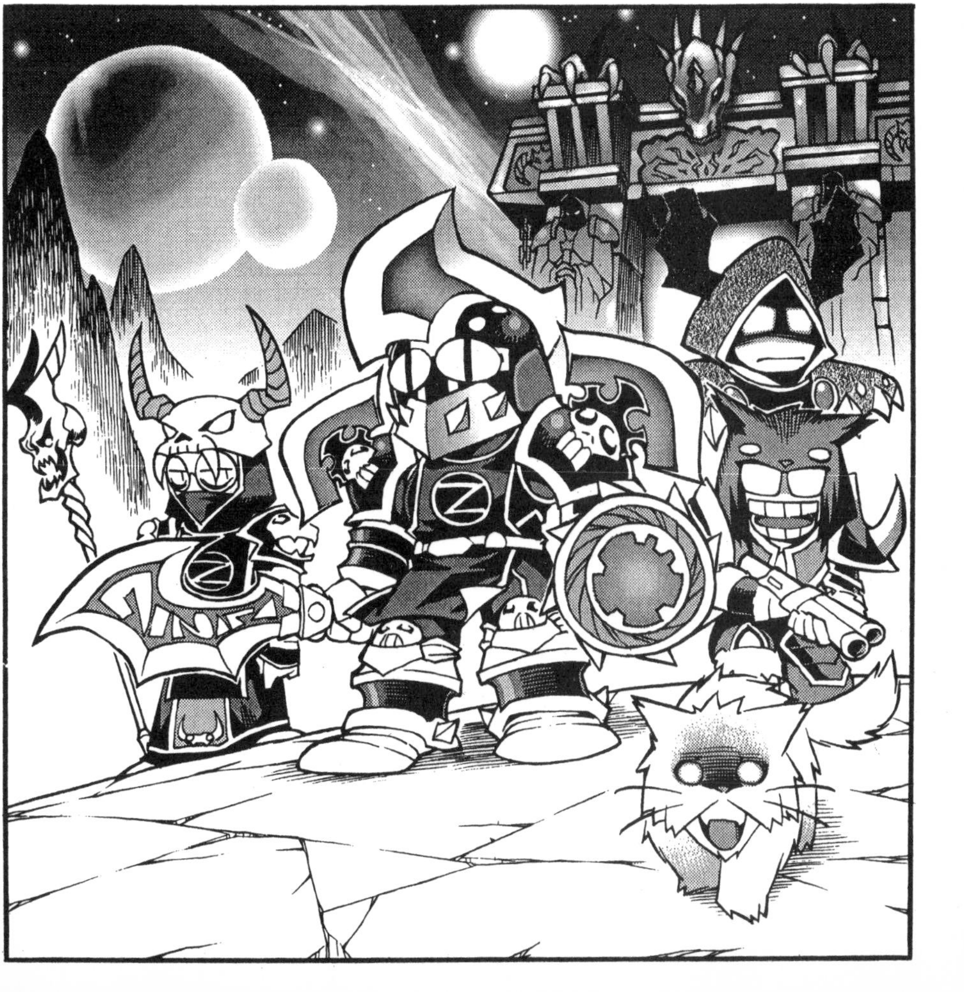

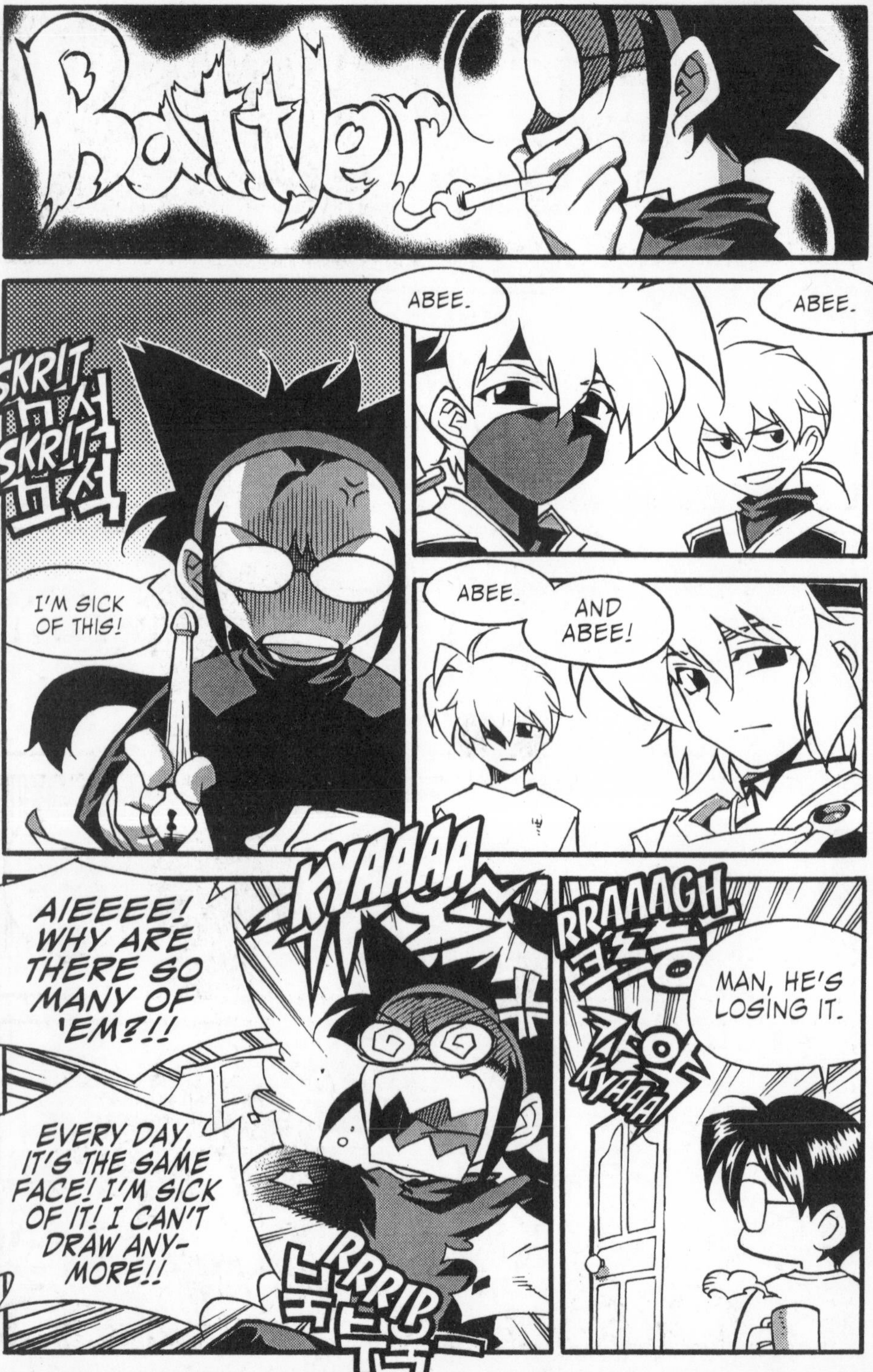
Battler
SKRIT
SKRIT
I'M SICK OF THIS!
ABEE.
ABEE.
ABEE.
AND ABEE!
KYAAAA
AIEEEEE! WHY ARE THERE SO MANY OF 'EM?!!
EVERY DAY, IT'S THE SAME FACE! I'M SICK OF IT! I CAN'T DRAW ANY-MORE!!
RRRRIP
RRAAAGH
KYAAA
MAN, HE'S LOSING IT.

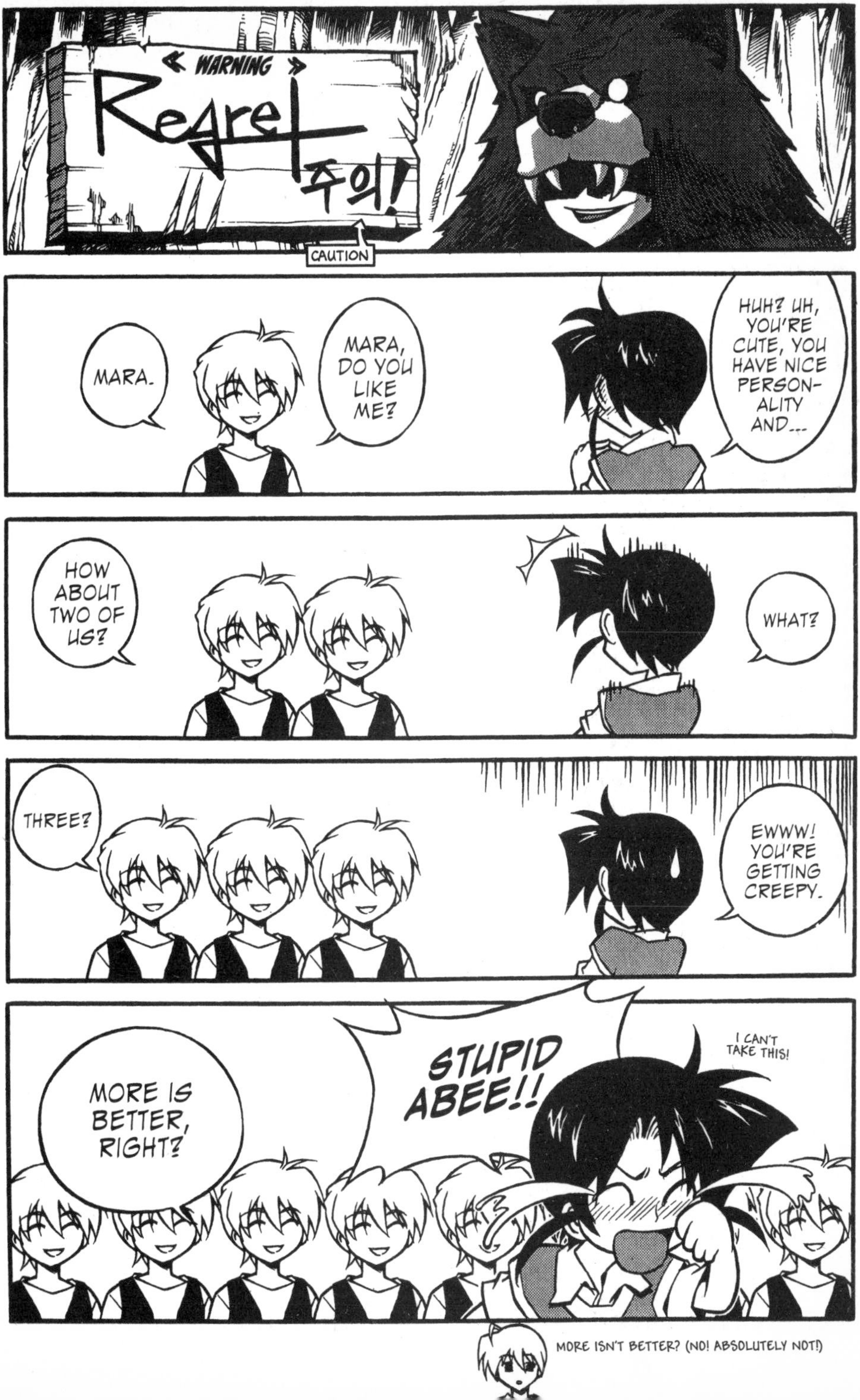
« WARNING »
Regret
주의!
CAUTION
MARA.
MARA, DO YOU LIKE ME?
HUH? UH, YOU'RE CUTE, YOU HAVE NICE PERSON-ALITY AND...
HOW ABOUT TWO OF US?
WHAT?
THREE?
EWWW! YOU'RE GETTING CREEPY.
MORE IS BETTER, RIGHT?
STUPID ABEE!!
I CAN'T TAKE THIS!
MORE ISN'T BETTER? (NO! ABSOLUTELY NOT!)

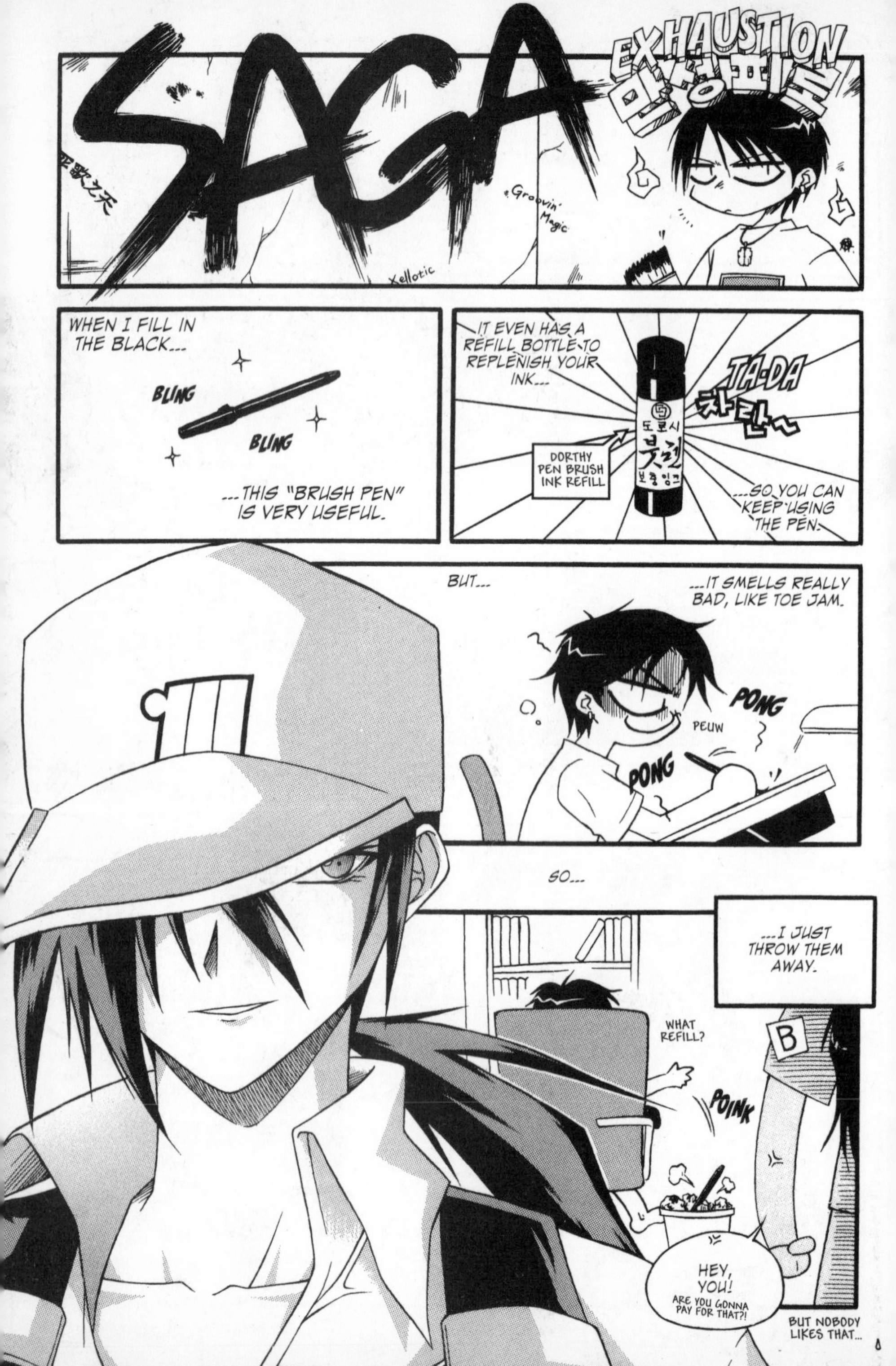
SAGA
EXHAUSTION
Groovin' Magic
Xellotic
WHEN I FILL IN THE BLACK...
BLING
BLING
...THIS "BRUSH PEN" IS VERY USEFUL.
IT EVEN HAS A REFILL BOTTLE TO REPLENISH YOUR INK...
TA-DA
DORTHY PEN BRUSH INK REFILL
...SO YOU CAN KEEP USING THE PEN.
BUT...
...IT SMELLS REALLY BAD, LIKE TOE JAM.
PONG
PEUW
PONG
SO...
...I JUST THROW THEM AWAY.
WHAT REFILL?
B
POINK
HEY, YOU!
ARE YOU GONNA PAY FOR THAT?!
BUT NOBODY LIKES THAT...

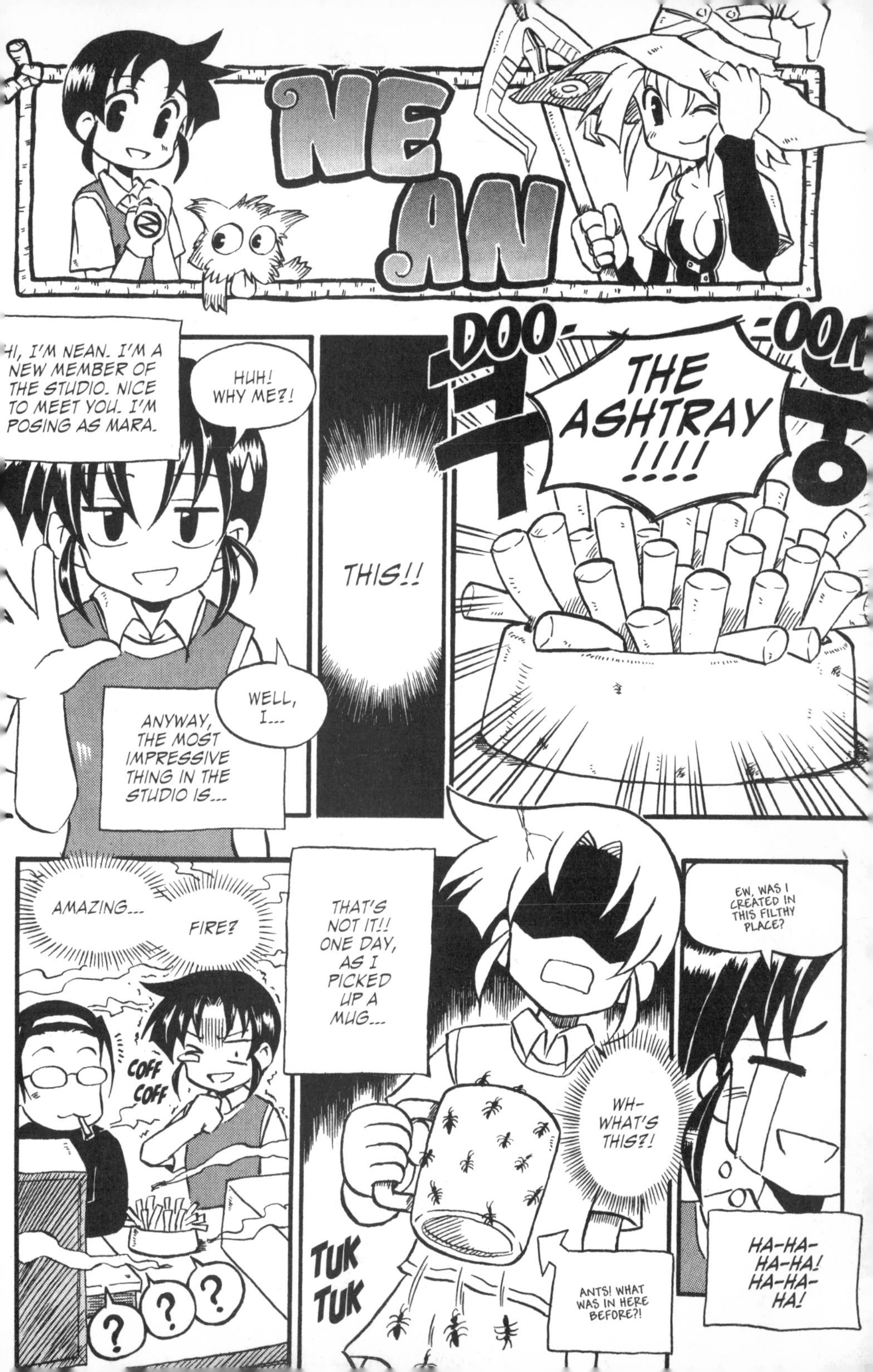
NE
AN
HI, I'M NEAN. I'M A NEW MEMBER OF THE STUDIO. NICE TO MEET YOU. I'M POSING AS MARA.
HUH! WHY ME?!
WELL, I...
ANYWAY, THE MOST IMPRESSIVE THING IN THE STUDIO IS...
THIS!!
DOO-
-OOM
THE ASHTRAY !!!!
AMAZING...
FIRE?
COFF COFF
???
THAT'S NOT IT!! ONE DAY, AS I PICKED UP A MUG...
WH-WHAT'S THIS?!
TUK TUK
ANTS! WHAT WAS IN HERE BEFORE?!
EW, WAS I CREATED IN THIS FILTHY PLACE?
HA-HA-HA-HA! HA-HA-HA!

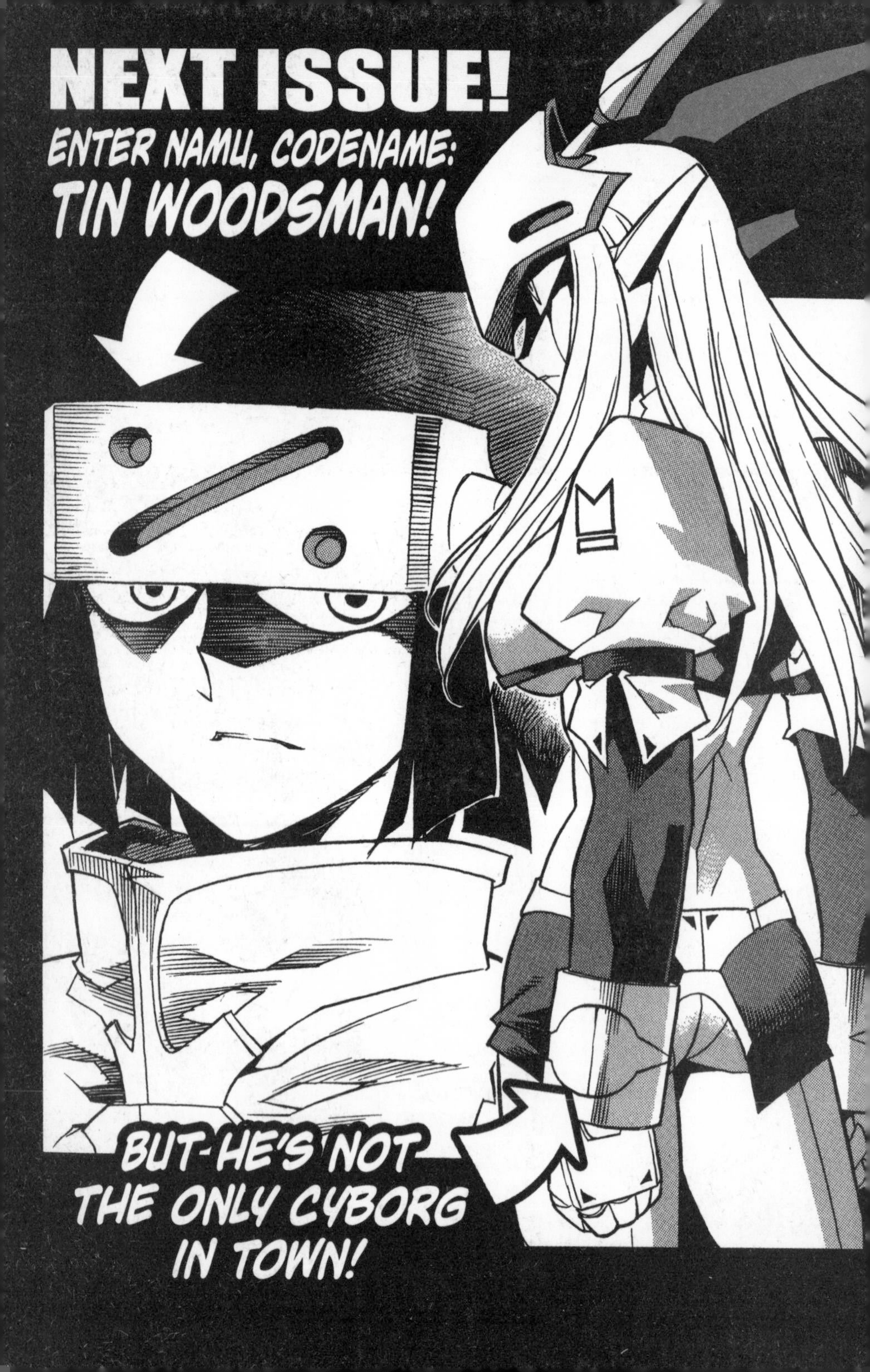
NEXT ISSUE!
ENTER NAMU, CODENAME:
TIN WOODSMAN!
BUT-HE'S NOT THE ONLY CYBORG IN TOWN!

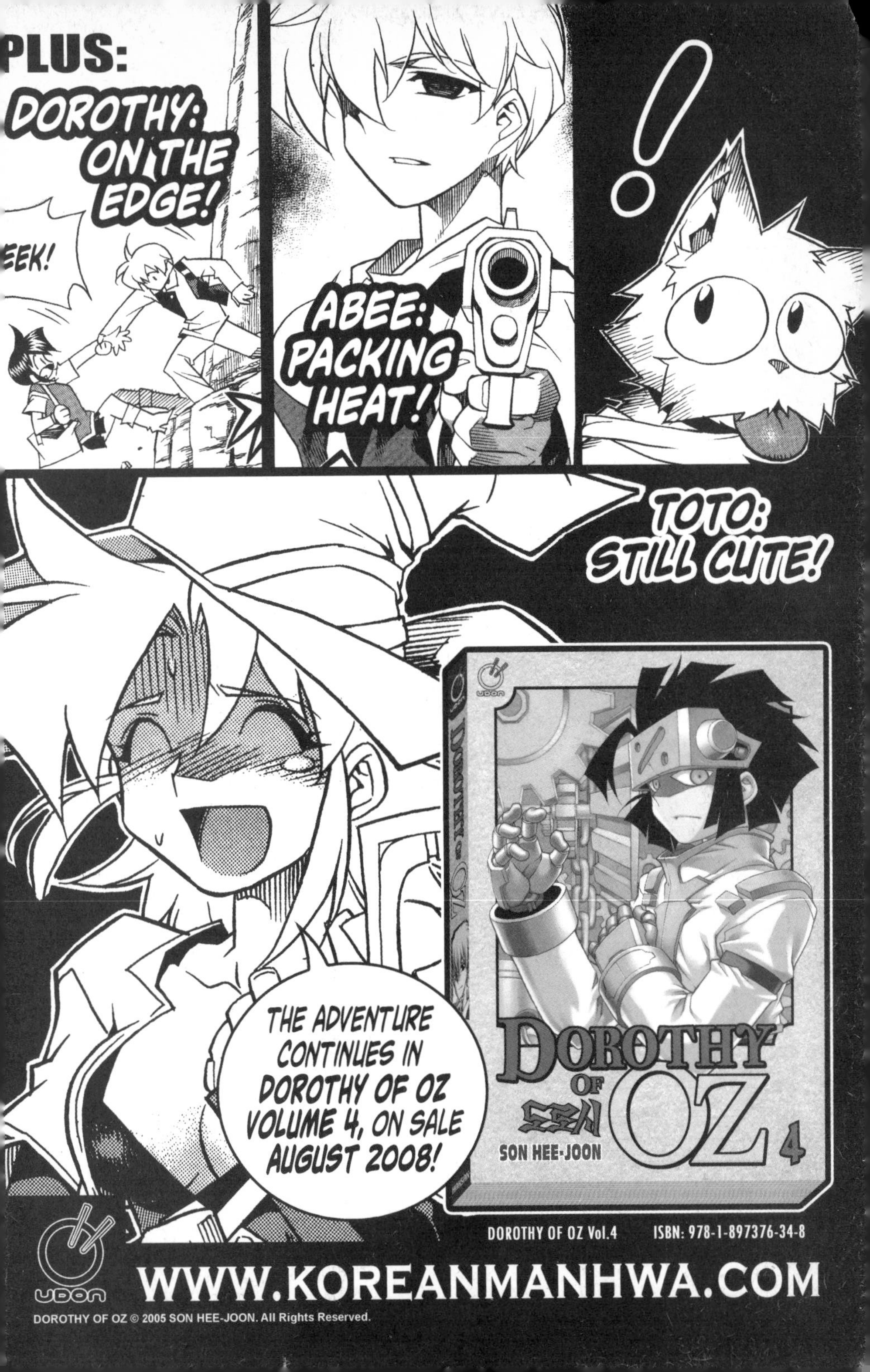
PLUS:
DOROTHY: ON THE EDGE!
EEK!
ABEE: PACKING HEAT!
!
TOTO: STILL CUTE!
THE ADVENTURE CONTINUES IN DOROTHY OF OZ VOLUME 4, ON SALE AUGUST 2008!
DOROTHY OF OZ
SON HEE-JOON
4

DOROTHY OF OZ Volume 3

Story and Art : Son Hee-Joon

English Translations : Nahee Jung
English Adaptations : Kevin M. Kilgore

Editorial Consultant: J. Torres
Coordinating Editor: Hye-Young Im

Lettering : Marshall Dillon

Cover & Graphic Design :
Erik Ko with Matt Moylan

English Logo : Alex Chung

DOROTHY OF OZ #3
©2007 SON HEE-JOON.
All Rights Reserved. First published in Korea by Haksan Publishing Co., Ltd.
This translation rights arranged with Haksan Publishing Co., Ltd.
through Shinwon Agency Co. in Korea.
English edition ©2008 UDON Entertainment Corp.

English launguage version produced and published by UDON Entertainment Corp.
P.O. Box 32662, P.O. Village Gate, Richmond Hill, Ontario, L4X 0A2, Canada.

www.udonentertainment.com

First Printing: May 2008   ISBN-13 : 978-1-897376-33-1   ISBN-10 : 1-897376-33-2
Printed in Canada